Understanding and Treating Obsessive-Compulsive Disorder

A Cognitive-Behavioral Approach

Understanding and Treating Obsessive-Compulsive Disorder

A Cognitive-Behavioral Approach

Jonathan S. Abramowitz
Mayo Clinic

LAWRENCE ERLBAUM ASSOCIATES, PUBLISHERS

2006   Mahwah, New Jersey   London

Lawrence Erlbaum Associates, Inc., Publishers
10 Industrial Avenue
Mahwah, New Jersey 07430
www.erlbaum.com

Cover design by Kathryn Houghtaling Lacey

Library of Congress Cataloging-in-Publication Data

Abramowitz, Jonathan S.
Understanding and treating obsessive-compulsive disorder :
a cognitive behavioral approach / Jonathan S. Abramowitz.

p. cm.

Includes bibliographical references and index.
ISBN 0-8058-5184-4 (alk. paper)
1. Obsessive-compulsive disorder. 2. Obsessive-compulsive
disorder—Treatment. 3. Cognitive therapy. I. Title.

RC533.A27 2005
616.85'22706—dc22   2005041406
                                                          CIP

Books published by Lawrence Erlbaum Associates are printed on acid-
free paper, and their bindings are chosen for strength and durability.

Printed in the United States of America
10 9 8 7 6 5 4 3 2 1

*To my dearest Stacy,
and our wonderful children—Emily and Miriam.*

*To the memory of my grandparents:
Morris Abramowitz and Dorothy Gerber—I know they would be proud.
And to their surviving spouses: Robert Gerber and Mildred Abramowitz.*

Contents

About the Author

Jonathan S. Abramowitz, PhD, is an Associate Professor of Psychology at the Mayo Clinic College of Medicine and Consultant (Staff Psychologist) in the Mayo Clinic Department of Psychiatry and Psychology, where he has worked since 2000. He is a recognized expert on the treatment of obsessive–compulsive disorder (OCD) and serves as Director of the OCD/Anxiety Disorders Treatment and Research Program at Mayo. Dr. Abramowitz conducts research on the psychopathology and treatment of OCD and other anxiety disorders and has authored more than 50 research articles and book chapters on these topics. He regularly presents papers and workshops at regional, national, and international professional conferences, and served on the *DSM–IV–TR* Anxiety Disorders Work Group. Dr. Abramowitz was awarded a Diplomate in Behavioral Psychology by the American Board of Professional Psychology in 2003. He is a member of the Obsessive Compulsive Foundation's Scientific Advisory Board, a member of the Anxiety Disorders Association of America's Clinical Advisory Board, and also serves on the editorial boards of several professional journals. In 2003, Dr. Abramowitz received the Outstanding Contributions to Research Award from the Mayo Clinic Department of Psychiatry and Psychology. In 2004, he received the David Shakow Early Career Award for Outstanding Contributions to Clinical Psychology from Division 12 (Clinical Psychology) of the American Psychological Association. He lives in Rochester, Minnesota, with his wife Stacy, and daughters Emily and Miriam.

Preface

Obsessive–compulsive disorder (OCD) has captured the attention of authors for more than a century. The seemingly bizarre thoughts and senseless repetitive behaviors featured in this disorder were refractory to unscientific psychoanalytic and psychodynamic therapies, leading to the view that it was an unmanageable condition. However, beginning with Solomon's work on animal models of avoidance learning in the 1950s, and Rachman and colleagues' eloquent studies on the phenomenology of OCD in the 1970s, we have seen the development and refinement of scientifically based behavioral models of OCD. This approach has led to the development of treatment procedures, namely exposure and response prevention, that are highly effective for reducing overt compulsive behaviors such as checking, washing, and other repetitive behaviors. Thus, in the last few decades, the prognosis for the 2% to 3% of the population suffering with OCD has dramatically improved.

The focus of this book reflects an even more recent transformation in the ethos of understanding obsessions and compulsions. Clinical and research interest has broadened from an exclusive emphasis on overt behavior to an increased appreciation for the role of *cognition* in the development and maintenance of these symptoms. In parallel fashion, a shift in focus from *overt* compulsive behaviors to *covert* symptoms, such as obsessions and mental rituals, has occurred. For example, we now know that most people with OCD deploy mental, as well as behavioral, strategies (not all of which are "compulsive") in response to obsessional fear. Studies also demonstrate that it is these "neutralizing" or "safety-seeking" responses which maintain obsessional preoccupation. Most importantly, from this research has sprung forth promising new approaches to treating OCD that rely on both traditional behavioral and novel cognitive approaches.

I have written this book for the mental health care provider who wishes to engage in the challenging yet rewarding pursuit of helping individuals with OCD overcome their disorder. The aim of the first part of the book is to present a scientifically based theoretical framework for understanding obsessions, compulsions, and related phenomena. The opening chapters help the clinician form a conceptualization of OCD that will guide the use of treatment procedures described in Part II. Chapter 1 covers the nature of obsessions and compulsions, and chapter 2 covers how to distinguish OCD from other similar disorders. In chapter 3, I critically examine various explanations of the causes of OCD, and in chapter 4, I outline a cognitive-behavioral model of the maintenance of OCD symptoms. Part I concludes with chapter 5, which presents a description and literature review concerning the two mainstream treatments for OCD: cognitive-behavioral therapy and serotonergic medication.

Within Part II, chapters 6 and 7 outline the procedures for providing assessment and consultation for OCD. Chapter 6 describes the initial assessment using interview and self-report questionnaire techniques, and chapter 7 aims to help clinicians offer the patient a proper recommendation and rationale for treatment. Chapter 8 describes how to begin preparing for cognitive-behavioral treatment by gathering information about the patient in a way that will guide the construction of an individualized case formulation and treatment plan. Chapters 9 through 12 constitute a manual for designing and implementing empirically supported cognitive and behavioral treatment procedures that are based on the conceptualization of OCD presented in the first part of the book. Treatment involves data collection at various stages and has an integrated educational component. Chapter 13 describes a follow-up and maintenance program to be implemented following the termination of treatment. Finally, in chapter 14, I discuss how to troubleshoot problems and complications that can arise in implementing the outlined treatment procedures. I have incorporated case examples throughout the book to illustrate phenomenology, assessment, and treatment (of course, the names of patients have been changed to protect confidentiality). Worksheets and handouts to be used in therapy are also provided in several of the chapters.

Finally, let me offer some words pertaining to treatment manuals in general, and manuals for the treatment of OCD in particular. An important aim of treatment manuals is to encourage the standardization of empirically based therapy procedures across clinicians and patients. Optimally, manuals should delineate the essential principles of assessment and treatment and provide the clinician with procedural guidelines for their implementation. The challenge in developing such a manual is to specify abstract principles of treatment with enough detail that they can be applied to a variety of patients, but not in so much detail that the manual becomes unwieldy and cumbersome. Striking this balance is never more relevant than in the case of OCD because the phenomenology of this disorder is exceptionally heterogeneous and patient specific. Indeed no treatment manual could adequately address the implementation of cognitive and behavioral treatment procedures across the countless personal variations of OCD symptoms. Therefore, my solution in this book is to present reasonably standardized guidelines for case formulation and treatment for a number of common OCD presentations, noting the need for ongoing assessment, flexibility, and creativity in dealing with the more idiosyncratic symptom variations likely to be encountered in clinical practice. For the most part, unanticipated obstacles can be managed by falling back on the cognitive and behavioral principles (i.e., functional analysis) that form the basis of successful cognitive-behavioral therapy.

Acknowledgments

This book reflects how I understand, provide consultation for, and treat the problem of OCD. The conceptual model and intervention strategies are based on a firm foundation of scientific literature to which I am a contributor and of which I am a student. First, I wish to thank all of those who have helped me learn from and add to this knowledge: countless patients I have evaluated and treated, therapists I have supervised, and many wonderful teachers who have been instrumental in my growth and learning. Kathleen Harring, my undergraduate advisor at Muhlenberg College in Allentown, Pennsylvania, and T. Joel Wade, my master's thesis advisor at Bucknell University in Lewisburg, Pennsylvania, initiated my interest in psychological research and helped me understand the importance of science in the field of psychology. Arthur Houts, my PhD advisor at the University of Memphis in Tennessee, taught me to apply scientific principles to conceptualizing and treating psychological disorders.

While I was an intern and postdoctoral fellow at the Center for Treatment and Study of Anxiety, in Philadelphia, Pennsylvania, Michael Kozak and Martin Franklin stood out among numerous accomplished colleagues as being particularly generous with their time and expertise. They have helped me cultivate my professional career and I thank them for their continued insights and support through thick and thin. I hope they will see their influence in this book because they have had a profound impact on my work. Although I have not worked personally with Jack Rachman or Paul

Salkovskis, their elegant writings have also had a major bearing on my thinking and clinical work with OCD, and their conceptual models are the centerpiece of this book and my work as a clinical scientist.

I am enormously fortunate to have so many collaborative relationships with fine researchers and clinicians in the field of OCD and anxiety disorders. I would especially like to thank David Tolin, Brett Deacon, Sarah Kalsy, Katherine Moore, Kristi Dahlman, and Stephen Whiteside, who have assisted me in various ways with this book, including lending case examples, providing editorial suggestions, and helping me refine my thinking about the concepts and treatment techniques that are covered. Thanks also to Shawna Stussy and Marcia Redalen, whose clerical support was invaluable to this project. Finally, I wish to acknowledge Susan Milmoe and Marianna Vertullo from Lawrence Erlbaum Associates for their enthusiastic support and assistance throughout the writing process.

On a personal note, I am grateful for a wonderful family that gives me the inspiration for everything I accomplish. When I began writing this book, I was lucky enough (at the age of 34) to have all four of my grandparents still living. However, I lost two of them—Morris Abramowitz and Dorothy Gerber—during the year it took to complete this undertaking. This book is dedicated to their beloved memories and to their spouses, Mildred Abramowitz and Robert Gerber, who remain a lively force in our family. My parents, Leslie and Ferne Abramowitz, and my siblings Andrew Abramowitz and Michelle Clay have always been there for me with unconditional love and encouragement, even across the miles. Most of all, I am thankful for Stacy—my adoring wife and best friend—and for our wonderful little girls Emily and Miriam, who have all been so very patient with me while I labored over this project. I hope you are as proud of me as I am of you.

I

What We Know About OCD

1

Recognition and Diagnosis of OCD

Few emotional disorders are as devastating as obsessive–compulsive disorder (OCD). Patients often have difficulty with work or school, falter in maintaining social and emotional relationships, and struggle with daily life events that others take for granted. Moreover, the psychopathology is among the most complex of the emotional disorders. Sufferers undertake a measureless struggle against seemingly ubiquitous opponents: recurrent thoughts, images, impulses, and doubts that although senseless on the one hand, are perceived as danger signs on the other. If such thoughts cannot be avoided or suppressed, if they cannot be resisted or rationalized, individuals with OCD turn to superstitious behavior in an attempt to prevent being accountable for feared disasters. The wide array and intricate associations between behavioral and mental symptoms can perplex even the most experienced clinicians. To illustrate the elaborate and seemingly bizarre features of OCD, consider the following case example.

> Sarah was a 26-year-old graduate student who had recently become engaged to marry her longtime boyfriend, Alan. At her initial assessment, Sarah described "weird thoughts and worries" that she might cheat on (or might have already cheated on) Alan, even though she had absolutely no desire to do so and had no history of this sort of behavior. The thoughts were continually on her mind and had become increasingly persistent and dis-

tressing as their wedding day drew nearer. On further inquiry, Sarah revealed that she also experienced recurrent unwanted thoughts and images of hurting innocent people. For example, while shopping for silverware for her new house, Sarah became worried she might use her new knives to stab people. After babysitting for her 1-year-old niece, she had intrusive distressing thoughts that perhaps she had done something terrible to hurt this baby, such as feeding her poison. Sarah had always considered herself a very kind and gentle individual—someone others sought out for advice. She had no legal history of any kind, which made the occurrence of these terrible thoughts even more bewildering.

Indeed, Sarah felt very guilty for thinking these thoughts. She had begun locking the kitchen drawers where her knives were kept and avoiding small children. She had also started taking certain precautions out of the fear that she might cheat on her fiancé. For instance, she tried to avoid going out alone so that she would not impulsively "hook up" with strange men. She also kept a written log of all her activities from the time she woke up to the time she went to sleep. This entailed recording where she was, whom she was with, and what she was doing every 5 minutes throughout the day. Thus, whenever the doubts arose, Sarah could verify to herself that she had not cheated or committed violent acts. Only when she was with Alan or other close friends did she not feel the need to keep the log. Still, she spent excessive time trying to analyze her thoughts and recall whether she had cheated or acted violently. In addition, when experiencing the unpleasant thoughts and doubts, Sarah often asked her friends if they had heard any rumors about her cheating on Alan. She also watched the news to make sure there were no stories about random violence. Needless to say, these symptoms were interfering with Sarah's ability to concentrate in school, interact socially, and enjoy her leisure time. Alan was becoming frustrated with Sarah's attempts to seek reassurance that she had not cheated. At the time of her assessment, Sarah estimated that the unwanted thoughts occupied about 8 hours each day.

Sarah's obsessions and compulsions seem like extraordinary phenomena—ideas, images, doubts, and urges that are completely contrary to her benevolent history, future intentions, and personal moral integrity. Yet they recur despite her ongoing efforts to control, suppress, or avoid them. There are also bizarre, wasteful, repetitive behaviors that she acknowledges are senseless yet cannot resist performing. Certainly these rare and illogical symptoms are far removed from *normal* human experiences. Surely some gross *abnormality*, in one form or another, is responsible for producing the symptoms of OCD. Yet research findings suggest otherwise. To date there is actually little compelling evidence that OCD symptoms are caused by abnormal brain structures or functions (Craske, 2003). Whereas all of our behaviors and thoughts (including one's general vulnerability to anxiety) could be reduced to genetics, convincing evidence of specific genetic anomalies linked to OCD is lacking (Pato, Pato, & Pauls, 2002).

Instead, research suggests OCD symptoms occur on a continuum that includes mild obsessions and compulsions in the population at large. A seminal study by Rachman and de Silva (1978) found that 80% of a nonpatient sample reported occasional intrusive unwanted thoughts, the content of which was identical to obsessions reported by a group of OCD patients such as Sarah. Examples of "normal obsessions" among nonpatients included thoughts of harming one's family, ideas about unacceptable sexual behavior, impulses to harm babies and the elderly, and thoughts about germs. Whereas both OCD sufferers and nonpatients may describe their intrusions as distressing, clinical obsessions are of greater frequency, intensity, and duration, and they evoke greater distress and more resistance compared to everyday obsessions. Other studies of nonpatients (Ladouceur et al., 2000; Muris, Merckelbach, & Clavan, 1997) have demonstrated that most people engage in various strategies to deal with or resist unwanted intrusive thoughts; these strategies are remarkably similar to compulsive behaviors observed among people with OCD. Examples include superstitious behavior, rationalizing or analyzing, checking, reassurance seeking, and thought suppression. These studies provide convincing evidence that people with and without OCD differ *quantitatively*, but not *qualitatively*, in their experiences.

But what causes clinical OCD symptoms? That is, how do normal intrusive thoughts and compulsive behavior progress into the more bizarre, distressing, and uncontrollable symptoms that we call OCD? If OCD symptoms are illogical, why do sufferers not recognize this and change their behavior? I address these important questions in the first part of this book by discussing current clinical and research findings that relate to cognitive and behavioral aspects of obsessions and compulsions. Progress in understanding the development and persistence of clinical obsessional problems from a cognitive-behavioral perspective has enhanced approaches to conceptualizing, assessing, and treating OCD. The second part of the book illustrates how to use cognitive and behavioral assessment and treatment techniques that are based on the conceptual model presented in Part I to successfully reduce clinical obsessions and compulsions.

OCD ACCORDING TO THE DSM–IV

According to the *Diagnostic and Statistical Manual of Mental Disorders* (4th ed., text revision *[DSM–IV–TR]*; American Psychiatric Association, 2000), OCD is an anxiety disorder defined by the presence of obsessions or compulsions that produce significant distress and cause noticeable interference with various aspects of functioning such as academic, occupational, social, leisure, or family settings. Table 1.1 presents a summary of the *DSM–IV* criteria for OCD. *Obsessions* are defined as intrusive thoughts, ideas, images, impulses, or doubts that the person experiences in some way as senseless and that evoke affective distress (i.e., anxiety, doubt). Classic examples include preoccupation with contamination, doubts

TABLE 1.1
DSM–IV **Diagnostic Criteria for OCD**

A. Either obsessions or compulsions.

 Obsessions are defined by (1), (2), (3), and (4):

   (1) Repetitive and persistent thoughts, images or impulses that are experienced, at some point, as intrusive and inappropriate and that cause marked anxiety or distress.

   (2) The thoughts, images, or impulses are not worries about real-life problems.

   (3) The person tries to ignore or suppress the thoughts, images, or impulses, or neutralize them with some other thought or action.

   (4) The thoughts, images, or impulses are recognized as a product of one's own mind and not imposed from without.

 Compulsions are defined as (1) and (2):

   (1) Repetitive behaviors or mental acts that one feels driven to perform in response to an obsession or according to certain rules.

   (2) The behaviors or mental acts are aimed at preventing or reducing distress or preventing feared consequences; however the behaviors or mental acts are clearly excessive or are not connected in a realistic way with what they are designed to neutralize or prevent.

B. At some point during the disorder the person has recognized that the obsessions or compulsions are excessive or unreasonable.

C. The obsessions or compulsions cause marked distress, are time-consuming (take more than 1 hour a day), or significantly interfere with usual daily functioning.

D. The content of the obsessions or compulsions is not better accounted for by another Axis I disorder, if present (e.g., concern with appearance in the presence of body dysmorphic disorder, or preoccupation with having a serious illness in the presence of hypochondriasis).

E. Symptoms are not due to the direct physiological effects of a substance or a general medical condition.

 Specify if:

   With poor insight: If for most of the time the person does not recognize that his or her obsessions and compulsions are excessive or unreasonable.

Note. *Diagnostic and Statistical Manual of Mental Disorders* (4th ed., text revision), by American Psychiatric Association, 2000, Washington, DC: Author. Copyright 2000 by the American Psychiatric Association. Adapted with permission.

about making terrible mistakes, and unwanted sexual and violent impulses. *Compulsions* are urges to perform behavioral (e.g., checking, washing) or mental rituals (e.g., praying) in response to obsessions. It is important to keep in mind that compulsive rituals are performed deliberately and in response to a sense of pressure to act. Compulsive behavior is usually perceived as senseless or excessive.

The *DSM–IV* definition implies that obsessions and compulsions are independent phenomena in that one or the other is necessary and sufficient for a diagnosis of OCD; yet this issue has been a matter of debate. To address this question, a large multisite field study of OCD patients was conducted during the early 1990s (Foa & Kozak, 1995). Among the 411 field study participants, 96% reported both obsessions and compulsions on the symptom checklist of the Yale–Brown Obsessive Compulsive Scale (Y–BOCS–SC; Goodman, Price, Rasmussen, Mazure, Delgado, et al., 1989; Goodman, Price, Rasmussen, Mazure, Fleischmann, et al. 1989; see chap. 6), only 2.1% reported predominantly obsessions, and only 1.7% reported predominantly compulsions. Moreover, of those who reported both symptoms, 84% indicated that they performed compulsive rituals to either reduce the likelihood of harm or to reduce subjective distress in general. These data suggest that the overwhelming majority of OCD patients have both obsessions and compulsions, and that for the most part, compulsions are performed deliberately with the aim of reducing obsessional distress.

Further support for the idea that obsessions and compulsions are closely related in a functional manner comes via a number of studies that have identified symptom dimensions and subtypes of OCD. These investigations consistently find that specific types of obsessions and compulsions load together on the same symptom-based factors and clusters (e.g., contamination obsessions with washing rituals; e.g., Abramowitz, Franklin, Schwartz, & Furr, 2003; Leckman et al., 1997; Summerfeldt, Richter, Antony, & Swinson, 1999) as well as on measures of symptom severity (e.g., Deacon & Abramowitz, 2005b). Moreover, there is evidence that the persistence of obsessional preoccupations is linked to the repeated performance of compulsive behavior (discussed further in chap. 4). So, as much as the distinction between obsessions and compulsions is intuitively appealing, the clinician should consider that OCD phenomenology does not necessarily distill neatly into these two categories.

The *DSM*'s emphasis on the *repetitiveness* and *persistent nature* of obsessions and compulsions falls short of helping the clinician fully understand the essential nature of OCD. Whereas these characteristics are the most readily observable signs of the disorder, the defining characteristic of OCD is actually in the functional relationship between obsessions (which evoke distress) and efforts to reduce this distress (e.g., compulsions). In treating individuals with OCD it is useful to view the disorder as one in which obsessional thoughts have become the focus of concern; compulsive behavior is a means of resisting or controlling intrusive thoughts (and the feared consequences of these thoughts). Moreover, as I discuss later, it is now well known that compulsive rituals such as washing and checking represent only one class of overt and covert tactics that patients use in response to their distressing obsessional thoughts.

The balance of this chapter introduces the reader to obsessions, compulsions, and other phenomena present in OCD that are important in understanding the disorder's complexity. Five symptom dimensions (e.g., contamination, harming, hoarding) that have been identified and studied are also discussed. The overall aim here is to help the clinician develop an approach to thinking about the symptoms of OCD that leads to the effective assessment and delivery of cognitive-behavioral treatment.

OBSESSIONS

One of the most striking features of OCD is its heterogeneity—obsessions present as endlessly personalized variations on a somewhat restricted number of themes. Foa and Kozak (1995) found that over time, most patients evidence multiple types of obsessions, as well as shifts in the content of these phenomena. In general, obsessions are experienced as unwanted, repugnant, threatening, obscene, blasphemous, nonsensical, or all of the above. Using a sample of 145 individuals with OCD evaluated at the Mayo Clinic, we examined the prevalence of various obsessional themes as categorized by the Y–BOCS–SC. These findings, along with representative examples of our patients' specific obsessions, are summarized in Table 1.2.

Aside from their thematic content, obsessions may take various forms, including doubts, images, impulses, fears, obsessional thinking, and miscellaneous forms (Akhtar, Wig, Varma, Pershad, & Verma, 1975). Descriptions and examples of the various forms are presented in Table 1.3.

Characteristics of Clinical Obsessions

It might be tempting to label any kind of repetitive thought or preoccupation as an obsession. Indeed this term is used indiscriminately in everyday language to refer to many types of repetitive thinking such as worries about everyday circumstances, a fascination with a certain type of car, a romantic or sexual crush, or the tendency to pay close attention to details. Each of these forms of cognition could be described as repetitious, and some might fall into the categories of obsessions listed in Tables 1.2 and 1.3. However, in the clinical sense, the term *obsession* is reserved for a very specific type of thinking. In fact, it is helpful for the clinician to become accustomed to recognizing obsessions less by their repetitiveness or thematic content, and

TABLE 1.2
Primary Obsessions Reported by 145 Patients With OCD

Category	n	%	Case Example
Contamination	84	57.9	My boss has a cold sore and touched my stapler; now I will get a cold sore.
			If I touch this bottle I will never feel clean again.
			I might have stepped in dog feces and then spread some of the germs to the floor of my house.
Aggressive	82	56.6	Image of my parents in a fatal car accident.
			If I don't correct other people's carelessness (at work in a factory), it will be my fault if something terrible happens.
			Impulse to yell curse words out loud during class.
			Maybe I didn't fully document the patient's symptoms, and as a result they will not get proper care.
			Other people will think I was dishonest.
Symmetry/ Order	62	42.8	Odd numbers are "wrong." The pictures must be evenly spaced on the wall.
Religious/ Morality	54	37.2	Is it OK to swallow saliva on Yom Kippur (a Jewish fast day) if you are thirsty?
			Unwanted image of Jesus masturbating on the cross.
			Maybe I cheated on the exam without realizing it.
Somatic	49	33.8	There is something wrong with my rectal sphincter muscle.
			One of my breasts is larger than the other.
Hoarding/ Saving	35	24.1	I need to save all of these art supplies in case the school system cuts back on spending for art classes.
			If I throw away pictures of dogs it's like I am being disrespectful to dogs.
			I might miss important information about my disorder.
Sexual	26	17.9	Urge to look in the direction of people's genitals.
			Unwanted image of my grandparents having sex.
			I could be gay since I admired that man's clothes.
Miscellaneous	60	41.4	If I say "cancer" someone in my family will get cancer.
			Odd numbers cause harm.
			Doubts that people don't completely understand what I say.

Note. Up to three primary obsessions were identified for each patient.

TABLE 1.3
Characteristics of the Six Forms of Obsessions

Form	Characteristics	Case example
Obsessional doubts	Persistent uncertainty over whether a task has been completed, or whether one is (or may come to be) responsible for harm	I may not have locked the doors, and someone could break in. I may have stepped in dog poop without realizing it. Was that a bump in the road or a person that I hit with my car?
Obsessional images	Persistent mental visualizations that are experienced as troubling or distressing	Images of loved ones seriously injured or dead. Unwanted images of one's grandparents having sex. Images of Christ's penis.
Obsessional impulses	Unwanted impulses or notions to behave in ways that would be inappropriate; often sexually or aggressively	Urge to push an elderly person to the ground. Urge to yell obscenities in church. Urge to jump in front of an oncoming car or train. Unwanted urge to sexually assault someone.
Obsessional fears	Excessive anxiety that one might lose control and act on impulses	What if I stabbed my wife in her sleep? What if I drowned my infant?
Obsessional thinking	Endless pondering over future negative outcomes	Maybe a person with herpes used this bathroom before I did and now I will get herpes and spread it to my family. What if God didn't appreciate the joke I just told and now I am damned to hell? Pondering over whether one is a "moral person."
Miscellaneous obsessions	Thoughts, tunes, numbers, and so on, that are distressing and difficult to dismiss	The number 666. The word cancer or death.

more by their functional properties—that is, how they are triggered, how they are experienced, and how the person responds to them.

To this end, three characteristics set clinical obsessions apart from other repetitive cognitive phenomena. First, obsessions are experienced as unwanted or uncontrollable in that they typically intrude into the sufferer's consciousness, often at what seem to be terribly inappropriate times. Although not deliberate forms of thinking, obsessions might be cued by certain situations or stimuli. For example, thoughts of screaming obscenities might arise at the library or in a place of worship, impulses to harm a child might be triggered by the sight of sharp objects, or the idea that one's hands are contaminated might surface at the sight of a garbage can or at mealtime. At other times, obsessional thoughts intrude without identifiable environmental cues. Examples include thoughts of having left the car door unlocked and unwanted images of loved ones being injured in accidents.

The second characteristic that distinguishes obsessions from other types of thinking is that although personally relevant, the content of obsessions is incongruent with the individual's belief system and is not the type of thought one would expect of himself or herself (sometimes referred to as *ego-dystonic*). Examples include a new mother's unwanted image of drowning her infant or a religious person's unwanted thought that God is dead. Such thoughts that directly conflict with one's sense of moral integrity often evoke high levels of anxiety and doubt because of their mere presence; for example: "What do the thoughts mean about who I really am?" or "Will I lose control and act on the impulses?" Obsessions might be at odds with the patient's sense of self in other ways as well; for example, contamination obsessions that occur among individuals who pride themselves on their cleanliness, obsessions with symmetry or orderliness that threaten one's feelings of perfection, or other senseless repetitive thoughts that represent a threat to one's idea of himself or herself as rational and in control of his or her thinking.

The third functional characteristic of obsessions is *subjective resistance*—the sense that the obsession must be dealt with, neutralized, or altogether avoided. Whereas compulsive behaviors are the most common (and observable) tactics used by individuals with OCD, a repertoire of other strategies may be used as well, including thought suppression, distraction, thought replacement, avoidance, rationalizing, and other mental or physical maneuvers (Freeston & Ladouceur, 1997). The motivation to resist is activated by the fear that if action is not taken, disastrous consequences, such as physical or mental harm to oneself or others, may occur. Less commonly, patients worry that if the obsession is not dealt with, anxiety, uncertainty, or a sense of imperfection will persist indefinitely or spiral to ever-increasing and unmanageable levels. Patients vary with respect to how easily they can articulate such concerns.

Lee and Kwon (2003) proposed two types of obsessions. *Reactive obsessions* are worry-like doubts evoked by situations or stimuli that carry a degree of uncertainty or risk that the person finds anxiety evoking (e.g., "I might have bathroom germs on my clothes"). Although reactive obsessions are usually recognized as excessive, the person might suspect that a feared consequence is likely. Thus, the occurrence or severity of a dreaded outcome is strongly resisted. Examples include concerns about contamination, making mistakes, accidents, and asymmetry. In contrast, *autogenous obsessions* are personally unacceptable intrusive thoughts, images, or urges that might either come to mind spontaneously or be prompted by external situations (i.e., the sight of a religious symbol may trigger an unwanted sacrilegious thought or image). Intrusive blasphemous or "immoral" thoughts and inappropriate sexual or aggressive impulses fall into this category. Because such thoughts are experienced as highly repugnant, they are readily perceived as irrational and the thoughts themselves are strongly resisted.

In summary, obsessions are doubts, thoughts, impulses, images, fears, or other types of cognitive phenomena that are personally relevant yet confined to a somewhat restricted range of topics. To varying degrees, people with OCD perceive their obsessions as intrusive and uncontrollable, inconsistent with their personal belief system or sense of self, and anxiety or distress producing. Given how obsessions are experienced it is not surprising that people with OCD engage in efforts to resist them with the aim of escaping from emotional discomfort. Traditionally, stereotyped compulsive rituals have been considered the primary means of resistance. Next, I encourage the clinician to think in line with current research indicating that compulsions represent only one of numerous overt and covert safety-seeking strategies that patients may deploy in their attempts to neutralize obsessional fear.

SAFETY-SEEKING BEHAVIOR: COMPULSIONS AND NEUTRALIZATION STRATEGIES

Salkovskis (1991) defined *safety-seeking behavior* as behavior that is performed to minimize or prevent a feared consequence. He further suggested that such behaviors explain why the nonoccurrence of a feared consequence fails to reduce the patient's fear. For example, a patient with contamination obsessions continues to fear becoming very sick from touching his shoes because every time he touches them, he ritualistically washes himself. When he does not become ill, he believes, erroneously, that his washing ritual is the reason this is so. The ritual prevents him from learning that shoes do not typically make people sick. The following text describes the various forms of safety behavior observed in OCD.

Overt Compulsive Rituals

Compulsive rituals are the most conspicuous features of OCD and, in many instances, account for most of the sufferer's functional impairment. Rachman (2002) proposed that the necessary and sufficient conditions for describing a repetitive behavior as compulsive are (a) performance of the behavior in response to an urge or pressure to act, and (b) attribution of the urge to internal sources. Some OCD patients make strong efforts to resist or delay their compulsive rituals (with occasional success), whereas others make little or no effort. Resistance may be strongest in the early stages of the disorder, with patients relaxing their fight against compulsive urges the longer they struggle with OCD (Tallis, 1995). When not bothered by obsessional fears, patients can often recognize that their compulsive urges are senseless and excessive. Although a relationship between obsessions and compulsions is the norm, some compulsive behaviors may not be directly connected to obsessions, yet they are still clearly senseless and excessive.

Form and Function. The DSM specifies that compulsions in OCD are motivated and intentional, in contrast to mechanical, robotic, repetitive behaviors (e.g., tics) as observed in disorders such as Tourette's syndrome. Moreover, compulsions are performed to reduce distress, in contrast to repetitive behaviors in addictive or impulse-control disorders (e.g., sexual addiction, trichotillomania), which are carried out because they produce pleasure or gratification.

Table 1.4 displays the various thematic categories of compulsions as assessed on the Y–BOCS–SC, as well as the percentage of individuals seen in our clinic with each category. The far right column of Table 4.1 presents examples of compulsive rituals from patients in our sample. In many instances it is clear that compulsive rituals are performed to reduce obsessional anxiety about particular feared consequences. Examples include compulsively checking appliances to reduce fears of electrical fires, or cleaning rituals intended to remove contaminants and thereby avoid sickness. In other cases, patients have difficulty articulating the presence of particular feared consequences, and instead perform rituals to reduce anxiety (or other forms of distress) or to achieve an ill-defined feeling of completeness.

Although rituals are intended to reduce distress, patients sometimes report that performing compulsive behavior evokes additional distress (Rachman & Hodgson, 1980). This may occur as a result of frustration with not being able to control seemingly senseless compulsive urges, or if there is obsessional doubt over whether the ritual was performed to completion. For example, one woman we evaluated found her showering ritual extremely distressing because she was unable to decide when she was clean

TABLE 1.4
Primary Compulsions Reported by 145 Patients With OCD

Category	n	(%)	Case Example
Checking	86	59.3	Checks locks, windows, lights, appliances
			Checks that sleeping child is still breathing
			Rechecks work assignments
			Checks with doctors or nurses to rule out serious illness
			Carefully inspects all empty envelopes before discarding
Cleaning/ Washing	80	55.1	Ritualized shower and toilet routine
			Uses rubber gloves to handle laundry
			Cleans shower stall before taking a shower
			Rinses hands in excess of 40 times per day
Ordering/ Arranging	64	44.1	Arranges books in particular manner
			Puts on clothes in a particular order
Mental rituals	61	42.1	Repeats the phrase "nothing, no one, nowhere" to himself
			Repeats "I love Jesus Christ with all my heart" three times to herself
			"Cancels out" unacceptable thoughts with "good" thoughts
			Reviews conversations to ensure she didn't say curse words
Repeating	49	33.8	Rewrites bank checks
			Turns light switch on and off repeatedly until feels just right
Counting	43	29.7	Counts breaths to avoid odd numbers
Hoarding	32	22.1	Collects empty grocery bags and envelopes
			Collects items that could be used as art supplies
Miscellaneous	73	50.3	Confesses all "bad" thoughts to his mother
			Asks the same questions to gain reassurance
			Confesses the same sins repeatedly to priest

Note. Up to three primary compulsions were identified for each patient.

enough. Thus, she remained in the shower until the hot water ran out—sometimes as long as 2 hours. In some instances rituals become so burdensome that patients try to avoid situations that would evoke compulsive urges. For instance, the woman just described eventually refrained from leaving her home to avoid feeling contaminated because that would trigger the irresistible urge to shower.

Less is understood about senseless and excessive compulsive behaviors that are performed to reduce discomfort yet are not linked with obsessional fears of danger or harm. Rachman (1974) described a subgroup of OCD patients with obsessional slowness who spend exceptional lengths of time repeating routine tasks such as reading and writing, dressing, arranging items, or walking through doorways. The reason for their slowness was the need to perform these activities "perfectly." Rasmussen and Eisen (1992a) proposed that such patients have "an inner drive that is connected with a wish to have things perfect, absolutely certain, or completely under control" (p. 756). More recently, Coles, Frost, Heimberg, and Rheaume (2003) hypothesized that compulsive rituals that are not performed to reduce specific fears of harm may be carried out in response to distress associated with obsessional concerns about things (including mental states) not being "just right" or perfect.

Rachman and his colleagues examined the functional properties of compulsions in a series of elegant experiments in which patients were exposed to stimuli that provoked compulsive urges and asked to report their level of anxiety and urge to ritualize. The findings of these studies can be summarized in the following way: For patients with washing rituals that were evoked by fears of dirt and germs, exposure to contaminants led to an increase in subjective anxiety and urges to ritualize, whereas completion of a washing ritual rapidly reduced this distress. A more gradual spontaneous reduction in both anxiety and compulsive urges was also observed when the performance of rituals was delayed for 30 minutes (Hodgson & Rachman, 1972). Similar results were obtained in two studies of patients with checking rituals that were evoked by exposure to potentially harmful stimuli such as knives (Roper & Rachman, 1976; Roper, Rachman, & Hodgson, 1973).

These studies are of utmost importance because they empirically demonstrate the functional link between obsessional anxiety and compulsive behavior in OCD. In behavioral terms, this research sheds light on how compulsive rituals are negatively reinforced by their consequences. That is, because rituals bring about a more rapid decline in obsessional anxiety than if the ritual was delayed or not performed, the patient is likely to resort to compulsive behavior as a habitual response to obsessional anxiety. This relationship between anxiety-evoking obsessions and anxiety-reducing compulsions (although not always readily apparent) is what sets OCD apart from most other disorders that involve repetitive thinking and behavior—it is the essence of OCD. For this reason, during assessment it is critical to ascertain the presence and nature of this relationship.

Although compulsions reduce anxiety in the short term, they are maladaptive in the long run because of how patients interpret their outcome. Specifically, when obsessive fears do not materialize patients believe that it was their rituals that prevented such disasters. This strengthens the obsessional fear (and the ritualistic urge) by fostering the notion that rituals are necessary to prevent catastrophe. Patients might also believe that without performing the ritual, obsessional anxiety would have continued indefinitely. Put another way, compulsive behavior in OCD blocks patients from finding out that their obsessional fears are unrealistic. For example, suppose David, who has an obsessional fear that his mother will die unless he counts to 10, dares to resist performing this counting ritual and his mother does not die. His obsessional fear will have been invalidated. If he repeatedly has similar experiences, David will accumulate disconfirmatory evidence that will weaken his belief that the counting ritual prevented his mother from dying. However, if David continues to engage in compulsive counting and his mother does not die, he will continue to attribute this to the compulsive counting and his fear will be strengthened. In similar situations, patients often say things such as, "If I had not washed my clothes, I would have become ill," "If I don't check that the door is locked, there will be a burglary," or "If I didn't get dressed the right way I would never feel right."

Because compulsive rituals bring about an immediate reduction in obsessional fear (i.e., they are an escape tactic), they are negatively reinforced and likely to be repeated. This repetition serves to strengthen the self-perpetuating vicious cycle displayed in Fig. 1.1. Understanding this pattern of phenomenology leads to the use of certain treatment procedures that can weaken this cycle. In particular, repeated exposure to obsessional cues while simultaneously refraining from compulsive behavior will teach patients two things. He or she will learn, first, that the feared consequences are unlikely to occur even if no compulsive behaviors are performed, and second, that compulsive rituals are unnecessary to reduce obsessional fear.

Mental Rituals

As Table 1.4 indicates, a substantial proportion of individuals with OCD engages in mental compulsions—repetitive mental acts aimed at preventing a negative outcome (also called *covert* or *cognitive* rituals). Because mental rituals are purely cognitive phenomena and therefore less tangible than overt rituals such as checking and washing, they may be difficult to distinguish from obsessions. However, as with behavioral rituals, mental rituals

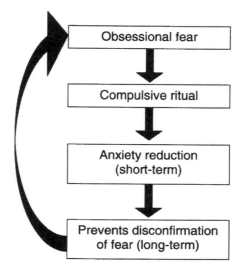

FIG. 1.1.   The self-perpetuating cycle of obsessions and compulsions in OCD.

are intentional acts that are performed to reduce distress (de Silva, Menzies, & Shafran, 2003). Obsessions, in contrast, are involuntary anxiety-evoking thoughts. Examples of common mental rituals include repetition of special phrases, prayers, or numbers in a specific manner, and ritualistically going over (mentally reviewing, analyzing) one's behavior or conversations to reassure oneself that one has not made egregious mistakes or said anything offensive. The following example illustrates a somewhat elaborate mental ritual.

> Stefanie was an unmarried department store clerk who lived with her parents. Her severe OCD symptoms interfered substantially with social, leisure, and work functioning. Among her symptoms was a complex mental ritual that she referred to as "being born again." This ritual was evoked by obsessional doubt associated with unacceptable thoughts such as "my life will always be out of control," or "OCD will run my life forever," that often came to mind and caused significant distress. To execute the ritual, Stefanie had to undress and lie, in the nude, on her parents' bed in a fetal position with her eyes closed. She then had to conjure up the following mental images in order: (a) her parents having intercourse, (b) herself being conceived from a sperm and egg, (c) herself as a fetus growing in her mother's womb, and (d) her birth.
>
> At first, completing this ritual took Stefanie only about 3 minutes. However, she became increasingly uncertain about whether she was visualizing the images "perfectly" enough to make the ritual "really count" and began starting over from the beginning if she even slightly lost her train of thought during the ritual. When Stefanie came to our clinic she reported spending over 2 hours getting through this ritual each day.

Mental rituals are functionally equivalent to overt rituals in that the urge to perform them is evoked by obsessional fear, and successful performance of the ritual results in an immediate reduction of fear and of the compulsive urge (de Silva et al., 2003). As with overt compulsions, urges to perform mental rituals decline on their own over time if the ritual is not performed. In fact, de Silva et al. (2003) found that urges to carry out mental rituals subsided within 15 minutes even if the mental ritual was not performed. As with behavioral rituals, mental compulsions (a) are maintained by negative reinforcement because they reduce distress, and (b) prevent the disconfirmation of obsessional fear.

Compulsive Reassurance Seeking

Many individuals with OCD engage in repeated attempts to gain "ultimate" certainty that the feared consequences featured in obsessions will not (or did not) occur. Requests for assurance may take various overt and covert forms and are evoked by obsessional doubt and intolerance for uncertainty. The most straightforward style is overt questioning. For example, Hayden had been with his parents at the bedside of his grandfather who was dying of cancer. Even though the event was a peaceful one, Hayden continued to be tormented with obsessional thoughts that perhaps when no one was looking, he had killed his grandfather by smothering him with a pillow. When these intrusions occurred, they evoked doubt and distress, which the patient dealt with by frequently asked his parents, "Are you sure I didn't kill Grandpa?" Some patients try to disguise their reassurance seeking by asking the same question in a slightly different way (e.g., "How did Grandpa die?").

Reassurance seeking provides the patient with no new information and is therefore simply an attempt to reduce anxiety. That is, the person can usually guess correctly the answers to his or her reassurance-seeking questions; yet he or she feels very anxious and engages in emotional reasoning wherein logic is dictated by emotions ("There might be something wrong because I feel anxious"). Although seeking reassurance may bring about short-term relief from obsessional doubt, patients rarely get the ultimate guarantee they are looking for. This is, of course, because complete certainty is rarely an option, especially for patients who tend to want reassurance about obscure doubts such as "Am I going to heaven when I die?" "How hard do I need to concentrate when saying my wedding vows to make them count?" and "How long must I wash my hands to be sure I have no germs?" A useful way of understanding urges to seek reassurance is to consider that whereas people without OCD tolerate acceptable levels of risk and uncertainty all the time (e.g., driving, crossing the street), those with OCD have trouble taking such risks when it comes to their obsessional fears. They wish to have a 100% guarantee of safety. The following example illustrates an elaborate form of reassurance seeking.

Steve, a 25-year-old medical student, described obsessional doubts that some years earlier he had injured his rectal sphincter muscle while having a bowel movement. Although a series of medical examinations suggested no abnormalities, Steve's need for assurance that he would not become bowel incontinent persisted. In addition to compulsively checking his rectal muscle tone using his fingers, Steve regularly sought guarantees from his physician and his medical school professors that one cannot permanently injure one's sphincter in this way. Notwithstanding his doctors' initially sincere efforts to provide the most accurate medical and logical reassurance, Steve could not be convinced. He began tracking down his professors or calling them at home when desperate for relief from obsessional doubt. The continual pestering of faculty members for an "absolute guarantee" became irritating to the point that Steve was asked to take a leave of absence. Despite all of his attempts to gain certainty, and despite no evidence of unhealthy muscle tone whatsoever, Steve saw himself as relegated to a life of horrible embarrassment. He was avoiding intimacy, using adult incontinence products, and having problems with depression.

A more clandestine method by which patients may seek reassurance is to closely observe how others respond to certain situations or stimuli. For example, one patient with contamination fears surreptitiously cajoled others to accompany him to public bathrooms. The patient then watched the other person's reaction to the bathroom very closely to gauge whether the bathroom was "safe enough" for him. It is important for the clinician to be cognizant of subtle attempts to obtain reassurance because these behaviors, like overt compulsions, strengthen obsessional fear.

Neutralization

Most people with OCD use additional overt and covert strategies that do not meet *DSM* criteria for compulsions (i.e., they are not stereotyped or repeated according to rigid rules) to control, remove, or prevent their obsessions (Freeston & Ladouceur, 1997; Ladouceur et al., 2000). On one hand, these *neutralization* strategies resemble compulsive rituals in that they are attempts to reduce anxiety. However, whereas compulsions are intended to prevent negative outcomes, patients use neutralization to offset obsessional thoughts; and this may or may not be an attempt to prevent a feared outcome (Rachman & Shafran, 1998; Salkovskis, 1985). Individuals may use different strategies to neutralize different thoughts and different strategies to cope with the same thought (Freeston & Ladouceur, 1997).

Researchers have identified several general categories of neutralization responses including overanalyzing and rational self-talk (i.e., to convince oneself of the unimportance of the thought), seeking reassurance, replacing the thought with another thought, performing a brief mental or behavioral act, distraction, and thought suppression (Ladouceur et al., 2000). The choice of neutralizing strategy may be influenced by the intensity of the obsessional thought, the context in which it occurs, how the thought is appraised, and how well particular strategies have "worked" in the past (Freeston & Ladouceur, 1997). Neutralizing can take infinitely diverse forms, and some of these strategies may be remarkably subtle. The key to recognizing and understanding such symptoms is to identify their antecedents (i.e., obsessional thoughts) and consequences (i.e., escape from the thought; anxiety reduction). To this end, a thorough assessment of the patient's cognition and behavior, as is described in later chapters, is imperative.

The following examples illustrate various kinds of neutralization strategies.

- One man gripped the steering wheel more tightly (brief behavioral act) when he experienced distressing thoughts of intentionally killing his family by driving his car into opposing traffic.
- A young woman always removed her jacket and wore tight clothing when she shopped to neutralize obsessional thoughts that others might think she was stealing (brief behavioral act).
- A man with unacceptable thoughts of awakening during the night and urinating on his furniture neutralized the thoughts by picturing himself using the toilet and by leaving the bathroom light on (brief mental and behavioral acts).
- A heterosexual woman with unwanted thoughts about what it would be like to be a lesbian tried to suppress and dismiss such ideas as they came to mind (thought suppression).
- A woman with obsessional thoughts of harming her unsuspecting husband confessed these thoughts to him whenever they came to her mind (social strategy). She explained to her therapist, "If I tell my husband that I'm thinking about hurting him, he'll be ready to stop me if I start to act."

A number of studies confirm that neutralization and overt compulsive rituals have similar functional properties. Both are deliberate and effortful, and both serve as a temporary escape from obsessional distress (e.g., Rachman, Shafran, Mitchell, Trant, & Teachman, 1996; Salkovskis, Westbrook, Davis, Jeavons, & Gledhill, 1997). Indeed such strategies become habitual because they provide rapid escape from obsessional distress (i.e., negative reinforcement). However, in the long run, neutralizing is a maladaptive response because, as with compulsive rituals, patients attribute the nonoccurrence of disastrous consequences to their neutralization efforts, thereby preserving their obsessional fears.

Avoidance and Concealment

Passive avoidance is present to some degree in most individuals with OCD and is intended to prevent exposure to situations that would evoke obsessional thoughts and compulsive urges. For some patients the aim of avoidance is to prevent specific consequences such as contamination or illness, whereas in other instances avoidance is focused on preventing obsessional thoughts from occurring in the first place. For example, one woman avoided using public staircases because they evoked thoughts and fears of impulsively pushing unsuspecting people down the steps. Other patients engage in avoidance so that they do not have to carry out tedious compulsive rituals. For instance a young man with obsessional fears of contamination from his family's home computer (because it had been used to view pornography) engaged in elaborate and time-consuming compulsive cleaning and showering rituals. During the morning and afternoon he avoided the computer room so that he would not have to perform these rituals during the day. In the evening, however, he relaxed his avoidance and allowed himself to enter the room and become contaminated knowing that he could "work in" his ritualistic showering before bedtime.

Newth and Rachman (2001) elaborated on a different form of avoidance in which patients deliberately conceal from others the content and frequency of their intrusive and repugnant obsessions. Usually it is unacceptable sexual, blasphemous, and violent images; impulses to harm loved ones; and senseless thoughts about contamination that are hidden from others. This concealment may occur for a variety of reasons, the most obvious of which is the fear that others will respond negatively to hearing about the thoughts or regard the person as dangerous or sick.

As with the various forms of compulsive behavior and neutralization, avoidance and concealment are maladaptive in that they provide short-term protection or relief from obsessional fear, yet have insidious longer term effects. By avoiding or concealing, the individual never has the opportunity to find out that obsessional situations are not high risk, and that obsessional thoughts are not as significant as is feared. Thus, in the end, these two strategies contribute to the persistence of obsessional fear. Concealment of obsessions also increases preoccupation with the concealed thought and ensures that the person will not receive corrective feedback about the normalcy of such thoughts. Therefore, the sufferer continues to believe that his or her intrusive thoughts are rare or dangerous.

SUBTYPES AND DIMENSIONS OF OCD

Although there are grounds for conceptualizing OCD as a homogeneous disorder, the prominence of particular features in particular patients is an obvious clinical reality. Whereas some patients are overly concerned with contamination and compulsively wash their hands to modulate distress, others who are equally impaired spend inordinate amounts of time repeating mundane activities to achieve "just right" feelings. Still others may be tormented by intrusive unacceptable thoughts of blasphemy, sex, or violence, or have to repeatedly check to allay persistent obsessive doubt. Although thematic shifts are common over time, the symptoms occurring at any given point are internally consistent and have meaning to the patient. That is, patients with washing rituals feel they must wash to reduce contamination. Those with compulsive praying rituals describe fears of punishment from God. Individuals who check say that they fear being responsible for harm. Observations that some symptom themes are less responsive to treatment than others suggest that it is useful to distinguish between different presentations of OCD (for a review see McKay et al., 2004).

A number of researchers have used multivariate statistical methods to derive symptom subtypes or dimensions using the Y–BOCS–SC. The findings from these studies, which have examined hundreds of patients with OCD, indicate that the following thematic presentations of OCD exist: contamination obsessions with washing rituals; aggressive/sexual/religious obsessions with checking rituals; symmetry obsessions with ordering/repeating/counting compulsions; and hoarding obsessions and compulsions (e.g., Leckman et al., 1997). One problem with these studies is that the Y–BOCS–SC does not adequately assess the full range of safety behaviors. For example, mental compulsions and neutralization are left out. Because about 80% of OCD patients report mental rituals, and about 10% report mental rituals as their most common compulsions (Foa & Kozak, 1995), the thematic schemes that are reported in these studies are incomplete.

In a more definitive study of the various presentations of OCD, my colleagues and I at Mayo Clinic and the University of Pennsylvania used an updated version of the Y–BOCS–SC that incorporated a separate *mental rituals* category (Abramowitz, Franklin, Schwartz, & Furr, 2003). This allowed us to more carefully study how mental rituals such as repeating "safe" phrases, numbers, images, prayers, mental counting, list making, and mentally reviewing (e.g., conversations) were related to other types of OCD symptoms. Using a large sample of patients ($N = 132$) we found five stable presentations of OCD with predominant patterns of obsessions and compulsions, including (a) harming, (b) contamination, (c) symmetry, (d) unacceptable thoughts with covert rituals, and (e) hoarding. Table 1.5 shows the percentage of patients in our sample with each presentation. Although we

TABLE 1.5
Frequency and Percent of Patients With Different OCD Symptom Subtypes

Subtype	Number of Patients	%
Harming	29	22.0
Contamination	33	25.0
Symmetry	13	9.9
Hoarding	16	12.0
Unacceptable thoughts	41	31.1

Note. Total sample size was 132. From "Symptom Presentation and Outcome of Cognitive-Behavior Therapy for Obsessive–Compulsive Disorder," by J. S. Abramowitz, M. E. Franklin, S. A. Schwartz, & J. M. Furr (2003), *Journal of Consulting and Clinical Psychology, 71*, 1049–1057. Copyright 2003 by American Psychological Association. Reprinted with permission.

clustered patients into groups according to their symptom presentation, it is probably more useful to think about the heterogeneity of OCD in terms of *symptom dimensions* because a given patient may experience different presentations to varying degrees (i.e., high, medium, or low on each dimension; Taylor, 2005). Moreover, the majority of patients evidence multiple symptom themes. Next, the essential phenomenology of each symptom dimension is discussed.

Harming

The chief obsessional symptoms in the harming dimension include unrealistic fears of responsibility for inflicting physical or emotional injury to oneself or to others. Patients may be overly concerned about possible accidents, mistakes, fires, burglaries, or hurting others' feelings. They have obsessive doubts such as "Am I absolutely certain I unplugged the iron?" or "What if I hit someone with my car and didn't realize it?" Some patients display obsessional fear of "unlucky" words, numbers, colors, or serious illnesses that they magically associate with disastrous consequences (e.g., saying the word *cancer* makes cancer more likely).

In an attempt to gain certainty that harm is unlikely, individuals with this presentation of OCD typically engage in compulsive checking. Checking occurs when individuals who believe they have a responsibility for preventing harm feel uncertain about whether a perceived risk has been adequately reduced or removed (Rachman, 2002). Such rituals may be elaborate and involve repeated checking of all doors, windows, lights, and electrical outlets before going to bed or leaving the house. Inordinate amounts of time may be spent checking for mistakes, such as when paying bills, addressing envelopes, or completing forms and school assignments. Checking might also involve compulsive reassurance seeking, mentally reviewing past behavior to check for feared mistakes, or counting to ensure avoidance of unlucky or harmful numbers (e.g., 13, 666). As Rachman (1976) noted, checking occurs predominantly in the person's home environment and when the person is alone. It may be more intense when the person is under additional distress or is experiencing depression, yet is most severe when the person feels highly responsible. Some patients perform repeating rituals, such as rereading or rewriting, or the repetition of routine behaviors (e.g., going through a doorway, looking twice at something) because they believe such rituals prevent harm or bad luck. There might be a certain safe number of times that such checking or repeating rituals must be repeated (e.g., multiples of 7).

Case Description.

Marcia and her husband managed a dog kennel. Marcia's most prominent obsessions included thoughts that the dogs might get injured or become ill (i.e., with ringworm) and that the dog owners would hold her and her husband liable. Such fears motivated Marcia to engage in a range of checking rituals including excessively examining each of the 20 to 30 dogs in the kennel multiple times each day and enlisting others to check on the status of the dogs if she was away from the kennel for more than an hour at a time. At intake, Marcia was spending more than 3 hours each day checking the kennel dogs' health. She acknowledged that her behavior was extreme compared to what other kennel managers do. However, she also described feeling compelled to know "for sure" that the dogs had not been injured. Marcia also checked locks, appliances, and water faucets before leaving the house and every night before going to bed. She noted that her checking rituals always took longer if her husband was away from home.

Contamination

Obsessions in the contamination dimension commonly include excessive and unreasonable fears of diseases from bodily fluids (e.g., blood, sweat, urine, feces, saliva, semen), harm from dirt, or germs, and pollution from environmental toxins such as asbestos or household items such as bleaches or solvents. Some individuals fear becoming sick from contaminants and a subset worry that they will contaminate others. In some instances it is as if the idea or feeling of being contaminated is the focus of concern over and above any specific illnesses. The transmission of contamination is typically by contact and Tolin, Worhunsky, & Maltby (2004) found that contamination could be "spread" from object to object without a reduction of the intensity of the contamination. More than other OCD presentations, contamination fears seem similar to the symptoms of specific phobia in which individuals go to great lengths to avoid confronting discrete anxiety-evoking stimuli (e.g., restrooms, floors, shoes). This may be contrasted with the harming subtype in which fear is evoked primarily by doubts regarding possible negative consequences. Most patients with contamination symptoms display hypervigilance for sources of contamination and may retain a precise memory of the nature and exact location of such stimuli going back many years (Rachman, 2004).

Contact with the contaminants just described (sometimes even imagined contact) evokes a sense of dirtiness and instigates attempts to remove the pollutant. The primary compulsive "decontamination" behaviors are excessive cleaning and washing (of oneself or inanimate objects), including ritualized showering, bathing, bathroom routines, and excessive use of handy wipes or disinfectant hand gels. Whereas some patients with washing and cleaning compulsions perform higher frequencies of brief rituals (e.g., 50 brief hand rinses per day), others engage in fewer, yet more time-consuming rituals (e.g., daily 90-minute showers). The function of these behaviors is to prevent the spread of contaminations or to reduce the chances of harm. However, over time such behaviors can become stereotyped and robotic (Rachman, 2004). The feeling of contamination also evokes avoidance behavior and attempts to prevent contamination. Some patients establish sanctuaries (e.g., one's own room) that they take especially great care to keep uncontaminated. The use of barriers (e.g., paper towels, gloves) when touching surfaces or opening doors is common, yet patients may also take more exorbitant measures to prevent or remove contact with feared contaminants, including changing clothes or bed linens more often than necessary.

In some ways, decontamination rituals resemble checking rituals in that both are intended to reduce obsessional distress, uncertainty, and the chances of harm. For patients with cleaning rituals, the source of uncertainty is that the feared contaminants are typically microscopic. Thus, the extent of possible contamination and how much cleaning must be done to decontaminate are both unknowns. Whereas situations in which definite contact with contaminants has occurred will likely evoke rituals, so may situations where there *might have been* contact. Rituals and avoidance are often performed in accordance with "rules" acquired (and often exaggerated) from outside sources (e.g., to avoid sickness one should wash for 30 seconds after using the bathroom; the herpes virus can live for 18 hours on a toilet seat). A difference between checking and cleaning rituals is that whereas checking is intended to *prevent* future harm, the goal of cleaning rituals is often to *remove* potential danger (e.g., contamination from germs). In addition, whereas checking rituals often serve to protect others from danger, cleaning usually serves to protect oneself. In our study, patients with this presentation of OCD were unique in that they evidenced very few non-contamination-related obsessions and compulsions.

Case Description.

Matt, a 35-year-old unmarried man, worked as a repairman for a cable TV company. His current obsessional fears concerned becoming sick via contamination from feces. He worried about stepping in dog feces while at work and therefore avoided grassy areas or homes where he thought there might be dogs. Compulsive behavior included frequent hand washing and changing his shoes or clothes. Even if he saw dog feces without stepping in it, Matt worried whether he had come close enough to get any germs. Such situations evoked irresistible urges to change his shoes and wash his hands. Other sources of contamination included the mail and certain public places he associated with dog feces. Matt's apartment was his "safe haven." Except for his bathroom, he considered everything in his living space to be clean. Before going into his apartment, Matt would perform a decontamination ritual that included removing his shoes and some of his clothing before entering, and not touching anything until he reached the bathroom. Once in the bathroom Matt showered and then avoided touching the toilet or shower curtain because these were considered contaminated. Anything he brought into his apartment, such as groceries, had to be cleaned in the bathroom before it could be placed in other rooms. All mail was opened in the bathroom as well. When Matt was evaluated at our clinic he was spending a total of more than 8 hours each day performing compulsive cleaning rituals.

Incompleteness

Research indicates that most individuals with and without OCD at some time experience the feeling that something is not "just right"; that is, they have "not just right experiences" (NJREs; Coles, Frost, Heimberg, & Rheaume, 2003; Leckman, Walker, Goodman, Pauls, & Cohen, 1994). In OCD, incompleteness primarily involves obsessions with order, neatness, symmetry, and feelings of discomfort evoked by the NJREs. Compulsive behavior largely involves ordering and arranging or repeating behaviors until the "just right" feeling is achieved. Calamari et al. (1999) asserted that patients with this symptom profile have a high need for certainty that things are just so. Coles, Frost, Heimberg, and Rheaume (2003) suggested these symptoms represent a specific form of perfectionism that is unique to OCD.

The clinician must be careful to distinguish between symmetry or exactness symptoms that are associated with NJREs and those associated with magical thinking. The latter is characterized by a belief that if objects are not in the "correct" position, disastrous consequences will result (e.g., bad luck, someone will die). Other patients with incompleteness symptoms perform ordering rituals to achieve a perfect state of cleanliness. Patients with this symptom subtype might also repeatedly check to ensure that something has been done perfectly for the sake of perfection, rather than to prevent disastrous consequences. Coles, Frost, Heimberg, and Rheaume (2003) proposed that for patients with incompleteness symptoms, the feeling of imperfection or incompleteness may be a feared consequence in its own right.

Case Description.

Karen's chief OCD symptoms involved ordering and arranging items until she was satisfied that they looked "perfect." This included making sure that photos in all of her albums were arranged just right, that pictures were hung evenly on the wall, that her closet was perfectly arranged (clothes folded perfectly), and that her writing was perfect. Even casual writing tasks were impaired. For example, she was unable to write love notes to her boyfriend, send cards during the holidays, or balance her checkbook without having to erase or rewrite many times before being satisfied with how her handwriting looked. Karen reported that her compulsive urges were motivated by a sense of imperfection that was somewhat difficult to describe, but which was associated with fairly intense affective distress. She felt that if she did not achieve a sense of completeness, her level of discomfort would persist indefinitely and increase to intolerable levels. She strongly wished not to rewrite or arrange items, yet was unable to resist her urges to do so.

It is important to distinguish between incompleteness symptoms in OCD from those observed in obsessive–compulsive personality disorder (OCPD). Patients with OCD describe their need for perfection and ordering or arranging rituals as unwanted and distressing (i.e., ego dystonic). They emphasize how such problems interfere with functioning and they wish not to be bothered by them. In contrast, people with OCPD view their perfectionism as worthwhile. They strive to attain perfection because they have imposed unrealistically high standards for themselves. Thus, they do not view their symptoms as problematic and often do not welcome the urging of others that they become more flexible. Whereas the treatment procedures described in this book are likely to be of help to people with OCD symptoms, they are not designed to reduce symptoms of OCPD.

Unacceptable Thoughts and Covert Rituals

This symptom dimension is characterized by autogenous obsessions that primarily (but not exclusively) concern violence, sex, or religion. Examples include intrusive ideas of loved ones injured in accidents; unwanted impulses to attack or harass innocent people or open the emergency exit of an airplane during flight; unspeakable thoughts of murdering one's own infant; "forbidden" or "perverse" sexual impulses; unwelcome images of unattractive people nude or having sex; and unacceptable blasphemous thoughts (e.g., God is dead), images (e.g., of Jesus' penis), or impulses (e.g., to defile the synagogue). These are experienced as senseless, repugnant, and difficult to dismiss. Moreover, the obsessional content is highly uncharacteristic of the person's moral, ethical, and behavioral tendencies and therefore causes high levels of distress and efforts to resist. In particular, patients worry about the presence, significance, and consequences of these thoughts (e.g., I might act on the thought; I'm an evil person for thinking this; I must be crazy because of my senseless thoughts) and conclude that they must take preventative measures or banish the thought from consciousness.

In an effort to reduce the discomfort or perceived risk of danger associated with having unacceptable intrusive thoughts, patients with this OCD presentation often resort to covert (mental) rituals such as trying to replace a "bad" thought with a "good" one. Other safety behaviors include reassurance seeking (to diffuse responsibility), avoidance, thought suppression, and concealment. For example, one happily married woman complained of unwanted sexual thoughts about her priest that occurred whenever she entered her church. She believed that it was terribly immoral to have adulterous thoughts in a place of worship, and that God would ultimately punish her for having such thoughts about a priest. She tried to stop the thoughts by thinking about more spiritual things (e.g., picturing a large cross), avoiding the priest, and repeating a special prayer to ask for forgiveness. Moreover, she refrained from telling anyone else of her "dirty little secret."

Some patients describe the sense that "naughty" or otherwise unacceptable or senseless thoughts can contaminate or ruin stimuli in the environment. To illustrate, one patient seen in our clinic reported that if certain senseless thoughts (e.g., germs coming out of the television) or evil images (e.g., the Devil) came to mind while he was engaged in an action (e.g., turning the page of a book, walking into a room, eating), he had to repeat the action 12 times to neutralize the thought. Otherwise, he feared, everything else he did would be "tainted" by the unwanted thought.

Based on the scarcity of prototypical observable rituals such as washing or checking, patients with this symptom presentation have traditionally been labeled as *pure obsessional* (e.g., Baer, 1994). This implies that only obsessions are present. However, as I described earlier, careful assessment reveals that as with other presentations of OCD, two processes are present here as well: (a) involuntary anxiety-evoking thoughts (obsessions) and (b) deliberate anxiety-reducing strategies (mental rituals, neutralizing). Even experienced clinicians sometimes find it a challenge to distinguish between these two forms of mental phenomena. Nevertheless, this distinction is highly important for successful treatment using cognitive-behavioral methods, as we will see in later chapters. The following example illustrates how obsessions and mental rituals can appear to be very similar when only their form and content are considered. A careful functional analysis of the antecedents and consequences of each phenomenon is required to gain a complete understanding of the symptomatology.

Case Description.

Dale, a 19-year-old man with no history of violent behavior, described persistent unacceptable intrusive images of physically attacking his mother and father. The images sometimes occurred spontaneously, but were often evoked by the sight of potential weapons such as knives, and by certain words such as *kill, murder,* and *thrash.* For some time, Dale's treatment providers had labeled him as a pure obsessional because there appeared to be no anxiety-reducing compulsive rituals—just constant violent images. However, on conducting a functional analysis, it was discovered that Dale's intrusive images of attacking his *mother* were involuntary and unwanted, but that he was deliberately and carefully conjuring up the images of attacking his *father* to neutralize the images of attacking his mother. On careful inquiry, Dale explained that he felt the need to replace his mother with his father in his intrusive images to reduce the intense distress he felt when thinking of harming a woman. Imagining attacking his father—another man—on the other hand, was more acceptable to Dale. Thus, the images of attacking mother were conceptualized as obsessions, and those of attacking father were considered mental rituals.

Hoarding

Patients with hoarding symptoms collect or save items that realistically have little or no practical value. The patients are subsequently unable (or unwilling) to discard such items. Examples of commonly hoarded items include obsolete newspapers and magazines, old clothes, bags and containers, pictures, letters, old schoolwork, junk mail, and the like. The resulting clutter may render entire rooms unusable and jeopardize personal safety or hygiene (Thomas, 1997). Obsessional concerns among patients with hoarding symptoms include thoughts about the potential use of saved objects, excessive emotional attachment to them (i.e., hypersentimentality), and the sense that objects have intrinsic value despite having no practical value (e.g., It's too nice to throw away). Whereas some individuals actively acquire items, hoarding is perhaps best conceptualized as avoidance behavior tied to indecisiveness, uncertainty, and perfectionism (Frost & Gross, 1993). That is, hoarding serves to avoid or postpone (a) the anxiety-evoking decision of whether to discard certain items, and (b) the feared negative consequences of discarding "important" items (Frost & Hartl, 1996).

Case Description.

Jill, a 52-year-old divorced art teacher, had severe hoarding symptoms that began when she was in her 20s. Although she saved a variety of things such as old mail, children's books, pictures of animals, and plastic containers, Jill's main hoarding behavior revolved around her art classes. Her home was strewn with unclaimed projects from students from as far back as the 1980s, including drawings, paintings, collages, and even larger sculptures and scenery from school plays that she felt she might use again at some point as examples of good artwork. Jill also had an entire room of lesson plans that she had downloaded off the Internet or copied from textbooks. Although she planned to one day use these lesson plans with her classes, this had never actually happened. She was also accumulating a collection of art supplies to use "just in case" there were funding cuts to the school's art program. Thus, countless rolls of masking tape, bottles of glue, magic markers, popsicle sticks, beads, and reams of paper were scattered throughout the house in no particular order. Jill refused to discard these items, asserting that some day she might need them, or could sell them. Meanwhile she was unable to keep relationships and was embarrassed to have anyone visit her home.

Is Hoarding a Symptom of OCD?   Collecting and the inability to discard unneeded items are actually observed across many organic and psychological disorders including dementia, developmental disability, eating disorders, and psychosis (e.g., Frost, Krause, & Steketee, 1996). Adams (1973) and Greenberg (1987) first hypothesized an association between hoarding and OCD. Coles, Frost, Heimberg, and Steketee (2003) argued that hoarding is a specific symptom of OCD on the basis of (a) correlations between OCD and hoarding symptoms, (b) the presence of hoarding factors in structural analyses of OCD symptoms, and (c) the preponderance of hoarding among individuals with OCD. Although such findings suggest a strong relationship between hoarding and OCD, they must be interpreted with caution due to selection biases that favored the inclusion of OCD patients with hoarding symptoms. Clinical observations suggest functional similarities between some presentations of hoarding and OCD. For example, among individuals whose hoarding symptoms are accompanied by other OCD symptom dimensions, hoarding appears to be motivated by obsessional doubt regarding the possibility that something important could be discarded by mistake. The task of painstakingly checking all potential garbage for important items becomes so daunting that the person gives up and retains all sorts of unnecessary materials. Conceptualized in this way, hoarding appears to fit with the harming symptom dimension described earlier.

There is mounting empirical evidence that hoarding itself is heterogeneous, and not necessarily a specific symptom of OCD. For example, Grisham, Brown, Liverant, and Campbell-Sills (in press) found factor analytic evidence that hoarding, although frequently associated with OCD, constitutes a distinct symptom. Cognitive aspects of hoarding appear somewhat distinct from cognitions in other OCD symptoms (Steketee, Frost, & Kyrios, 2003). Moreover, in contrast to patients with OCD and those reporting mixed OCD and hoarding, those with pure hoarding symptoms reported lower levels of negative affect, anxiety, depression, and worry. Two studies of nonclinical samples by Wu and Watson (2005) indicated that whereas prototypical OCD symptoms such as washing and checking are strongly correlated with one another, hoarding is only moderately associated with other OCD symptoms. Moreover, individuals with OCD can be distinguished from patients with other disorders and from nonpatients on the basis of prototypical OCD symptoms, but not on the basis of hoarding. Finally, whereas OCD symptoms show consistent relationships with negative affect, hoarding does not.

Although additional research is needed to clarify the relationship between OCD and hoarding symptoms, the data just reviewed cast doubt on the notion of a distinct hoarding symptom dimension. Most likely, when hoarding occurs along with other OCD symptoms, the hoarding is secondary to harming-related doubts regarding the possibility of terrible mistakes as previously described. Evidence also suggests that hoarding that occurs in isolation of other OCD symptoms is functionally distinct from OCD. Given these findings, and considering that cognitive-behavioral treatment that is usually effective for OCD is less helpful for hoarding (e.g., Abramowitz, Franklin, Schwartz, & Furr, 2003), the discussion of OCD psychopathology and treatment in this book assumes that hoarding symptoms as observed in OCD exist as part of the harming symptom dimension. Clearly, however, additional research on this topic is needed.

A Comment on Symptom Dimensions

It is important to note that the symptom dimensions illustrated here are descriptive, rather than functional. That is, they are based primarily on what the patient does, as opposed to why or what motivates such behavior. An example of how this approach can be misleading is the fact that some incompleteness symptoms involve the fear of disastrous outcomes whereas others involve concern with perfectionism and not-just-right feelings. Thus, although these dimensions can be useful for understanding a patient's OCD symptoms on a superficial level, they do not substitute for a thorough functional assessment of cognitive and behavioral phenomenology as is described in later chapters.

POOR INSIGHT AND OVERVALUED IDEATION

The *DSM–IV* criteria for OCD include the specifier "with poor insight" to denote individuals who view their obsessional fears and compulsive behavior as reasonable. These patients are also said to have *fixed beliefs* or *overvalued ideas* (OVI), defined as "almost unshakable beliefs that can be acknowledged as potentially unfounded only after considerable discussion" (Kozak & Foa, 1994, p. 344). To illustrate poor insight, consider the case of Charles, who had been on a scuba diving trip to the Caribbean with his 15-year-old son. In the year since this trip, Charles had been tormented with the obsessional thought that his son's scuba gear had been used by someone with AIDS and was not sufficiently cleaned. He was sure that it was only a matter of time until his son became an AIDS victim. Charles's conviction in this belief was remarkably unshakable despite six negative HIV tests. He had even begun planning for his son's bout with AIDS by writing a eulogy to deliver at the funeral. Even following numerous attempts to help Charles logically challenge his fears, he remained steadfast in his belief.

Although the majority of OCD patients recognize at some point that their obsessions and compulsions are senseless and excessive, evidence suggests OCD is characterized by a continuum of insight into the irrationality of these symptoms. In the *DSM–IV* field study described earlier, Foa and Kozak (1995) found that of 250 patients with obsessional fears of harmful consequences, 13% were completely certain their feared consequence would not occur, 27% were mostly certain, and 30% were uncertain of whether such consequences would occur. Another 26% were mostly certain that the feared consequences would materialize, and 4% were convinced that feared consequences would happen. When clinicians were asked to categorize patients on the basis of their insight, 5% of the patients were judged to have never recognized that their symptoms are senseless (i.e., have poor insight).

In a further analysis of this data, my colleagues and I (Tolin, Abramowitz, Kozak, & Foa, 2001) found that levels of fixity of belief vary depending on the obsessional theme. In particular, poorer insight seems to be associated most strongly with religious obsessions, fears of making mistakes, and unwanted obsessional impulses to act aggressively. A number of additional studies suggest patients with somatic obsessions (e.g., fears of serious illnesses, obsessions with physical appearance) have poorer insight and greater overvalued ideation compared to those with other kinds of OCD symptoms (Abramowitz, Brigidi, & Foa, 1999; McKay, Neziroglu, & Yaryura-Tobias, 1997; Neziroglu, McKay, & Yaryura-Tobias, 2000). It is important to know about insight in OCD patients because there is evidence that poor insight is related to attenuated treatment outcome with behavioral therapy (e.g., Foa, Abramowitz, Franklin, & Kozak, 1999).

PREVALENCE AND COURSE

Prevalence

OCD was once considered extremely rare in the general population. However, results from large-scale epidemiological surveys now suggest it is among the more common adult psychological disorders. The Epidemiological Catchment Area survey conducted in five U.S. communities in the 1980s estimated the lifetime prevalence in adults to be 2.6% (range across the five sites was 1.9%–3.3%) and the 1-month prevalence at 1.3% (range was 0.7%–2.1%; Karno, Golding, Sorenson, & Burnam, 1988). In Canada (Edmonton), Kolada, Bland, and Newman (1994) reported a 2.9% prevalence rate. A cross-national study estimated the lifetime prevalence of OCD at 2% worldwide (range = 0.7%–2.5%; Weissman et al., 1994).

Clinic-based and community studies from around the world report a slight preponderance of females with OCD (e.g., Weissman et al., 1994; Rasmussen & Eisen, 1992b) and there appears to be a rarity of minority groups among these research samples (e.g., Karno et al., 1988). Weissman et al. (1994) found substantially lower lifetime rates of OCD in Taiwan compared to other countries surveyed (0.7% vs. 2.0%). Reasons for racial and ethnic differences are unclear and may reflect variability in symptom reporting or differential utilization of mental health care.

Onset

OCD typically begins by the age of 25, and often in childhood or adolescence. Only rarely does it onset after age 50 (Rachman & Hodgson, 1980; Rasmussen & Tsuang, 1986). Large studies indicate that the mean age of onset is earlier in men (about age 21) than in women (age 22–24; Rasmussen & Eisen, 1992b). Rasmussen and Eisen (1992b) found that among a sample of 512 patients, primary OCD symptoms began before the age of 15 in about one third, before age 25 in about two thirds, and after age 35 in less than one fifth of patients.

Although most individuals with OCD do not identify clear-cut precipitants to symptom onset, researchers have found evidence that stressful or traumatic events and experiences may play a role for some patients (de Silva & Marks, 1999; Kolada et al., 1994). Accumulating data also suggest that OCD symptoms occur at higher than expected rates among childbearing women and their partners (Abramowitz, Moore, Carmin, Wiegartz, & Purdon, 2001; Abramowitz, Schwartz, Moore, & Luenzmann, 2003). Moreover, the content of obsessional thoughts among new parents typically concerns unwanted thoughts and fears of harming their children (Wisner, Peindl, Gigliotti, & Hanusa, 1999). It seems likely that in this case the abrupt increase in stress and responsibility that comes with caring for a newborn infant gives rise to exaggerated obsessional thinking (Abramowitz, Schwartz, & Moore, 2003).

Course

OCD is a chronic condition with a very low rate of spontaneous remission. Left untreated, symptoms fluctuate, with worsening during periods of increased life stress. In an early study by Rasmussen and Eisen (1988) that was conducted prior to the widespread availability of effective treatments, 85% of 560 patients had a continuous course with waxing and waning of symptoms, 10% had a deteriorating course, and only 2% had an episodic course marked by 6-month periods of full remission. More recently, Skoog and Skoog (1999) completed a 40-year follow-up study of 144 individuals with OCD, many of whom had received treatment. These authors found that 83% of this cohort had improved and 48% no longer met diagnostic criteria for OCD, although about half of the nonclinical individuals reported some residual symptoms. Steketee, Eisen, Dyck, Warshaw, and Rasmussen (1999) found a 15% probability of full symptom remission at 1 year and a 22% probability after 5 years. Collectively, these findings suggest that although OCD symptoms are likely to improve with treatment, full recovery is the exception, not the rule.

Quality of Life

Individuals with OCD show impaired social and role functioning, troubled romantic and family relationships, diminished academic performance, increased unemployment, and increased receipt of disability income (Koran, 2000). Although the severity of obsessions and coexisting depressive symptoms were the best predictors of poor quality of life in one study (Masellis, Rector, & Richter, 2003), the direction of causality (particularly for depression) remains unclear. Koran, Thienemann, and Davenport (1996) found that despite a reduced quality of life, people with OCD did not differ substantially from the general U.S. population in rates of alcohol abuse, suicide, or marriage. The relatives of OCD patients suffer as well, because symptoms may result in restricted access to certain rooms, involvement of others in compulsive rituals, and difficulty in taking vacations (Black, Gaffney, Schlosser, & Gabel, 1998; Calvocoressi et al., 1995; Magliana, Tosini, Guarneri, Marasco, & Catapano, 1996). Data from our own sample of 50 patients indicate that a diagnosis of OCD is related to increased (nonmental health) medical utilization, and that more severe OCD and depressive symptoms are associated with greater impairment in work or school, social, and family functioning.

Dupont, Rice, Shiraki, and Rowland (1995) estimated that the direct cost of OCD on the U.S. economy in 1990 was $2.1 billion, and the indirect cost (e.g., in lost productivity) was $6.2 billion. Moreover, OCD accounted for about 6% of the estimated cost of all psychiatric disorders in 1990. Still, only about 1 in 15 individuals with OCD receive treatment for their condition (Nestadt, Samuels, Romanoski, Folstein, & McHugh, 1994); and the delay between symptom onset and obtaining a correct diagnosis and treatment may be as long as 10 years (Marks, 1992; Rasmussen & Eisen,

1988). Reasons for the lag between onset and treatment initiation include patients' concealment of their seemingly bizarre thoughts and behaviors, and the underrecognition by professionals. Many sufferers only recognize their symptoms as part of OCD after being exposed to media coverage about the disorder.

Comorbidity

Individuals with OCD are at an increased risk for additional Axis I and Axis II psychopathology. Depressive disorders are among the most commonly co-occurring difficulties (e.g., Crino & Andrews, 1996a; Nestadt et al., 2001; Steketee et al., 1999). Weissman et al. (1994) found that the lifetime prevalence of major depressive disorder (MDD) among OCD patients ranged from 12.4% to 60.3% across seven countries ($M = 29\%$). In the eastern United States, Nestadt et al. (2001) reported a lifetime comorbidity rate of 54.1% and Steketee et al. (1999) reported a concurrent comorbidity rate of 36%. In Canada (Toronto), Antony, Downie, and Swinson (1998) found that 24.1% of a large OCD sample presently met criteria for MDD. For the most part, OCD predates MDD (Demal, Lenz, Mayrhofer, Zapotoczky, & Zitterl, 1993). This suggests that depressive symptoms usually occur in response to the distress and functional impairment associated with OCD. Depressive symptoms seem to be more strongly related to the severity of obsessions than to compulsions (Ricciardi & McNally, 1995).

A number of studies indicate that OCD is often compounded by additional anxiety problems (Weissman et al., 1994). Table 1.6 shows comorbidity rates for particular anxiety disorders from three research samples. Nestadt et al. (2001) found significantly higher lifetime rates of social phobia, panic and general anxiety disorder (GAD), but not specific phobia or agoraphobia, among individuals with OCD compared to non-OCD controls. We (Abramowitz & Foa, 1998) found that 20% of the *DSM–IV* OCD field study sample ($n = 381$) also had a concurrent diagnosis of GAD. Two studies examined the rates of various proposed OCD spectrum disorders among individuals with OCD. As Table 1.7 indicates, with the exception of somatoform disorders (hypochondriasis and body dysmorphic disorder), the proposed spectrum disorders only rarely occur among OCD patients. The relationship between OCD and proposed spectrum disorders is discussed further in chapter 2.

A number of studies have reported the prevalence of personality disorders among individuals with OCD (e.g., Black, Noyes, Pfohl, Goldstein, & Blum, 1993; Crino & Andrews, 1996b; Steketee et al., 1999). Estimates of comorbidity with at least one personality disorder vary widely (from 8.7%–87.5%) depending on the methodology used to assess Axis II psychopathology. However, studies generally agree that personality disorders belonging to the anxious cluster (e.g., obsessive–compulsive, avoidant) are more common than those of other clusters.

TABLE 1.6
Percentages of OCD Patients With Other Anxiety Disorders

Anxiety Disorder	Crino & Andrews (1996a)[a] (N = 108)	Antony et al. (1998)[b] (N = 87)	Nestadt et al. (2001)[a] (N = 80)
Social phobia	42	41.4	36.0
Specific phobia	—	20.7	30.7
Panic disorder	54	11.5	20.8
Agoraphobia	—	—	16.7
Generalized anxiety disorder	41	11.5	13.0

[a]Concurrent diagnosis.
[b]Lifetime comorbidity rate.

TABLE 1.7
Percentages of OCD Patients With Proposed Obsessive–Compulsive Spectrum Disorders[a]

Proposed Spectrum Disorder	Jaisoorya et al. (2003) (N = 231)	Nestadt et al. (2001) (N = 80)
Somatoform disorders		
Hypochondriasis	13	15
Body dysmorphic disorder	3	16
Impulse control disorders		
Trichotillomania	3	4
Sexual compulsions	0.4	—
Compulsive buying	0.4	
Kleptomania	0	3
Pyromania	—	0
Pathological gambling	0	0
Eating disorders		
Anorexia nervosa	0.4	9
Bulimia nervosa	0	4
Neurological disorders		
Tourette's syndrome	3	—

[a]Lifetime comorbidity rates.

2

Differential Diagnosis: What Is OCD and What Is Not?

The clinical picture of OCD presented in chapter 1 characterizes a specific and unmistakable pattern of thinking and behavior. Obsessions are unwanted, unacceptable, and intrusive repetitive thoughts, ideas, images, urges, or doubts that give rise to affective distress—typically in the form of anxiety over some feared consequence(s). For example, the sufferer doubts whether germs are present or whether he or she has made (or will make) a catastrophic mistake. In response to the obsessional distress, individuals with OCD deploy various safety-seeking strategies, some of which could be regarded as compulsive, to reduce uncertainty over the perceived risk of negative consequences. These strategies may take the form of overt, stereotyped, repetitive rituals such as checking to prevent a possible threat or washing to remove an existing one. However, they may also be subtle, brief, covert, and unobservable.

Gaining widespread acceptance is the notion that a number of psychological and neuropsychiatric disorders from various *DSM* diagnostic categories are related to OCD. Collectively, these conditions have been referred to as *obsessive–compulsive spectrum disorders* (OCSDs). Some authors have proposed, largely on the basis of clinical observation, that the OCSDs are linked by shared clinical features (i.e., repetitive thoughts and behaviors), courses of illness, family history, comorbidity, and treatment response

(Hollander & Wong, 2000). Its intuitive appeal and popularity aside, the OCSD concept has conceptual and practical difficulties. As we will see in this chapter, although OCD and the OCSDs have some overlaps in symptom presentation, not all OCSDs are characterized by the kind of phenomenology that is present in OCD. Clinicians working with individuals with OCD must therefore be able to differentiate OCD phenomenology from that which is distinct. After placing current conceptualizations of OCD within a historical context, this chapter closely examines the clinical phenomenology of some of the proposed spectrum conditions.

APPROACHES TO OCD THROUGH HISTORY

The earliest accounts of OCD were rooted in a religious context. Demons were thought to possess people who complained of repetitive, unwanted distressing thoughts, and who exhibited compulsive behavior. Treatment usually entailed exorcism. The first nonreligious explanations held that obsessions and compulsions developed from "psychic fatigue" in which an individual's mental and behavioral dyscontrol was caused by an imbalance of "mental energy" (Janet, 1903). The psychoanalytic point of view held that obsessions were unconscious impulses, and compulsions were ego defenses against these impulses (Salzman & Thaler, 1981). Although unsubstantiated by research, these early conceptualizations represented attempts to understand the phenomenology of OCD.

The behavioral approach followed in the tradition of emphasizing phenomenological mechanisms, yet advanced the methodology for doing so by applying functional analysis, which clarified observable (and therefore measurable) antecedents and consequences of obsessions and compulsions (e.g., Dollard & Miller, 1950; Mowrer, 1960; Rachman & Hodgson, 1980). Behavioral (learning) models of OCD propose that obsessions develop as classically conditioned fear responses to previously neutral stimuli. Compulsions are conceptualized as escape responses that are negatively reinforced by the reduction in obsessional anxiety that they engender. Most recently, the cognitive-behavioral approach, discussed in the chapters that follow, has expanded the study of obsessive–compulsive phenomenology to maladaptive beliefs and assumptions thought to underlie obsessional fear (Salkovskis, 1985, 1989). Strengths of both the behavioral and cognitive-behavioral approaches are that they are derived from a vast clinical and laboratory research base, and therefore are probably accurate.

Unfortunately, theoretically driven approaches to understanding the complex phenomenology of OCD are all but abandoned in current diagnostic schemes, such as the *DSM*, which promote an understanding of disorders as merely lists of signs and symptoms. With this shift toward a reductionistic medical model, an appreciation for psychological mechanisms (e.g., learning and cognitive mediation) is replaced by a more superficial "checklist" approach that merely collects signs and symptoms according to their form or topography, as opposed to their function. For example, a complete understanding of safety behaviors as efforts to mitigate obsessional distress that paradoxically strengthen obsessions is lost in the *DSM*'s definition of compulsions as described in chapter 1. Thus, recognition of the rich phenomenology of OCD is diminished in favor of a more cursory view of the disorder as characterized by the presence of repetitive thoughts and behavior.

Perhaps a main cause of the shift in emphasis toward identifying overt signs and symptoms of mental disorders was the desire to improve on the poor diagnostic reliability of early versions of the *DSM*. However, this has led to a blurring of the distinction between the symptoms of OCD and those of various other disorders that also involve repetitive thoughts or actions, even in cases where clear phenomenological (functional) differences exist. The OCSD approach provides the hallmark example: A dizzying array of problems from across the *DSM* are all proposed to be related to OCD based on the presence of irresistible repetitive impulses and actions (Hollander & Wong, 2000). I argue that this has had deleterious effects. For example, it is relatively common to see patients given a diagnosis of OCD when they have problems such as repetitive skin picking, hair pulling, and compulsive sexual behavior, which are actually phenomenologically distinct from OCD. Next I consider a number of disorders often confused with OCD in this way. Pulling from research on these various conditions I evaluate the extent to which each condition may be said to be related to OCD. Further, I discuss methods for distinguishing these disorders from OCD.

IMPULSE CONTROL DISORDERS

Trichotillomania

Trichotillomania (TTM) provides an excellent example of how an emphasis on lists of signs and symptoms can be misleading in differentiating OCD from other disorders. The chief *DSM–IV–TR* diagnostic criteria for TTM include: (a) recurrent pulling of one's hair resulting in noticeable hair loss; (b) increase in tension immediately before pulling, or when attempting to resist pulling; and (c) pleasure, gratification, or relief when pulling out the hair (APA, 2000). Going by this list of features alone, TTM appears to share characteristics with OCD, namely, repetitive, compulsive behaviors. However, despite some overlap in the way that these symptoms are described, intrusive anxiety-evoking obsessional thoughts that occur in OCD are not present in TTM. This is an important difference because, as we saw in chapter 1, obsessional fears and doubts evoke the compulsive behavior in OCD. That is, patients with OCD wash compulsively to escape from fears of contamination or illnesses, they repeat actions because of intrusive thoughts that things must be "just right," and they compulsively check to assure themselves that danger has not (or will not) occur. In contrast, urges to pull one's own hair in TTM are precipitated by feelings of general tension, depression, anger, boredom, frustration, indecision, or fatigue (Christensen, Ristvedt, & Mackenzie, 1993; Stanley & Mouton, 1996). Moreover, the hair pulling leads to pleasurable feelings, a phenomenon not reported by OCD patients after completing compulsive rituals (Rachman & Hodgson, 1980; Stanley, Swann, Bowers, & Davis, 1992).

Some shared characteristics between OCD and TTM that deserve mention include that both are frequently comorbid with mood, anxiety, eating, personality, and substance use disorders; both may involve embarrassment due to their symptoms; and both may impact the sufferer's functioning. Although TTM tends to affect females more often than males, an earlier age of onset seems to be more common for males, and this is similar to the demographic pattern found in OCD. Importantly, the characteristics just mentioned are present among many emotional disorders, not just OCD and TTM. Therefore, the presence of these features does not suggest a specific relationship between the two disorders. Thus, aside from the fact that hair pulling in TTM can be described as compulsive, TTM and OCD actually have little that is uniquely in common in terms of their phenomenology. Nevertheless, the keys to differentiating these two disorders lie in a thorough examination of the precursors (triggers) and aftereffects (consequences) of the compulsive behavior. To this end, clinicians may find the information provided in Table 2.1 helpful in making the distinction and explaining this difference to patients.

Nonparaphilic Sexual Disorders

Sometimes referred to as sexual addictions, sexual compulsions, or hypersexuality, nonparaphilic sexual disorders (NPSDs) are problems involving repetitive sexual acts comprised of conventional, normative, or nondeviant sexual thoughts or behavior that the person feels compelled or driven to perform, often in an exploitative way, which may or may not cause distress (Goldsmith et al., 1998). Examples include the incessant use of Internet pornography, frequent masturbation, and continuous sexual encounters with prostitutes to the detriment of one's marital relationship. Although NPSDs are not *DSM* diagnoses, people for whom this pattern of behavior persists for at least 6 months and interferes with functioning meet diagnostic criteria for impulse-control disorder not otherwise specified.

Because repetitive thoughts of a sexual nature are observed in both NPSDs and OCD, some have proposed that NPSDs are a variant of OCD and

TABLE 2.1
Differentiating Between Compulsive Behaviors in Trichotillomania and OCD

Question	Trichotillomania	OCD
What is the compulsive behavior?	Hair pulling, including manipulating or biting and eating the hair	May take various forms (e.g., washing, checking, etc.)
What triggers provoke the compulsive urges?	Boredom, being alone, general stress or tension, physical sensation (e.g., scalp itches)	Obsessional thought or other specific fear cues (e.g., knives, toilets)
Are obsessions present?	No	Yes
What is the outcome of the compulsive behavior?	General stress relief, relaxation, feels good	Escape from specific obsessional anxiety, reassurance
What time of day do the compulsive behaviors occur?	Often only at night	Night or day

therefore OCSDs (e.g., Hollander & Wong, 2000). To examine this proposal empirically, my colleague Stefanie Schwartz and I conducted careful interviews with individuals with NPSDs and others with OCD who reported "sexual obsessions" (Schwartz & Abramowitz, 2003). As Fig. 2.1 shows, there were considerable differences in the phenomenology of the repetitive thoughts and behaviors reported by people with these two conditions. Patients with OCD reported more fear and avoidance related to sexual thoughts than did those with NPSDs. Conversely, individuals with NPSDs evidenced greater sexual arousal associated with repetitive thoughts and behaviors compared to those with OCD. This is consistent with clinical observations that logging onto Internet chat rooms, for example, is not aimed at reducing uncertainty or the probability of feared outcomes. Instead, these sexual habits appear to be motivated by the physically and emotionally enjoyable states they produce (e.g., sexual arousal, orgasm). This impulsive behavior is phenomenologically distinct from compulsive behaviors in OCD, which the individual feels driven to perform to reduce anxiety or fear, and which do not involve actual sexual activities.

The fact that both NPSDs and OCD involve repetitive sexual thoughts can be a source of confusion in distinguishing between the two conditions. As is described above, the clinician must carefully assess the antecedents and consequences of such thoughts to determine whether the thought is an obsession as in OCD, or a sexual fantasy as in NPSDs. The following examples illustrate this distinction.

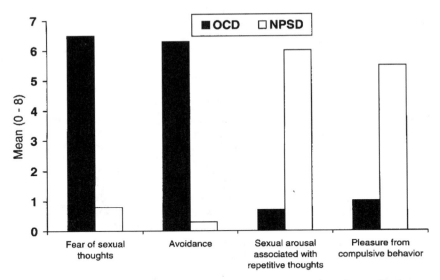

FIG. 2.1. Phenomenological characteristics of repetitive thoughts and behaviors in OCD and nonparaphilic sexual disorders. Adapted from "Are Nonparaphilic Sexual Addictions a Variant of Obsessive-Compulsive Disorder: A Pilot Study," by S. Schwartz and J. Abramowitz, 2003, *Cognitive and Behavioral Practice, 10*, pp. 372–377. Copyright 2003 by the Association for Advancement of Behavior Therapy. Adapted with permission.

OCD patient:

Howard, who had been married to the same woman for 14 years, presented with severe sexual obsessions as his primary OCD symptom. Whenever he saw an attractive woman, Howard experienced recurrent images about what she might look like without her clothes on. The thoughts were utterly repugnant to Howard and he perceived them as immoral and inconsistent with his strong love and attraction to his wife. He did not want to think about or have sex with these other women, they did not sexually arouse him, and he engaged in attempts to "cancel out" or control the unwanted images whenever they came to mind using strategies such as thought suppression. Howard was afraid that if he could not control his sexual thoughts it meant that he was an unfaithful husband and an adulterer. Thus, he tried to avoid places where there might be many women (e.g., shopping malls, the health club) and confessed his unwanted thoughts to his wife just to be sure she would stop him if he began to act on them.

NPSD patient:

Robert, an accountant who had been married for 5 years, described often thinking about attractive females he had seen recently. He imagined what such women looked like undressed or wearing only their underwear, sometimes spending hours each day with such thoughts in his mind. These images were highly sexually arousing to Robert and they often led to erections and the urge to masturbate. Robert engaged in daily masturbation sessions during which he purposely conjured up sexual images involving women he had seen in places such as shopping malls or health clubs. Currently, he was masturbating in the bathroom at work for up to 30 minutes at a time and this was interfering with his productivity and his desire to have sex with his wife, who had become upset with Robert's behavior.

These two case examples portray the key phenomenological differences between sexual thoughts and repetitive behavior in OCD and NPSDs. In OCD, sexual thoughts (i.e., obsessions) are perceived as unacceptable and they lead to anxiety, avoidance, and urges to neutralize or control the thought, or prevent feared consequences. People with OCD are exquisitely sensitive to the potential for harm and it is this that makes the occurrence of unwanted sexual thoughts especially unacceptable. In contrast, for the person with NPSD, the sexual thought itself is not experienced as distressing. In fact, it may be intentionally conjured up on a repeated basis because it is associated with sexual excitement or release. In addition, such thoughts often lead to sexual behavior and devaluation of the object of the thought (e.g., members of the opposite sex) in NPSDs, but not in OCD. Although both OCD and NPSDs involve repetitive thinking or behavior concerning sex, the underlying functional aspects of these signs and symptoms suggest clear differences between the two disorders in how these symptoms are experienced.

Kleptomania

Kleptomania involves the failure to resist urges to steal objects that are not needed for personal use or monetary value (APA, 2000). Often referred to as *compulsive*, the stealing behavior is actually *impulsive* as it occurs without extensive planning. Moreover, the stolen items are typically of little value and might never be used. People with kleptomania report no obsessional fear or anxiety before stealing, but may describe a sense of general tension. Also unlike in OCD, people with kleptomania report a "rush," "thrill," or "manic high" associated with their stealing (McElroy, Keck, & Phillips., 1995). Thus, the function of compulsive stealing in kleptomania is quite different from that of compulsive rituals and neutralizing in OCD. This important phenomenological distinction leads to the conclusion that kleptomania is not related to OCD.

Pathological Gambling

The essential features of pathological gambling include a preoccupation with gambling; the need to gamble with increasing amounts of money to achieve the desired excitement; unsuccessful efforts to curtail the gambling behavior; and a history of lying, fraud, theft, and relationship problems associated with gambling (APA, 2000). The gambling often occurs on a repetitive basis, hence the proposed relationship to OCD. However, whereas obsessional preoccupations in OCD are unwanted, unacceptable, resisted, and lead to anxiety or fear, the thoughts about gambling evoke feelings of excitement. Moreover, patients with pathological gambling report pleasure or gratification during and after gambling (Hollander & Wong, 1995), which is in contrast to compulsive behavior in OCD that serves to reduce anxiety about feared outcomes. Thus, the drive to gamble, and the emotion associated with this experience, is qualitatively different from that which is present in OCD.

Compulsive Buying

Characterized by repeated, excessive, and inappropriate spending, and frequent thoughts about shopping and buying, compulsive buying is not officially recognized as a mental disorder. This behavior, however, is considered to fall in the category of impulse-control disorder not otherwise specified. In contrast to obsessions and compulsions in OCD, preoccupation with buying and urges to make purchases are neither anxiety evoking nor typically resisted, and the actual purchasing behavior is experienced as gratifying and pleasurable (until long-term negative financial consequences occur; McElroy et al., 1995). Thus, as with other impulse-control conditions, the repetitive symptoms of compulsive buying are mediated by vastly different psychological mechanisms than are compulsions in OCD.

Compulsive Skin Picking and Nail Biting

Parallels have been drawn between OCD and compulsive skin picking and nail biting because these all involve senseless, repetitive behavior (Hollander & Wong, 2000). However, as we have seen with the repetitious activity associated with other impulse-control problems, skin picking and nail biting are performed in response to general tension rather than in response to specific obsessional fears. Additionally, these habits are often associated with gratification and tension relief, as opposed to escape and avoidance of disastrous consequences. From a behavioral analytic perspective, repetitive behavior in impulse-control disorders is primarily positively reinforced by its consequences (i.e., gratification). In OCD, however, compulsive behavior is maintained by a process of negative reinforcement (i.e., escape). Thus, the drive to pick one's skin and bite one's nails, and the emotional experiences associated with these behaviors, are qualitatively different from those present in OCD, even if they are all repetitious. Table 2.2 compares the antecedents and consequences of repetitive behaviors observed in OCD and in impulse-control disorders.

TABLE 2.2
Comparison of Repetitive Behaviors in OCD and in Impulse-Control Disorders Included in the OC Spectrum

	OCD	*Impulse-Control Disorders*
Antecedents	• Specific fears of undesirable consequences • Unwanted, intrusive obsessional thoughts, doubts, images, and impulses	• General tension, sexual arousal, depression, being alone, boredom, indecision, fatigue, thoughts about the behavior, excitement (e.g., sexual)
Characteristics of the behavior	• Usually deliberate • May or may not be repeated • May be carried out by a proxy • Usually intended to reduce the chances of harm • May involve avoidance, covert ritualizing, or neutralization • Typically resisted (at least early in the disorder's course)	• May be deliberate or indiscriminant • May or may not be repeated • Often performed by oneself • May be damaging or hurtful to self or others • Typically overt • Typically not resisted
Consequences	• Short-term escape from (or avoidance of) obsessional distress	• Emotional arousal; manic-like high, pleasure, gratification, or satisfaction

TICS AND TOURETTE'S SYNDROME

Tics are involuntary, rapid, repetitive, and stereotyped movements of individual muscle groups (APA, 2000). Characterized as *motor* or *vocal* and either *simple* or *complex*, tics are easier to recognize than they are to precisely define. Urges to perform tics can sometimes be resisted, but usually only for a matter of minutes or seconds. Table 2.3 presents characteristics of various classes of tics. Tourette's syndrome (TS) is a neurological disorder involving chronic and persistent motor and vocal tics that occur daily and result in functional impairment. Some have likened tics to compulsions (and therefore view TS as related to OCD) because both are repetitive, stereotyped, and seem senseless (Hollander & Wong, 2000). Others have reported a high prevalence of OCD symptoms (i.e., compulsions) among samples of patients with TS and other tic disorders (e.g., Pauls, Towbin, Leckman, Zahner, & Cohen, 1986), suggesting an apparent overlap.

On the other hand, researchers have acknowledged that comorbidity estimates between tic disorders and OCD may be artificially inflated due to the difficulty in distinguishing (particularly complex) motor tics from compulsions (e.g., Shapiro & Shapiro, 1992). Understanding and discriminating between the two phenomena requires close attention to functional aspects (as opposed to the mere repetitiveness) of the target behaviors (O'Connor, 2001). As described previously, compulsive rituals in OCD are not movements per se, but rather purposeful responses to obsessional stimuli, and there is the sense that feared consequences may occur if the compulsive ritual is not performed. In contrast, tics are spontaneous movements devoid of purpose. Unlike compulsions, which are evoked by obsessional thoughts and affective states, tics are evoked by physical tension and

TABLE 2.3
Characteristics of Different Classes of Tics

Behavior	Type of Tic	
	Simple	*Complex*
Motor	Fast, darting, and meaningless (e.g., eye blinking, head shaking)	Stereotyped series of movements that may appear purposeful (e.g., clapping, touching people)
Vocal	Meaningless sounds and noises (e.g., barking, throat clearing)	Linguistically meaningful utterances (e.g., words, phrases)

feelings of sensory incompleteness or insufficiency (Leckman et al., 1995; Leckman et al., 1994). The person with tics experiences a *premonitory urge* that may be anatomically located, although not necessarily present with every tic. People with tics report a feeling of tension release after performing tics. Although TS and OCD share some superficial similarities, assessment of the functional characteristics of tics and compulsions summarized in Table 2.4 suggests important differences between these symptoms.

SOMATOFORM DISORDERS

Hypochondriasis

Hypochondriasis (HC) is classified as a somatoform disorder in *DSM–IV–TR* and is characterized by a preoccupation with fears of having (or the conviction that one already has) a serious disease (e.g., cancer). The fears are based on a catastrophic misinterpretation of benign bodily sensations (e.g., "This headache means I have a brain tumor") and persist despite appropriate medical evaluation and frequent reassurance from authorities such as doctors or medical texts. The intrusive, incessant health-related preoccupations in HC have been compared to obsessional thoughts or fears in OCD; and the repetitive attempts to seek reassurance in HC have been likened to compulsive checking rituals (Fallon, Javitch, Hollander, &

TABLE 2.4
Functional Characteristics of Tics and Compulsions

Characteristic	Tics	Compulsions
Antecedents and triggers	Sensory tension; urge to release energy	Cognitive or affective distress (obsessional thought, doubt, image, impulse)
Description of the behavior	Spontaneous movements with no apparent meaning	Purposeful responses to a perceived threat
Outcome of the behavior	Release of physical tension	Escape or avoidance of feared consequences; reduction in anxiety or distress
If resisted	Difficult if not impossible to resist completely; can be delayed momentarily with effort	Mounting autonomic anxiety symptoms; fear of catastrophes

Liebowitz, 1991). Research findings suggest functional similarities as well: affective states (e.g., anxiety and depression) and the degree of resistance to obsessional phenomena in HC are comparable to those in OCD (Neziroglu et al. 2000). However, as a group, individuals with HC present with a less diverse range of obsessional themes (i.e., they are restricted to somatic concerns) and show less insight into the senselessness of their fears compared to those with OCD (Abramowitz et al., 1999; Neziroglu et al., 2000).

Fine-grained functional analyses of HC symptoms (e.g., Abramowitz, Schwartz, & Whiteside, 2002; Warwick & Salkovskis, 1990) also point to similarities with OCD. Intrusive thoughts about illness in HC are associated with perceived threat and evocation of subjective anxiety as are obsessions in OCD. Repetitive checking behavior in HC is performed in response to intrusive stimuli and function as a means of acquiring reassurance about health status in a way that reduces distress, at least in the short term. Thus, checking in HC serves as an escape from preoccupation with disease much as compulsive rituals in OCD (e.g., washing, checking) serve as an escape from obsessional anxiety (e.g., concerning germs, danger). Although classified as a somatoform disorder because of the focus on bodily concerns, HC appears to feature signs and symptoms that are comparable in both form and function with those in OCD, as reviewed in Table 2.5. Some authors have recast hypochondriasis as "health anxiety disorder" (Taylor & Asmundson, 2004).

Body Dysmorphic Disorder

Another somatoform disorder with features similar to OCD is body dysmorphic disorder (BDD). BDD involves excessive preoccupation with an imagined defect in appearance (e.g, "my nose is off-center"). Thoughts of unsightliness occur in the absence of any noticeable physical defect, are often resisted, and lead to significant anxiety about how the person appears to others. In this way, preoccupations in BDD are functionally similar to obsessions in OCD (Neziroglu & Yaryura-Tobias, 1993). To circumvent anticipated embarrassment, individuals with BDD may avoid particular social situations or engage in behaviors that are aimed to reduce distress or the visibility of their imagined defect. Examples include excessive checking in mirrors, grooming, hiding the perceived defect, and comparing one's body with others' bodies (Rosen, 1996; Veale & Riley, 2001). These behaviors bear functional similarities to safety-seeking behaviors, such as compulsive rituals, in OCD; namely, both are performed as a means of escape from anxiety or threat when no actual danger is present. Although BDD appears to involve similar levels of general anxiety and depression as OCD, people

Table 2.5
Comparison of Symptoms in OCD, Hypochondriasis, and BDD

Characteristic	OCD	Hypochondriasis	BDD
Focus of intrusive thoughts or fears	Variable (aggression, sex, religious, contamination)	Possible illnesses	Imagined physical defect and others' perceptions
Emotion associated with intrusive thoughts	Anxiety	Anxiety	Anxiety
Response to intrusive thoughts	Variety of overt or covert neutralizing and compulsive behaviors and avoidance	Check with doctors, medical resources, friends or family, own body; avoidance of fear cues	Check mirrors, compare oneself to others, camouflage, grooming, cosmetic surgery; avoid interactions
Meaning of the response	Escape from anxiety or distress, avoid feared disasters	Gain certainty or reassurance about health status	Examine extent of "disfigurement," gain certainty about appearance
Short-term outcome of the response	Anxiety reduction	Anxiety reduction	Anxiety reduction or increase
Long-term outcome of the response	Persistence of obsessional fear	Health anxiety persists	Fear of negative evaluation persists

with BDD seem to be singly obsessed with their imagined defect whereas obsessional themes in OCD vary more widely (McKay et al., 1997). Table 2.5 also compares the symptoms of OCD and BDD on a functional level.

GENERALIZED ANXIETY DISORDER

The main features of GAD include chronic, exaggerated worry and tension that is unfounded or much more severe than the normal anxiety that most people experience. People with GAD are unable to relax and often suffer from insomnia and other physical symptoms including fatigue, trembling, muscle tension, headaches, irritability, and hot flashes.

Worries in GAD can be intrusive, unwanted, repetitive, and highly distressing to the individual. Therefore it is common for the worrying symptoms of GAD to be mistaken for obsessions as in OCD. The clinician should therefore be aware of the differences between worries and obsessions, shown in Table 2.6. First, whereas the content of worries in GAD is focused

TABLE 2.6
Distinguishing Characteristics of Obsessions and Worry

Characteristic	Obsessions	Worry
Focus	Bizarre, not everyday concerns (e.g., serious illness from touching surfaces, unknowingly hitting a pedestrian)	Real-life circumstances (e.g., finances, relationships, health)
Form	Images, impulses, ideas, urges, thoughts, doubts	Thoughts, doubts (verbal content)
Content	Improbable negative outcomes Stable or "fixed" content	Generally pessimistic and ruminative Content often shifts
Resistance	Strongly resisted, evoke neutralizing responses and safety behaviors	Often ego-syntonic, little or no neutralizing responses

on real-life circumstances such as finances, social and family relationships, work, and school performance, obsessional content in OCD is typically somewhat bizarre and does not concern actual life problems. Second, worries tend to involve verbal content, whereas obsessions often involve imagery and impulses along with thoughts and doubts. Third, worry is often ruminative with general pessimistic ideas about oneself, the world, and the future that frequently shift in content from one topic to another. In contrast, obsessions are typically stable (fixed) and concern improbable disastrous consequences. Finally, whereas obsessions elicit neutralizing responses such as compulsive rituals, worries and ruminations are not associated with neutralizing.

OBSESSIVE–COMPULSIVE PERSONALITY DISORDER

It is unfortunate that OCD and OCPD share a similar name because these problems have very little else in common. The main features of OCPD are an enduring pattern of perfectionism, rigidity, stubbornness, and orderliness that interferes with task completion; preoccupation with rules, organization, and schedules so that the point of activities are lost; overconscientiousness and inflexibility regarding ethical or moral issues (not accounted for by normal cultural or religious values); and excessive devotion to work and productivity to the exclusion of friendships or leisure time (APA, 2000).

Although some of these characteristics are informally referred to as *compulsive* and might be found among individuals with OCD, a closer examination reveals important differences in the cognitive mediation of these symptoms. In OCD, compulsive or perfectionistic behavior is resisted. Although the person wishes he or she did not feel compelled to behave this way, the threat of disastrous consequences if he or she does not looms large (e.g., "Things must be arranged alphabetically or else Mom and Dad's plane will crash"). In contrast, people with OCPD do not have obsessional fears and instead perceive their compulsive traits as functional, agreeable, and consistent with their worldview (i.e., ego syntonic). From a cognitive perspective, people with OCPD appear to harbor core beliefs and assumptions such as, "Feelings, decisions, and behaviors are either morally right or wrong," "Making mistakes means I am bad, worthless, and a failure," and "Certainty and predictability are necessary to avoid mistakes; therefore I must always be in control." Whereas OCD symptoms are associated with subjective resistance, individuals with OCPD do not resist thinking and acting in this inflexible way and are often quite insurgent when it is suggested that they adapt a less rigid style.

SCHIZOPHRENIA AND DELUSIONAL DISORDERS

It is important to distinguish psychotic disorders, such as schizophrenia, and delusional disorders from OCD because these conditions possess certain superficial similarities that have led some to speculate a relationship (e.g., Enright, 1996; Insel & Akiskal, 1986). In particular, both OCD and psychotic disorders may involve repetitive, intrusive, highly fixed beliefs with bizarre, absurd, and unwanted content (i.e., delusions in psychosis, obsessions with poor insight [overvalued ideas] in OCD); for example, thoughts about harming loved ones (e.g., babies). Strange behavioral and mental rituals, such as repeating routine activities, may also accompany both conditions. Yet despite superficial similarities in how these symptoms are described, substantial differences exist in their phenomenology and in how they are experienced as discussed next and summarized in Table 2.7.

Primarily, people with psychotic disorders do not resist their bizarre, intrusive, unwanted thoughts. Moreover, such thoughts do not produce anxiety or give rise to safety-seeking behavior. Instead, patients with delusional problems typically distort reality to conform to their bizarre belief systems. In contrast, obsessions in OCD are resisted, experienced as anxiety evoking, and elicit urges to perform safety behaviors. Other differences include that the senseless repetitive behavior in schizophrenia and other psychotic disorders is truly pointless; its purpose cannot be explained by the person. In contrast, even seemingly bizarre, extensive compulsive rituals and avoidance behavior in OCD are purposeful and grounded in the sufferer's reality. That is, the sufferer can typically explain why he or she performs

TABLE 2.7
Distinguishing Characteristics of OCD
and Psychotic and Delusional Disorders

Characteristic	Obsessions	Delusions
Resistance to intrusive thoughts	Obsessions are strongly resisted. They evoke neutralizing responses and safety behaviors.	Delusions do not evoke anxiety or distress. They are not resisted or neutralized. The person might distort reality to conform to the delusion.
Repetitive behavior	Safety-seeking maneuvers performed to reduce obsessional fear. The patient can explain the purpose of rituals.	Pointless behavior. The individual cannot explain its purpose.
Other features	Individuals with OCD do not display other signs of psychosis (e.g., loosening associations, negative symptoms).	Other signs of severe mental illness might be present (e.g., reduced self-care, poverty of speech, flat affect).

safety behaviors, even if the explanation is based on miscalculations of risk, misinterpretations of thoughts, and irrational fears. Finally, negative symptoms (e.g., loose associations, flat affect, poverty of speech) often present in schizophrenia are not found in people with OCD.

OBSESSIONS VERSUS SOCIOPATHY

When violent obsessions are encountered, it is important to establish that the obsession is part of OCD and not an indicator of antisocial tendencies. Although one cannot predict with absolute certainty whether a person will act on violent thoughts at some point in the future, clinicians can attain an acceptable level of confidence by assessing whether or not the obsessions are ego-syntonic or ego-dystonic. People who engage in antisocial or sociopathic behavior experience their violent thoughts as ego-syntonic (i.e., they are welcomed). They have histories of acting on thoughts about committing actions. They also voluntarily generate fantasies about committing such behaviors, seek out situations in which such thoughts could be acted out, and devalue the victims (or potential victims) of such acts. In contrast, people with OCD experience such thoughts as ego-dystonic and distressing. Such patients worry not only that they might harm others, but that the mere occurrence of thoughts about violence indicates something personally abhorrent. This demonstrates their sincere respect for others. Avoidance behavior, neutralizing, and thought suppression are aimed at stopping the thought and reducing the perceived chances that they might impulsively act on such thoughts. Because an individual's past behavior is the best predictor of his or her future behavior, one way a clinician can assess the probability that someone will act on his or her violent thoughts is to find out about his or her history (e.g., "What's the most violent thing you've ever done?")

3

What Causes OCD?

In this chapter we explore three of the leading hypotheses proposed to account for the development of OCD: neuropsychiatric models, cognitive deficit models, and the cognitive-behavioral perspective.[1] In addition to describing the central tenets of each theory, I review the relevant research and provide critical remarks. As of yet, there is no definitive answer to the question of what causes OCD. However, it is important to consider that from the perspective of cognitive-behavioral therapy, the causes of OCD are less important than are the factors that maintain the problem. Indeed the aim of treatment is to reverse such *maintenance processes*. In chapter 4 we will see that despite a lack of clarity regarding the causes of OCD, significant advances have been made in understanding how obsessional symptoms are maintained.

---

[1]A psychoanalytic model of OCD exists, yet as psychoanalytic theories in general have largely been discredited in recent years (e.g., Eysenck, 1985) there is little need to deal with it here. The theory contributes trivially, if at all, to the current understanding of OCD and its treatment. Moreover, as is true for most of psychoanalysis, it has met its demise largely due to the lack of recent contributions and its failure to demonstrate therapeutic effectiveness.

NEUROPSYCHIATRIC MODELS

The Serotonin Hypothesis

Biologically inclined theorists have proposed that neurochemical and neuro-anatomical abnormalities are implicated in the development of OCD. The leading neurochemical theory posits that OCD symptoms are caused by abnormalities in the serotonin system. In particular, Zohar and Insel (1987) pointed to the hypersensitivity of postsynaptic serotonergic receptors. Rosenberg and Keshavan (1998) also proposed that glutamate–serotonin interactions underlie the disorder. Three lines of evidence are proposed to support the serotonin hypothesis of OCD: medication outcome studies, biological marker studies, and challenge studies in which OCD symptoms are evoked using serotonin agonists and antagonists. The most consistent findings come from the pharmacotherapy literature, which suggests that serotonin reuptake inhibitor medications (SRIs; e.g., fluoxetine, sertraline, escitalopram) are more effective than medications with other mechanisms of action (e.g., desipramine, imipramine) in reducing OCD symptoms (e.g., Abramowitz, 1997). In contrast, studies of biological markers, such as blood and cerebrospinal fluid levels of serotonin metabolites, have provided inconclusive results regarding a relationship between serotonin and OCD (e.g., Insel, Mueller, Alterman, Linnoila, & Murphy, 1985). Similarly, results from studies using the pharmacological challenge paradigm are largely incompatible with the serotonin hypothesis (e.g., Hollander et al., 1992)

There is some skepticism regarding the exact mechanism of action of the SRIs. For example, because neurotransmitter systems do not work in isolation, serotonergic neurons in one area of the brain may have synaptic relationships with, say, dopaminergic neurons elsewhere in the brain. Therefore, increasing serotonin levels in one region (e.g., by administration of SRIs) may effectively increase or decrease (depending on the relationship) dopamine levels elsewhere. Ironically, one of the great scientific, as opposed to practical, problems with the SRI drugs is that they seem to work for such a wide variety of disorders. The fact that OCD responds to SRIs but not to other types of antidepressant medicine is not, by itself, convincing evidence that serotonin reuptake inhibition is the key to symptom improvement, or that serotonin is the culprit in OCD.

Neuroanatomy

Prevailing neuroanatomical models of OCD hypothesize that obsessions and compulsions are caused by structural and functional abnormalities in particular areas of the brain, specifically, the orbitofrontal-subcortical circuits (Saxena, Bota, & Brody, 2001). These circuits are thought to connect regions of the brain involved in processing information with those involved in the initiation of behavioral responses that are implemented with little conscious awareness. The classical conceptualization of this circuitry consists of a direct and an indirect pathway. The direct pathway projects from the cerebral cortex to the striatum to the internal segment of the globus pallidus/substantia nigra, pars reticulata complex, then to the thalamus and back to the cortex. The indirect pathway is similar, but projects from the striatum to the external segment of the globus pallidus to the subthalamic nucleus before returning to the common pathway. In individuals with OCD, overactivity of the direct circuit purportedly leads to OCD symptoms.

These structural models have largely been derived from the results of neuroimaging studies in which activity levels in specific brain areas are compared between people with and without OCD. Investigations using positron emission tomography (PET) have found increased glucose utilization in the orbitofrontal cortex (OFC), caudate, thalamus, prefrontal cortex, and anterior cingulate among patients with OCD as compared to nonpatients (e.g., Baxter et al., 1987; Baxter et al., 1988). Studies using single photon emission computed tomography (SPECT) have reported decreased blood flow to the OFC, caudate, various areas of the cortex, and thalamus in OCD patients as compared to nonpatients (e.g., Crespo-Facorro et al., 1999). The fact that studies using PET and SPECT have found differences between individuals with OCD and controls in the opposite directions is not necessarily contradictory, and probably arises because these methods measure different processes. Finally, studies comparing individuals with OCD to healthy controls using magnetic resonance spectroscopy have reported decreased levels of various markers of neuronal viability in the left and right striatum, and in the medial thalamus (e.g., Ebert et al., 1997; Fitzgerald, Moore, Paulson, Stewart, & Rosenberg, 2000). Although findings vary across studies, a meta-analysis of 10 PET and SPECT studies found reliable differences in the orbital gyrus and the head of the caudate nucleus between patients with OCD and nonpatients (Whiteside, Port, & Abramowitz, 2004).

Limitations of Neurobiological Models

Neurobiological theories of OCD have a number of problems that should be considered. First, they are contentless and provide little coherent account of the phenomenology of OCD—that is, they do not address the empirically demonstrated relationships between obsessional fear and compulsive behavior or neutralizing. Second, there is little correspondence between the patterns of symptoms that patients report and the biological mechanisms proposed to account for them. For example, no coherent explanation has been offered to explain how neurotransmitter or neuroanatomical abnormalities translate into OCD symptoms (e.g., why does hypersensitivity of postsynaptic receptors cause intrusive obsessional thoughts, anxiety, compulsive rituals, or neutralizing?). Third, purely biological models are unable to account for the restriction of OCD symptoms to particular types of stimuli. As Rachman (1997) noted, obsessions of causing harm to others invariably target the defenseless—the elderly, disabled, and babies—whereas there are no "Arnold Schwartzenegger obsessions." That there are many stimuli about which OCD patients do not obsess suggests that general biological deficits, if present at all, must interact with learning and environmental factors in the etiology of OCD.

A fourth problem with biological models is the way that outcome data from studies on the effects of SRIs have been interpreted. Because the serotonin hypothesis originated from the findings of preferential efficacy of clomipramine (an SRI) over nonserotonergic tricyclic antidepressants (e.g., imipramine, desipramine; Zohar & Insel, 1987), the assertion that the effectiveness of SRIs supports the serotonin hypothesis is circular. Further still, models of etiology cannot be derived solely from knowledge of successful treatment response. This is an example of the logical error known as *ex juvantibus* reasoning, or reasoning backward from what helps, which is a variation of the fallacy known as *post hoc ergo propter hoc*, or *after this, therefore because of this*. The logical fallacy is clear if you consider the following example: When I take aspirin, my headache goes away. Thus, the reason I get headaches is because my aspirin level is too low. Just as there may be many possible mechanisms by which aspirin makes headaches go away, there may be many possible mechanisms by which SRIs decrease OCD symptoms.

Of course, the serotonin hypothesis could be supported by evidence from controlled studies demonstrating differences in serotonergic functioning between individuals with and without OCD. Especially convincing would be a demonstration that the administration of serotonin agonists produces the onset (or exacerbation) of OCD symptoms. Yet the numerous biological marker and pharmacological challenge studies that have been conducted to date provide remarkably inconsistent results (for a review, see Gross, Sasson, Chorpa, & Zohar, 1998). So, although it is likely that obsessive–compulsive symptoms involve the serotonin system at some level (one is hard-pressed to find many human processes that do not involve the serotonin system), the existing evidence does not suggest that OCD is caused by an abnormally functioning serotonin system.

A fifth problem is that results from brain scanning studies are not convincing. For example, SPECT studies reporting differences in blood flow to the OFC between OCD patients and nonpatients do not necessarily provide evidence for a neuroanatomical abnormality; nor do they implicate the OFC as involved in the production of OCD symptoms. This is because such correlational study designs cannot address whether true abnormalities exist (abnormal compared to what?), or whether observed associations are even related to the causes of OCD. In fact, some data suggest that it is the act of obsessing that causes changes in brain functioning (e.g., Cottraux et al., 1996; Mataix-Cols et al., 2003). For instance, Cottraux et al. (1996) compared PET scans of 10 patients with OCD with checking rituals while obsessing and while resting to 10 nonpatients while thinking about normal obsessions and while resting. Results indicated that both groups showed increased activity in the OFC during evocation of obsessional thoughts. In another study, when patients with OCD received successful treatment, there were corresponding decreases in OFC activity (Baxter et al., 1992). Most recently, Mataix-Cols and colleagues (2003) found that the brain systems implicated in the mediation of anxiety in healthy study participants are similar to those identified in OCD patients during symptom provocation. Moreover, anxiety associated with different OCD symptom dimensions was associated with differential patterns of activation in these neural systems. Taken together, data from brain scanning research in OCD seem to be showing nothing more than neurophysiological, neuropsychological, and biochemical correlates of normally functioning cognitive systems.

Summary

Neuropsychiatric models of OCD endorse the idea that the kinds of thoughts and behaviors displayed by people with OCD are so strange that they defy any explanation short of an appeal to disease processes. Yet claims that OCD is caused by neuropsychiatric irregularities are premature. Ultimately, biological research may prove important in furthering our understanding of OCD. As of yet, however, a comprehensive neurobiological theory that can be subjected to and can pass experimental scrutiny has yet to be clearly articulated.

COGNITIVE DEFICIT MODELS

Memory Deficits

On another level, some theorists have considered that OCD symptoms might be caused by abnormally functioning cognitive processes, such as memory. For example, perhaps compulsive checking arises as a consequence of not being able to remember whether or not one has locked the door, turned off the oven, or unplugged the iron. However, despite its intuitive appeal, this hypothesis has not received strong support (for a review see Muller & Roberts, 2005). Savage et al. (1996) found evidence of impaired recall for nonverbal stimuli in OCD patients compared to nonpatient controls, although this deficit was not found for verbal stimuli or on recognition tasks. Other investigations have found no evidence of an overall memory deficit among individuals with OCD (e.g., Abbruzzese, Bellodi, Ferri, & Scarone, 1993; Tolin, Abramowitz, Brigidi et al., 2001).

In a meta-analysis of 22 studies (including 794 participants) on memory in compulsive checking, Woods, Vevea, Chambless, and Bayen (2002) found small to medium effect sizes, suggesting that compulsive checkers do not perform quite as well as noncheckers on tests of short-term/working memory and episodic long-term memory. However, Woods et al. (2002) also cautioned that mediating variables, such as self-doubt, could account for the apparent memory deficits in checkers. For example, Clayton, Richards, and Edwards (1999) found that individuals with OCD performed more poorly than healthy controls and individuals with panic disorder on timed, but not on untimed tasks. This raises the possibility that excessive caution or slowness in responding, rather than a memory deficit per se, hindered performance.

Conceding largely equivocal evidence for an across-the-board memory deficit, some theorists have proposed that individuals with OCD have memory problems only where their obsessional fears are concerned. This would explain, for example, why a patient who fears burglaries might spend hours rechecking that doors to the outside (e.g., the garage door) are securely locked, yet have no urges to check closet or bathroom doors. However, results from the few studies that have examined this selective memory hypothesis suggest just the opposite: Patients appear to have enhanced memory for threat-relevant (OCD-related) information. In one study, Radomsky and Rachman (1999) had healthy individuals and OCD patients with washing compulsions look at everyday (neutral) objects, such as a ruler, that had been touched with either a "clean" cloth or a "dirty" cloth. In a subsequent surprise recall test, the OCD patients recalled more "contaminated" objects than "clean" objects, and they recalled fewer "clean" objects than did the nonpatient participants. Radomsky, Rachman, and Hammond (2001) replicated their earlier findings in a study with compulsive checkers. Together, these two studies strongly suggest that individuals with OCD have a selectively better memory for anxiety-relevant events. Such a memory bias for threatening stimuli is adaptive and can be conceptualized as part of the normal fight-or-flight response that functions to protect organisms from harm. That is, paying attention to and being able to remember characteristics of stimuli perceived to be harmful serves a protective function.

Reality Monitoring Deficits

If abnormal working memory per se does not underlie OCD, perhaps the symptoms are caused by deficits in *reality monitoring*—the ability to discriminate between memories of actual and imagined events (Johnson & Raye, 1981). It seems plausible that ritualistic checking, for example, is prompted by problems discerning whether an action (e.g., locking the door) was really carried out or merely imagined. However, studies examining the reality monitoring skills of OCD patients also report inconsistent results. Whereas two investigations (Ecker & Engelkamp, 1995; Rubinstein, Peynircioglu, Chambless, & Pigott, 1993) found that OCD patients did not discriminate between real and imagined actions as well as did healthy controls, the majority suggest that OCD is not characterized by a deficit in reality monitoring ability (Brown, Kosslyn, Breiter, Baer, & Jenike, 1994; Constans, Foa, Franklin, & Matthews, 1995; Hermans, Martens, De Cort, Pieters, & Eelen, 2003; McNally & Kohlbeck, 1993). In their meta-analytic review, Woods et al. (2002) found virtually no differences in reality monitoring between OCD patients and control groups across five studies (effect sizes = 0.02 and 0.03).

Inhibitory Deficits

The intrusive, repetitious, and seemingly uncontrollable quality of obsessional thoughts has led some researchers to hypothesize that OCD patients have deficits in their ability to dismiss or attend to extraneous mental stimuli (i.e., cognitive inhibition). For example, Wilhelm, McNally, Baer, and Florin (1996) used a directed forgetting procedure to test whether OCD patients have a dysfunction in their ability to forget disturbing material. In this study, OCD patients and healthy control participants were presented with a series of negative, positive, and neutral words, and given instructions to either remember or to forget each word after it was presented. Tests of recall and recognition showed that OCD patients had more difficulty forgetting negative material relative to positive and neutral material, whereas control participants did not. Tolin, Hamlin, and Foa (2002) replicated and extended this finding by demonstrating that relevance to OCD, rather than threat relevance alone, predicted impaired forgetting.

Poor cognitive inhibition might lead to a greater frequency of intrusive thoughts, making deliberate attempts to suppress such thoughts more difficult. The directed forgetting results reviewed earlier are complemented by another study in which we gave participants with OCD, social phobia, and healthy controls instructions to suppress thoughts of "bears," and measured how quickly they could recognize the word *bear* in comparison with other words that had not been suppressed (Tolin, Abramowitz, Przeworski, & Foa, 2002). We found that the individuals with OCD had faster recognition times compared to the other groups, suggesting a deficit in thought suppression ability in OCD.

Synthesis of Cognitive Deficit Research

It is easy to understand how one might reach the conclusion that OCD patients (especially those with compulsive checking symptoms) suffer from general cognitive deficits such as memory or reality monitoring impairments. However, the research findings reviewed thus far provide only weak support for global memory problems in OCD. Interestingly, the most consistent finding emerging from the research on memory and reality monitoring in OCD is that compared to nonpatients, individuals with OCD have less confidence in their own memory (e.g., Foa, Amir, Gershuny, Molnar, & Kozak, 1997; MacDonald, Antony, MacLeod, & Richter, 1997; McNally & Kohlbeck, 1993; Woods et al, 2002; for a review, see Muller & Roberts, 2005). However, reduced confidence in one's (normally functioning) memory is not a deficit per se; rather, it is an erroneous interpretation (e.g., "I recall having locked the door, but I can't trust that my memory is accurate"). Interestingly, Radomsky et al. (2001) found that reduced memory confidence was enhanced under conditions of experimentally induced responsibility. Moreover, Tolin, Abramowitz, Brigidi, Amir, Street, & Foa (2001) found that confidence in memory for threat-relevant (but not irrelevant) stimuli declined over time. Thus, there is strong evidence that compulsive checking results, at least in part, from decreased memory confidence, particularly in situations where there is the perception of responsibility for mistakes.

Astutely, Radomsky and Rachman called attention to the difference between *memory deficits* and *memory bias*. They demonstrated that individuals with OCD show normal overall memorial abilities, yet have a bias toward remembering feared objects that is amplified in situations of heightened responsibility (Radomsky & Rachman, 1999; Radomsky et al., 2001). Moreover, feeling responsible was associated with reduced memory confidence. These findings are consistent with research suggesting that increased attentional and memorial resources are allocated to processing information relevant to a person's current emotional state (e.g., Kovacs & Beck, 1978). In the case of anxiety, this is particularly adaptive and can be conceptualized as part of the normal body's normal response to perceived danger. Radomsky and Rachman's results are also consistent with the idea that, fearing responsibility for negative outcomes, people with OCD become highly concerned about their memory and try to compensate by checking.

This memory bias hypothesis is consistent with clinical observations. One patient in our clinic described spending hours checking to make sure she did not write curse words in notes she was sending to business colleagues, whereas she could send notes to close family members without any checking. This common phenomenon would be difficult to explain as a general problem with reduced memory or even as a deficit in memory confidence: Why is there better memory for notes being sent to some people as opposed to others? More likely, the checking of only certain letters results from feeling an increased sense of responsibility that (because of the higher stakes) leads to reduced memory confidence in that particular situation (Radomsky et al., 2001). A similar observation is how the presence of trusted others (e.g., therapist, spouse) reduces compulsive urges, as in the patient who only checks that the garage door is closed when her husband is away on business.

Interestingly, Radomsky and colleagues suggested a reconciliation with previous research reporting apparent neuropsychological deficits in OCD (e.g., Tallis, 1997). Given that individuals with OCD may be distracted by obsessional thinking, and may delay or withhold their responses due to uncertainty, it seems plausible that low scores on neuropsychological tests are secondary to OCD-related symptoms and not simply the result of actual memory problems. Therefore, research attempting to understand the etiology of OCD by studying general cognitive and neuropsychological deficits has two caveats. First, the results of such studies are likely attributable to the effects of being anxious as opposed to etiologically significant variables. Second, such research severely confounds salience of cues with etiological factors. For example, the fact that patients have slower reaction times during neuropsychological tests is easily attributable to their problems with indecision. This is not to say that research on information processing in OCD is valueless; it may be highly important in helping to understand the processes that maintain (rather than cause) obsessions and compulsions.

Additional problems with cognitive deficit models include their inability to explain the effectiveness of exposure and response prevention treatment, their inability to account for the heterogeneity of OCD symptoms, and the fact that mild neuropsychological deficits have been reported in a number of mood, eating, and anxiety disorders (Alarcon, Libb, & Boll, 1994). All of this suggests that even if deficits such as poor memory functioning or cognitive dyscontrol were involved at all in the production of obsessions and compulsions, they likely are involved in a nonspecific way.

Summary

The idea that OCD arises from general cognitive deficits does not add to the understanding of the disorder. Apparent memory and other processing deficits are better accounted for by cognitive biases in which obsessional anxiety leads to preferential processing of threat relevant stimuli. In the case of compulsive checking, it is likely that reduced confidence in memory, and therefore concern over whether the seeming memory problems will lead to misfortune, are evoked by the perception that one may be (or may come to be) responsible for negative outcomes. Hence, checking results as a way of reducing doubts that have arisen because of mistaken beliefs about one's memory, ability to manage doubts and uncertainty, and pathological estimates of responsibility for harm.

THE COGNITIVE-BEHAVIORAL MODEL

In contrast to the models already presented, which emphasize the presence of biological or functional abnormalities, cognitive-behavioral models of the development of OCD posit that obsessional symptoms develop from essentially normal (albeit biased) thinking and learning processes. Moreover, the model emphasizes *specificity* in that it proposes that obsessional problems arise from a pattern of idiosyncratic responses to key stimuli to which the individual has become sensitive. Observations such as apparent neuropsychiatric irregularities and memory problems are regarded as consequences of the emotional arousal and counterproductive strategies the sufferer uses to manage anxiety.

Obsessions and Compulsions Originate From Normal Experiences

Although it is an intuitively appealing hypothesis, the development of OCD cannot be attributed to the mere presence of intrusive thoughts, ideas, images, or impulses. This is because unwanted and senseless thoughts are a universal experience (e.g., they occur in 80% of the general population; Rachman & de Silva, 1978; Salkovskis & Harrison, 1984), yet the prevalence of OCD is only about 2% to 3%. Even the presence of intrusions with highly bizarre, upsetting, or unacceptable content does not predict who develops OCD. Indeed, studies on unwanted thoughts indicate that so-called normal obsessions closely resemble clinical obsessions in terms of their form and content. In fact, Rachman and de Silva (1978) found that even experienced mental health professionals had difficulty distinguishing the intrusive thoughts of OCD patients from those of nonpatients. Patients and nonpatients alike reported unwanted impulses to attack or harm people they were not upset with, thoughts about family members being harmed in accidents, images of personally unacceptable or violent sexual acts, and ideas of contamination. Subsequent work has consistently replicated Rachman and de Silva's initial findings (e.g., Abramowitz, Schwartz, & Moore, 2003; Freeston, Ladouceur, Thibodeau, & Gagnon, 1991; Ladouceur et al., 2000; Salkovskis & Harrison, 1984). Table 3.1 shows a sample of the kinds of intrusions reported by non-treatment-seeking individuals. The universality of intrusive thoughts also applies to compulsive rituals. Over 50% of the population exhibits ritualistic behavior in one form or another (Muris et al., 1997), and 10% to 27% report significant compulsive behavior (e.g., Frost, Lahart, Dugas, & Sher, 1988).

TABLE 3.1
Examples of Intrusive Thoughts Reported
by Nonclinical Individuals

Thought of catching a disease from a public swimming pool

Image of my home burning down and I lose everything I own

Impulse to blurt out curse words when everyone is praying silently in the synagogue

Idea of gouging my infant's eyes out

Thought that I would be less likely to have a car accident if my brother had one first

Thought of smashing a wine bottle over my frail father's head

Thought that I didn't lock the door before leaving the house

Impulse to shout racial slurs when in the company of minorities

Doubt about whether I wrote something inappropriate in an important e-mail message

Idea of purposely poisoning my child by putting harmful substances in his milk

Idea that I will get sick from shaking hands in a receiving line

Thought about the baby's genitals

Unwanted image of relatives having sexual intercourse

Doubts about whether I really have faith in God

Thought that I'd be able to do more social activities if the baby hadn't been born

Idea that the baby has cerebral palsy

Imagining what it would be like if my wife died in a car accident

Impulse to throw the baby off the balcony

Idea that others think I am responsible for the workplace robbery that occurred

Image of the baby's dead body lying in the crib

Idea of reaching for a police officer's gun

Feeling "bad" for a toy that got broken

Thought that the room must be in perfect order before I leave

Idea of saying something very nasty that would ruin my boyfriend's day

Thought of driving into oncoming traffic

Image of a patient dying because I made an error in their medical records

Image of the neighbor's dog attacking the baby

Idea that the furnace or other electrical appliances will catch fire while I am not home

Note. List adapted from Rachman and de Silva (1978), Abramowitz, Schwartz, and Moore (2003), and unpublished research.

There is good reason to think that life events, current concerns, and present interests influence the occurrence and themes of intrusive thoughts. For example, Horowitz and colleagues (e.g., Horowitz, 1975) found that exposure to films with distressing content increased the incidence of intrusive upsetting thoughts. Parkinson and Rachman (1980) reported increases in unwanted thoughts among mothers of children who were about to have surgery. Other authors have reported that OCD patients with trauma histories had obsessions related to their traumatic experiences (de Silva & Marks, 1999). Accumulating evidence suggests that intrusive thoughts that develop following the birth of a child (for both new mothers and fathers) typically involve unwanted ideas of harming the baby or making terrible mistakes regarding the infant's care (e.g., Abramowitz et al., 2001; Abramowitz, Schwartz, Moore, & Luenzmann, 2003). My colleagues and I found that 69% of postpartum women and 58% of new fathers experience intrusive distressing thoughts and impulses regarding their newborn infant (Abramowitz, Schwartz, & Moore, 2003). These findings correspond with clinical observations suggesting that external stimuli spark spontaneous intrusions. For example, some people report that just the sight of objects that could be used to commit violence, such as knives, guns, scissors, or wine bottles, provokes unwanted ideas or impulses about harm. Thus, threatening intrusions may follow exposure to (or anticipation of) threatening material, especially if one is sensitive to external danger signs.

Despite their similar content, the intrusive obsessional thoughts of OCD patients differ from those of nonpatients along other parameters. People with OCD experience their obsessions more frequently, for longer duration, and as more distressing and more difficult to control (Rachman & de Silva, 1978). Thus, a viable causal theory of OCD must account for the fact that while practically everyone experiences unwelcome intrusive, obsessional thoughts from time to time, only a small proportion of the population develops clinically significant symptoms.

Misinterpretations and Other Dysfunctional Cognitions Lead to Obsessions

Mindful of the fact that intrusive thoughts—even those about extremely senseless, upsetting, vulgar, dirty, violent, disgusting, or blasphemous topics—pose no realistic threat, most people confer little (if any) significance on such intrusions and consequently do nothing about them. As a result, such thoughts proceed harmlessly and unceremoniously in and out of consciousness. However, Rachman (1976, 1993) and Salkovskis (1985, 1989) proposed that if a person appraises such thoughts as highly significant or threatening, the harmless intrusions will come to evoke distress and develop into clinical obsessions. Salkovskis (1985, 1989) emphasized the role of *responsibility appraisals,* meaning that the individual interprets intrusive thoughts as an indication that (a) harm to himself or herself or someone else is particularly likely, and (b) the person may be responsible for such harm (and for preventing the harm). Rachman (1997, 1998) later suggested that misinterpretations of intrusive thoughts were not limited to responsibility appraisals, but could be any interpretation of the occurrence or content of the intrusion as personally significant, revealing, threatening, or catastrophic. For example, one might believe that the occurrence of the thought "I could spread germs to my family and make them very sick" means that there is a strong probability that this will happen unless something is done to prevent it, such as avoidance, hand washing, or reassurance seeking. Misinterpreting intrusive thoughts in this way evokes obsessional fear.

The idea that obsessional distress would result from misinterpreting common intrusive thoughts as threatening draws on Beck's (1976) cognitive specificity model of emotion. The cognitive specificity model stipulates that emotions are caused not by situations or stimuli per se, but rather by how the person ascribes meaning to the situation or stimuli. Moreover, particular emotions (and corresponding behaviors) are linked with specific interpretations. For example, interpretations concerned with loss lead to depression and crying, whereas the perception that one has deliberately been treated with disrespect leads to anger and hostility. When an individual blames himself or herself for failing to achieve a goal, the result is guilt. Interpretations concerned with perceived threat lead to anxiety and taking action to reduce the perceived threat, as we observe in OCD.

As a clinical illustration let us consider the example of Becky, who reported intrusive obsessional thoughts that her young children might accidentally consume her medication and become terribly ill or die. As a result of her fear, Becky spends hours each day checking the floors for lost pills and recounting the pills in her containers. Essentially, Becky's thoughts about accidental deaths can be regarded as normally occurring stimuli. Thus, it is not the occurrence or content of these thoughts per se, but rather how Becky interprets their occurrence or content, that leads to obsessional distress. In particular, Becky's obsessional distress is caused by her erroneous beliefs that just because she has the intrusive thoughts, it means that a negative outcome is likely and that she is responsible for preventing it. This process is depicted in Fig. 3.1.

The cognitive-behavioral model also proposes that once intrusive thoughts are misinterpreted as threatening, they naturally become the target of preoccupation (i.e., vigilance) and safety-seeking behavior such as avoidance and compulsive rituals (e.g., Becky's checking and counting). These, as well as other processes, in turn maintain the threat value of the intrusions and give rise to a self-perpetuating cycle of obsessional distress and safety-seeking behaviors that increase the vulnerability toward contin-

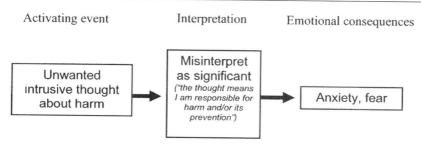

FIG. 3.1. The cognitive theory of emotion as applied to Becky's intrusive thoughts.

uing anxiety. The specific factors that maintain OCD symptoms are the topic of chapter 4.

Misinterpreting intrusive mental stimuli, as well as external situations and stimuli, as significant, threatening, and having implications for responsibility for harm (or the prevention of harm) appears to be linked to more general dysfunctional beliefs and attitudes that people with OCD hold. An international group of researchers, the Obsessive Compulsive Cognitions Working Group (OCCWG), which has spearheaded the study of cognition in OCD, has described six categories of dysfunctional beliefs. These are summarized in Table 3.2 and discussed in detail next:

An Inflated Sense of Responsibility. Responsibility refers to the belief that one has the pivotal power to cause or prevent particular unwanted outcomes. Individuals with OCD often view themselves as responsible for the content featured in their intrusive thoughts. They may be as concerned about failing to prevent bad outcomes (sins of omission) as they are with directly causing them (sins of commission; Wroe & Salkovskis, 2000). Excessive responsibility evokes feelings of anxiety and guilt.

Responsibility appraisals may be observed across the range of OCD symptom dimensions. For example, a patient we evaluated described obsessional thoughts of contaminating his family with germs from the funeral home where he worked. He felt responsible for seeing to it that none of his relatives became ill. Another individual reported obsessional thoughts of people being injured and felt compelled to absolve himself of any responsibility by excessively warning others (even strangers) of potential hazards such as icy walkways, flat tires, and untied shoelaces.

The Overimportance of Thoughts. Individuals with OCD often reason (erroneously) that the mere presence of unwanted intrusive thoughts indicates that such thoughts are significant and meaningful. Thought–action fusion (TAF) refers to two particular beliefs: (a) that intrusive thoughts are morally equivalent to the corresponding actions (moral

TABLE 3.2
Domains of Dysfunctional Beliefs in OCD

Category	Description
Excessive responsibility	Belief that one has power to cause or the duty to prevent negative outcomes featured in intrusive thoughts
Overimportance of thoughts	Belief that the mere presence of a thought indicates that the thought is significant
Moral TAF	Belief that thoughts are morally equivalent to the corresponding action
Likelihood TAF	Belief that thinking about an event makes the event more likely
Need to control thoughts	Belief that complete control over one's thoughts is both necessary and possible
Overestimation of threat	Belief that negative events associated with intrusive thoughts are likely and would be insufferable
Perfectionism	Belief that mistakes and imperfection are intolerable
Intolerance for uncertainty	Belief that it is necessary and possible to be 100% certain that negative outcomes will not occur

Note. TAF = thought–action fusion. From *Cognitive Approaches to Obsessions and Compulsions: Theory, Research, and Treatment*, by R. O. Frost & G. S. Steketee (Eds.), 2002, New York: Pergamon. Copyright 2002 by Pergamon. Reprinted with permission.

TAF), and (b) that thinking about something makes the corresponding event more likely (likelihood TAF; Shafran, Thordarson, & Rachman, 1996). For example, "It is just as immoral to think about cursing in church or synagogue as it is to actually curse, and because I am thinking about cursing, I will probably do it." People with OCD also attach exaggerated significance to intrusive unwanted thoughts by regarding them as repugnant, horrific, dangerous, disgusting, sinful, alarming, insane, or criminal (Freeston, Ladouceur, Gagnon, & Thibodeau, 1993; Rachman, 2003). Many patients believe their intrusive thoughts reveal important but hidden aspects of their personality or character, such as, "These thoughts mean that deep down I am an evil, dangerous, and unstable person." One patient concluded, "Thinking about my parents having a car accident means that I must really want this to happen."

The Need to Control Unwanted Thoughts. Related to perceiving intrusive thoughts as important, individuals with OCD may believe that it is both possible and necessary to maintain complete control over their unwanted thoughts (Purdon & Clark, 1994). A related assumption is that it is important to track and "keep a look out" for intrusive or unwanted mental events. Such beliefs are usually associated with repugnant obsessions concerning aggression, violence, unwanted sexual themes, and blasphemous or taboo subjects (religious or morality obsessions), and may be accompanied by the fear that not controlling such thoughts will have disastrous moral, behavioral, or psychological consequences. The resistance to obsessions that is commonly observed in OCD occurs as a result of such beliefs.

Overestimation of Threat. People with OCD tend to exaggerate the probability and costs of negative events associated with their obsessions (e.g., mistakes, sickness, or harm). Whereas most people take for granted that a situation is safe unless there are clear signs of danger, those suffering from OCD assume obsessional situations are dangerous or insufferable unless they have a guarantee of safety. For example, someone with contamination fears might exaggerate the probability of infection, as well as the severity of the resulting illness. Those with fears of making errors may overestimate the probability of discarding important information and the negative consequences of such a mistake. Many patients also hold the belief that anxiety itself will persist indefinitely and lead to physical or psychological damage. Overestimates of threat likely arise from anxious patients' inaccuracies in judgment. Rather than using objective evidence, these individuals frequently rely on publicized cases or the content of obsessional thoughts to make such predictions. Excellent examples include obsessional fears of relatively rare conditions that often gain media attention such as West Nile virus, SARS, or Lyme disease.

Perfectionism.   OCD is associated with an inability to tolerate mistakes or imperfection (Frost & Steketee, 1997). The perfectionism may relate to external stimuli, such as a need to fill out a form without making a single mistake; or to internal stimuli, such as a need to repeat a routine action until it feels "just right" (Coles, Frost, Heimberg, & Rheaume, 2003). Such beliefs are often observed among patients with symmetry and ordering OCD symptoms; for example, the belief that "I must keep working at something until it is exactly right" and "Even minor mistakes mean a job is not complete" (OCCWG, 1997).

Intolerance of Uncertainty.   Individuals with OCD often hold the erroneous belief that it is both important and possible to be absolutely (100%) certain that negative outcomes will not occur. Even the remote possibility of highly unlikely events can become a source of great concern. As a result, harmless intrusive doubts evoke great distress and urges to make sure that, for example, one did not commit a sin, leave the oven on, make a terrible mistake, cause something terrible to happen, or get close enough to blood to contract HIV. If senseless intrusive thoughts about violence and aggression, sex, or mistakes are appraised as highly significant, these stimuli activate intolerance for uncertainty, leading patients to worry whether they yelled curses out loud, put the cat in the freezer, violently raped a coworker, cheated on their spouse, changed their sexual preference, or committed a terrible crime. Intolerance for uncertainty in OCD is also characterized by specificity. At once, a patient who is unable to accept uncertainty associated with his or her idiosyncratic obsessional fear might be perfectly able to live with uncertainties associated with everyday activities; for example, the possibility of having a car accident on the way to the therapy session. Thus, intolerance for uncertainty plays a central role in obsessions and underlies the pathological decision making and need for reassurance that patients often display (Foa et al., 2003; Tolin, Abramowitz, Brigidi, & Foa, 2003).

Data from three lines of evidence—self-report questionnaire research, laboratory experiments, and naturalistic longitudinal studies—support the notion that misinterpretations of intrusive thoughts underlie OCD symptoms. Numerous questionnaire studies consistently indicate that people with OCD are more likely than those without OCD to interpret intrusive thoughts as significant, threatening, or in terms of responsibility for harm (e.g., Abramowitz, Whiteside, Lynam, & Kalsy, 2003; Freeston et al., 1993; OCCWG, 2003; Salkovskis, et al., 2000; Shafran et al., 1996). For example, my colleagues and I found higher likelihood TAF scores among OCD patients as compared to anxious and nonanxious control groups (Abramowitz, Whiteside, Lynam, & Kalsy, 2003). Although studies like this one show relationships between cognitive biases and OCD symptoms, they are merely correlational and therefore do not address whether cognitive biases play a causal role in OCD (it cannot be ruled out that cognitive biases result from the presence of OCD symptoms).

Several laboratory experiments have prospectively addressed the effects of interpretations of intrusive thoughts on OCD symptoms (Ladouceur et al., 1995; Lopatka & Rachman, 1995; Rachman et al., 1996; Rassin, Merckelbach, Muris, & Spaan, 1999). Perhaps the most clever of these was the study by Rassin et al. (1999) that addressed the role of TAF in the etiology of OCD. The researchers connected 45 psychologically naive participants to electrical equipment that, participants were told, would monitor their thoughts for 15 minutes. To induce TAF, participants who had been randomly assigned to the experimental condition were told that thinking the word *apple* would automatically result in a mild electric shock to another person (a confederate of the experimenter) they had met earlier. Participants were also informed that by pressing a certain button immediately after having an apple thought, they could prevent the shock—this was intended to be akin to a neutralizing response. On the other hand, participants in the control group were told only that the electrical equipment would monitor their thoughts. Results indicated that during the 15-minute monitoring period, the experimental group reported more intrusive apple thoughts, more guilt, greater subjective discomfort, and more intense resistance to thoughts about apples compared to the control group. Moreover, there was a strong association between the number of reported apple thoughts and the number of button presses. Thus, experimentally induced TAF (i.e., the belief that one's thoughts can produce harmful and preventable consequences) evoked intrusive distressing thoughts and neutralizing behavior profoundly similar to clinical OCD symptoms.

The causal effects demonstrated under highly controlled laboratory conditions might or might not extend to the development of OCD in naturalistic settings. Thus, longitudinal studies in which individuals who are likely to experience an increase in responsibility are assessed for vulnerability and then followed up after some critical event are apt to be particularly informative. In one such prospective study, my colleagues and I administered the Obsessive Beliefs Questionnaire (OBQ; OCCWG, 2003) to 75 expecting parents before the birth of their first child (Time 1). The OBQ assesses the domains of dysfunctional beliefs summarized in Table 3.2. Between 2 and 3 months after childbirth (Time 2), we assessed the presence and intensity of parents' unwanted intrusive thoughts about their newborn. Sixty-six of the 75 new parents (88%) reported unwanted infant-related thoughts at Time 2 (e.g., an image of dropping the child down the stairs or off the balcony). As shown in Fig. 3.2, after controlling for trait anxiety, individuals who scored in the highest quartile on the OBQ at Time 1 had significantly more intense OCD symptoms (as rated by

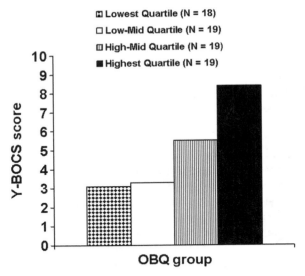

FIG. 3.2. Mean Yale– Brown Obsessive Compulsive Scale (Y–BOCS) score by Obsessional Beliefs Questionnaire (OBQ) quartile controlling for scores on the State–Trait Anxiety Inventory (STAI–Trait version), $F(3, 65) = 4.95, p < .005$. Post hoc analysis indicated that the highest OBQ quartile group scored significantly higher than the other three groups ($p < .05$).

the Y–BOCS) at Time 2 compared to those scoring in the other three quartiles. This suggests that the tendency to interpret the presence or meaning of intrusive thoughts as significant or threatening is a risk factor for the development of more severe OCD symptoms.

Foundations of Misinterpretations

What predisposes people to magnify the significance of their intrusive thoughts? A number of studies have examined the possible contributions of parental rearing practices to the development of OCD, yet these have yielded largely conflicting results. For example, some researchers have found high levels of parental overprotection in OCD patients (Hafner, 1988; Merkel, Pollard, Wiener, & Staebler, 1993; Turgeon, O'Connor, Marchand, & Freeston, 2002), whereas others have reported more rejection and less caring as compared to nonpatients (e.g., Hoekstra, Visser, & Emmelkamp, 1989), or no significant differences between individuals with and without OCD (Alonso et al., 2004; Vogel, Stiles, & Nordahl, 1997). Thus, there is not convincing evidence that certain styles of parental rearing cause OCD.

Other authors (Rachman, 1997; Salkovskis, Shafran, Rachman, & Freeston, 1999) have proposed that strict religious orthodoxy might give rise to overvaluation of thoughts if certain standards for behaving and thinking are repeatedly admonished by authority figures (e.g., learning from clergy that it is a sin to think aggressive, blasphemous, or adulterous thoughts). The influence of cultural and religious background on OCD symptoms has been examined in several studies with largely consistent results lending support for this hypothesis. For example, my colleagues and I found that the fear of God and fear of committing sin were associated with more severe OCD symptoms (particularly doubting and checking) in a nonclinical sample (Abramowitz, Huppert, Cohen, Tolin, & Cahill, 2002). In a subsequent study, highly religious Protestants reported more obsessionality, contamination concerns, intolerance of uncertainty, beliefs about the importance of thoughts, beliefs about the need to control thoughts, and inflated responsibility, compared to atheists and less religious Protestants (Abramowitz, Deacon, Woods, & Tolin, 2004). A similar investigation of Catholics revealed almost identical results (Sica, Novara, & Sanavio, 2002).

Cultural influences are also apparent in the heightened frequency of contamination obsessions in India, for example, where purity and cleanliness are emphasized as part of Hindu religious doctrines (Akhtar et al., 1975; Khanna & Channabasavanna, 1988). Similarly, studies of OCD in Egypt and Turkey find obsessions related to Muslim culture, including contamination and moral or ethical obsessions. Further evidence for the role of cultural influences can be found in how the content of obsessional concerns has undergone shifts over time that correspond with changes in societal concerns. For example, the heightened awareness of anthrax poisoning following the 2001 terrorist attacks in the eastern United States gave rise to increased obsessions about this particular contaminant.

Salkovskis et al. (1999) proposed several paths to the evolution of inflated responsibility beliefs, including learning experiences. For example, a childhood in which one's parents convey the message that certain situations or objects are very dangerous, or that the child is incapable of dealing with the resulting harm, could lead to obsessions regarding the specific harbinger of perceived danger. This idea is consistent with previous research finding that patients with severe contamination obsessions came from families in which cleanliness and perfectionism were emphasized (Hoover & Insel, 1984). Shafran et al. (1996) proposed that certain experiences, such as a chance pairing between a thought and a negative event, could lead to a heightened threat value for intrusive mental processes. Although research has not yet addressed this possibility, the following clinical example demonstrates how coincidental incidents in which it seems that one's thoughts or actions contribute to a disastrous consequence can make one vulnerable to developing obsessions.

> Brett, an 18-year-old college student and devout Christian, had suffered with manageable OCD symptoms involving unrealistic fears of making mistakes since he was a child. On the morning of Saturday, February 1, 2003, while working on an assignment, his computer crashed and Brett lost all of his work. At the same time, he heard a television news anchor say that the space shuttle *Columbia* was due to land shortly. In his anger over the loss of his assignment, Brett exclaimed, referring to the space shuttle, "I hope the damn thing blows up!" Shortly thereafter, news that the *Columbia* had exploded on re-entry into Earth's atmosphere was broadcast. Brett became extremely anxious and worried that perhaps his thoughts and words had something to do with the shuttle disaster. He developed intense guilt and the obsessional fear of causing additional tragedies if he let himself think any more "bad" thoughts. At his evaluation some months later, Brett stated that he realized the senselessness of his obsessional fear, but that he recalled a particular sermon by his pastor about how God knew everyone's thoughts, and how thinking about a sin was as morally reprehensible as committing the sin itself.

Summary

The cognitive-behavioral theory of the development of OCD assumes that obsessions begin as normal phenomena that come to acquire special negative significance when they are appraised as threatening. Once perceived in this way, obsessions evoke distress and become the natural target of safety-seeking behavior such as avoidance and compulsive rituals, aimed at reducing distress and the probability of feared consequences. Several lines of research support this hypothesis and collectively suggest that people with OCD are not abnormal in terms of the occurrence of obsessional thoughts. Rather, they are experiencing anxiety over ordinary distressing intrusive thoughts in much the same way that people with social phobia worry about scrutiny from others and those with panic disorder catastrophically misinterpret harmless anxiety-related body sensations. The origins of catastrophic beliefs about intrusive thoughts remain speculative, with the possible exception of certain forms of religiosity. In the next chapter the factors that serve to maintain OCD symptoms are discussed.

4

The Maintenance
of Obsessions and Compulsions

Within a theoretical framework it is necessary to distinguish between etiological and maintenance processes because maladaptive thinking and behavior might begin for one reason, yet persist for other reasons. Knowledge of *causal* factors is helpful for the purposes of prevention or relapse prevention following successful treatment. Understanding factors that *maintain* a disorder is most useful in psychological treatment because reversing these factors will weaken existing symptoms. Patients also benefit from understanding the psychological processes involved in the maintenance of their problem, as this understanding provides them with a compelling rationale for undertaking therapy (as discussed in chapter 5). Moreover, understanding this rationale appears to play a role in the successful treatment of OCD (Abramowitz, Franklin, Zoellner, & DiBernardo, 2002).

As presented in chapter 3, the cognitive-behavioral model of OCD posits that clinical obsessions develop when normally occurring intrusive cognitions are appraised in ways that lead them to acquire negative emotional significance. Avoidance, compulsive rituals, and other forms of neutralization are undertaken as natural safety-seeking responses that function to reduce obsessional distress. However, if OCD patients' dysfunctional beliefs and interpretations are mistaken in the first place, why do these thinking and behavioral patterns persist? That is, if unwanted intrusive thoughts and other feared stimuli such as numbers, doorknobs, floors, imperfection, uncertainty, and so on are not really as dangerous as patients anticipate, why do patients not recognize this, correct their flawed thinking, and stop performing senseless and redundant rituals? The first part of this chapter seeks to answer these questions by explaining the factors that maintain OCD symptoms. Next, particular maintenance processes associated with each of the OCD symptom dimensions are described. The chapter closes with a discussion of treatment implications of the cognitive-behavioral conceptualization. The conceptual model I present is largely based on the pioneering work of Rachman (e.g., Rachman, 1997, 1998) and Salkovskis (e.g., Salkovskis, 1985, 1989).

MAINTENANCE FACTORS

Selective Attention to Threat Cues

Once an intrusive thought or other stimulus is appraised as threatening it, takes on negative emotional significance and, like all threat cues, becomes a mental priority. This phenomenon is a more or less automatic part of the body's innate danger detection system—the *fight-or-flight response*—that kicks into gear whenever threat is perceived. By causing us to scan our surroundings and become hypervigilant for danger cues, this mechanism helps us figure out how to protect ourselves in the event that actual danger is lurking. Although this is often an involuntary process, some patients adopt a more deliberate anticipatory strategy of hypervigilance and scanning if they believe such tactics are necessary to avoid perceived threat. As a result of this heightened cognitive self-consciousness, the individual becomes exquisitely sensitive to his or her unwanted thoughts. It is as if the threshold for a thought to be "unacceptable" has been lowered. Thus, someone concerned with immoral sexual thoughts begins to notice more sexual thoughts. Similarly, someone with concerns about symmetry and orderliness is primed to identify things that are not "just right." An individual who fears contamination from urine looks carefully for (and often finds) yellow stains that could be urine. A person with somatic obsessions becomes highly sensitive to bodily sensations as would someone with panic disorder.

The tendency to selectively attend to obsessional stimuli also helps to explain the uncontrollable and repetitive nature of obsessions, as well as the common complaint among people with OCD that their particular feared situations and intrusive thoughts seem to confront them at every turn. This experience is typified by one patient with contamination obsessions who remarked that "God must be toying with me by placing so many piles of dog shit along my jogging route everyday." Of course, this person's overconcern with feces has led him to become increasingly hypervigilant of such stimuli (whereas others do not give such experiences much mental priority). A related effect is that the tendency to closely monitor and thereby notice more "danger signs" leads the person to conclude that danger is on the increase, which reinforces dysfunctional beliefs about the hazards of obsessional stimuli.

Physiologic Factors

Anxiety associated with obsessional thoughts also elicits autonomic (sympathetic) arousal as part of the body's physiological reaction to stress (fight or flight). This instinctive and highly adaptive response serves to protect the organism from danger by preparing it for immediate action (i.e., attack or run) if danger becomes imminent. When danger is anticipated, adrenaline is released into the bloodstream, producing noticeable physiologic effects including (but not limited to) an increase in heart rate and breathing, muscle tension, onset of cold or hot flashes, dilation of the pupils, and gastrointestinal distress (Barlow, 2002). What is the relevance of the physiology of anxiety to the maintenance of OCD? Clinical observations and research findings suggest that anxiety patients often adopt a type of emotional reasoning in which anxiety-related physiological effects are used to validate beliefs about danger (Arntz, Rauner, & van den Hout, 1995). For example, "I feel anxious, therefore there must be something to fear." This is called *ex-consequentia reasoning* because the person concludes not only that perceiving danger results in feeling anxious, but that feeling anxious implies the presence of danger. For individuals with OCD, inferring danger on the basis of anxiety evoked by mistaken beliefs about objectively safe situations and thoughts serves to reaffirm the mistaken beliefs, thereby maintaining OCD symptoms.

Safety-Seeking Behavior: Rituals and Neutralization

A person experiencing obsessional anxiety (or any other perceived threat) is motivated to take action to reduce the probability of anticipated negative outcomes or neutralize the anxiety or discomfort (Salkovskis, 1985). As I described in chapter 1, strategies such as compulsive rituals, mental compulsions, reassurance seeking, and various other neutralizing responses to obsessional distress can be jointly conceptualized as safety-seeking behaviors because they are performed with the intent of minimizing, or altogether preventing feared consequences of exposure to obsessional cues (Salkovskis, 1991). Safety seeking is a normal and adaptive response to threatening circumstances. If the building you are in was on fire, you would try to escape as quickly as you could. However, in OCD, the obsessive fear is irrational. That is, the risk of harm is objectively low. There is therefore no actual need for escape from obsessions. From the standpoint of conditioning theory, safety behaviors contribute to the persistence of irrational fear because they prevent the natural extinction of anxiety (and compulsive urges) that occurs through prolonged encounters with feared stimuli in the absence of disastrous consequences. By using safety behavior to terminate exposure to feared stimuli, the individual with OCD never has the opportunity to learn that danger is not actually present.

The cognitive-behavioral model proposes that the choice of a particular safety strategy (or strategies) is linked to beliefs about feared outcomes associated with obsessional thoughts, situations, or stimuli. These examples illustrate the relationship between beliefs and safety-seeking behavior:

- A man who interprets his intrusive thoughts of violence as meaning that he is a sinful person might compulsively pray or covertly "cancel out" the thoughts with a mental ritual.
- A woman who overestimates the risk of danger from contact with a public toilet will engage in ritualistic washing or cleaning after using the bathroom.
- Someone who believes his or her intrusive doubts about discarding important information signify that he or she is likely to make such mistakes might compulsively check to achieve certainty about the absence of such errors.
- A patient who perceives that he or she did not perform an activity "just right" might repeat the activity until it is carried out perfectly.

To explain the habitual (repetitive, compulsive) use of safety behaviors, the cognitive-behavioral model adopts an operant conditioning explanation: Performance of safety-seeking behaviors is negatively reinforced by the short-term reduction in obsessional fear it produces. Thus, under similar circumstances of obsessional fear, the behaviors are increasingly likely to be performed again. The model also draws attention to two incidental and counterproductive long-term effects of safety behaviors. First, performance of safety-seeking behaviors prevents an unambiguous disconfirmation of faulty beliefs (e.g., misappraisals of obsessional thoughts). That is, when the feared outcome does not occur, the person is prone to believing that he or she narrowly escaped disaster by performing the safety behavior. Thus the safety behavior interferes with learning that the fear was unrealistic to begin with. Second, the very effort put toward performing safety-seeking behavior leads to increased preoccupation with the obsessional thoughts or stimuli that evoked the safety behavior. Thus, the very safety-seeking behaviors that develop into habitual strategies for reducing fear in the short term actually serve to maintain this fear in the long run.

Results from a number of empirical studies support the hypothesis that safety-seeking behaviors have deleterious effects. In one elegant experiment using 29 individuals with OCD, Salkovskis, Thorpe, Wahl, Wroe, and Forrester (2003) ascertained each patient's most disturbing obsessional thought and preferred strategy for neutralizing the particular obsession. Each patient then made an audiotape recording of a written version of his or her most disturbing obsessional intrusion. During the first phase of the experiment, patients listened to the tape while being instructed to either use their preferred neutralizing strategy (e.g., mental rituals) or simply count backwards from 20 (a distraction task). During the second phase, which occurred 15 minutes later, all participants again listened to their obsessional thoughts for 8 minutes, this time without any neutralizing or distraction. Ratings of subjective discomfort were obtained throughout both phases of the study.

The findings from this study can be summarized as follows: During the first phase of the experiment (neutralizing or distraction), only the patients who used their typical neutralizing strategies experienced a decrease in subjective discomfort while listening to their obsession. However, during the second phase, patients who had previously neutralized reported an increase in their discomfort while listening to their obsession. Moreover, these patients evidenced stronger urges to neutralize during the second phase relative to patients in the distraction condition. Salkovskis et al.'s (2003) findings are consistent with the cognitive-behavioral model and replicate the earlier work of Rachman and his colleagues (e.g., Roper & Rachman, 1976), demonstrating that safety-seeking behavior, in this case neutralizing, is associated with short-term anxiety reduction. The results also demonstrate that neutralizing leads to increases in discomfort and urges to neutralize during subsequent encounters with obsessional thoughts.

As a clinical illustration let us consider Heidi, a nurse who reported recurrent intrusive doubts that she made mistakes in a patient's medical chart that could lead to the patient's death (e.g., recording the wrong medication dose). Although quite cautious and deliberate in her work, Heidi experienced persistent urges to recheck her work excessively. She often called her coworkers from home (e.g., on her days off) to ask that they review her charts for errors and reassure her that no patients had died. The coworkers typically complied with Heidi's requests for assurance, which temporarily alleviated her obsessional distress.

Despite the short-term success of her reassurance-seeking rituals, Heidi's intrusive doubts, obsessional distress, and compulsive behaviors grew more intense. According to the cognitive-behavioral model, her symptoms persisted because she (like most OCD patients) attributed the nonoccurrence of feared catastrophes and reduction of anxiety to the compulsive safety-seeking behavior. That is, she erroneously believed the absence of patient deaths was a direct result of her compulsive behavior: "Had I not been so careful, patients might have died because of me" (an inflated sense of responsibility is evident here). Put another way, Heidi's rituals prevented her from realizing that even if she did not check, terrible consequences would be unlikely and her anxiety would eventually dissipate. In addition, performing compulsive behavior increased the frequency of obsessional thoughts simply by drawing increased undue attention toward the intrusions (e.g., "If I have to call my coworkers so much, these doubts must be important"). Thus, as shown in Fig. 4.1, safety-seeking behavior contributes to a vicious cycle that maintains OCD symptoms and gains habit strength with repetition.

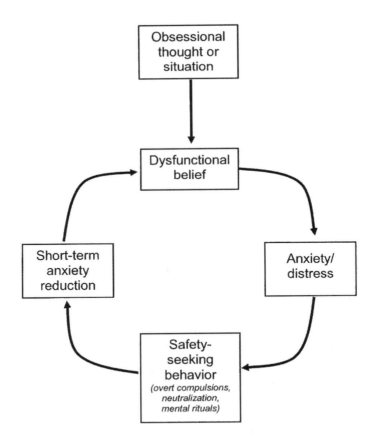

FIG. 4.1.   Vicious cycle resulting from the use of safety-seeking behaviors to reduce obsessional distress.

Passive Avoidance

As discussed earlier, behavioral retreat from obsessional fear cues also contributes to the maintenance of OCD. In the short term, avoidance clearly results in a decrease or termination in exposure to threat. This reduction in fear negatively reinforces future avoidant responses; therefore avoidance sustains itself over time. However, consistent avoidance also prevents the person from having corrective experiences that might otherwise modify dysfunctional beliefs and interpretations of intrusive thoughts and other fear-related stimuli. Moreover, patients tend to misinterpret the effects of their habitual avoidance. For example, a man who uses only self-flush urinals in public restrooms (thereby avoiding having to touch the flushing device) continues to believe that flushing the toilet is dangerous and that he has remained healthy only because he uses self-flush toilets. Thus, the dysfunctional appraisals and overestimates of threat that fuel obsessional fear remain intact.

Concealment of Obsessions

Concealing from others the content and regularity of obsessional thoughts is a form of avoidance that deserves elaboration because it is frequently overlooked by clinicians. If a person attaches negative personal meaning and significance to their unwanted intrusive thoughts, images, impulses, or ideas, it is understandable that they will want to keep these "dirty little secrets" hidden from other people (Newth & Rachman, 2001). Typically, it is unacceptable religious, sexual, and aggressive or violent obsessions (as opposed to contamination concerns or fears of mistakes) that are concealed. Patients with these types of obsessions worry about others' negative reactions to the content and frequency such thoughts. For example:

- The pastor would think I was a fake if he found out that I have so many intrusive doubts about God's existence.
- What would my family think if they knew I had thoughts about sleeping with Heather (the patient's first cousin)?
- My doctor would have me committed if I told him I was having intrusive ideas of suffocating the baby.

The habitual concealment results in the preservation of the patient's perception that his or her intrusions indicate some deep, dark, unspeakable personality defect. Patients continue to believe that they are the only ones experiencing such thoughts. More specifically, it reduces the likelihood of their learning (perhaps through socialization) that others (a) most likely do not become horrified on learning of the thoughts, (b) presumably can relate to these experiences themselves, and (c) probably hold alternative (healthier) explanations of the meaning and significance of the intrusions.

Paradoxical Effects of Thought Control

Active resistance to intrusive obsessional thoughts takes many forms. In addition to compulsive rituals and other safety-seeking behaviors, patients with OCD often engage in an ongoing struggle for mental control in which they attempt to dismiss or regulate their unwanted distressing thoughts. These efforts are no doubt motivated by dysfunctional beliefs regarding the importance of controlling one's own thoughts; for example "Losing control of my thoughts is as bad as losing control of my behavior," and "Control over thoughts is an important part of self-control" (e.g., Purdon & Clark, 1993). As I describe later, efforts to suppress or gain control over cognitive intrusions are generally counterproductive, resulting in a paradoxical increase in the unwanted thought and maintenance of OCD symptoms.

Consider the example of Joseph, an Orthodox Jew who described obsessional thoughts of curse words that came to mind each time he entered a synagogue, read the Torah, or tried to pray. Joseph was terrified that these intrusions meant that he was a fraud who harbored a deep-seated hatred of God, Judaism, and the Torah. He felt extremely guilty and fearful that others would find out about the thoughts and label him a "bad Jew." He wondered what God thought of him for having such blasphemous thoughts. In addition to a number of compulsive rituals aimed at neutralizing the feared effects of such thoughts, Joseph tried desperately to suppress the intrusions when they came to mind; yet he had little success doing so. Eventually giving up his struggle, he started avoiding the synagogue and became intensely depressed. At the urging of his wife, he came to our clinic for consultation and treatment.

Interest in the relationship between thought suppression and OCD was generated by the work of Wegner and his colleagues (e.g., Wegner, Schneider, Carter, & White, 1987), who asked their research participants (undergraduate students) to spend 5 minutes trying not to think of a white bear. Results indicated that attempts to suppress such thoughts were often futile and even led to an increase in the frequency of white bear thoughts after suppression instructions were relaxed—a phenomenon termed the *rebound effect*. To determine whether this paradoxical phenomenon extended to individuals with OCD, we (Tolin, Abramowitz, Przeworski, & Foa, 2002) designed a study similar to that of Wegner et al. (1987) and found that patients indeed reported difficulty suppressing white bear thoughts. A large body of research on thought suppression in clinical and nonclinical samples has accumulated since Wegner's initial work. Our own comprehensive meta-analytic review of this research (Abramowitz, Tolin, & Street, 2001) revealed support for the hypothesis that deliberately trying to suppress a thought leads to an increase in that particular thought (although not all studies have found consistent results; e.g., Purdon, Rowa, & Antony, 2005). Thus, attempting to suppress intrusive thoughts probably plays an important role in obsessional problems (e.g., Rachman, 1997; Salkovskis, Forrester, & Richards, 1998; Wegner, 1994). Just when patients are trying to expel unwanted thoughts from consciousness, they are priming themselves to experience an increase in the unwanted thoughts. The "solution" has become part of the problem.

Thought Suppression Failure.   It also appears that maladaptive interpretations of thought suppression failure, apart from negative appraisals of intrusive thoughts in general, contribute to the maintenance of OCD (Janeck, Calamari, Riemann, & Heffelfinger, 2003; Purdon et al., 2005). Examples of such appraisals include, "Since I can't stop these thoughts even when I try very hard, deep down I must really want something bad to happen," and "I must really be a terrible person if I keep thinking this way despite trying to stop." Consistent with this idea, we (Tolin, Abramowitz, Hamlin, Foa, & Synodi, 2002) found that people with OCD interpreted their thought suppression failures as a sign of personal weakness (i.e., "I am mentally weak") rather than attributing them to realistic situational factors (i.e., "It is often difficult to suppress unwanted thoughts"). Beliefs that one is personally weak, in turn, lead to a decline in mood (Purdon, 2001) and the perceived need to intensify suppression efforts. The result, as in Joseph's case presented earlier, is a sense that catastrophic beliefs about the consequences of failing to control thoughts are coming true, leading to a self-perpetuating cycle of suppression, intrusion, and self-defeating beliefs. Therefore, it is important to accurately identify and target patients' appraisals of thought recurrences (Purdon et al., 2005).

Thought Control Strategies.   Patients with OCD seem to use additional maladaptive strategies when attempting to regulate intrusive thoughts. The Thought Control Questionnaire (TCQ; Wells & Davies, 1994) measures the tendency to use five different strategies: (a) distraction (e.g., "I keep myself busy"), (b) social control (e.g., "I talk to a friend about the thought"), (c) worry (e.g., "I think about past worries instead"), (d) punishment (e.g., "I tell myself something bad will happen if I think the thought"), and (e) reappraisal (e.g., "I challenge the thought's validity"). In one study, we gave this measure to groups of OCD patients, panic patients, and healthy controls, finding that compared to the other groups, individuals with OCD reported more frequent use of worry and punishment strategies, and less frequent use of distraction (Abramowitz, Whiteside, Kalsy, & Tolin, 2003). Because punishment and worry (in contrast to social, distraction, and reappraisal strategies) likely evoke negative affect and selective attention to the intrusive thought, these data suggest that such strategies serve to maintain mistaken beliefs and distress associated with intrusive thoughts.

Summary of Maintenance Factors

A summary of the maintenance factors just described appears in Table 4.1. From the cognitive-behavioral perspective, OCD is largely a problem in which otherwise harmless unwanted intrusive thoughts have become a focus of concern. Threat-related appraisals and interpretations of such thoughts (and other related stimuli) evoke an array of responses that inadvertently increase the frequency of cognitive intrusions and reinforce maladaptive beliefs about their potential for harm. This leads to a self-sustaining vicious cycle of intrusions, maladaptive beliefs, anxiety, ill-fated responses, intrusions, and so on that becomes more and more insidious with repetition. Observations that some individuals with OCD spend their entire day engaged in ritualistic behavior or devise elaborate avoidance strategies that so restrict their ability to function are a testament to the insidiousness of the vicious cycle. In a very real sense, the means by which individuals with OCD appraise and attempt to manage their intrusive thoughts eventually become more perilous than the intrusions themselves. A graphical depiction of the cognitive-behavioral model is presented in Fig. 4.2.

The cognitive-behavioral approach provides a clearly articulated, logically sound, and empirically verifiable account for the symptoms of OCD that is derived from normal human learning principles (i.e., conditioning) and normal cognitive processes. There is no appeal to chemical imbalances, disease states, or general deficits to explain the origin or maintenance of obsessions and compulsions. Even the kinds of biased thinking implicated in the transformation of normal intrusions into obsessions are not in themselves "disturbed" because everyone makes incorrect judgments about situations and stimuli from time to time. And when faced with a perceived threat it is highly adaptive to take action to avoid or reduce the anticipated danger. So, the safety-seeking behavior observed in OCD is neither mysterious nor uniquely pathological. It is, however, self-preserving in that it prevents the person from correcting their faulty beliefs and judgments.

THE COGNITIVE-BEHAVIORAL MODEL
AND SYMPTOM DIMENSIONS

The cognitive-behavioral conceptual framework is fairly broad and therefore generalizes well to most individuals with OCD. However, al-

TABLE 4.1
Summary of Factors Involved in the Maintenance of OCD

Maintenance Factor	Description
Selective attention	Hypervigilance for threat cues is an adaptive response, yet it leads to noticing more threatening stimuli, including unwanted thoughts.
Physiological factors	The fight-or-flight response is an innate response to perceived threat. OCD patients often use emotional reasoning to infer that situations are dangerous on the basis of feeling anxious. This reaffirms mistaken beliefs that lead to feeling anxious.
Safety-seeking behavior	Efforts to reduce obsessional anxiety or prevent feared consequences of obsessions include overt compulsive rituals, mental rituals, and various overt and covert neutralizing strategies. These behaviors reduce distress in the short term and are thereby reinforced. In the long term, habitual use of safety behaviors prevents disconfirmation of mistaken beliefs because of how their outcomes are incorrectly interpreted (e.g., "If I didn't wash my hands I would have become very sick," "If I didn't say the prayer perfectly, my relatives would have died").
Passive avoidance	Leads to short-term anxiety reduction, but prevents extinction of anxiety and disconfirmation of overestimates of risk because the individual never has the opportunity to find out that danger is unlikely.
Concealment of obsessions	Prevents disconfirmation of mistaken beliefs about intrusive thoughts because the individual is never exposed to corrective information through social outlets.
Attempted thought control	Attempts to control or suppress unwanted thoughts paradoxically lead to an increase in the unwanted thoughts. Misappraisal of thought control failure leads to further distress.

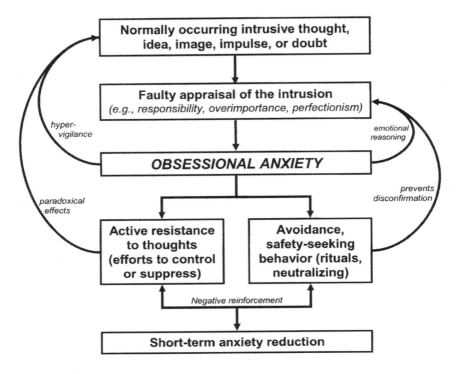

FIG. 4.2.   Cognitive-behavioral conceptual model of the maintenance of OCD.

though many of these cognitive and behavioral characteristics are present to some extent across the range of OCD symptom themes, different manifestations of the disorder may be typified by some features more than others. To help the clinician develop a specific conceptualization of patients presenting with different symptom themes, we briefly consider the cognitive characteristics and maintenance factors of the OCD symptom dimensions described in chapter 1: harming, contamination, incompleteness, and unacceptable thoughts. These characteristics are also summarized in Table 4.2.

Harming

Clinical and research observations indicate harm-related obsessions are associated with overestimation of the probability and "awfulness" of

TABLE 4.2

Prominent Cognitive and Behavioral Characteristics of Different OCD Symptom Dimensions

Dimension	Intrusive Thoughts	Prominent Appraisals of Intrusive Thoughts	Prominent Maintenance Factors
Harming	• Thoughts of mistakes, accidents • Thoughts or images of fires, burglaries, serious diseases	Overestimates of likelihood and cost of danger, exaggerated responsibility for preventing harm, intolerance for uncertainty, likelihood TAF	Checking for safety, seeking reassurance (asking questions), mental and behavior neutralizing, avoidance
Contamination	• I or others will become ill • Disgust • Thoughts or images of germs	Overestimates of the likelihood and costs of danger, responsibility for causing or preventing feared outcomes	Passive avoidance, compulsive washing
Incompleteness	• Sense that something is not just right • Feeling, thought, or sense of asymmetry	Imperfection and mistakes are intolerable	Compulsive ordering and arranging, repeating routine activities to achieve a sense of perfection or completeness
Unacceptable thoughts and covert rituals	• Unwanted violent, sexual, or blasphemous thoughts, ideas, images, impulses, and doubts	Overimportance of thoughts, overestimation of threat, exaggerated sense of responsibility for preventing harm, need to control thoughts	Mental rituals, overt and covert neutralization strategies, concealment, avoidance (when possible), thought control and suppression attempts

87

harm, an exaggerated sense of responsibility for preventing harm to one-self or others, and intolerance for uncertainty about the chances of mis-fortune (e.g., Rachman, 2002). TAF beliefs may also be present. The chief maintaining factors for harm-related obsessions include compulsive checking (e.g., for safety) and reassurance seeking (asking questions). Subtle rituals and other safety behaviors such as mental compulsions (prayer, reviewing) and repeating actions (retracing steps) may also be performed to magically prevent "bad luck" or to cancel out or neutralize the perceived danger. Although compulsive checking and other safety behaviors are intended to achieve a sense of certainty and reduce anxi-ety, they inadvertently cultivate obsessional fear as described in previ-ous sections.

Contamination

The most prominent cognitive features of contamination obsessions are overestimates of the likelihood and costs of illnesses associated with the feared contaminant (e.g., Jones & Menzies, 1997a). One patient feared she would easily get herpes (cold sores) from touching surfaces such as elevator buttons and door handles, and by using other people's pens or telephones (overestimate of likelihood). She also worried that if she had cold sores, she would be ostracized by her coworkers for being unclean and forsaken by her family for the rest of her life (overestimate of cost). Some patients do not articulate such specific feared consequences, but instead say they feel as if anxiety will persist indefinitely if exposed to sources of contamination (a form of perfectionism). Overestimates of danger and use of avoidance bring to light parallels between contamina-tion fears in OCD and specific phobias.

The distinguishing factor between contamination obsessions and phobias is the presence of responsibility cognitions in OCD. That is, pa-tients with contamination obsessions tend to believe that they can (and therefore must) act to prevent negative consequences by engaging in washing or cleaning rituals (Menzies, Harris, Cumming, & Einstein, 2000). The presence of responsibility cognitions is perhaps best illus-trated by contamination obsessions involving the fear that one will be accountable for infecting others with contaminants. For example, one woman was obsessed with concerns that her dishwasher might not do an adequate job of disinfecting the family dishes and silverware, and as a result, her family (particularly her young children) might become sick. To "prevent" sickness, she therefore scrubbed each item after it had been through the dishwasher and again before using it to serve food to her family. Interestingly, when preparing food only for herself, this patient was not nearly as concerned about becoming sick. In this example, the patient believed she held the pivotal power to prevent disastrous consequences from befalling others.

Incompleteness

Intrusive thoughts regarding symmetry, exactness, and the sense that something is not just right are relatively common experiences, yet may develop into obsessions if appraised as intolerable (Coles, Frost, Heimberg, & Rheaume, 2003). Thus, perfectionistic beliefs about mistakes, orderliness, and symmetry appear to dominate within this symptom dimension. Patients may not be able to articulate fears of specific negative catastrophes, and instead experience general distress associated with the imperfection they are confronted with (e.g., "the shoes don't feel even," "the clothes aren't arranged properly," "I didn't close the door just right"). Compulsive rituals such as ordering, arranging, and repeating actions serve the obvious purpose of reducing distress. However, from a learning standpoint, they maintain perfectionistic beliefs because they prevent the natural extinction of incompleteness-related distress. From a cognitive-behavioral perspective, rituals reinforce beliefs that imperfection, asymmetry, and disorderliness are distressing and intolerable, and that the only way to reduce this distress is by removing the not just right feeling. Thus, patients fail to learn that they would eventually stop worrying about the imperfection even if no rituals were performed.

Unacceptable Thoughts and Covert Rituals

Overly negative appraisals of the occurrence and content of intrusive violent or aggressive, sexual, and religious (blasphemous) thoughts, ideas, images, doubts, and urges characterize the unacceptable thoughts symptom dimension. Patients interpret their obsessional thoughts as morally unacceptable, indicative of some serious personal flaw, and in terms of personal responsibility for reducing or preventing harm to oneself or others (e.g., acting on the thought). As a result, sufferers often believe that they can and should control or suppress such repugnant, senseless thoughts. Common safety-seeking behaviors include mental compulsions and other neutralizing strategies, as well as concealment, avoidance (when possible), and various forms of thought control or suppression to minimize distress or the perceived probability of danger. The short-term success of safety behaviors in reducing anxiety reinforces distorted interpretations of the intrusive obsessional thoughts and prevents extinction of associated anxiety. As discussed previously, the general failure of thought control strategies often leads to secondary distress and an increase in the very intrusive thoughts that the person is trying to dismiss.

TREATMENT IMPLICATIONS
OF THE COGNITIVE-BEHAVIORAL MODEL

It follows from the cognitive-behavioral model that effective treatment of OCD must help patients (a) modify their erroneous interpretations of intrusive thoughts and other obsessional stimuli, and (b) eliminate avoidance, safety-seeking behavior, and other responses that serve as barriers to the natural extinction of obsessional fear and the self-correction of the erroneous interpretations. Patients must understand their problem not in terms of the risk of feared consequences, but in terms of how they are thinking and behaving in response to stimuli (e.g., intrusive thoughts) that objectively pose a low risk of harm. Individuals with washing compulsions must see their problem not as the need to prevent illness, but as the need to change how they respond to intrusive thoughts of germs, illness, or contamination as cued by situations that actually pose little risk of danger. Similarly, those with checking rituals are helped to view their problem not as how they are going to reassure themselves that dreaded mistakes will not occur, but as one in which they are lending too much significance to intrusive ideas, thoughts, doubts, and images about possible harm.

This conceptualization implies the need for a thorough assessment of the patient's obsessional cues (intrusive thoughts and external stimuli) and appraisals of these stimuli. In addition, particulars about the use of safety behaviors and other tactics for responding to obsessional stimuli must be precisely understood. Assessment culminates in the collaborative (i.e., the patient and therapist) development of an individualized account of the cognitive and behavioral mechanisms underlying the patient's OCD symptoms, and a plan for reversing these mechanisms using empirically validated treatment procedures.

Four such procedures are used in the cognitive-behavioral treatment of OCD. First, patients are educated about the normalcy of intrusive mental stimuli, the ways in which misinterpreting such stimuli leads to obsessions, and the ways in which obsessional fear is maintained. Second, cognitive therapy procedures similar to those used in the treatment of depression (Beck & Emery, 1985) are implemented to help patients identify and challenge distorted beliefs about intrusive thoughts and other obsessional stimuli. Exposure and response prevention, the third and fourth procedures, are incorporated as in traditional behavior therapy, with an emphasis on using these techniques to modify dysfunctional cognitions and weaken connections between obsessional stimuli and anxiety, and between safety behaviors and anxiety reduction. The next chapter provides an overview of these treatment procedures and reviews the strong evidence for their effectiveness. The second part of this book details the implementation of these evidence-based assessment and treatment techniques.

5

Overview of Cognitive-Behavioral Therapy for OCD

Cognitive-behavioral therapy (CBT) is a time-limited, structured, and active psychological treatment that is based on an empirically consistent relationship among symptoms, the treatment procedures, and a specified outcome. In contrast to some forms of psychotherapy where the emphasis is on elucidating the origins of the disorder, CBT targets the processes that maintain undesirable emotional and behavioral symptoms. In the case of OCD, the patient's symptoms are conceptualized as maladaptive patterns of thinking (i.e., misinterpreting the importance of obsessional stimuli in ways that evoke anxiety) and behaving (i.e., responding to obsessional distress using safety-seeking strategies). CBT helps to weaken these patterns by teaching patients to implement a repertoire of new (more effective) skills. Therapy represents a collaborative effort between the therapist and patient, yet in many ways it resembles education, coaching, or tutoring. The therapist, armed with understanding and expertise, takes the role of instructor; and the patient, the role of student. Whereas a positive therapeutic relationship is important for successful outcome in CBT, it alone is not considered to be the agent of change. Instead, the aim of the therapeutic relationship is to foster the development of the patient's new competencies.

When a person presents for psychological treatment, he or she assumes that the treatment provider possesses expertise that is superior to that available through consultation with friends, family members, clergy, or the local bartender. Clinicians therefore have a professional and ethical obligation to provide treatments that are likely to be beneficial, and not to provide treatments that are not likely to be helpful. For this reason it is important for practitioners to stay informed of the scientific evidence regarding the treatment techniques they use. Alas, an important strength of CBT for anxiety disorders is that it has stood the test of scientific scrutiny—it is evidence based. That is, the procedures applied in the treatment of anxiety problems such as OCD have been consistently demonstrated to be beneficial in controlled studies comparing them with other credible treatments of known value.

The major CBT techniques with proven effectiveness for reducing OCD symptoms are exposure, response prevention, and cognitive therapy (CT). This chapter provides a concise description of these procedures and reviews research substantiating their effectiveness. Findings from research on factors related to successful treatment response and the effects of CBT in comparison to (and in combination with) medications for OCD are also presented. Detailed guidelines for planning and implementing CBT techniques are provided in Part II of this volume.

EXPOSURE AND RESPONSE PREVENTION

Exposure and response prevention (ERP) are behavior therapy techniques that entail confrontation with stimuli that provoke obsessional fear, but that objectively pose a low risk of harm. Exposure can occur in the form of repeated actual encounters with the feared situations (situational or in vivo exposure), and in the form of imaginal confrontation with the feared consequences of confronting these situations (imaginal exposure). For example, an individual with obsessional fears of bad luck from the number 13 would be asked to practice writing the number 13 for situational exposure. She would also practice imaginal exposure to thoughts and images of being held responsible for causing bad luck. A patient with fears of becoming contaminated might be asked to touch objects of increasing "dirtiness"—a doorknob, the floor, a toilet—for situational exposure. He would then confront images of germs for imaginal exposure.

As would be expected, when an exposure task is begun, the patient's subjective sense of anxiety is evoked. In fact, patients are encouraged to engage in the exposure task fully and allow themselves to experience this obsessional distress. Over time, the distress (and the associated physiological responding) naturally subsides—a process known as *habituation*. With repeated exposure, habituation occurs more rapidly. The response prevention component of ERP entails refraining from compulsive rituals and other safety-seeking behaviors that serve as an escape from obsessive fear. Response prevention helps to prolong exposure and facilitate extinction of obsessional anxiety. In the preceding examples, the first patient might practice refraining from any strategies she typically uses to "undo" the effects of exposure to the number 13. She would also refrain from checking for reassurance that bad luck did not occur. The second patient would be instructed to refrain from decontamination rituals such as washing or cleaning.

The Delivery of ERP

The way ERP is delivered can vary widely, although two meta-analytic studies suggest that greater effectiveness is achieved when therapist-guided exposure sessions are held multiple times per week, as opposed to once weekly (Abramowitz, 1996, 1997). This is probably because changing the habits that maintain OCD requires a sustained effort that could be compromised by intersession intervals of longer than a few days. Research also indicates that substantial beneficial effects, which are also durable, can occur following a limited number of treatment sessions. It is therefore recommended that an initial course of therapy be limited to about 15 to 20 sessions. One format that has been found to produce particularly potent effects includes a few hours of assessment and treatment planning followed by 15 daily treatment sessions, lasting about 90 minutes each, spaced over about 3 weeks (e.g., Franklin, Abramowitz, Kozak, Levitt, & Foa, 2000). When pragmatic concerns render this regimen impractical, conducting the treatment sessions on a twice-weekly basis over 8 weeks works very well for many individuals with OCD (Abramowitz, Foa, & Franklin, 2003).

At our specialty clinic, patients who live within commuting distance typically receive the twice-weekly therapy program, whereas those who travel from out of town are offered the 3-week, daily sessions (intensive outpatient) option. Regardless of the therapy schedule, treatment sessions are spent doing exposure tasks with the therapist supervising these exercises. Self-supervised exposure homework practice is also assigned for completion between sessions. Depending on the patient's symptom presentation and the practicality of confronting actual feared situations, treatment sessions might involve varying amounts of situational and imaginal exposure practice.

A course of ERP ordinarily begins with the assessment of obsessions, safety-seeking strategies, avoidance behaviors, and anticipated consequences of confronting feared situations. Before treatment commences, however, the therapist provides a rationale regarding how ERP is helpful in reducing OCD. This psychoeducational component is an important step in therapy because it helps to motivate the patient to tolerate the distress that typically accompanies exposure practice. The treatment rationale communicates to the patient an explanation of OCD symptoms in terms that he or she will readily understand. It also prepares the patient for ERP by letting him or her know that treatment is likely to evoke anxiety, but that this distress is temporary and subsides with time. Information gathered during the assessment sessions is then used to plan the specific exposure exercises that will be pursued. Importantly, the term *response prevention* does not imply that the therapist actively prevents the patient from performing rituals or other safety-seeking behaviors. Instead, the therapist must convince patients to resist their own urges to carry out these behaviors. Self-monitoring—the keeping of a record of any response prevention violations—is also implemented.

The exposure exercises in ERP typically begin with moderately distressing situations, stimuli, and images, and progress to the most distressing situations—which must be confronted during treatment. Beginning with less anxiety-evoking exposure tasks increases the likelihood that the patient will learn to manage his or her distress and complete early exposures successfully. Mastery of initial exposures increases confidence in the treatment and helps motivate the patient to persevere during later, more difficult, exercises. At the end of each treatment session, the therapist instructs the patient to continue exposure for several hours and in different environmental contexts, without the therapist. Exposure to the most anxiety-evoking situations is not left to the end of the treatment, but rather, is completed during the middle third of the treatment program. This strategy allows the patient ample opportunity to repeat exposure to the most difficult situations in different contexts to allow generalization of treatment effects. During later sessions, the therapist emphasizes the importance of the patient's continuing to apply the ERP procedures learned during treatment.

The Development of Behavioral Treatments

Before the mid-1960s OCD was considered rare and highly resistant to treatment. The most common forms of psychotherapy used at that time were based on psychoanalytic and psychodynamic approaches that emphasized the role of unconscious motivation. However, these treatments were not particularly reliable in reducing obsessions and compulsions as evidenced by the reputation OCD had as an intractable problem. Early case histories reporting on the use of select behavioral procedures such as systematic desensitization, progressive muscle relaxation, flooding, thought stopping, aversion therapy, and covert sensitization also revealed little evidence of any substantial or durable treatment effects (for a review see Foa, Steketee, & Ozarow, 1985).

The prognostic picture for OCD began to improve in the mid-1960s and 1970s when Meyer first applied ERP procedures, which had been derived from learning models of OCD as a set of conditioned responses. Meyer's (1966) initial open trial study with 15 inpatients found that ERP led to sustained improvement in OCD symptoms. Ten patients responded extremely well, and the remaining five showed partial improvement. Follow-up studies conducted several years later revealed that only two of the successfully treated patients had relapsed (Meyer, Levy, & Schnurer, 1974). These findings generated extensive interest in ERP and led to additional studies worldwide using more advanced research methodology in both inpatient and outpatient settings. Studies in England (Hodgson, Rachman, & Marks, 1972; Marks, Hodgson, & Rachman, 1975; Rachman, Hodgson, & Marks, 1971; Rachman, Marks, & Hodgson, 1973), Holland (Emmelkamp & Kraanen, 1977), Greece (Rabavilas, Boulougouris, & Stefanis, 1976), and the United States (Foa & Goldstein, 1978) with a total of more than 300 patients and numerous different therapists affirmed the generalizability of ERP's beneficial effects. By the end of the 1980s, ERP was widely considered the psychological treatment of choice for OCD.

Mechanisms of Change

How does ERP reduce obsessional anxiety and compulsive urges? Foa and Kozak (1986) proposed that these treatment procedures help patients modify overestimates of the likelihood of negative outcomes that underlie obsessional anxiety. Therefore, it is incumbent on the therapist to engineer exposure tasks that involve fear-evoking experiences in which the patient expects (unrealistically) that something bad will happen, but where the feared consequences do not actually occur. Foa and Kozak (1986) drew attention to three indicators of successful outcome with ERP. First, physiological arousal and subjective fear must be evoked during exposure. Second, these fear responses must gradually diminish during the exposure session (within-session habituation). Third, the initial fear response at the beginning of each exposure session should decline across sessions (between-sessions habituation).

Let us consider the example of a patient who washes his hands compulsively because he is afraid that he has contracted "bathroom germs" that will lead to a serious illness. During ERP, this patient would be helped to (a) repeatedly contaminate himself with bathroom germs by touching objects that he fears are contaminated, such as the bathroom floor (exposure); (b) refrain from washing rituals (response prevention); and (c) observe that he does not become ill. Figure 5.1 depicts the pattern of habituation within and between four exposure sessions during which this patient confronted bathroom germs. During each session, the patient sat on the bathroom floor, abstained from all safety behaviors, and practiced eating with his hands. As illustrated, the initially high levels of discomfort during exposure were

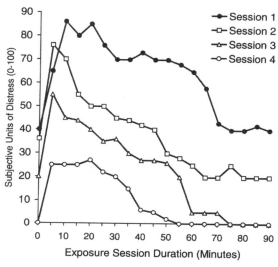

FIG. 5.1.   Ratings of subjective distress for an individual with OCD during four sessions of exposure to "bathroom germs." The figure illustrates the reduction of anxiety both within individual sessions as well as across treatment sessions.

temporary, and gave way to the extinction of obsessional anxiety in the long term. In fact, during the fourth exposure session, the patient's level of distress was very minimal.

Dismantling Studies

Dismantling studies, which examine the individual effects of specific treatment procedures in multicomponent therapy programs, have addressed three questions with respect to ERP. First, what are the differential effects of exposure and response prevention? Second, how do these individual treatment components compare to the complete ERP package? Third, is adding exposure in imagination to situational (in vivo) exposure superior to situational exposure alone?

Differential Effects of Exposure and Response Prevention.   Two studies that examined the separate effects of exposure and response prevention found similar results (Foa, Steketee, Grayson, Turner, & Lattimer, 1984; Foa, Steketee, & Milby, 1980). For example, Foa et al. (1984) randomly assigned 32 OCD patients (all with contamination obsessions and washing rituals) to one of three treatment groups: exposure only, response prevention only, or the combination (ERP). At posttreatment, patients in the exposure-only group evidenced greater reductions in contamination fears than did those in the response-prevention-only group. In contrast, response prevention was superior to exposure in reducing washing rituals. These results suggest that exposure and response prevention have differential effects on OCD symptoms: Response prevention is superior to exposure in decreasing compulsive rituals, and exposure is superior to response prevention for decreasing obsessional fear.

Exposure With Response Prevention vs. the Individual Treatment Procedures. Foa et al.'s (1984) study also revealed an additive effect of combining exposure and response prevention. As shown in Fig. 5.2, ERP was more effective than either of its individual components and led to the greatest short- and long-term reduction of anxiety and urges to ritualize. To explain this finding, Foa et al. (1984) proposed that response prevention helps render information learned during exposure more incompatible with the patient's expectations. For example, without response prevention, a patient who repeatedly practices exposure to public bathrooms, yet does not contract herpes, may attribute the nonoccurrence of herpes to her continued compulsive washing. In this case, the maladaptive beliefs that bathrooms are dangerous and washing rituals prevent herpes will persist. However, if response prevention is implemented along with exposure, good health cannot be attributed to washing rituals and thus the patient's overestimates of risk must change.

Imaginal and in Vivo Exposure. As discussed in previous chapters, anxiety-evoking stimuli in OCD are not limited to external cues. Indeed, most patients experience intrusive anxiety-evoking thoughts, images, ideas, or impulses that elicit excessive anxiety and therefore must also be dealt with in ERP. Whereas exposure to tangible fear cues such as dirt or unlucky numbers can be conducted in vivo (real life), confrontation with imagined disasters obviously cannot. A woman afraid of causing fires, and therefore constantly checking light switches, can be exposed in vivo by requiring her to leave lights on. However, she cannot be exposed to actually causing a fire as a result of not carefully checking. Confrontation with such situations must, therefore, be conducted in imagination. It follows from Foa and Kozak's (1986) proposition regarding the importance of matching the exposure stimulus with the patient's fear that obsessional fears of disastrous consequences should improve when imaginal exposure is added to in vivo exposure.

To examine the additive effect of imaginal exposure, Foa, Steketee, Turner, and Fischer (1980) assigned 15 OCD patients with checking compulsions to either 10 daily sessions of ERP with all exposure conducted in vivo, or a similar regimen of ERP that incorporated both situational and imaginal exposure. Imaginal exposure consisted of repeated and prolonged confrontation with thoughts of anxiety-evoking scenes related to particular obsessional fears. For example, a woman who performed rituals

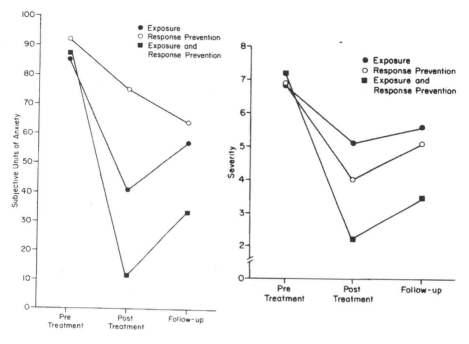

FIG. 5.2. Differential effects of exposure, response prevention, and combined treatment on the mean highest subjective levels of anxiety (left), and severity of rituals (right). From "Deliberate Exposure and Blocking of Obsessive-Compulsive Rituals: Immediate and Long-term Effects," by E. B. Foa, G. S. Steketee, J. B. Grayson, R. M. Turner, & P. R. Lattimer, 1984, *Behavior Therapy*, *15*, pp. 450–472. Copyright 1984 by the Association for Advancement of Behavior Therapy. Reprinted with permission.

to protect her family from death purposely imaged that her husband died as a result of her failure to perform her rituals. At posttreatment, both groups of patients improved substantially, but did not differ significantly from one another. However, at follow-up (3 months–2.5 years), the group that received imaginal and situational exposure maintained their improvements more than did the group that had conducted only situational exposure. Thus, imaginal exposure to the consequences of not ritualizing is an important adjunct to situational exposure.

The Efficacy of ERP

Results From Meta-Analysis. Data from a large number of controlled and uncontrolled outcome trials consistently indicate that ERP is extremely helpful in reducing OCD symptoms. A comprehensive meta-analysis of this literature (Abramowitz, 1996) that included 24 studies conducted between 1975 and 1995 (and involving more than 800 patients) revealed very large treatment effects as assessed by various measures of OCD. At posttreatment, the mean effect sizes were 1.16 on self-report measures and 1.41 on interview measures. Follow-up effect sizes were similarly large: 1.10 and 1.57 for self-report and interview scales respectively. Using a different meta-analytic approach, Foa and Kozak (1996) calculated the percentage of patients in each study that were "responders" (usually defined as achieving a pre- to posttreatment improvement of at least 30%). They found that across 13 ERP studies, 83% of patients were responders at posttreatment, and across 16 studies, 76% were responders at follow-up (mean follow-up was 29 months). In concert, these findings suggest that the majority of OCD patients who undergo treatment with ERP evidence substantial short- and long-term benefit.

Randomized Controlled Trials.   Because meta-analysis combines controlled and uncontrolled studies, the aggregated treatment effect sizes are influenced by both specific (ERP procedures themselves) and nonspecific (e.g., time, expectancy) factors and therefore may be overstated. We therefore examine more closely several randomized controlled trials (RCTs) that are designed to assess the specific efficacy of ERP procedures over and above nonspecific effects.

Interpreting the results of OCD treatment research is aided by the fact that most studies have used the 10-item Yale–Brown Obsessive Compulsive Scale (Y–BOCS; Goodman, Price, Rasmussen, Mazure, Delgado, et al., 1989; Goodman, Price, Rasmussen, Mazure, Fleischmann, et al., 1989) as the primary outcome measure. This has not only enabled comparisons between different studies, but it has also provided readers with a means of deriving clinically meaningful data from study results. The Y–BOCS (described in detail in chapter 6) yields a total score ranging from 0 (*no symptoms*) to 40 (*extremely severe*). Scores of 0 to 7 indicate subclinical symptoms, 8 to 15 indicate mild OCD, 16 to 25 represent moderate symptomatology, 26 to 30 represent severe symptoms, and 31 to 40 indicate profound or extreme symptoms. Because the Y–BOCS is so widely used and possesses adequate psychometric properties, I focus primarily on this measure in the literature review presented next.

Table 5.1 summarizes the results of four RCTs that examined the efficacy of ERP. Two studies compared ERP with a credible psychotherapy control condition. Fals-Stewart, Marks, and Schafer (1993) randomly assigned patients to individual ERP, group ERP, or a progressive relaxation control treatment. All treatments included 24 sessions delivered on a twice-weekly basis over 12 weeks. Although both ERP regimens were su-

TABLE 5.1
Effects of ERP in Randomized Controlled Trials

				Y–BOCS Total Score										
			ERP Group						Control Group					
			Pre		Post				Pre		Post			
Study	Control Condition	n	M	SD	M	SD	n		M	SD	M	SD		
Fals-Stewart et al. (1993)[a]	Relaxation	31	20.2	—	12.1	—	32		19.9	—	18.1	—		
Lindsay et al. (1997)	Anxiety management	9	28.7	4.6	11.0	3.8	9		24.4	7.0	25.9	5.8		
Van Balkom et al. (1998)	Waiting list	19	25.0	7.9	17.1	8.4	18		26.8	6.4	26.4	6.8		
Foa et al. (2005)	Pill placebo	29	24.6	4.8	11.0	7.9	26		25.0	4.0	22.2	6.4		

Note. Y–BOCS = Yale–Brown Obsessive Compulsive Scale; ERP = exposure and response prevention.

[a] Standard deviation not reported in the study.

perior to relaxation, there were no differences between group and individual ERP. Average improvement in the ERP groups was 41% on the Y–BOCS, and posttreatment scores fell within the mild range of severity. In the second study, Lindsay, Crino, and Andrews (1997) compared ERP to anxiety management training (AMT), a credible placebo treatment consisting of breathing retraining, relaxation, and problem-solving therapy. Both treatments were intensive: 15 daily sessions conducted over a 3-week period. On average, patients receiving ERP improved almost 62% from pre- to posttreatment on the Y–BOCS, with endpoint scores again in the mild range. In contrast, the AMT group showed no change in symptoms following treatment. The clear superiority of ERP over credible placebo therapies such as relaxation and AMT indicates that improvement in OCD symptoms can be attributed to the ERP procedures themselves, over and above any nonspecific factors such as time, attention, or expectancy of positive outcome.

In the Netherlands, Van Balkom et al. (1998) examined the relative efficacy of four active treatments and a wait-list control. Treatment conditions included (a) ERP, (b) cognitive therapy (CT), (c) ERP plus fluvoxamine, and (d) CT plus fluvoxamine. All psychotherapy involved 16 weekly sessions. As Table 5.1 indicates, ERP fared somewhat less well in this study than in other RCTs. A likely explanation for the relatively disappointing improvement rate of 32% is that the ERP protocol was less than optimal: All exposure was conducted as homework assignments rather than in session and under the therapist's supervision. Moreover, therapists were not allowed to discuss expectations of disastrous consequences during the first 8 weeks of ERP because this would have overlapped substantially with CT procedures.

Finally, Foa et al. (2005) conducted a multicenter double-blind RCT examining the relative efficacy of (a) intensive (15 daily sessions) ERP (including in-session exposure), (b) clomipramine (CMI), (c) combined treatment (ERP + CMI), and (d) pill placebo. ERP produced a 50% Y–BOCS reduction, which was far superior to the effects of pill placebo. Moreover, endpoint Y–BOCS scores fell within the mild range of OCD severity. ERP was also more effective than CMI, but not CMI + ERP (which was equivalent to ERP alone). Overall, the findings from RCTs suggest that ERP produces substantial and clinically meaningful improvement in OCD symptoms and that symptom reduction is due to the specific effects of these treatment procedures and not to nonspecific or "common" factors of psychotherapy.

COGNITIVE THERAPY

Enthusiasm for ERP is dampened somewhat by the 13% to 25% refusal rate among patients (Foa et al., 1983; Stanley & Turner, 1995), which if considered along with the additional 15% to 25% discontinuation and failure rates reported in many studies, suggests room for improvement. Some clinicians and researchers have turned to CT approaches to address shortcomings of ERP because cognitive techniques incorporate less prolonged exposure to fear cues and have led to advances in the treatment of other disorders such as depression and panic disorder (e.g., Jones & Menzies, 1997b). The basis of CT is the rational and evidence-based challenging and correction of faulty and dysfunctional thoughts and beliefs that underlie emotional upset (Beck & Emery, 1985). As you recall from earlier chapters, individuals with OCD hold characteristic faulty beliefs that lead to obsessive fear. It is these beliefs that are targeted in CT, including overestimates of the probability and severity of danger and misinterpretations of intrusive thoughts as having implications for responsibility for harm (D. A. Clark, 2004).

Delivery of CT

CT typically begins with the therapist presenting a rationale for treatment that incorporates the notion that intrusive obsessional thoughts are normal experiences and not harmful or indicative of anything important. Problems with OCD are thought to arise because of how the patient appraises his or her intrusions as significant in a way that is distressing (e.g., thoughts of violence are equivalent to committing violent acts). Misappraisal of intrusions in this way leads to preoccupation with the unwanted thought as well as responses such as avoidance and safety behaviors that unwittingly maintain the obsessional preoccupation and anxiety.

The experienced clinician may recognize that this conceptualization of OCD parallels the established cognitive-behavioral formulation of panic disorder proposed by D. M. Clark (1986). This model proposes that individuals with panic disorder experience innocuous arousal-related physical sensations (e.g., racing heart), which they misinterpret as indicating that some catastrophic internal event is taking place (e.g., a heart attack). The therapeutic implication is that correcting the way physical sensations are perceived will reduce panic. Similarly, the cognitive formulation of OCD assumes that unwanted intrusive thoughts are normal (Rachman & de Silva, 1978), and that it is their misinterpretation as signs of possible danger that underlies OCD. The rationale for the use of CT procedures is therefore that OCD symptoms may be reduced by helping the patient correctly view his or her unwanted intrusions as nonthreatening and not needing to be controlled.

Various techniques are used to help patients correct their erroneous appraisals, such as didactic presentation of educational material and Socratic dialogue aimed at helping patients recognize and correct dysfunctional thinking patterns. *Behavioral experiments*, in which patients enter situations that exemplify their fears, are often used to facilitate the acquisition of corrective information about the realistic risks associated with obsessional fears. Although the rationale for behavioral experiments in CT is somewhat (but not altogether) different than the rationale for exposure exercises in ERP, there is a good deal of procedural overlap.

Van Oppen and Arntz (1994) outlined a 16-session CT program for OCD that was aimed specifically at modifying overestimates of threat and perceptions of inflated responsibility associated with obsessions. Steps in this intervention included: (a) considering obsessive intrusions as stimuli, (b) identifying and challenging anxiety-provoking thoughts associated with obsessions with Socratic questioning, (c) changing the dysfunctional assumptions to nondistressing ideas, and (d) behavioral experiments. van Oppen and her colleagues later found that their CT program was effective in reducing OCD symptoms (Van Oppen et al., 1995).

Jones and Menzies (1997b) developed a separate CT program specifically for patients with contamination and washing symptoms. Their eight-session treatment called Danger Ideation Reduction Therapy (DIRT) consisted of procedures designed to reduce expectations of danger concerning feared contaminants. Components included (a) cognitive restructuring along the lines of Beck (1976), (b) watching filmed interviews with people regularly exposed to feared stimuli (e.g., nurses who are exposed to blood, bank tellers who handle money), (c) presentation of results from microbiological experiments, (d) presentation of corrective information regarding rates of illnesses and the effects of hand washing, (e) discussions about the probability of feared catastrophes, and (f) practice with focusing attention away from threat cues (i.e., attentional training). In an RCT with 21 patients, Jones and Menzies (1998) found that DIRT was superior to wait list (Jones & Menzies, 1998), thus indicating the utility of this program.

CT Versus ERP

How does the efficacy of CT measure up to that of ERP for ameliorating OCD symptoms? Six studies have addressed this question by directly comparing variants of the two treatments. In two early investigations, Emmelkamp and colleagues compared rational emotive therapy (RET, which is a form of CT) to ERP (Emmelkamp & Beens, 1991; Emmelkamp, Visser, & Hoekstra, 1988). RET (Ellis, 1962) involved identifying anxiety-evoking thoughts (e.g., "Not washing my hands would be 100% awful"), challenging the basis of these thoughts, and replacing them with alternative beliefs and assumptions that do not lead to anxiety; however, no behavioral experiments were performed. Exposure in the ERP condition was completely *self-controlled*, meaning patients completed all exposure practice on their own as homework assignments. In both studies, RET and self-controlled ERP produced roughly similar results. Limitations of these studies included the relatively small sample sizes and use of an ERP format that was less than optimal (no therapist-supervised exposure). In addition, these investigations were conducted before the Y–BOCS was available. Given the problems with these studies, it is difficult to draw from them firm conclusions regarding the relative efficacy of ERP and RET.

Four additional studies that used the Y–BOCS compared contemporary cognitive interventions similar to Van Oppen and Arntz's (1994) program to variations of ERP. The results of these investigations are summarized in Table 5.2 and discussed next. Van Oppen et al. (1995) randomly assigned patients to either 16 sessions of CT or 16 sessions of self-controlled ERP. Both treatments led to an improvement in OCD symptoms and CT was more effective than ERP (Y–BOCS reductions of 53% and 43%, respectively). Importantly, the brief and infrequent therapist contact (weekly 45-minute sessions), along with reliance on patients to manage all exposure practice on their own, likely accounted for the relatively modest effects of ERP in this study. Moreover, CT involved behavioral experiments that resembled exposure, which blurred the distinction between the two study treatments. Only after behavioral experiments were introduced (at the sixth session) did symptom reduction in the CT group approach that of ERP. Thus, it is possible that the exposure component of behavioral experiments is key to the efficacy of CT. Using a sample that overlapped with van Oppen et al.'s, Van Balkom et al. (1998) found no significant difference between CT with behavioral experiments and self-controlled ERP.

Cottraux et al.'s. (2001) study seems to provide the fairest comparison between CT and an adequate ERP regimen. Both treatments involved 20 hours of therapist contact over 16 weeks. CT was based on Salkovskis's (1985) cognitive model of OCD and included psychoeducation, modification of unrealistic interpretations of intrusive thoughts (i.e., cognitive restructuring), and behavioral experiments to test dysfunctional assumptions (both in session and for homework). ERP involved therapist-supervised and homework exposure and complete response prevention. As shown in Table 5.2, the two programs produced comparable outcomes at posttreatment (Y–BOCS reductions = 42%–44%). Interestingly, ERP resulted in changes in cognitions (e.g., TAF) that were not explicitly addressed in therapy. At 1-year follow-up, patients treated with ERP had continued to improve from their posttreatment status (follow-up Y–BOCS = 11.1), whereas this was not the case with CT (follow-up Y–BOCS = 15.0). Finally, McLean et al. (2001) compared the two treatment approaches as conducted in group settings. Patients received 12 weekly 2.5-hour group sessions (6–8 participants per group) of either CT (similar to the program used by Cottraux et al.'s [2001] study) or ERP involving in-session and homework exposures. Both treatments were more effective than a wait-list

TABLE 5.2
Comparisons Between Contemporary CT and ERP

Study	Comments	Y–BOCS Total Score										
		CT Group					ERP Group					
			Pre		Post			Pre		Post		
		n	M	SD	M	SD	n	M	SD	M	SD
Van Oppen et al. (1995)	No therapist-supervised ERP	28	24.1	5.5	13.3	8.5	29	31.4	5.0	17.9	9.0
Van Balkom et al. (1998)	Patients overlapped with Van Oppen et al. (1995)	25	25.3	6.6	13.5	9.7	22	25.0	7.9	17.1	8.4
Cottraux et al. (2001)	Both treatments included exposure-like procedures	30	28.6	5.1	16.1	8.2	30	28.5	4.9	16.4	7.8
McLean et al. (2001)	All treatment in groups	31	21.9	5.8	16.1	6.7	32	21.8	4.6	13.2	7.2

Note. Y–BOCS = Yale–Brown Obsessive Compulsive Scale; CT = cognitive therapy; ERP = exposure and response prevention.

control condition, and ERP was associated with greater improvement than CT at both posttreatment (40% and 27% Y–BOCS reductions, respectively) and follow-up (21% and 41% Y–BOCS reductions).

Although the results of several comparison studies suggest that ERP and CT were of similar efficacy for OCD, one should not conclude that well-executed ERP is only as effective as CT. Particularly in the earlier studies, both ERP and CT yielded minimal improvements in OCD symptoms. The efficacy of ERP was likely attenuated by the use of suboptimal procedures, such as the lack of therapist-supervised exposure. Moreover, CT programs were likely enhanced by behavioral experiments, which probably have similar effects to supervised exposure. Using meta-analytic methods, we found that behavioral experiments improve the efficacy of CT for OCD (Abramowitz, Franklin, & Foa, 2002). Thus, CT may have been systematically advantaged, and ERP systematically disadvantaged, in these investigations.

The Addition of CT to ERP

Perhaps the addition of CT can enhance the effects of ERP. To examine this possibility, Vogel, Stiles, and Götestam (2004) conducted a controlled study in which 35 individuals with OCD were randomly assigned to receive either ERP plus CT ($n = 16$) or ERP plus relaxation ($n = 19$). Relaxation was added as a placebo procedure to control for the effects of adding additional techniques to ERP. For 12 patients, a 6-week wait list preceded active therapy. Treatment entailed 12 twice-weekly 2-hour sessions with 90 minutes dedicated to therapist-supervised exposure, and the remaining 30 minutes for either CT or relaxation. Response prevention was partial: Patients were required not to ritualize for 2 hours following exposure. Results indicated that both therapy programs were superior to wait list. Among treatment completers, Y–BOCS scores for the ERP + CT group were reduced from 25.1 to 16.4, and for the ERP + REL group, from 23.4 to 11.3 posttreatment. At 1-year follow-up, the ERP + CT group had a mean Y–BOCS score of 13.3, and the ERP + REL group had a mean score of 10.2. Statistical analyses indicated a nonsignificant trend toward superiority of ERP + REL at posttreatment, but this difference disappeared at the follow-up assessment. Importantly, the inclusion of CT was useful in reducing dropout. Thus, there appear to be benefits to incorporating CT techniques along with ERP—perhaps CT techniques improve the acceptability of ERP.

Combining CT procedures with ERP might be particularly helpful for individuals high on the unacceptable thoughts OCD symptom dimension. In a controlled study, Freeston et al. (1997) obtained excellent results with a treatment package that entailed (a) education about the cognitive-behavioral model of OCD; (b) ERP consisting of in-session and homework exposure to intrusive thoughts using audio loop tapes and refraining from neutralizing behaviors; and (c) CT targeting exaggerated responsibility, perfectionism, and inflated estimates of the probability and severity of negative outcomes. Compared to a wait-list control group, treated patients achieved substantial improvement: Among all patients ($n = 28$) Y–BOCS scores improved from 23.9 to 9.8 after an average of 25.7 sessions over 19.2 weeks. Moreover, patients retained their gains at 6-month follow-up: The mean Y–BOCS score at follow-up was 10.8. This study demonstrates that ERP and CT can be successfully combined in the treatment of a presentation of OCD that had previously been considered resistant to psychological treatment (Baer, 1994).

Clinically speaking, just as exposure adds to the benefits of CT (Abramowitz, Franklin, & Foa, 2002), cognitive techniques surely play a critical role in ERP. It is unfortunate that most published accounts of ERP (e.g., Kozak & Foa, 1997) fail to fully describe the informal cognitive procedures that likely contribute to its efficacy. For example, patients often need to be persuaded that the evocation of fear that occurs during ERP will be beneficial for them in the long term. As I describe in later chapters, encouraging patients to engage in treatment often relies heavily on discussions about dysfunctional beliefs, the consequences of risk taking, the costs of avoidance behavior, and the futility of attempts to gain complete certainty via compulsive ritualizing. Importantly, the research reviewed previously suggests that discussions about mistaken cognitions should accompany, rather than replace, systematic prolonged and repeated therapist-supervised exposure. Thus, in the CBT program I outline in Part II of this volume, the role of CT is primarily to pave the way for ERP exercises. That is, cognitive interventions are used to encourage patients to take acceptable risks (i.e., to undertake ERP exercises) that will help weaken their dysfunctional beliefs.

Acknowledging the overlaps in implementation and beneficial effects of treatment procedures derived from behavioral (ERP) and cognitive (CT) formulations of OCD, it has become conventional to collectively describe these procedures as "cognitive-behavioral therapy." Therefore, when referring generally to treatment programs incorporating variations of ERP and CT, I use the term *CBT*. Yet when referring to specific techniques and procedures used in treatment, I continue to apply the most descriptive terms available (e.g., CT, ERP).

THE EFFECTIVENESS OF CBT: BEYOND THE BOUTIQUE

Whereas numerous RCTs substantiate the efficacy of ERP and CT in well-controlled academic research settings and specialty clinics (i.e., "boutiques"), some authors have cautioned that results from such rigorously conducted studies may not generalize to typical service settings (e.g., Silbershatz in Persons & Silberschatz, 1998). For example, RCTs frequently exclude patients with comorbid conditions to achieve homogenous diagnostic samples. Yet people with OCD often suffer from comorbid mood and anxiety disorders. RCTs often exclude patients who have failed the treatments under study. Yet, most people with OCD have lengthy treatment histories. Thus, RCT patient samples may not be representative of treatment-referred outpatients who present with multiple problems. Other differences between RCTs and routine clinical practice include rigorous therapist training and supervision, manualization of therapy (including a fixed number of sessions), and random assignment. It is no wonder that many practicing clinicians doubt whether the treatments found efficacious in highly controlled studies do not work as well with "typical" OCD patients as encountered in routine practice.

A promising solution to this apparent generalizability problem is effectiveness research in which empirically supported treatments are evaluated in clinical service contexts with representative patients and treatment providers. Four effectiveness studies have examined CBT for OCD as delivered in nonresearch settings. Kirk (1983) reported on 36 OCD patients treated by non-research-oriented behavior therapists in England. Therapy was neither manualized nor time limited, yet generally involved variations of ERP procedures. Kirk reported that over 75% of these patients were at least moderately improved at posttreatment, and 81% had sought no further treatment at follow-up (between 1–5 years). Unfortunately, no standardized outcome measures were used to assess outcome, thus it is difficult to ascertain the clinical significance of the reported improvement.

My colleagues and I (Franklin, Abramowitz, Foa, Kozak, & Levitt, 2000) conducted a large effectiveness study in which we examined outcome for 110 consecutively referred individuals with OCD who received ERP on a fee-for-service outpatient basis. Treatment was intensive—15 daily sessions over 3 weeks—and no individuals were excluded for reasons of age, comorbidity, previous treatment failure, or medical problems. In fact, half of the sample had comorbid Axis I or Axis II diagnoses and 61% were medication nonresponders. Patients were only denied ERP if they were actively psychotic, abusing substances, or suicidal (all reasons not to begin ERP in any setting; see chapter 7). The results were encouraging: Mean Y–BOCS scores improved from 26.8 to 11.8 (60% reduction in OCD symptoms). Moreover, only 10 patients dropped out of treatment prematurely.

Although the Franklin et al. (2000) study demonstrated that unselected OCD patients respond well to CBT, the therapy setting was not naturalistic: Treatment took place in an anxiety disorders specialty clinic where many of the therapists were highly experienced with ERP, or received regular supervision from ERP experts. In addition, the intensive treatment regimen was highly demanding and unlikely to be used in most outpatient settings. To address these issues, Warren and Thomas (2001) reported on 26 individuals with OCD treated in a private practice psychotherapy clinic with ERP and formal cognitive techniques. Treatment sessions were held weekly for 1 hour and the total number of therapy hours across patients varied ($M = 16.4$ hours). Thirty-two percent of the patients in this study had comorbid conditions and 50% had previously received treatment for their OCD. Results were highly consistent with Franklin et al.'s (2000) study: Y–BOCS scores improved from 23.0 to 11.6 (48% reduction in OCD symptoms).

In a multicultural naturalistic study, Friedman et al. (2003) presented treatment outcome results for a community sample of African American ($n = 15$), Caribbean American ($n = 11$), and White ($n = 36$) patients with OCD. Therapy involved twice-weekly 45- to 90-minute sessions ($M =$ about 20 sessions) of ERP and termination was decided by the clinician when it appeared that maximal gains had been achieved. Treatment was informed by an ERP manual, yet therapists were not required to adhere strictly to the protocol if specific patient difficulties required alternate interventions. Although treatment was effective in reducing OCD and depressive symptoms, many patients reported significant residual symptoms after therapy: Mean Y–BOCS scores for African American patients were 23.5 (pretreatment) and 17.2 (posttreatment; 27% reduction), and for Whites were 26.03 (pretreatment) and 17.65 (posttreatment; 23% reduction). There were no between-group differences in treatment outcome. The authors attributed the reduced effectiveness of ERP in this study to the use of less frequent treatment sessions (twice weekly compared to daily), although Warren and Thomas (2001) obtained better results with a once-weekly ERP regimen.

Figure 5.3 compares the pre- and posttreatment Y–BOCS mean scores reported in effectiveness studies to those from RCTs. As can be seen, the effectiveness study samples—which contained individuals with substantial comorbidity and histories of treatment failure who received therapy in nonresearch contexts—fared comparably to the highly selected "rarified" samples treated under controlled conditions in RCTs. This indicates that the substantial and clinically significant effects of CBT for OCD are transportable from research to clinical contexts.

IMPACT OF CBT ON FUNCTIONAL DISABILITY

This chapter has emphasized CBT's effects on OCD symptoms; however, OCD is associated with significant disability and therefore diminished quality of life. Disability in this context refers to the extent to which the person's occupational, social, and family functioning are impaired by OCD symptoms. Data collected from 66 patients in our OCD specialty clinic using the Sheehan Disability Scale (SDS; Sheehan, 1983) indicate that persons

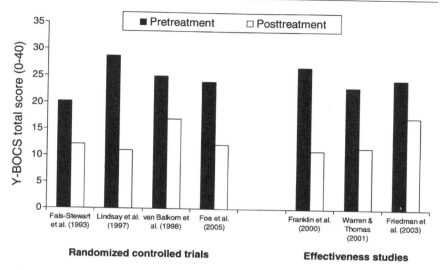

FIG. 5.3. Effects of CBT as measured by the Yale–Brown Obsessive Compulsive Scale in randomized controlled trials and effectiveness studies.

with OCD report much more disability compared to a normative sample, and that increased disability is related to the severity of OCD, general anxiety, and depressive symptoms. Moreover, as is shown in Fig. 5.4, patients had made significant improvements in functionality immediately following an 8-week (16 twice-weekly sessions) course of CBT. Although this is good news to be sure, these improved scores on the SDS remained above those of the normative sample. Thus, it appears that although we are able to help patients with OCD improve their functioning, we are not yet able to get them all the way home.

FACTORS ASSOCIATED WITH THE OUTCOME OF CBT

A number of predictors of response to CBT for OCD have been identified; most of the research has examined response to ERP. Predictor variables can be grouped into three broad categories: (a) ERP procedural variations, (b) patient-related characteristics, and (c) supportive factors.

ERP Procedural Variations

Meta-analytic studies have closely examined the relationship between treatment outcome and the manner in which ERP is delivered (Abramowitz, 1996, 1997). These results are directly applicable to clinical practice and may be summarized as follows: First, across the literature, ERP

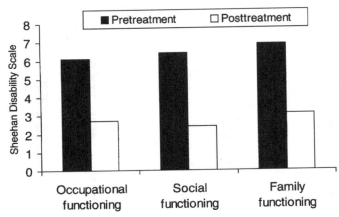

FIG. 5.4.   Effects of CBT on patients' ratings of functional disability ($N = 66$). Higher scores represent more severe disability.

programs that involved more in-session, therapist-supervised exposure practice produced greater short- and long-term improvements compared to programs in which all exposure was performed by the patient as homework assignments. Second, combining in vivo and imaginal exposure was superior to in vivo exposure alone in reducing anxiety symptoms. Third, programs in which patients refrained completely from ritualizing during the treatment period (i.e., total response prevention) produced superior immediate and long-term effects compared to those that involved only partial response prevention.

If in-session exposure practice is an important component of ERP, what is the optimal session frequency? To examine whether the robust effects of intensive (daily) therapy are substantially compromised by reducing the session frequency, my colleagues and I compared 15 sessions of intensive ERP to 15 sessions of ERP delivered on a twice-weekly basis (Abramowitz, Foa, & Franklin, 2003). Whereas intensive therapy was minimally superior to the twice-weekly regimen immediately following treatment (posttreatment Y–BOCS scores were 10.4 [intensive] and 12.7 [twice weekly]), this difference disappeared at 3-month follow-up (Y–BOCS = 13.13 [intensive] and 14.25 [twice-weekly]). Results of this study suggest that a twice-weekly therapy schedule provides clinicians with a more pragmatic, yet equally effective, alternative to the highly demanding and often impractical intensive protocol.

There also appears to be a relationship between adherence with ERP instructions and treatment outcome (Abramowitz, Franklin, Zoellner, et al., 2002; Lax, Basoglu, & Marks, 1992). For example, we (Abramowitz, Franklin, Zoellner, et al., 2002) found that better outcomes were associated with understanding the rationale for ERP techniques and adhering to the therapist's instructions for exposure practice (both in-session and homework assignments). As discussed in subsequent chapters, these findings suggest that it is important for clinicians to provide a compelling explanation for using ERP procedures and to elicit the patient's input when developing an exposure plan.

Patient Characteristics

A number of patient characteristics have been identified as predictors of poorer treatment response. These include the presence of extremely poor insight into the senselessness of obsessions and compulsions (Foa, 1979; Foa et al., 1999), severe depression (Abramowitz & Foa, 2000; Abramowitz, Franklin, Street, Kozak, & Foa, 2000; Steketee, Chambless, & Tran, 2001), GAD (Steketee et al., 2001), extreme emotional reactivity during exposure (Foa et al., 1983), and severe borderline personality traits (i.e., borderline; Steketee et al., 2001). Whereas some studies found that more severe OCD symptoms predicted poorer outcome (e.g., Franklin et al., 2000), others did not (e.g., Foa et al., 1983). However, consistent evidence is emerging to suggest that patients who present with primarily hoarding symptoms respond less well to traditional CBT techniques (Abramowitz et al., 2003; Mataix-Cols, Marx, Greist, Kobak, & Baer, 2002).

Supportive Factors

Results have been conflicted as to whether the level of marital satisfaction impacts the efficacy of CBT for OCD (Emmelkamp, de Haan, & Hoogduin, 1990; Hafner, 1982; Riggs, Hiss, & Foa, 1992). What is clearer is that hostility from relatives toward the identified patient is associated with premature dropout from ERP and with poor response among patients who complete treatment (Chambless & Steketee, 1999). Interestingly, Chambless and Steketee (1999) found that when relatives express dissatisfaction with patients' symptoms, but do not express personal rejection, such constructive criticism may have motivational properties that enhance treatment response. This underscores the importance of educating family members about OCD and how to assist with ERP, as discussed in subsequent chapters.

COMPARISON OF CBT AND MEDICATIONS FOR OCD

Efficacy of Pharmacotherapy for OCD

Pharmacotherapy using SRIs (clomipramine [Anafranil], sertraline [Zoloft], fluoxetine [Prozac], fluvoxamine [Luvox], citalopram [Celexa], paroxetine [Paxil]) has been found effective for reducing OCD symptoms in a number of double-blinded, randomized, placebo controlled trials (e.g., DeVeaugh-Geiss, Landau, & Katz, 1989; Montgomery et al., 1993. Studies of SRIs suggest average improvement rates of about 20% to 40% (reductions of about 5–8 points on the Y–BOCS; Greist, Jefferson, Kobak, Katzelnick, & Serlin, 1995) in comparison to placebo. Meta-analytic results (Abramowitz, 1997; Greist et al., 1995) suggest that clomipramine is superior to other SRIs (fluoxetine, fluvoxamine, and sertraline), and that the latter do not differ from one another in their efficacy. However, it is important to point out that, on average, posttreatment Y–BOCS scores of patients taking SRIs would have qualified for entry to the respective studies. Long-term improvement with SRIs is reliant on continuation of treatment because relapse occurs on stoppage for most patients (e.g., Pato, Zohar-Kadouch, Zohar, & Murphy, 1988). A list of the medications evaluated in RCTs for the treatment of OCD is presented in Table 5.3

Relative Efficacy of CBT and Pharmacotherapy

Given two effective treatments for OCD, researchers have attempted to examine the relative efficacy of CBT and SRIs (e.g., Cottraux et al., 1990; Foa et al., 2005; Marks et al., 1988; Marks, Stern, Mawson, Cobb, & McDonald, 1980), although many of these studies used complex designs that confound direct comparisons between these two forms of treatment. An exception is the large multisite study by Foa et al. (2005) in which 122 patients were randomly assigned to treatment by (a) ERP, (b) clomipramine, (c) the combination of ERP and clomipramine, or (d) pill placebo. ERP treatment lasted 12

TABLE 5.3
Medications Evaluated for Use With OCD

Brand Name	Generic Name	Manufacturer	Effective Dose
Anafranil[a]	Clomipramine	Novartis	Up to 250 mg/day
Luvox[a]	Fluvoxamine	Solvay	Up to 300 mg/day
Paxil[a]	Paroxetine	GlaxoSmithKline	40–60 mg/day
Prozac[a]	Fluoextine	Lilly	40–80 mg/day
Zoloft[a]	Sertraline	Pfizer	Up to 200 mg/day
Effexor	Venlafaxine	Wyeth-Ayerst	75 mg/day
Celexa	Citalopram	Forest	Up to 60 mg/day

[a]Approved by the U.S. Food and Drug Administration for the treatment of OCD.

weeks (4 weeks of intensive treatment followed by 8 weekly maintenance sessions) and involved in-session (therapist-supervised) and homework exposure along with complete response prevention. Clomipramine treatment lasted 12 weeks. Immediately following treatment, all active therapies were superior to placebo, and ERP (mean 50% Y–BOCS reduction) was superior to clomipramine (mean 35% Y–BOCS reduction). Important caveats for these findings are that the active phase of ERP was intensive (daily treatment sessions), provided by expert therapists, and that patients with comorbid conditions (e.g., depression, anxiety disorders) were excluded. Thus this sample of patients, and the psychological treatment they received, were not highly representative of typical clinical practice.

COMBINING CBT AND MEDICATION IN THE TREATMENT OF OCD

Although the concurrent use of medication and psychotherapy is common in clinical settings, relatively few studies have examined whether this approach affords advantages over monotherapy with either CBT or SRIs. Three different outcomes are possible with combination treatment for OCD. The desired outcome is, of course, a synergistic effect in which combined therapy is superior to either CBT or SRIs alone. This could occur if adding one treatment increases the magnitude of response to the other. A second possibility is that medication and CBT add little to each other. This would be the case if either form of therapy were sufficiently powerful that the other had little room to contribute. Third, it is conceivable that one treatment detracts from the efficacy of the other. This could happen, for example, if patients attributed their improvement to taking medication and subsequently failed to comply with CBT procedures.

For the most part, the available studies suggest that simultaneous treatment with CBT and SRIs yields superior outcome compared to SRI monotherapy, but not compared to CBT alone (Cottraux et al., 1990; Foa et al., 2005; Franklin, Abramowitz, Bux, Zoellner, & Feeny, 2002; Hohagen et al., 1998; Marks et al., 1988; Marks et al., 1980; O'Connor, Todorov, Robillard, Borgeat, & Brault, 1999; Van Balkom et al., 1998). That is, adding medication to CBT does not improve the effectiveness of CBT. One exception was reported by Hohagen et al. (1998), who found that combined ERP and fluvoxamine offered an advantage over ERP monotherapy for seriously depressed OCD patients. Importantly, many of the available studies have limitations. For example, some did not use reliable outcome measures such as the Y–BOCS, sample sizes in some investigations were too small to detect modest differences between treatments, and many studies excluded patients with comorbidity—perhaps the very patients who would show the greatest benefit from combined treatment. The use of CBT to augment medication treatment is discussed next.

CBT AS AN ADJUNCT TO PHARMACOTHERAPY

Recall that on average, the effects of medication leave many patients clinically symptomatic. Four investigations, all of which used the Y–BOCS as an outcome measure, have examined whether supplemental CBT results in additional benefit in cases where patients with OCD experience only partial (or no) improvement following one or more adequate trials of SRIs. The results of these studies are presented in Table 5.4 and briefly summarized next.

Simpson, Gorfinkle, and Liebowitz (1999) offered twice-weekly ERP (17 sessions) to six individuals who had shown only minimal improvement despite at least 12 weeks on an adequate dose of an SRI. At the completion of ERP, scores on the Y–BOCS were substantially further reduced, indicating that ERP augments the effects of SRIs in medication-resistant patients. Similar results were reported by Kampman, Keijsers, Hoogduin, and Verbank (2002), who conducted 12 sessions of CBT with 14 individuals who evidenced less than 25% symptom reduction after 12 weeks on fluoxetine. In a third study, my colleague Lori Zoellner and I (Abramowitz & Zoellner, 2002) examined whether these findings reported extended to OCD patients with primarily obsessions and covert (e.g., mental) neutralizing strategies. Following 15 sessions of twice-weekly CBT, the six patients in our study improved substantially compared to the minimal gains they had made during the 12 weeks on an SRI before beginning CBT. Finally, Tolin, Maltby, Diefenbach, Hannan, and Worhunsky (2004) selected 20 individuals with

TABLE 5.4
Summary of Studies Examining the Effects of CBT for Medication-Resistant Patients With OCD

| Study | N | Y–BOCS Mean Score | | | | | |
| | | Premedication | | Postmedication/ pre-CBT | | Post-CBT | |
		M	SD	M	SD	M	SD
Simpson et al. (1999)	6			23.8	2.6	12.2	4.3
Kampman et al. (2002)	9	28.1	5.6	25.7	5.3	15.0	6.5
Abramowitz & Zoellner (2002)	6			23.3	2.7	8.7	4.5
Tolin, Maltby, et al. (2004)	15			25.2	5.7	15.9	9.0

Note. Y–BOCS = Yale–Brown Obsessive Compulsive Scale; CBT = cognitive-behavioral therapy.

OCD who had a high rate of comorbid psychological diagnoses and who had not responded adequately to multiple adequate medication trials. After a 1-month wait-list period, these patients received 15 sessions of ERP. Results indicated a statistically significant drop in OCD symptoms following psychological treatment although posttreatment Y–BOCS scores remained somewhat high. Still, those who completed the study maintained their gains as far out as 6 months after the end of treatment (follow-up M Y–BOCS score = 18.7).

Together, these studies indicate that CBT is an appropriate strategy to use for OCD patients who have residual symptoms despite having tried SRI medications. The clinical implications of this research are substantial because medication is the most widely available (and therefore the most widely used) form of treatment for OCD, yet it typically produces only modest improvement. This means that psychotherapists are very likely to encounter patients who have already attempted treatment with medication, yet desire additional help. Thus, an important role for CBT is that it works well for medication nonresponders.

II

How to Conduct Consultation and Treatment for OCD

6

Consultation I: Diagnosis and Assessment

Psychological consultation entails obtaining a thorough assessment of a patient's problem and providing education, information, and recommendations to that individual and his or her family or support network (Brown, Pryzwansky, & Schulte, 2001). Consultative services are based on the consultant's education, training, and experience, as well as on knowledge of the relevant scientific literature. This chapter provides a detailed description of how to conduct a diagnostic interview, assess the nature and severity of OCD symptoms, and provide feedback to the patient regarding his or her symptoms. Collection and discussion of this information constitutes one portion of the initial consultation that should precede therapy. The second portion of the consultation, described in chapter 7, involves discussing and recommending an effective treatment. The assessment procedures covered in this chapter can be conducted over a 2- to 3-hour period, and may be divided across multiple sessions if necessary. More time may be required in complex cases or for therapists new to working with individuals with OCD. The case of Susan T., described next, will be used to illustrate the consultation and treatment procedures throughout the second part of this book.

Susan T., a 33-year-old elementary school teacher, had been married for 6 years. She and her husband, Steve, have a 3-year-old son, Brian, and a 3-month-old infant, Jennifer. Susan's primary care physician has referred her to a psychologist because of persistent washing and checking rituals that were not responding to various serotonergic medications. Susan had also undergone numerous trials of talk therapy that had not been particularly helpful in alleviating her symptoms.

OVERVIEW AND PURPOSE OF ASSESSMENT

Assessment is an ongoing and conceptually driven pursuit where theories of the causes, maintenance, and treatment of OCD determine what is important to evaluate. Initial assessment begins with a clinical interview to substantiate a diagnosis of OCD, identify possible comorbid conditions, and rule out problems that are sometimes mistaken for OCD. Next, the content and severity of the individual's obsessions and safety-seeking behaviors are determined. The presentation of OCD symptoms, range of comorbid psychopathology, and impact of the disorder on the individual's functioning vary widely from patient to patient. Thus, assessment should encompass the individual's level of functioning, support network, and treatment goals. Understanding this broad context helps the clinician identify factors that might exacerbate or ameliorate OCD symptoms, or impact adherence to treatment recommendations. It also helps with recognizing additional forms of psychopathology that warrant clinical attention or that might impact treatment planning.

DEVELOPING A THERAPEUTIC RELATIONSHIP

Careful assessment provides an excellent opportunity to begin developing an alliance with the patient and engaging him or her in the process of goal setting. Many patients with OCD come to their initial consultation embarrassed about their symptoms, perhaps having hidden their obsessional thoughts and compulsive rituals from friends or relatives for many years. In such cases, the clinician can destigmatize these symptoms by recasting them as manifestations of a clinical disorder, rather than eccentric or "mad" behavior. It might help to point out that about 1 in 40 people have OCD, and to provide examples of obsessions and compulsions reported by others. In contrast to those who conceal their symptoms, other patients will have become caught up in vicious cycles of mutual irritation or coercion with family members. Here, the assessment process provides a chance to encourage collaboration and cooperation in implementing a jointly agreed on treatment program.

IMPORTANCE OF ONGOING ASSESSMENT

Continually assessing the nature and severity of OCD and related symptoms throughout the course of treatment assists the therapist in evaluating whether, and in what ways, the patient is responding. This is consistent with the emphasis on objective measurement of treatment effectiveness within evidence-based practice. It is not sufficient for the clinician simply to think, "He seems to be less obsessed," or "It sounds like she has cut down on her compulsions"; or even for the patient (or a relative) to report that he or she "feels better." Instead, progress should be assessed systematically by comparing current functioning against the baseline obtained at the outset of treatment. Thus, periodic assessment using the psychometrically validated instruments described later in this chapter should be conducted to clarify in what ways treatment has been helpful and what work remains to be done.

ASSESSMENT AS PSYCHOEDUCATION

Helping the patient understand why his or her seemingly bizarre and senseless thoughts and behaviors persist despite strong resistance enhances the value of assessment for the patient. For example, learning that most everyone normally experiences odd or upsetting unwanted thoughts helps normalize these experiences. Frequently, patients fail to see the connections between their obsessional fears and their avoidance or safety-seeking behaviors. Pointing out that these responses are means of coping with obsessional fear helps validate such behaviors, even if they are excessive; for example, "I know you think it's a bit strange, but if you are afraid of catching germs from dead bodies, I can see why you'd want to shower after driving past a cemetery." Linking avoidance and safety behaviors to obsessional thoughts in this way also makes the patient increasingly aware that his or her behaviors are consistent and predictable. In turn, this awareness helps patients identify their obsessions and compulsions more accurately.

ESTABLISHING THE DIAGNOSIS OF OCD

The clinician should begin with unstructured inquiry into the present symptoms, history, family issues, and feelings about treatment. This information will guide the structured component of the assessment described later in this chapter.

Assessing the Chief Complaint and History

The assessor's initial job is to determine whether the patient's symptoms fit into the category of OCD and whether comorbid conditions are present. Chapter 2 provides useful guidelines for distinguishing between OCD and other disorders that, although just as disturbing, are not the same as OCD. It is useful to begin by asking the patient to describe his or her chief complaint and purpose for coming to the session. The patient might also be asked to describe a typical day, highlighting the frequency, intensity, and duration of OCD symptoms. The interviewer can probe for information about how the problem is managed and how symptoms interfere with functioning. Table 6.1 contains a list of additional questions for eliciting more information about the presence of obsessions, compulsions, avoidance, and other safety-seeking strategies. Information about the onset, historical course of the problem, comorbid conditions, social and developmental history, and personal and family history of psychiatric treatment should also be obtained.

> Susan T. described intense fears of becoming ill from germs, particularly from bodily fluids and secretions such as urine and sweat. She awakened at 4 a.m. each morning to complete a 2-hour bathroom routine before leaving for work. Her ritualistic behavior included extensive decontamination of the toilet and shower using heavy-duty cleansers, the need for half of a roll of toilet paper to wipe herself when using the toilet, and a 45-minute shower routine that included washing her body according to specific rules she had devised. Hand washing occurred throughout the day and Susan was spending over an hour cleaning the dishes after dinner. She also described a fear of fires and break-ins, and often got "stuck" checking that doors and windows were locked, and that appliances were off and unplugged. At work she re-checked paperwork extensively, which often caused her to be late for picking up her son from day care. Soon after the birth of her daughter, Susan began having scary unwanted thoughts of hurting this child. For example, she was afraid to carry Jennifer for fear of dropping her down the stairs, and at times, asked her husband, Steve, to bathe the baby because of unwanted thoughts about drowning her in the bathtub. Although Susan was able to work, she was constantly behind in her paperwork and felt as if things were getting worse.

Insight

When assessing the patient's ability to recognize the senselessness of his or her symptoms, the clinician should keep in mind that this capability often fluctuates. Some individuals will willingly concede that their obsessional fears are irrational, yet they still cause distress and urges to perform rituals. A smaller group firmly believes that their obsessions are realistic and compulsive rituals serve to prevent feared disasters. In most patients, however, the strength of belief changes depending on the situation, making it diffi-

TABLE 6.1
Examples of Open-Ended Questions to Help
in Assessing the Presence of OCD Symptoms

- How often do the obsessional thoughts come to mind? How long do they last?
- What kinds of activities or situations trigger the obsessional thoughts or urge to ritualize?
- What kinds of activities do you avoid to prevent yourself from worrying about accidents or mistakes?
- What do you do to avoid coming into contact with _____ (triggers)?
- What do you do to prevent yourself from thinking thoughts that upset you or make you worried?
- When you come into contact with _____ (trigger), what do you do?
- How many times a day do you feel the urge to _____ (insert safety-seeking ritual)?
- How long does each ritual last?
- After you have completed this safety-seeking ritual how do you feel? How anxious are you?
- When you are worrying about accidents, mistakes, or harm, how do you assure yourself that things are OK?
- What precautions do you take to make sure you don't make terrible mistakes, have an accident, or hurt anyone?
- What do you do to keep yourself from acting on unwanted thoughts?
- If you were unable to _____ (give examples of rituals), how would you feel? What are you afraid might happen?
- How much do you think these rituals are senseless or excessive?
- How often do you resist or delay your rituals? What happens when you try?
- How else are these fears and rituals interfering with your life? What are you avoiding because of your fears?
- How does your family react to your symptoms? What do they think of your situation?
- Are other people involved in your rituals? Do they help you avoid feared situations?

cult to pin down the precise degree to which they recognize the symptoms are irrational. For example, in the session, a patient might be able to state that the risk of acting on an intrusive impulse to stab someone is quite low. However, when the impulse occurs at home as triggered by watching a sleeping child, it might evoke intense fear that the dreaded consequences will occur. Assessment of insight is illustrated by the following exchange between Susan and her therapist:

Therapist: Can you tell me how likely it is that a fire would start if you left the toaster plugged in while you were away from your house for a few hours?

Susan: I wouldn't do that. I definitely think it would cause a fire.

Therapist: So, you are saying that there is a 100% chance that leaving the toaster plugged in will cause a fire; right?

Susan: Well ... I guess so.

Therapist: Hmmm. Most people leave appliances like toasters plugged in even when they are not using them. For example, in my house, the toaster stays plugged in all the time whether someone is home or not. In fact, it's probably been plugged into the electrical outlet continuously for several years. But what you're saying is that by now, my house should have burned down; and probably lots of others' homes too. How do you explain that house fires are less common than that, and that fire prevention guidelines don't say that you should unplug toasters every time you leave the house?

Susan: Hmm. I hadn't thought about it that way. Maybe it's not 100% likely. Maybe it's less likely, like 10% or even less.

Because Susan was able to notice the inconsistency in her thinking and revise her probability estimate (although it remained excessively high), she was considered to have good insight into the senselessness of her symptoms.

Mood

Because most individuals with OCD also suffer from depressive symptoms it is important to assess mood state. Clinicians should inquire about the chronological history of mood complaints to establish whether such symptoms should be considered as a primary diagnosis or as secondary to OCD symptoms. Primary depression develops in parallel with OCD, and might precede OCD onset. In contrast, when depressive symptoms develop subsequent to OCD, and when the patient describes being depressed about having OCD, the depression is considered secondary to OCD.

Social Functioning

Clinicians should assess the degree of impairment in leisure and social, family, and occupational or academic functioning. Where appropriate, this information should be incorporated into the treatment plan so that difficulties can be addressed in the appropriate context. As an example, Susan experienced difficulties grading students' paperwork and entering these grades into her computer because she repeatedly checked for possible errors. Thus, treatment could include practicing performing these tasks at work without checking. In cases where the patient is not working (i.e., a temporary leave of absence), work situations may be simulated as closely as possible.

History

Circumstances surrounding the onset of the problem and the course of symptoms should be assessed. Typically, symptoms wax and wane over time, yet some patients describe a general worsening over the years. Many patients cannot describe the particulars surrounding the origin of their OCD symptoms, either because onset was not discrete or because the symptoms began so long ago that the memory has since faded. Fortunately, it is not essential to know the exact causes or predisposing factors of OCD for CBT to be successful. If previous treatment has been unsuccessful, obtain the patient's explanation for this failure, and discuss how the planned course of therapy will differ in ways that might yield a better response.

Previous Treatment

It is important to collect information about previous attempts to treat OCD symptoms to determine whether the patient has received adequate treatment. Perhaps he or she has been prescribed medications that are not known to be helpful with OCD, or low dosages of potentially helpful medicines. Many patients seek CBT because they wish to augment any gains achieved with medication, or so that they can discontinue using drugs altogether. Another issue is whether psychodynamic or analytic psychotherapy has been tried. If so, former therapists might have told the patient that his or her OCD was caused by intrapsychic conflicts from childhood, and that insight into the nature of such phenomena is required for improvement. If this is the case, the clinician should explain that there is no evidence OCD is caused by internal conflicts, nor is there evidence that working on resolving conflicts reduces symptoms.

If the patient has previously received CBT, a determination should be made of whether or not the treatment regimen was satisfactory. Adequate CBT involves prolonged and repeated exposure to the patient's most feared situations along with complete response prevention. Many patients describe therapy in which they were never exposed to their most feared stimuli, in which response prevention was only partial (e.g., stopping some rituals but not others), or in which therapy sessions occurred infrequently (e.g., every 2 weeks) allowing for a return to avoidance and safety-seeking behaviors between sessions. Appendix A includes the OCD Treatment History Form, which clinicians can use to determine whether a patient has previously received an adequate trial of CBT. If a satisfactory CBT regimen has occurred, closely examining the reasons for failure may shed light on potential obstacles to the current treatment. For example, was the patient reluctant to try difficult exposure tasks? Did he or she not adhere to response prevention instructions? If compliance and adherence were not issues in previous failures, it might mean that the previous treatment plan was deficient.

Medical History and Review of Systems

It is useful to obtain a brief medical history. What (if any) major medical issues or treatments has the patient had? If the patient has not seen a doctor within the last year, a yearly check-up should be recommended. Has OCD or its treatment been discussed with the patient's general physician? Significant medical concerns should be addressed with a physician before beginning treatment for OCD. In addition, it is important to assess the following areas: daily and weekly exercise amounts, daily caffeine use, and daily alcohol and drug use. If substance usage is a concern, it should be determined whether the use of alcohol or drugs is associated with OCD symptoms. As we will see in the next chapter, substance abuse and dependence can impact decisions about treatment for OCD.

Family Issues

The therapist should ask the patient about his or her family of origin. What was growing up like? Did relatives suffer with OCD or other anxiety disorders? Did parents or other authority figures (e.g., teachers, clergy) reinforce extreme regidity, cleanliness, order, ideas about danger, or the importance of thoughts? Although there is no way to verify whether such experiences set the stage for the development of OCD, they may lead to core beliefs that influence how certain situations and stimuli are interpreted. For example, one man with fears of contamination from blood said that, as a young boy, he recalled an incident in which his mother became very upset that there was blood on her pillow. She resorted to washing all of the bed linens several times to make sure the blood was cleaned away because "blood is dangerous."

Assessment should also address relatives' emotional responses to the patient's OCD symptoms. In some families, relatives are highly critical and express hostility toward their loved one with OCD. This may be manifested as meddling or intrusiveness into the patient's daily activities. Asking patients to rate how critical relatives are using a scale from 1 (*not at all critical*) to 10 (*extremely critical*) can help determine whether family issues require further assessment or intervention (Chambless & Steketee, 1999).

In other families, relatives may enable or accommodate patients' OCD symptoms by helping with checking and cleaning rituals, providing frequent reassurance to ease obsessional anxiety, and by avoiding situations that evoke obsessional distress (e.g., contact with contaminants). In one extreme example, the parents of a 30-year-old patient purchased a new home to alleviate their son's fears of contamination following an incident in which dirty laundry had fallen on the floor in their former home. In most cases, accommodation occurs either to avoid confrontation over OCD symptoms, or because family members do not want to see loved ones suffer with extreme anxiety. However, such behavior reinforces obsessional fear and, if not addressed, adversely impacts treatment outcome.

Including family members in the assessment process and gaining their perspective on the problem can shed light on family reactions and the degree to which symptoms are accommodated. Sometimes relatives observe avoidance and safety-seeking behavior that the patient has not reported. This also affords an opportunity to view how the relatives respond to the patient. Are they supportive, constructively critical, or hostile? In an open-ended fashion, relatives should be asked about the extent to which they participate in the patient's compulsive rituals and avoidance habits. How do they respond when repeatedly asked questions for reassurance? What consequences do they fear if symptoms are not accommodated (e.g., will the patient leave home, commit suicide, or "go crazy")? To what extent are the family's activities modified because of OCD symptoms? The clinician should explain that the purpose of involving family members in the interview is to collect information from a variety of viewpoints. We typically invite relatives into the session after all information has been collected from the patient, but before reviewing this information or presenting recommendations for treatment.

Individual Strengths and Areas of Difficulty

To help attain a more global impression of the patient, he or she can be asked what he or she views as personal strengths and shortcomings. Has she or he ever had legal difficulties? How does the person view himself or herself in light of the fact that he or she has OCD? How does he or she perceive his or her ability to manage symptoms? Other questions should pertain to strengths and difficulties with managing OCD symptoms. That is, which situations, fears, or rituals are he or she best able to resist or control; and which do he or she most struggle to manage?

Motivation for Treatment

Because compliance with CBT procedures requires a great deal of effort on the patient's part, it is critical to assess his or her motivation for therapy. Was it his or her or someone else's idea to seek treatment? If the patient is presenting on his or her own volition, what was it that drove him or her to ask for help now? If others have "forced" the patient into seeking therapy, what is the patient's understanding of why this is the case? Determination of how hard an individual is willing to work to reduce OCD symptoms may present clinicians with a challenge, and straightforward questioning is not always the best strategy because individuals may be tempted to give the socially desirable response (e.g., "very hard"). As we will see in chapter 7, one strategy is to describe CBT procedures and ask the patient whether he or she would agree to participate. Miller and Rollnick (2002) described some excellent ways of conceptualizing and assessing motivation for change. These motivational interviewing techniques are directly applicable to the treatment of OCD.

Structured Diagnostic Interview

If it appears from the unstructured assessment that OCD symptoms are present, a standardized diagnostic interview should be used to confirm this diagnosis, as well as to determine the presence of any other comorbid anxiety and mood disorders. A number of instruments exist for this purpose, including the Anxiety Disorders Interview Schedule for *DSM–IV* (ADIS–IV; DiNardo, Brown, & Barlow, 1994), the Structured Clinical Interview for *DSM–TR* (SCID; First, Spitzer, Gibbon, & Williams, 2002), and the Mini International Neuropsychiatric Interview (MINI; Sheehan et al., 1998). In our clinic we use the MINI to establish diagnoses because it is a fairly brief interview that possesses very good reliability and validity. The section of the MINI for diagnosing OCD is reprinted for use in Appendix B.

> The MINI confirmed that Susan met the diagnostic criteria for OCD. She recognized that her obsessional fears and compulsive rituals were excessive, and therefore was not diagnosed with poor insight. Although Susan reported depressive symptoms, these did not rise to the level of a major depressive episode. Moreover, her mood symptoms were clearly secondary to her difficulties with OCD. She also endorsed persistent worry, but because her worries were confined to OCD-related topics she did not meet the criteria for generalized anxiety disorder.

ASSESSING THE TOPOGRAPHY OF OCD SYMPTOMS

The broad range of possible obsessions and safety-seeking behaviors as discussed in Part I present a challenge during assessment. Because patients often do not spontaneously report all of their symptoms the clinician is advised to use the Symptom Checklist of the Yale–Brown Obsessive Compulsive Scale (Y–BOCS–SC; see Appendix C) to gain a more thorough and comprehensive picture of the symptom presentation. The Y–BOCS–SC is a very useful clinical interview that begins with instructions for providing the patient with practical definitions of obsessions and compulsions to help in identifying these symptoms. Next, the interviewer proceeds through a checklist of more than 50 common obsessions and compulsions that the patient indicates as *currently present, absent,* or *present only in the past.* Clinicians should ask for examples of each symptom the patient endorses to confirm that only OCD symptoms are recorded. The role of family members in performing particular compulsions can also be assessed during administration of the Y–BOCS–SC (e.g., Do other people in your family help with your checking?). After completing the checklist, the clinician and patient generate a brief list of the most severe (primary) obsessions, compulsions, and OCD-related avoidance behaviors to be targeted in treatment.

A limitation of the Y–BOCS is that it largely assesses symptoms on a superficial descriptive level without concern for functionality. For example, patients are asked whether or not they have an excessive showering or grooming routine. Although it is important to know whether such rituals exist, it is also meaningful to understand the relationship between these rituals and the patient's obsessions. That is, some patients' ritualistic showers involve washing various parts of their body very thoroughly to reduce contamination fears. For other individuals, however, showers might be ritualistic because the patient has to repeat certain behaviors a certain number of times (or avoid performing them in certain numbers) to magically prevent feared disasters such as car accidents or plane crashes. The point here is that to gain a true understanding of the patient's symptoms, the clinician must inquire about the functionality of symptoms endorsed on the Y–BOCS–SC—not simply whether or not the symptom is present. A related issue is that care should be taken to ensure that only OCD symptoms are rated as such. The Y–BOCS–SC contains a number of items (e.g., hair pulling) that are not genuine obsessions or compulsions.

The Y–BOCS–SC identified numerous specific obsessions and compulsions for Susan. She endorsed contamination obsessions and washing compulsions, obsessions of making mistakes that would lead to terrible outcomes and checking compulsions, and unacceptable thoughts and mental rituals. Primary obsessions, compulsions, and avoidances included:

Primary Obsessions	Primary Compulsions	Avoidance
1. Contamination from body waste	1. Excessive bathroom rituals	1. Public restrooms
2. Responsibility for mistakes and disasters	2. Excessive ritualized washing	2. Trash cans
3. Violent, horrific impulses	3. Checking locks, appliances, papers	3. Bathroom floors

MEASURING SYMPTOM SEVERITY

Measuring the severity of current symptoms provides a way of quantifying the patient's experience and comparing his or her level of distress and impairment with the population of OCD sufferers at large. It also helps the clinician offer a rationale for considering treatment and discuss what might be expected in terms of treatment response. A multitrait, multimethod approach to assessing symptom severity is suggested. This involves the use of clinician-administered and self-report instruments that tap into various facets of OCD, depression, general anxiety, and functional disability. Table 6.2 includes a list of recommended measures. These measures, as well as other interviewing techniques, are discussed in the text that follows.

TABLE 6.2
**Suggested Instruments for the Assessment of OCD Severity
and Related Symptoms**

Measure	No. of Items	Assessment Method	Symptom Focus
Y–BOCS severity scale	10	Interviewer	OCD
Obsessive Compulsive Inventory–Revised	18	Self-report	OCD
Brown Assessment of Beliefs Scale	7	Interviewer	Insight in OCD
Hamilton Depression Scale	17	Interviewer	Depression
Beck Depression Inventory	21	Self-report	Depression
Beck Anxiety Inventory	21	Self-report	General anxiety
Sheehan Disability Scale	3	Self-report	Functional disability

Note.   y–BOCS = Yale–Brown Obsessive Compulsive Scale.

Clinician Administered Measures

Severity of Obsessions and Compulsions. The Y–BOCS severity scale is regarded as the gold standard measure of OCD symptoms (Appendix C). It contains 10 items (5 that assess obsessions and 5 that assess compulsions), each of which is rated on a 5-point scale from 0 (*no symptoms*) to 4 (*extremely severe*). Items address (a) the time occupied by current symptoms, (b) interference with functioning, (c) associated distress, (d) attempts to resist obsessions and compulsions, and (e) the degree of control over symptoms. Scores on each of the 10 items are summed to produce a total score ranging from 0 to 40. In most instances, scores of 0 to 7 represent subclinical OCD symptoms, those from 8 to 15 represent mild symptoms, scores of 16 to 23 relate to moderate symptoms, scores from 24 to 31 suggest severe symptoms, and scores of 32 to 40 imply extreme symptoms. In clinical research, a score of at least 16 is commonly used to identify patients with symptoms severe enough to warrant inclusion in studies on OCD.

The Y–BOCS is unique among measures of OCD in that it is sensitive to multiple aspects of symptom severity independent of the number or types of different obsessions and compulsions. However, the clinician must be careful to ensure that only bona fide OCD symptoms are rated. Because administration of the Y–BOCS checklist and severity scale may require up to 45 minutes (perhaps more in complex cases), some clinicians opt to use the scale as a self-report measure. However, patients often require direction in responding to Y–BOCS items, so this practice is not recommended. Moreover, the discussion spawned by administration of the instrument as a semistructured interview provides pertinent information. Therefore, the time required to properly use the scale as a clinical interview may be considered well spent. Used in this way, the Y–BOCS also has good reliability and validity, and is sensitive to the effects of treatment (Goodman, Price, Rasmussen, Mazure, Delgado, et al., 1989; Goodman, Price, Rasmussen, Mazure, Fleischmann, et al., 1989).

Insight Into OCD Symptoms. The Brown Assessment of Beliefs Scale (BABS; Eisen et al., 1998) is a brief continuous measure of insight that has good reliability, validity, and sensitivity to change (see Appendix D). Administration begins with the interviewer and patient identifying one or two of the patient's specific obsessional beliefs that have been of significant concern over the past week (prior use of the Y–BOCS to identify target symptoms is helpful). Examples include, "If I don't carefully check the garbage, I will discard important items by mistake," "I will get herpes if I use a public toilet," and "I will act on the unwanted impulse to molest children." Next, individual items assess the patient's (a) conviction in this belief, (b) perceptions of how others view this belief, (c) explanation for why others hold a different view, (d) willingness to challenge the belief, (e) attempts to disprove the belief, (f) insight into the senselessness of the belief, and (g) ideas or delusions of reference. Only the first six items are summed to produce a total score. Eisen, Phillips, Coles, and Rasmussen (2004) reported a mean total score of 8.38 ($SD = 4.14$) on the BABS among 64 individuals with OCD.

Depressive Symptoms.   Because the majority of individuals with OCD report mood symptoms, and as many as half will meet criteria for a depressive disorder at some point in life (Crino & Andrews, 1996a), assessment of mood complaints should be routine. The Hamilton Rating Scale for Depression (HRSD; Hamilton, 1960) is a well-studied, semistructured interview that measures cognitive (e.g., feelings of guilt), affective (e.g., current mood state), and somatic (e.g., appetite, sleep) aspects of depression. The scale has adequate psychometric properties and is sensitive to the effects of treatment (Hedlund & Vieweg, 1979). It is used widely for assessing depressive symptoms in OCD patients.

Self-Report Measures

It would be convenient if clinicians could rely on patients to provide reliable and valid answers to queries about the frequency, intensity, and duration of their obsessive fears and compulsive behaviors. However, as this is not always the case, psychometrically validated self-report instruments should be used to supplement the clinical interview. Self-report measures have the advantage of using carefully worded questions that are consistent over time. Moreover, they allow the clinician to compare the patient's responses to well-established norms for other people with and without OCD. Accordingly, questionnaires are valuable for screening purposes, to corroborate information obtained in a clinical interview, and to monitor symptom severity during treatment, but not as a substitute for careful clinical interviewing.

Severity of Obsessions and Compulsions.   Numerous self-report inventories have been developed to measure the content and severity of OCD symptoms (for a comprehensive review see Taylor, Thordarson, & Sochting, 2002). The difficulty is that many were devised to measure the more quintessential features of OCD, such as washing and checking compulsions. Therefore, not all of these instruments adequately assess the full range of obsessions and compulsions. An exception is the Obsessive Compulsive Inventory (OCI; Foa, Kozak, Salkovskis, Coles, & Amir, 1998), a 42-item measure that assesses the frequency and distress associated with a comprehensive range of obsessional and compulsive phenomena. Some practical problems with the OCI (it is long and the scoring procedure is arduous) led to a subsequent revision, the OCI–R (see Appendix E), which consists of only 18 items (Foa, Huppert, et al., 2002). Each item (e.g., I check things more often than necessary) is rated on a 5-point scale (0–4) of distress associated with that particular symptom. The OCI–R has six subscales—washing, checking, ordering, obsessing, hoarding, and neutralizing—each containing three items that are summed to produce subscale scores (range = 0–12). A total score (range = 0–72) may be calculated by summing all 18 items. The OCI–R is psychometrically sound (Foa et al., 2002) and is useful for measuring response to treatment (Abramowitz, Tolin, & Diefenbach, 2005). A cutoff score of 15 can often differentiate OCD patients from nonpatients.

Depression and Anxiety.   The Beck Depression Inventory (BDI; Beck, Ward, Mendelsohn, Mock, & Erlbaugh, 1961) is one of the most widely used measures of depressive symptoms in research and clinical settings. It contains 21 items that measure the cognitive, affective, and somatic features of global distress. The BDI has good psychometric properties, is sensitive to treatment, and is easy to administer and score. Patients typically need about 5 minutes to complete the scale and scores of 20 or greater usually indicate the presence of clinical depression.

The Beck Anxiety Inventory (BAI; Beck, Epstein, Brown, & Steer, 1988) is an ideal measure of general anxiety that enjoys widespread clinical and research use. It consists of 21 items that assess the severity of clinical anxiety symptoms over the past week on a 4-point (0–3) severity scale. Items measure physiological responses (e.g., sweating), affective states (e.g., scared), and anxious cognitions (e.g., fear of losing control). The BAI was designed to assess anxiety symptoms independently from depressive symptoms. It has good reliability and validity (Beck et al., 1988) and requires about 5 minutes for patients to complete.

Functional Disability.   The Sheehan Disability Scale (SDS; Sheehan, 1983) is a brief and face valid measure of functional impairment that is routinely used in clinical research. It consists of three 0-to-10 ratings of the extent to which symptoms interfere with work, social, and family life.

Susan's Y–BOCS score was 27, placing her OCD symptoms in the severe range. She had a score of 6 on the BABS, indicating good insight, and a score of 10 on the HRSD, suggesting subclinical depressive symptoms. A number of self-report inventories had been completed before the assessment session and Susan's responses on these instruments were consistent with the information obtained through the clinical interviews. Susan indicated that while her social life was only moderately impaired by her OCD symptoms, her work and family life were seriously handicapped.

PROVIDING FEEDBACK AND ADDRESSING FREQUENTLY ASKED QUESTIONS

Very often, patients are accompanied to the initial consultation by a close relative or friend (e.g., spouse, parent) who is interested in being included in the assessment. To preserve confidentiality and maximize the patient's comfort with disclosing what are often perceived as "bizarre" or embarrassing symptoms, we recommend conducting the initial interview individually, and including relatives (at the patient's discretion, of course) when it comes time to discuss the results of the interview and provide education and recommendations. Before inviting relatives or friends into the session, the clinician and patient should discuss whether there are any symptoms that the patient prefers not be discussed in front of others.

> Susan's initial interview was conducted individually with the therapist. However, because Susan's husband, Steve, had expressed interest in being involved with treatment, the therapist suggested that he be invited into the office to hear the summary of Susan's symptoms and to raise any questions or concerns that he had. Susan agreed and said that Steve knew about all the details of her symptoms; thus it was all right to openly discuss them.

To address the patient's (and relatives') questions about his or her problem, feedback should include an explanation of (a) the diagnosis of OCD and scores on relevant assessment measures, (b) a brief functional description of the patient's particular OCD symptoms, and (c) a brief review of the etiological theories of OCD (making treatment recommendations is also an important part of this process, but is discussed in chapter 7). The clinician should be prepared to address these issues directly and honestly. The following are some exemplary ways to review clinical impressions and discuss the nature of OCD with patients. Susan's case is again used as an example, but clinicians can adapt these discussions for any patient with OCD.

Summarizing the Interview Results

Patients are typically eager to find out the assessor's impressions of their problem. Thus, feedback should begin with a review of the interview results. First, the clinician should summarize the information that has been collected and discuss the diagnosis of OCD.

Therapist: Now that I have collected information about your symptoms, I would like to review my impressions with you. First, the problems you are describing fit into the category of obsessive–compulsive disorder, or OCD for short. You might already know this, but it is important for me to interview you carefully to make an accurate diagnosis because this will influence my recommendations for treatment. Your main problem areas include fears of contamination and washing and cleaning rituals, fears of making mistakes and repetitive checking, and upsetting thoughts about your baby girl, Jennifer. Everyone's OCD symptoms are a little different, yet the kinds of symptoms you are experiencing are fairly common ones.

To find out how severe your symptoms are, I gave you the Yale–Brown Obsessive Compulsive Scale, or Y–BOCS for short, which is the gold standard measure of OCD symptoms. Based on what you told me about your symptoms, your score is 27 out of a possible 40. We consider this in the severe range of OCD. However, you seem able to recognize that your fears and rituals are senseless, even though they don't seem senseless when you are anxious. I also asked you about symptoms of depression, and based on how you described your mood at this time, it appears that although you feel down from time to time, you do not meet criteria for clinical depression right now. How does this fit with your experience of these problems?

Explaining the Symptoms of OCD

Patients and their confidants often have misunderstandings about the nature of OCD. Therefore, it is appropriate to begin providing psychoeducational material to correct such misperceptions. For example, most laypeople define obsessions as thoughts, and compulsions as behaviors. As we have seen, this is an inaccurate way to differentiate between such phenomena. Instead, patients should learn to distinguish between obsessions and compulsions on the basis of whether they evoke or reduce anxiety. Clarifying this functional relationship will help the patient better understand his or her own symptoms and how they can be reduced with CBT. Using the patient's own symptoms to illustrate the phenomenology of OCD, the clinician can begin to instill an understanding of the problem as a set of patterns that adhere to the rational laws of learning. As patterns, the symptoms can be weakened with CBT.

Therapist: I want to review with you some information about OCD so that we are all on the same page when it comes to how we understand this complex problem. First, OCD is part of a larger group of disorders called the anxiety disorders. It is also one of the more common psychological disorders, affecting about 1 in 40 people. As you know, it can have a very negative impact on life functioning.

As we have talked about during the evaluation, OCD involves two major symptoms: obsessions and compulsions. Obsessions are unwanted thoughts that may be triggered in different situations, such as your thoughts of getting sick when you use the bathroom, the idea that you graded a student's paper incorrectly, and your unwanted thoughts about hurting Jennifer. The most important aspect of obsessions is that they *provoke* anxiety. Compulsions, on the other hand, are urges to do things like rituals to *decrease* obsessional anxiety. Rituals can be visible behaviors like washing and checking, or they can be subtle mental actions like having to think a special "good thought."

Obsessions and compulsions are related. So, each time you have obsessive fears about germs, your reaction is to wash your hands to reduce your fear. It is human nature to try to avoid feeling anxious, or do something that reduces the discomfort if it can't be avoided. What you have learned to do to restore a state of comfort is to wash and clean, and to avoid situations to minimize exposure to feared contaminants; for example, by avoiding public bathrooms. Similarly, you have developed a pattern of rechecking paperwork before handing it back to your students to deal with your doubts that you made a mistake. Checking reassures you that you haven't made any terrible errors, and this reassurance makes you feel better. Now, as you know, compulsive rituals often bring you some relief from obsessional fear—but the relief is only temporary. Before long, obsessional fears return and you get stuck ritualizing over and over. This is because the feeling of relief you experience after you complete a ritual is very powerful. So, the more relief you feel, the more you want to ritualize the next time you feel anxious. You have learned to use rituals to reduce your obsessional fears. They make you feel safe. Do you see the way that your obsessions and rituals are connected in a pattern?

Susan: Yes. No one has ever explained it to me this way before, but it makes a lot of sense.

Therapist: I'm glad it makes sense. So, what you need is to learn a way of dealing with obsessional thoughts that doesn't involve doing rituals. Rituals are traps.

Susan: I would probably go insane if I didn't wash or check. I feel like something very bad would happen.

Therapist: That's because you usually do the rituals to make you feel safe. But, realistically, the risk of harm is very low in these situations—you said so yourself. It's just that you have learned that ritualizing is a quick, easy, and very powerful way to reduce anxiety. Unfortunately, the ritualizing prevents you from overcoming your obsessional fear.

Susan: If I learned to do rituals, can I "unlearn" them?

Therapist: Yes, but it requires help. We know from research studies that OCD symptoms do not typically go away on their own. In fact, most people who seek treatment for OCD say that things tend to get worse over time; although, depending on stressful events in your life, your symptoms may improve or get worse from day to day or week to week. So, I highly recommend that you consider receiving treatment for your OCD symptoms.

Discussing Etiological Theories of OCD

Naturally, patients often speculate as to what causes problems such as OCD. Many form their own theories, perhaps influenced by consumer-oriented educational materials they have encountered, or information provided by previous professionals they have seen. Because CBT more or less requires the adoption of a particular conceptual model, it is important to begin socializing the patient to this approach from the outset. This often involves correcting faulty perceptions of what causes OCD and why certain treatments will or will not hold promise.

Susan said that a psychiatrist once told her that OCD was caused by a "chemical imbalance" in her brain that was similar to, but not as severe as, that which causes schizophrenia. This was highly disconcerting to Susan, who had been a psychology major in college and imagined that people with schizophrenia often lived out their lives isolated and institutionalized. Susan had also been told that to treat OCD required medications that correct the imbalance of serotonin in her brain, and that because people with OCD have many problems with brain functioning, she should expect to suffer from OCD symptoms for the rest of her life. Susan was hopeful that there was a better prognosis. Still, she was somewhat skeptical of what she perceived as "yet another try at psychotherapy." During the consultation, the clinician began laying the foundation for a cognitive-behavioral conceptualization by confidently presenting the following information.

Susan: If my OCD symptoms are learned patterns, why did my psy-
            chiatrist tell me that OCD is a brain disease?

Therapist: I don't know about that, but I can tell you that there has been a
            lot of research on the causes of OCD and presently there are no
            clear answers. There are probably many different factors that
            interact to cause OCD. But, even though we don't know for
            sure what causes OCD, we do have some good leads. Two the-
            ories that have been well studied are the biological theory and
            the learning theory. Let me talk for a minute about each theory.

            First, the biological theory proposes that OCD is a medical
            or genetic disease that is caused by a problem with the neuro-
            transmitter serotonin, which works in the brain and nervous
            system. Usually people take this to mean that having OCD is
            like having other medical conditions, like diabetes; the body
            is simply not producing the right amounts of certain chemi-
            cals. Lots of research has been conducted in which the brains
            of people with OCD have been compared to the brains of peo-
            ple without OCD. While some studies have found differences
            that point to deficient serotonin levels in OCD, just as many
            studies have not found any differences. These inconsistent
            findings suggest that it is premature to assume at this point
            that OCD is caused by serotonin problems. Plus, this expla-
            nation is overly simplistic because it ignores the fact that our
            experiences in the world affect the very complex chemical
            systems and neural pathways in the brain. In fact there is re-
            search showing that people's brains change when they are
            treated successfully with either psychological treatment or
            medication for OCD. So, the cause of OCD is probably not en-
            tirely biological, although it appears that some people are
            more vulnerable than others to developing anxiety problems
            like OCD, and this vulnerability might be biological.

            The other leading theory is that experiences people have
            while growing up affect the development of OCD. For exam-
            ple, someone raised in a family where the parents worried a
            lot, or washed their hands a lot, could be vulnerable to getting
            OCD. Some researchers think that being taught very strict
            rules about how to think and behave, and how *not* to think
            and behave, could lead to OCD; especially if these rules are
            nearly impossible to follow and if there is the threat of pun-
            ishment for breaking the rules. Finally, situations where a
            person's thoughts or behavior seemed to contribute to bad

luck or to a serious tragedy might play a role. For example, let's suppose that you think about your dog dying, and then the next day, your dog coincidentally dies. This might make you worry that perhaps your thoughts had something to do with causing the dog's death. Researchers think that such experiences could trigger OCD. As with the biological theory, there have been many studies of the learning theory. Yet there is not enough evidence to confirm that OCD is caused entirely by these environmental factors.

So, as you can see, the jury is still out on what exactly causes OCD. The most reasonable conclusion at this time based on the available research is that OCD is probably caused by a complex combination of factors—biological and environmental. One metaphor that helps people to understand this is that of a blizzard. To get a severe snowstorm, the atmosphere must have cold air and moisture. Either of these ingredients by itself cannot produce snow. They both must be present, but perhaps in varying amounts. The same is true for how biology and the environment give rise to OCD. In fact, the exact cause—how much biology versus environmental influence is present—is probably different for each person. So, it is not a good idea to worry about what caused your OCD, or to blame your parents, your brain, or your genes for creating this problem. Most likely, it is not possible to figure this out with much accuracy.

Do we have to know about the causes of OCD to treat it effectively? The answer is "no." But we do have to understand the *symptoms* of OCD. Fortunately, we know a great deal about these symptoms. A comparable situation is that of treating cancer. If you went to the doctor for cancer treatment, he or she would not be too concerned with trying to figure out exactly why you got cancer in the first place. This is because cancer treatments—surgery, radiation therapy, and chemotherapy—work based on what we have learned about how to stop cancer cells (tumors) from growing, and this is different from knowing exactly why the cancer started in the first place. OCD is the same way. Through research, we now know a great deal about the symptoms of OCD. We know how they develop into strong patterns that are difficult to weaken without the right kind of help. The goal of treatment, therefore, is to weaken these patterns.

Susan: So I don't have a disease of my brain?

Therapist: That's probably right. If you had real problems with your brain, they would manifest themselves in more ways than just OCD. You wouldn't be able to teach, keep a marriage, or raise children; and you'd probably have all sorts of other problems, too. OCD is a set of maladaptive patterns that become worse on their own. The treatment program that I can offer you is based on weakening these patterns.

It is helpful to pause at this point and address patients' questions about the etiological theories. Regardless of which model is favored, the clinician should emphasize the importance of understanding the function of symptoms and draw on specific examples of the patient's obsessions and rituals to highlight how obsessional thoughts and situations evoke anxiety, and how compulsions become habitual responses because they reduce anxiety. In the next chapter we consider factors that influence treatment recommendations and the procedures for describing the effective forms of therapy for OCD.

7

Consultation II: Recommending a Treatment Strategy

Treatments for OCD that have been empirically tested can be divided into two broad categories: cognitive-behavioral and biological. CBT, which was discussed in chapter 5, includes the use of exposure, response prevention, and cognitive therapy techniques and can be delivered in a variety of formats and settings. Biological treatments include pharmacotherapy with SRIs and neurosurgery. The first part of this chapter provides an overview of the CBT program described in this book. Next, I present descriptions of the available biological treatments for OCD. The third section discusses factors to be considered when recommending a particular treatment or treatments to an individual patient. The chapter ends with examples of responses to frequently asked questions that patients and their families raise when discussing treatment options.

OVERVIEW OF CBT FOR OCD

There are five main components of the CBT program that I outline in chapters 8 through 13 of this book:

- Information gathering and case formulation.
- Cognitive therapy techniques.

- Exposure therapy.
- Response prevention.
- Maintenance and relapse prevention techniques.

The information-gathering and case formulation phase involves in-depth assessment of obsessional triggers; cognitive, behavioral, and emotional responses to triggers; and the derivation of a case formulation based on the cognitive-behavioral model of OCD described in Part I. Cognitive therapy techniques, which include educational modules and methods for challenging and restructuring problematic beliefs and assumptions, are aimed at directly weakening dysfunctional thinking patterns. Exposure therapy and response prevention (ERP) form the central elements of CBT. Although the primary aims of ERP include weakening patterns of avoidance and compulsive rituals, these techniques are also a powerful vehicle of cognitive change. Finally, relapse prevention techniques include strategies for maintaining and extending treatment gains, including methods for managing future episodes of obsessional fear.

The Recommended Treatment Regimen

The CBT regimen described here is a time-limited program that generally consists of 16 treatment sessions of 90 minutes in length. Typically, sessions are held on a twice-weekly basis with one session scheduled toward the beginning of the week and the other occurring toward the end (e.g., Monday and Thursday). Spacing the sessions in this way minimizes the intersession interval; thus, any gravitation toward dysfunctional thinking or behavioral habits can be addressed promptly. This program also affords the patient opportunities to practice the skills learned in therapy in a variety of settings (including in his or her own home), thus promoting the generalization of treatment effects.

During the first two to three sessions (information gathering and case formulation) the therapist conducts an in-depth functional assessment of the patient's specific triggers, and the cognitive and behavioral responses (i.e., safety seeking) associated with OCD. The culmination of this inquiry is the derivation of a patient-specific case formulation and treatment plan that is based on the cognitive-behavioral model of the persistence of OCD symptoms (see chapter 4). Simultaneously, the therapist uses educational modules to socialize the patient to the cognitive-behavioral model, the treatment interventions, and the goals for therapy. Psychoeducation specifically addresses the normalcy of intrusive obsessional thoughts and the relationship between catastrophic beliefs and anxiety. Understanding and "buying in" to the conceptual model helps patients recognize more subtle aspects of their OCD symptoms and increases collaboration, motivation, and compliance with later treatment interventions. The information gathering phase can therefore be regarded as an exchange of information between patient and therapist. The patient, who best understands his or her own OCD symptoms, educates the therapist about these symptoms. Simultaneously, the therapist, who knows how to synthesize from this information a viable treatment plan, teaches the patient how to think about his or her symptoms in a way that maximizes the effectiveness of therapy.

By Session 4, the treatment plan is developed and a rationale for using ERP techniques is provided. Exposure is implemented hierarchically, beginning with moderately distressing situations and stimuli. It may be helpful to frame ERP as a set of experiments to test the validity of erroneous probability estimates of harm. In other instances these procedures are used to demonstrate that anxiety recedes over time even if compulsive rituals are not performed. Gradual therapist-supervised exposure to anxiety-evoking situations and intrusive thoughts is planned for Sessions 4 though 16, and homework practice is assigned for completion between sessions. Patients are helped to refrain from safety-seeking behaviors during treatment.

Because ERP involves the purposeful evocation of obsessional fear, patients often require a great deal of encouragement to engage in such tasks, yet how to persuade patients to persist with exposure remains more of an art than a technology in CBT. By helping patients modify their catastrophic predictions about the outcome of exposure, cognitive therapy can help convince patients of the benefits of confronting mistakenly feared situations. Therefore, the chief role of cognitive therapy is to set the stage for ERP tasks, which are the "active ingredients" in treatment. As described in subsequent chapters, cognitive therapy is also used throughout a course of CBT when the therapist identifies mistaken beliefs as barriers to therapeutic exposure.

As the end of therapy draws closer, the therapist begins to incorporate procedures to enhance the maintenance of treatment gains. These include (a) education about the relationship between stress and OCD symptoms and the process of relapse, (b) instruction in how to choose situations for self-controlled exposure, (c) problem solving regarding how to spend time that was previously occupied by OCD symptoms, and (d) scheduling follow-up visits.

Other CBT Programs

Intensive Outpatient Treatment. A handful of OCD specialty clinics offer intensive outpatient CBT, involving 15 daily (Monday–Friday) 90- to 120-minute sessions (e.g., Franklin et al., 2000). The first two or three sessions are dedicated to information gathering and treatment planning. Next, daily sessions incorporate therapist-supervised in vivo and imaginal exposure with instructions for abstinence from compulsive rituals (response prevention). Daily exposure exercises are also assigned for the patient to practice outside of the sessions. A relapse prevention program consisting of four 90-minute sessions over 1 week may be applied following the intensive therapy period. Relapse prevention includes (a) a discussion of lapse versus relapse, (b) identifying stressors that could trigger OCD symptoms, and (c) cognitive therapy. A practical advantage of intensive CBT over less intensive treatment is that massed sessions allow for regular therapist contact and rapid correction of problematic between-session avoidance or compulsive habits. The primary disadvantage is the inherent scheduling demands for both the clinician and the patient. Intensive outpatient CBT is therefore an optimal program for patients seeking treatment from out of town and those with great difficulty resisting compulsive rituals.

A number of clinical variables should guide recommendations regarding treatment schedule. Daily sessions permit close supervision of exposure and rapid identification of problems with adherence. This is important because nonadherence can impede outcome. Thus intensive CBT is recommended when patients report extreme difficulty with confronting feared stimuli, poor insight, or difficulty grasping the rationale for using ERP techniques. Missed sessions, excessive bargaining over exposure instructions, difficulty refraining from ritualizing, and involvement of family members in avoidance and rituals are often signs that an intensive regimen should be considered over a less intensive schedule. Because we believe it is critical for individuals to practice self-guided exposure in a wide range of settings, twice-weekly treatment is the default for local patients in our clinic. Only when the obstacles just described are present do we suggest a more intensive regimen; and very rarely would we recommend that CBT occur on a one-session-per-week basis.

Group CBT. Conducting CBT in a group format can be helpful for OCD (Fals-Stewart et al., 1993; McLean et al., 2001). Advantages of this approach include the support and cohesion of a group atmosphere. Potential disadvantages include the relative lack of attention to each individual's symptoms, especially given the heterogeneity of OCD symptoms.

Residential CBT Programs. Although most inpatient psychiatric hospitals are equipped to provide standard care for patients with OCD, programming is often limited by the short duration of stay. Therefore, the initial focus is often on stabilizing patients via medication and supportive psychotherapy. Only a few specialized residential treatment programs for severe OCD exist. Therapy typically includes individual and group CBT, medication management, and supportive therapy for comorbid psychiatric conditions. Length of stay may vary from a few weeks to a month or more.

One advantage of specialized residential OCD programs is that they provide constant supervision for patients requiring help with implementing treatment (i.e., conducting self-directed ERP). This may be helpful in very severe cases hampered by functional disability, and those in which patients lack the support or assistance of family or friends. Drawbacks of inpatient treatment include the costs and the travel. The range of situations available for exposure practice may also be constrained by the hospital setting. For example, bathrooms in the patient's home environment cannot be confronted until the patient returns home. This could pose problems for patients whose symptoms are triggered by particular stimuli found only in certain places that cannot easily be transported to a hospital.

BIOLOGICAL TREATMENTS

Serotonin Reuptake Inhibitors

As reviewed in chapter 5, although they are the most widely available (and the most widely used) treatment for OCD, SRIs typically produce a modest 20% to 40% reduction in symptoms (Rauch & Jenike, 1998). The major strength of pharmacological treatment is its convenience. Limitations include a high rate of nonresponse (40%–60% of patients show little response), relatively modest improvement rates, high probability that residual symptoms will persist, and likelihood of side effects. Additionally, once SRIs are terminated, OCD symptoms typically return rapidly (Pato et al., 1988).

Neurosurgical Treatment

The clinician should be aware that currently, four neurosurgical procedures are available for use with OCD patients: subcaudate tractotomy, limbic leucotomy, cingulotomy, and capsulotomy. These operations involve severing interconnections between areas of the brain's frontal lobes and the limbic system. Recommended only in cases where severe and unmanageable OCD and depressive symptoms persist despite adequate trials of all other available treatments, the risks of neurosurgery include permanent alterations in cognitive functioning and personality. Although clinical improvement has been observed in some cases, it remains unknown why these procedures are only successful for a subset of OCD patients (Jenike, 2000). There is also an increased risk of suicide following failure with this approach.

FACTORS TO CONSIDER
WHEN RECOMMENDING TREATMENT

Let us now turn to a discussion of the factors to be considered when deciding on which treatment to recommend for a particular patient. As listed in

Table 7.1, these variables may be divided into two broad categories: (a) factors that are related specifically to aspects of the patient's presentation of OCD, and (b) nonspecific factors.

OCD-Related Factors

Primacy and Severity of OCD Symptoms

A defining characteristic of CBT is that the techniques used in therapy target specific symptoms. For instance, exposure procedures target obsessional fear. Thus, CBT for OCD should be recommended only when obsessions and compulsions cause clinical levels of distress and are among the patient's primary complaints. Because CBT programs (particularly intensive programs) require a substantial commitment to therapy, patients should not initiate this treatment if they are concurrently attending therapies likely to compete for time and energy. Examples would include intensive therapy for substance abuse or eating disorders. Commitment issues are less relevant to the use of pharmacotherapy. Thus, patients who have additional therapeutic undertakings that they are unwilling to discontinue would be advised to begin with medication until their schedule can accommodate CBT.

The clinical severity of OCD symptoms alone should not determine whether CBT or medication is recommended as the first-line treatment.

TABLE 7.1
Factors to Consider When Recommending Treatment for OCD

OCD-related factors

    Primacy and severity of OCD symptoms

    Symptom presentation

    Presence of feared consequences of obsessions and the degree of insight

    Comorbidity with Axis I and II psychopathology

    Treatment history

Nonspecific factors

    Demographic characteristics

    Educational level

    Availability of treatment

    Patient preference

    Social support

There is no evidence that either treatment (or combined treatment) is more effective for more severe obsessions and compulsions. Given the superior short- and long-term effectiveness of CBT, and the fact that improvement is typically achieved over less than 20 sessions, CBT should be considered before SRIs regardless of clinical severity. Greater symptom severity may necessitate a more intense regimen of whichever treatment is offered: a higher dose of medicine or more frequent CBT sessions. In cases where patients are practically incapacitated by their symptoms (e.g., cannot leave their home) or present a danger to themselves or to others, residential treatment should be recommended.

Symptom Presentation

Hoarding.   As reviewed in chapter 5, accumulating evidence suggests that hoarding symptoms are associated with poorer response to CBT (Abramowitz, Franklin, Schwartz, & Furr, 2003; Mataix-Cols et al., 2002) and SRIs (Mataix-Cols, Rauch, Manzo, Jenike, & Baer, 1999) typically used with OCD. This is likely because the factors that maintain hoarding symptoms extend beyond those that maintain other OCD symptoms as described in previous chapters. Because patients with primary hoarding exhibit deficits in decision making and organizational skills, appropriate treatment must target these areas. Hartl and Frost (1999) developed a cognitive-behavioral protocol for hoarding that involves training in organizational and decision-making skills as well as some cognitive and exposure-based techniques. Although still experimental, these newer approaches should be utilized when patients present with primarily hoarding symptoms (Frost, Steketee, & Greene, 2003). Because the treatment techniques presented in this book pertain less to hoarding than to other types of OCD symptoms, only limited discussion of their application to hoarding appears in subsequent chapters.

Pure Obsessions.   Patients (and clinicians) may have read or been told that mental rituals or "pure obsessions" fare less well in treatment compared to when the clinical picture involves overt compulsions such as washing and checking. However, owing to contemporary theoretical and research advances in understanding and treating obsessions without overt rituals (Rachman, 2003), both cognitive and exposure-based techniques have been adapted for use with patients presenting with this symptom picture (e.g., Freeston et al., 1997). These treatment procedures are described in subsequent chapters. Thus, the absence of prototypical compulsive behavior and the presence of severe mental rituals are not reasons to defer a recommendation of CBT. To the contrary, such symptoms often respond quite readily to cognitive and exposure-based interventions.

Feared Consequences and the Degree of Insight

Whereas some individuals with OCD clearly articulate fears of disastrous consequences associated with their obsessions (e.g., "If I touch the bathroom floor and do not wash my hands I will become very ill"), others do not verbalize specific feared outcomes (e.g., "I just wouldn't feel right unless I ritualized"). Research suggests patients who describe specific feared consequences fare better with CBT than do those without specific fears (Foa et al., 1999).

Clinical observations and research findings indicate that patients who have poor insight into the senselessness of their OCD symptoms improve less with CBT than do those who recognize that their fears and safety-seeking behaviors are excessive or unreasonable (Foa, 1979; Foa et al., 1999). Perhaps it is difficult for patients who are strongly convinced that their fears are realistic to consolidate disconfirming evidence gleaned from exposure exercises. Alternatively, those with poor insight may be more reluctant, because of their fears, to confront obsessional situations during exposure therapy. Thus, adherence may be a problem for such patients. To increase adherence to instructions for exposure, therapists might use cognitive techniques to "tenderize" strongly held dysfunctional beliefs. A second augmentative approach for patients with poor insight is SRI pharmacotherapy. Some psychiatrists will even prescribe antipsychotic medication for such patients despite no consistent research evidence that this augmentation strategy produces additional benefits over monotherapy (e.g., Bystritsky et al., 2004; Shapira et al., 2004).

Comorbidity

Certain comorbid Axis I conditions are known to interfere with the effects of CBT. For example, seriously depressed persons with OCD may become demoralized and have trouble complying with the demands of exposure therapy (e.g., Abramowitz & Foa, 2000; Abramowitz, Franklin, Street, Kozak, & Foa, 2000; Foa, 1979). Also, the strong emotional reactivity present in people with severe depression could interfere with habituation during exposure sessions and limit treatment gains (e.g., Foa et al., 1983). For individuals with OCD and comorbid GAD, pervasive worry might detract from the time and emotional resources needed to learn the skills for managing obsessional fear (Steketee et al., 2001). Whereas highly anxious patients, once engaged, often benefit from CBT, severe depression might be cause for postponing this approach to treatment until the depression can be brought under control (e.g., with antidepressant medication or psychotherapy aimed at depression). Given that the serotonergic medications used with OCD are also used in the treatment of both depression and GAD, these drugs represent another possible recommendation for patients with comorbidity.

Although research is scarce, our clinical observations suggest that psychotic and manic symptoms, as well as active substance abuse and dependence, attenuate the effects of CBT. Patients suffering from these symptoms have interference with normal perception, cognition, and judgment, which would impede their ability to follow treatment instructions or consolidate corrective information gleaned through exposure exercises. The use of mood-altering substances to manage distress evoked by exposure is of particular concern because this would prevent the natural habituation of obsessional fear and the learning of corrective information. Therefore, services aimed at bringing such conditions under control (e.g., detoxification, antipsychotic medications) should be sought prior to attempting CBT for OCD.

Severe personality disorders and traits can also hinder response to CBT and medication (Steketee et al., 2001). For example, anxious (e.g., obsessive-compulsive personality disorder) and dramatic (e.g., histrionic personality disorder) traits might interfere with developing rapport and adhering to instructions for EPR. However, if a therapeutic relationship can be developed, CBT can be successful despite these traits. Clinicians should also consider that some patients with dramatic traits gain reinforcement for their OCD symptoms. In such circumstances, CBT is unlikely to succeed because patients do not perceive themselves as gaining rewards for their efforts to reduce obsessions and rituals. Individuals with personality traits in the odd cluster (e.g., schizotypal personality disorder) present a challenge to CBT because of their reduced ability to profit from corrective information obtained during exposure or cognitive interventions. Clinicians are therefore advised to consider CBT for OCD patients with comorbid anxious or dramatic personality traits, while heeding the potential problems discussed previously. On the other hand, when OCD is comorbid with odd personality traits, intensive inpatient CBT along with medication is recommended.

Treatment History

Clinical observations suggest that for the most part, patients who have received an adequate length and dosage of one SRI (see Table 5.3 for recommended doses) are unlikely to respond to others, or to combinations of different SRIs. Thus, for medicated patients who have not had a course of CBT, psychological treatment is the obvious next choice. If, however, patients report that they have undergone CBT, the adequacy of this therapy course should be assessed before making additional recommendations (see Appendix A). If the previous treatment included infrequent sessions, lack of adequate exposures, little emphasis on refraining from rituals, or if patients were not given a clear rationale for the use of ERP techniques, an adequate trial of CBT should be considered.

There are various reasons that patients previously treated with adequate CBT seek additional help. Most commonly they require "booster sessions" to help with maintenance of earlier gains. In such cases, patients approach therapy having already been socialized to the cognitive-behavioral model and the intervention techniques, and often fare quite well. Other individuals seek an additional CBT trial due to the failure of an earlier trial. In such cases it is important to identify factors that might have contributed to failure so that these can be addressed in the current trial. The most common reason for unresponsiveness to exposure-based therapy is nonadherence with treatment procedures; particularly, the inability or unwillingness to confront feared stimuli or delay carrying out rituals and other forms of safety-seeking behavior (Rachman & Hodgson, 1980). Noncompliance with ERP procedures due to extreme fear may necessitate the increased use of cognitive and motivational interventions to prepare the patient for exposure.

Other, more subtle, reasons for nonresponse to CBT include the persistence of subtle avoidance tactics and covert safety behaviors. For example, one patient followed all instructions for exposure to feared contaminants as assigned by the therapist, but then, to make response prevention easier, avoided situations where casual exposure might occur. Another patient was able to refrain from her overt checking behavior, but persisted in compulsively mentally reviewing all of her actions to reassure herself that she had not made any bad mistakes. This type of problem highlights the need for patients to identify and understand the function of their symptoms as described in earlier chapters. Response prevention requires abstaining not just from overt compulsive rituals, but also from subtle tactics (safety-seeking behaviors) used to escape from obsessive fear. Finally, some patients make a transient, but not a permanent commitment to change. They might vow (secretly) to engage in treatment during the program, but as one patient with blasphemous obsessions told us, "In the back of my mind, I always knew I would start the praying rituals again the minute treatment was over." This individual had actually made excellent progress during his previous course of CBT, but relapsed within a short time.

A history of noncompliance due to motivational factors may suggest the need for either residential treatment or alternative methods altogether (e.g., medication, individual therapy for other difficulties). The motivational interviewing techniques described by Miller and Rollnick (2002) can be useful tools in such instances. Finally, for patients who have failed multiple adequate trials of both pharmacotherapy and CBT, the clinician can recommend individual supportive therapy, group support programs, or (if symptoms are unremitting and insufferable) psychosurgery.

Nonspecific Factors

Age, Gender, and Race.   For different reasons, the elderly have more difficulty with adherence to medication regimens than do young and middle-aged adults. Missed doses or overdoses may result in reduced benefit and unpleasant side effects. Older adults may be subject to more adverse side effects from SRIs because of reduced metabolic rates and interactions with medicine prescribed for other conditions. Thus, CBT is the best initial treatment option for older adults. Evidence that CBT is highly effective for elderly individuals with OCD is accumulating (Calamari & Cassiday, 1999). Nevertheless, older individuals may feel more comfortable with medication rather than attending outpatient psychotherapy. This issue should be discussed openly during consultation.

Gender should not affect treatment recommendations for OCD. Nevertheless, some patients may feel more comfortable with therapists of their same sex, especially if symptoms involve sexual (e.g., unwanted doubts about sexual preference) or contamination (e.g., semen) concerns that provoke self-consciousness. For example, a therapist of the same sex would be necessary to accompany the patient during exposure to public restrooms.

Some members of minority groups perceive a stigma in seeking psychotherapy and therefore obtain treatment, usually in the form of medication, through primary care physicians (Williams, Chambless, & Steketee, 1998). This sense of shame can also interfere with assessment and CBT by hindering the patient's self-report of symptoms and his or her performance of exposure exercises. In addition, members of minority groups may be reluctant to involve friends or relatives in their treatment (Hatch, Friedman, & Paradis, 1996), thus leaving them without benefit of outside support. The suggestion of residential treatment may induce further shame for members of minority groups; thus clinicians must address this topic with sensitivity. Although these issues may make pharmacotherapy a better initial treatment for some patients, Williams et al. (1998) reported clinically significant improvement for African American OCD patients treated with CBT.

Educational Level.   Successful CBT requires that the patient comprehend an abstract model of OCD and rationale for the treatment procedures. Moreover, the ability to consolidate information learned during exposure practice, complete written exercises, and implement these treatment procedures independently is necessary for improvement. These skills may be difficult for individuals who are overly concrete in their thinking. Because group CBT may proceed at a pace that is too rapid for individuals with cognitive impairment or severe learning disabilities, individual therapy is recommended for such patients. For those OCD patients too cognitively impaired to comprehend or profit from CBT, it may be more fruitful to explore other forms of psychotherapy to help the patient cope with his or her symptoms, or recommend pharmacotherapy options.

Availability of Treatment.   Geographic location limits the availability of CBT, but not medication, for OCD. Despite increasing numbers of professionals who are trained to deliver CBT, access to qualified therapists remains limited, especially in rural areas where there are no academic medical centers or universities with clinical psychology training programs. Thus, many patients must travel for adequate treatment. Insurance coverage may also dictate the availability of both CBT and pharmacotherapy, as some insurance providers do not adequately cover mental health treatment.

Two self-help CBT programs have been developed for OCD. Fritzler, Hecker, and Losee's (1997) 12-week bibliotherapy program involved using Steketee and White's (1990) self-help book, *When Once Is Not Enough,* and five sessions with a therapist to review information presented in the book. Improvement among the nine patients in this study was modest, yet three obtained clinically significant benefit. Greist et al. (2002) described an interactive and computerized telephone-based self-help behavioral therapy program called BT Steps. The intervention included education about OCD, treatment planning, instructions for ERP tasks, and relapse prevention. Patients who received this program improved about 25% in their OCD symptoms, yet whether these gains were maintained in the long term was not reported. Thus, although some degree of benefit may be obtained from self-help programs, the lack of therapist contact likely jeopardizes the integrity of exposure, and may compromise long-term outcome.

Patient Preference.   Pharmacotherapy and CBT involve dissimilar approaches to conceptualization and treatment. Pharmacotherapy is most consistent with biological theories that implicate the role of neurotransmitter dysregulation, whereas CBT is derived from models that emphasize the role of conditioning, avoidance, and cognitive biases in the maintenance of OCD. The chief practical considerations associated with each treatment were described previously. Research in our clinic suggests that OCD patients have generally favorable impressions of both treatment approaches, but strongly prefer CBT to medication as their treatment of choice (Deacon & Abramowitz, 2005a). Research has not clearly indicated whether it is most advantageous to match a patient's treatment to his or her preference, encourage the patient to accept one modality over another, or combine treatment methods. Therefore, it is worthwhile for the clinician to review the advantages and disadvantages of CBT and pharmacotherapy before assessing the patient's preference because greater adherence can be expected if the patient is agreeable with the particular treatment modality. For example, some individuals are unwilling to endure exposure to feared situations as would occur in CBT. If this is the case, it is important to ascertain the nature of such concerns so that they may be addressed during the consultation. An example of how to present treatment options for OCD patients is provided later in this chapter.

Social Support.   Although not a requirement for all patients, the effects of CBT may be enhanced by the involvement of a support person who becomes familiar with the treatment procedures and helps the patient complete therapy exercises outside of the session. This individual should be capable of providing firm, yet empathic, emotional support (Mehta, 1990). It is therefore important for the clinician to carefully evaluate family members' interactions with the patient before assuming that their assistance with CBT will be beneficial. If family members are unsupportive, meddling, ridiculing, or argumentative, involving them in CBT may be counterproductive. For patients who are in need of positive support, group CBT may be a good option.

When it is clear that family members' behavior is serving to maintain OCD symptoms, the clinician should address this issue in a straightforward yet sensitive manner and educate all parties about its potentially deleterious effects on treatment. In some instances the patient and family are able to align themselves together in addressing the patient's symptoms. In others, where family dynamics might undermine the benefits of CBT, family therapy or pharmacotherapy is suggested as a first-line treatment. Van Noppen and Steketee (2003) provide an excellent discussion of family considerations in the treatment of OCD. The following is an excerpt from Susan T.'s consultation in which the issue of Susan's husband's involvement in OCD symptoms was raised.

Therapist: So, it sounds like Steve sometimes helps you by checking that the appliances are unplugged before going to bed or leaving the house. Do you have to ask him to do these things?

Susan: Not so much anymore. He knows I get upset, so he just does them automatically.

Steve: That's right. I worry that if Susan got too anxious she might lose control or go crazy or something. I would just as soon do whatever I can to keep her from getting upset. It must be bad for her to be so anxious, so I do these things to help. It's not that big of a deal.

Therapist: Sure. I can understand that; you care about Susan and don't want her to get too upset. I'd probably want to do the same thing if I were in your position. Actually, many people with

OCD involve their spouses in rituals for the same reasons. Sometimes, though, we do things that we think are helpful, or that seem helpful to avoid an immediate problem, but which may be problematic in the long run. Let me explain so you can see what I mean.

As I said before, compulsive rituals are ways that Susan copes with her obsessional fears of being responsible for mistakes or causing disastrous consequences such as fires. But rituals are maladaptive strategies because even though they make her feel a little better for a short while, they prevent her from getting over her fear of mistakes or fires. This happens because if Susan checks, or if you check for her, she never has the chance to learn to cope with her anxiety or see that her fears are unlikely to come true. So, Steve, although you mean well by helping Susan with her rituals, and although it makes her more comfortable in the short run, the long-term effect is that it is actually preventing her from overcoming her illogical fear. Do you see that?

Susan
and Steve: Yes.

Therapist: If Susan decides to begin treatment with me, I will help her to learn to manage her obsessional fears in more healthy ways so that she does not need to repeatedly check or wash, or ask you to do these things. Also, I will teach you how to be supportive of Susan in a way that will help her become less dependent on checking. Rather than cooperating with Susan's OCD, you will practice helping her see that compulsive rituals are unnecessary and wasteful. Of course, not doing rituals for Susan anymore probably seems like a difficult task. Some families worry that this will make the person with OCD even more upset. This is understandable, and I will work with you both so that you, Susan, can overcome your reliance on these rituals.

HOW TO DISCUSS TREATMENT OPTIONS WITH PATIENTS

After considering the patient's clinical presentation and motivation for treatment, and the numerous factors described earlier, treatment recommendations are discussed in an open and evidence-based format. Most patients are aware that medications and psychological treatment are available for OCD. Less understood is that only certain types of drugs, and certain forms of therapy, are likely to be helpful. The excerpts presented next are taken from Susan T.'s initial consultation.

The Effectiveness of Medications

The clinician should rely directly on research results (see chapter 5) when addressing questions about the effectiveness of treatment.

> Therapist: One form of treatment for OCD is medication. The specific kinds of medication that are known to help OCD are called serotonin reuptake inhibitors, or SRIs, and a psychiatrist who is knowledgeable about OCD would prescribe them for you. Examples of SRIs include Paxil, Prozac, Luvox, Zoloft, Anafranil, and Celexa. There have been many studies conducted to evaluate the effectiveness of these medicines, and this research shows that about half of those who take these drugs for OCD do fairly well. The research also shows that on the average, symptom relief is between 20% and 40%. So, for many people, the SRIs are helpful to the point that there is noticeable improvement in their lives. It is hard to say which of the SRIs is best for OCD, but most psychiatrists have their preferences as far as which drug they tend to prescribe. Also, because everyone responds a little differently, it would be difficult to make a prediction about how helpful an SRI would be for you. The SRIs are actually antidepressants that have been found to also help with anxiety problems. And the truth is that we do not understand exactly how they work to reduce OCD. Some experts think that SRIs correct serotonin problems. But remember that we are not certain of the role serotonin plays in OCD.

Advantages and Disadvantages of Medication

Practical considerations weigh heavily in patients' preference for a treatment. With pharmacotherapy, the main advantages are accessibility and ease of administration. Disadvantages include the modest improvement rate, need for long-term use, and side effects.

> Therapist: Medication treatment for OCD has some important advantages. Many people like this treatment because it is so convenient. It is easy to obtain from a drug store once it is has been prescribed, and there are no therapy sessions to go to. If you were to leave town for an extended period of time, you could take the medication with you. Usually, your doctor gives you instructions for how much of the drug to take and when to take it, and once you swallow the pill, the drug does all of its

work internally. At the beginning, you might have to visit the psychiatrist a few times to establish the best dose for you. Then, you return for monitoring every few months.

Susan: But if I take medication, do I have to stay on it for the rest of my life?

Therapist: Well, let's talk about some of the disadvantages of SRIs. First, as I mentioned, the average person achieves only modest improvement. So, in other words, even with an optimal response, most people who take SRIs still have noticeable OCD symptoms. A second drawback is that to keep up any improvement in symptoms, you must continue to take the medication. That is, OCD symptoms typically return if the medication is stopped; even if you've been taking it for a long time. While some people don't mind taking medicine, others prefer not to be on drugs for a long time. The third disadvantage of SRIs is that they can produce unwanted side effects such as dry mouth, sleep changes, weight gain, and sexual dysfunction. This is because SRIs act on serotonin functioning all over the body, not just in the brain, and serotonin is involved in many bodily functions. In most cases, side effects can be tolerated, or managed by having the psychiatrist change the dose of the drug. It is hard to predict the kinds of side effects you might have because everyone responds to medication a little differently.

The Effectiveness of CBT

Summarizing the treatment outcome research reviewed in chapter 5 provides a basis for the effectiveness of CBT and demonstrates to the patient that the clinician is knowledgeable. Clinicians should also point out how the assumptions underlying the specific CBT techniques are distinct from those underlying serotonergic medication. Moreover, it is helpful to link each treatment procedure to its intended effect (e.g., response prevention is aimed at reducing compulsive urges). The following discussion, which occurred during Susan's consultation, could be adapted for any individual with OCD.

Therapist: CBT is based on understanding OCD at the symptom level, rather than on a biological level. As we talked about before, we understand a great deal about the symptoms of OCD and how they develop into maladaptive thinking and behavior patterns. In CBT, you learn skills that weaken these patterns. For example, you practice techniques that weaken your pattern of becoming very anxious over obsessional thoughts and situations. You also learn skills to weaken the pattern of using compulsive rituals to reduce obsessional anxiety. CBT is highly effective for OCD and we know this from the many studies that have been conducted around the world on this treatment. In the research on CBT, most patients typically show a reduction in obsessions and compulsions of 50% to 70%. So, we would expect you to show a great deal of improvement with this treatment.

Four techniques are used in CBT. The first is education, which means that you learn about your obsessions and compulsions and how CBT is used to reduce these symptoms. Another technique is called cognitive therapy, which involves helping you identify and correct problematic thinking styles that lead to anxiety. The two most powerful techniques in CBT are called exposure and response prevention. Exposure means gradually confronting the situations and thoughts that trigger obsessional fear, such as public bathrooms or upsetting thoughts about Jennifer. Response prevention means that you practice staying in the situation until the anxiety decreases on its own, rather than escaping by doing rituals. For example, not washing or checking. Although these techniques are highly effective, they are also challenging. You have to face situations that you've been working hard to avoid. Although this is done gradually and with the therapist's help and encouragement, you would almost certainly become anxious at the beginning of exposure practice. However, by practicing exposure and response prevention, you would learn that your anxiety actually lessens the more you remain exposed—even if you resist doing rituals. This is called habituation. So, exposure therapy helps reduce obsessional anxiety and response prevention helps you to weaken the habitual pattern of using rituals to reduce obsessional anxiety.

Advantages and Disadvantages of CBT

Clinicians should emphasize that CBT requires a great deal of work up front, but this effort is likely to pay off in the long run. It may be helpful to provide assurance that the therapist will carefully titrate these exercises so that distress is minimized. The transitory nature of exposure-induced distress can also be explained using a plot similar to that in Fig. 7.1, which illustrates the phenomena of within- and between-session anxiety reduction (habituation).

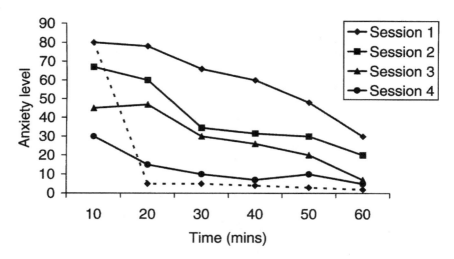

FIG. 7.1. Graphical illustration of anxiety reduction within and between exposure therapy sessions. This graph can be used to illustrate for patients considering CBT the transient nature of distress that is likely to accompany systematic exposure to fear-evoking cues during treatment. The dashed line depicts the immediate reduction in anxiety that occurs if a safety-seeking ritual
is performed. Rituals prevent the reduction in obsessional anxiety that would
occur naturally over time if no rituals were performed. It is important for patients to experience the natural habituation of anxiety to reduce obsessional
fear.

Therapist: The greatest advantage of CBT is that it is the most effective
treatment for OCD. Of course, I cannot guarantee you success, but it is certainly likely that CBT will lead to appreciable
levels of improvement for you. Another advantage is that
CBT is brief. Typically, improvement occurs within about 15
to 20 sessions. Third, the effects of CBT are long lasting. So,
once therapy is over you will have learned skills that no one
can take away from you. In other words, you will become
your own therapist and be able to apply these skills as necessary in your life. So, CBT is a brief treatment that is more effective than medication in the short term and in the long run.

However, there are also some disadvantages to CBT. First,
as you have probably noticed, CBT requires a great deal of
work. You will have to come to regular treatment sessions
and practice confronting situations that you have been trying
to avoid—situations that will most likely make you anxious.
You will also be practicing exposure exercises outside the of-

fice between sessions. For example, based on what you told me, you would probably practice touching surfaces such as bathroom doorknobs, toilets, and the like, which might make you worry about germs. Of course, you would receive help with these tasks and there will never be any surprises. Nor will anyone force you into doing exposures. What I mean is that you would play a big role in deciding on when you do exposure to different situations.

As I said, you will almost definitely feel uncomfortable during exposure exercises, but you should know that your therapist will work with you to minimize your distress. For example, you would start slowly and begin with exposure to less distressing situations, gradually working your way up to more challenging ones. Also, your anxiety will subside as time goes by. So, each time you repeat exposure to these situations you will experience less and less distress. That is how exposure therapy works. It is hard to say how much discomfort you might have during exposure because it varies from person to person. However, I can tell you that the anxiety will be temporary, and that with practice you will see that it decreases.

So, as you might have guessed, how much improvement you get out of CBT is related to how much effort you put into doing the therapy exercises. You must decide to invest the time and energy in CBT to gain control over your OCD symptoms. You have to choose to become anxious to learn that you really have very little to fear. CBT can be exhausting, but the reward for your hard work up front is that you are likely to see improvement that will last over the long term. This is different from medication where there is less of an effort involved, yet the improvement is not likely to be as substantial.

Combining Medication With CBT

The effectiveness of combination treatments for OCD is discussed in chapter 5. Despite the intuitive appeal of combining two effective treatments, concurrent medication use is not necessary for patients to gain substantial benefits from CBT. An exception to this would include patients with severe co-occurring depression and perhaps those with very poor insight into the senselessness of their OCD symptoms.

Therapist: Patients and their families often ask whether a combination approach—using CBT and medication together—produces a better outcome than either treatment alone. Unlike what you might expect, the several research studies that have looked at this question indicate that for most patients, medication is not required to see substantial benefits with CBT. In other words, using both treatments is not likely to produce a better outcome than you would have with CBT alone. But you should also know that medication does not *interfere* with the effects of CBT. So, you do not need to stop your medicine, especially if you feel it has been helpful. If you have been on SRI medication and are still having obsessions and compulsions, the research suggests there is a good chance that adding CBT will lead to added improvement. So, I would say that if you begin CBT, you should not start or stop any OCD medication right before or during psychotherapy, because then we would not be able to tell which treatment was responsible for any beneficial or adverse effects, in case we had to change the treatment plan.

Making a Recommendation

A review of the procedures, effectiveness, and the pros and cons of each treatment provides a compelling rationale for recommending CBT in most cases. Exceptions would be instances in which patients have not responded to previous adequate trials of CBT, do not have the time to commit to therapy, are otherwise motivated, or are unwilling to tolerate the temporary evocation of obsessional distress during exposure practices. We find patients and their families often feel comforted by our knowledge and expertise regarding the various treatment options and appreciate being included in the decision process. We also let the patient know that although our decision is guided by expertise, we remain flexible regarding the course and regimen of treatment depending on how therapy progresses.

> Therapist: My recommendation is that you consider beginning CBT because it is likely to be most helpful and long lasting. It is true that you will need to work hard and even endure some initial distress during therapy, but I can tell you that this will be temporary and we will do everything we can to help you succeed. I believe that if you are willing to invest some anxiety up front, the chances are good that you will have a more relaxed future. What thoughts do you have about what I've said?

8

Information Gathering
and Case Formulation

The initial phase of CBT involves a detailed assessment of the cognitive-behavioral phenomenology and maintenance processes involved in the patient's particular obsessional fears and safety-seeking responses. From this information, the therapist synthesizes an individualized cognitive-behavioral formulation of the problem. It is this formulation that will guide treatment planning and the implementation of therapeutic procedures described in subsequent chapters. The first part of this chapter presents a detailed description of how to conduct a cognitive-behavioral (functional) analysis of OCD symptoms. This includes instructing the patient in self-monitoring his or her safety-seeking behaviors. In the second part, the reader will learn how to synthesize information gleaned through functional analysis and derive a case formulation that informs treatment planning. Susan's case, introduced in chapter 6, is used throughout this chapter to illustrate the assessment and case conceptualization procedures.

INFORMATION GATHERING

The initial assessment and diagnostic procedures described in chapter 6 set the stage for a more comprehensive *functional assessment* in which idiosyncratic circumstantial, cognitive, and behavioral features of the patient's symptoms are carefully identified, and the links between these features are understood. Assessment may be considered an exchange of information between the patient—who enters treatment presumably able to describe his or her own OCD symptoms—and the clinician—who is able to draw on a conceptual template of OCD phenomenology to derive a treatment plan that addresses the patient's particular symptoms. Therefore, the therapist must ascertain the specific nuances of the patient's obsessions and rituals, and the patient must learn how to understand these symptoms from a cognitive-behavioral (functional) perspective to optimize assessment and treatment. The composition of a cognitive-behavioral assessment for OCD is summarized in Table 8.1, and the steps involved in obtaining this information are outlined later. Special issues related to assessment of the various OCD symptom dimensions are also addressed. Forms for recording information obtained during this part of the assessment appear in Fig 8.1.

Review of Recent Episodes

To gain additional insight into the patient's experience and how he or she copes with symptoms, the clinician can ask for a "play-by-play" description of a few specific instances of obsessional fear, avoidance, and com-

TABLE 8.1
Components of Functional Assessment of OCD Symptoms

Obsessional stimuli

    Situations and stimuli that trigger obsessions

    Obsessional thoughts, impulses, images, and doubts

Cognitive features

    Dysfunctional beliefs and interpretations of obsessional situations and stimuli (feared consequences)

    Catastrophic misinterpretations of intrusive thoughts

    Intolerance for uncertainty

    Not-just-right experiences

    Fears of harm from experiencing long-term anxiety

Safety-seeking (responses to obsessional distress)

    Passive avoidance

    Compulsive behavior (rituals)

    Covert neutralizing strategies

Self-monitoring of obsessional situations and safety behaviors

FUNCTIONAL ASSESSMENT OF OCD SYMPTOMS

Patient's name: _____

Age: _____

Duration of symptoms: _____

Educational level: _____

I. OBSESSIONAL STIMULI

A. External situations and stimuli that trigger obsessions (people, places, things, and circumstances that evoke anxiety; e.g., sweat, knives, the number 6, doing paperwork)

B. Obsessional thoughts, impulses, images, doubts (e.g., "I could be contaminated,"   "Jesus is sexy," "I could kill this baby")

FIG. 8.1.   Forms for conducting a functional assessment of OCD symptoms.

(continued on next page)

II. COGNITIVE FEATURES (DYSFUNCTIONAL BELIEFS)

A. Dysfunctional Beliefs about obsessional situations and stimuli (feared consequences of exposure)

B. Catastrophic misinterpretations of intrusive thoughts (e.g., "thinking about it is the same as actually doing it")

C. Describe the patient's difficulties with intolerance for uncertainty

D. Not-just-right experiences/perfectionism (e.g., "If it's not perfect, it's worthless")

E. Fears of long-term anxiety/discomfort ("I will be anxious forever unless I ritualize")

FIG. 8.1.   *continued.*

FUNCTIONAL ASSESSMENT OF OCD SYMPTOMS (continued)

III. SAFETY-SEEKING BEHAVIORS (RESPONSES TO OBSESSIONAL DISTRESS)

A. Passive avoidance and its relationship to obsessional fear (e.g., avoids churches to keep from having blasphemous thoughts; avoids public restrooms to remain clean)

B. Overt compulsive behavior (describe in detail) and its relationship to obsessional fear (e.g., checking the stove three times to prevent fires; retracing steps until bad thought is dismissed to prevent bad luck)

C. Mental rituals, covert neutralizing strategies, and their relationship to obsessional fear (e.g., thought suppression to prevent acting on thoughts; repeating the phrase "God is good" to neutralize blasphemous thoughts)

FIG. 8.1. *continued.*

pulsive behavior. This technique could also be used to focus the assessment on a particular symptom the clinician is having difficulty understanding. What was the context in which obsessional distress was evoked? What was the first sign of trouble? Then, the patient is asked to step through the situation and report his or her emotional and cognitive responses. What was he or she feeling and thinking? What happened next? How anxious did he or she become and what was done to reduce this anxiety (e.g., compulsive rituals, avoidance)? How did the situation resolve itself and how did the patient feel afterward? The clinician should be sure to point out for the patient the functional relationships between obsessions and increased distress, and between safety-seeking rituals or avoidance and anxiety reduction. For example:

- That's a great example of how your obsessional doubt about causing a fire evoked a high degree of anxiety. Then, when you drove all the way back home to check and you saw that the toaster was unplugged, you said that you felt relieved. Do you see how your checking rituals reduce your anxiety?
- It sounds like when you have one of these unacceptable thoughts about the devil, it makes you feel uneasy and afraid, but then you pray to God and tell him you're devoted to him and it makes you feel relieved.

Identifying Obsessional Stimuli

Next, the therapist begins collecting specific information on the full range of OCD symptoms. It is important that assessment is thorough so that treatment can address all situations and thoughts that present problems for the patient. Information gathered using the Y–BOCS symptom checklist can be used to guide the assessment.

Assessing Situational Triggers

Specific information about the range of situations and objects that evoke the patient's obsessional fears should be identified first. The most straightforward way to identify such triggers is to inquire about situations that are avoided or that elicit urges to perform rituals. Notably, different situations and stimuli may elicit the same fundamental fear for different patients. For example, two individuals concerned with other people's saliva may have distinct triggers: One might fear contamination only from people known to be sick, whereas another may fear all public surfaces because of the possible presence of saliva. In addition, the same stimulus might be associated with different fundamental fears for different patients. For example, some individuals fear pornographic magazines because they may be contaminated with body fluids, whereas others fear such material because it evokes unacceptable sexual thoughts and images. Thus, it is important to clarify why a situation or stimulus evokes fear.

Contamination.   The most common feared contaminants are bodily wastes and fluids (e.g., urine, feces, blood, sweat, semen, saliva), garbage (and garbage receptacles), chemicals (e.g., pesticides), dirt, animals, and corpses. Many (but not all) patients assume that contamination is easily spread to nearby surfaces (e.g., urine gets on the floor), thus secondary and tertiary triggers of contamination obsessions need to be identified. For example, recall that urine was a primary source of contamination for Susan. However, her fear extended to secondary sources such as one of her students who she believed failed to wash his hands after using the bathroom. As a result, anything this student handled—his assignments, books, doors, pencils, and even his parents—also triggered obsessional fear. Some secondary sources have less of a logical connection to the primary source. For example, patients afraid of contamination from blood occasionally fear anything that is the color red. Questions such as, "What things make you feel contaminated or want to wash or clean?" are useful ways to elicit pertinent information.

Harming.   Situations that activate obsessional guilt and anxiety concerning responsibility for harm or mistakes are highly idiosyncratic. Routine activities such as leaving the house ("What if I left an appliance on and a fire starts?") or turning off a light switch ("What if I only imagined turning it off?") might be triggers. Other possible cues include driving (for fear of hitting pedestrians), discarding bags or envelopes (for fear of throwing away money or important papers, often observed in patients with hoarding problems), seeing broken glass (which could result in injury if not picked up), or completing paperwork (fears of errors resulting in negative consequences). Words (e.g., *accident, cancer*) or numbers (e.g., 13) that the patient associates with danger, harm, or bad luck may also trigger obsessional fear. For Susan, grading papers and entering grades into the computer were significant sources of distress. She worried about assigning poor grades by mistake, which might lead to "ruining a student's life." She also described mild to moderate fear evoked by leaving her home—she worried that she would be responsible for a fire.

Incompleteness.   The most common triggers of incompleteness obsessions are a sense of asymmetry, imbalance, or disorderliness. This may pertain to situations, objects, feelings, or words and numbers; for example, having books arranged "out of order" on a bookshelf, having "messy" handwriting, or finding one's clothes not folded perfectly. One woman became distressed if she was touched or brushed on one side of her body but not the other. Simply hearing the word *left* without hearing *right* evoked discomfort for this individual. Another patient became anxious over odd numbers, for example, on the odometer or when balancing the checkbook. There was no sense of danger, just the idea that odd numbers were "wrong."

Unacceptable Thoughts and Covert Rituals. Intrusive unacceptable thoughts about violence, sex, and blasphemy are often classically conditioned to external triggers such as knives or baseball bats, horror movies, Halloween, cemeteries, holding a baby, pornography, information about homosexuality, specific people, words, numbers, and religious icons. One patient was afraid of anything having to do with the New Jersey Devils hockey team for fear of "devil thoughts." In fact, he avoided everything regarding the state of New Jersey (e.g., maps, postcards, license plates). Another feared places of worship because they evoked unwanted blasphemous intrusions such as, "Jesus is gay." Still another patient feared women's lingerie stores (e.g., Victoria's Secret) for fear of seeing attractive women and experiencing unwanted doubts about her sexual preference. A more dramatic example is that of a man who feared going to sleep at night because he once dreamed of having sex with his father and feared having such a dream again. Susan T.'s unwanted thoughts of harming her infant daughter were evoked by the sight of knives and by bathing the baby in the bathtub.

Assessing Obsessional Thoughts

Intrusive, senseless, and unacceptable thoughts, ideas, images, impulses, and doubts that evoke feelings of anxiety, shame, terror, or disgust are hallmarks of OCD and every patient experiences them in one form or another. Although these are often overlooked in strictly behavioral models and treatment of OCD, cognitive-behavioral models regard these internal stimuli (often triggered by situational cues) as normal experiences that evoke inappropriate fear and uncertainty because of how they are appraised. Some patients conceal their obsessions, believing that to vocalize such thoughts would increase the probability of the corresponding negative event. As an example, one man refused to talk about his unwanted impulse to kiss his male boss because he thought that verbalizing this idea somehow brought him closer to acting on the impulse. Other patients conceal because they are ashamed or embarrassed by the content and frequency of the obsessional intrusion. On the one hand, the therapist must understand that describing these noxious thoughts may be a great challenge for patients. Nevertheless, because the aim of treatment is to weaken the connection between such thoughts and anxiety, patients need to be encouraged to disclose the content of even their most disturbing obsessions.

Patients are often comforted (and surprised) when they see that the therapist is neither alarmed nor disgusted by the content and frequency of the obsessions. Many individuals seem to scrutinize the therapist's reactions for any signs of horror. Responding genuinely, but in a "matter-of-fact" way, reinforces the notion that even the most bizarre or obscene obsessions are normal, nonthreatening, and do not necessitate any extraordinary emotional response. This is illustrated in the following dialogue.

Patient: (with trepidation) I know this sounds crazy, but I often think about "what if I stabbed my wife in her sleep?"

Therapist: Um hmm, sure [nods empathically]. I'll bet that's pretty scary for you.

Patient: Yes, it is. Now, you must think I'm some sort of psychopath.

Therapist: (matter-of-factly) No, not really. Does it look like I'm worried about you killing your wife in her sleep? [A thorough assessment had been conducted to rule out any history of actual aggressive behavior.]

Patient: Well, no. But all the other therapists I've had were shocked and wanted to try and figure out why I was thinking those things.

Therapist: I see. My approach is much different than theirs, for sure. We know from lots of scientific research that everyone has those kinds of thoughts, and that they are not dangerous or significant, especially given your history of not being a violent person. So, instead of trying to figure them out, we're going to help you realize that those thoughts are not at all threatening or psychopathic. They're not worth figuring out. It might help you to know that I've also had these kinds of thoughts.

Contamination.   Patients with contamination fears typically report persistent thoughts, images, and doubts regarding germs and illness attributable to contact with feared contaminants. Some entertain obsessions about being responsible for contaminating others and thereby causing them harm. Rachman (1994) described a phenomenon known as *mental pollution,* which is a more or less obscure sense of internal "dirtiness" seldom traceable to a specific source, but which may be induced by circumstances such as memories of traumatic events, unwanted unacceptable thoughts (e.g., images of molesting children), or humiliation. Susan reported some of the most common contamination obsessions: images of germs on her hands, thoughts of being sick, and doubts about whether she really was contaminated.

Harming.   Persistent doubts are the chief obsessional thoughts for this symptom presentation. The individual might question whether he or she has accidentally injured or killed someone (e.g., while driving) or did enough to prevent catastrophes. Doubts about mistakes, negligence, or mishaps, such as inserting inappropriate or hurtful language into conversations or e-mail messages, are also common. Individuals with scrupulosity entertain nagging doubts about largely unanswerable questions of whether they have acted morally or followed religious doctrines to the letter of the law. Susan had doubts about whether she had assigned grades correctly or recorded them accurately on students' report cards. Perhaps she would be responsible for a promising student not being accepted to a private school or college. Doubts about whether she might cause (or had caused) a house fire were also present. Lastly, Susan had obsessional thoughts about not doing enough to keep her husband and children from becoming very sick or dying because of feared contaminants. This last example illustrates an overlap between the contamination and harming symptom dimensions.

Incompleteness.   Specific obsessions may be difficult to identify within this symptom presentation. Most patients report the sense that something is "not just right," or images of themselves "going crazy" or "out of control" due to experiencing prolonged anxiety or distress.

Unacceptable Thoughts and Covert Rituals.   This dimension of OCD represents the purest example of obsessional thoughts, impulses, and images that evoke discomfort. Violent or aggressive obsessions include unwanted ideas such as "I could burn my child with the iron," the thought of pushing one's wife onto the tracks when the train is approaching, or "what if I yell racial slurs at my friend who is an ethnic minority?" Sexual obsessions can take several forms, including unwanted ideas of molesting or raping others, thoughts or images of consensual yet personally undesirable sexual behavior (e.g., incest, homosexuality), unwelcome thoughts of improper sexual activity (e.g., with someone other than your spouse), and unacceptable images such as that of one's grandparents having sex. Religious obsessions may include blasphemous images (e.g., of Jesus with an erection on the cross) or other thoughts and doubts that create the feeling of having sinned (e.g., unwanted thoughts questioning the existence of God). Susan experienced unwanted thoughts of violence against her infant, Jennifer. The most distressing thoughts were those of losing control and stabbing Jennifer, and of drowning her in the bathtub. It is interesting to note that virtually any thought has the potential to become an obsession if its presence or meaning is appraised as threatening or significant in a negative way. Next, we turn to the appraisal component of obsessions.

Identifying Dysfunctional Beliefs
and Interpretations of Obsessional Stimuli

As I described in Part I, the cognitive-behavioral model of OCD distinguishes between obsessional stimuli and the meaning that patients give to these stimuli. The model proposes that obsessional fear results from dysfunctional appraisals, interpretations, and perceptions of situations and stimuli that objectively pose a low risk of harm. Because CBT aims to modify these dysfunctional beliefs, the therapist must be aware of such thinking patterns. Figure 8.1 includes space for recording patients' feared consequences of exposure to obsessional situations and thoughts.

Examples of questions to elicit dysfunctional cognitions include the following:

- What is so bad for you about using public bathrooms? What bad things do you expect to happen?
- What do you tell yourself before leaving the house that makes you feel like you need to check all the appliances?
- Why is it so bad for you to have thoughts about sex while you are in church?
- What might happen if you are holding a knife and you think about stabbing your child?
- What are you afraid would happen if you touched your shoes and didn't wash your hands?

The downward-arrow technique (Burns, 1980) is a useful way of identifying specific dysfunctional beliefs (overestimates of severity, likelihood, and the need to prevent harm) about obsessional situations and thoughts. This method involves asking the patient to describe an episode of obsessions and compulsions, followed by probe questions to identify the fundamental or core beliefs that evoke fear, avoidance, or neutralization (e.g., "If that were so, what would be the worst thing that could happen?").

Susan described an episode in which she avoided shaking hands with people in a reception line at her church. The following transcript illustrates the use of the downward-arrow method to identify Susan's feared consequences of contact with other people.

Therapist: Can you tell me what you were worried about when you were going through the reception line?

Susan: I was afraid that people's hands were sweaty. It was very hot in the church that day and I didn't want to get other people's sweat on me. I felt like I had to wash my hands as soon as possible.

Therapist: I see. What would have happened if you shook their hands and touched their sweat without washing your hands afterward?

Susan: There would be other people's germs on me.
Therapist: OK. And what would happen next?
Susan: I would probably get sick, or spread the germs to my kids and make *them* sick.
Therapist: And what do you imagine that would be like? How sick would everyone become?
Susan: Well, it could depend. Probably just a cold, but perhaps worse.
Therapist: How much worse?
Susan: I don't know … salmonella poisoning, bacterial infections? Someone could get really sick.
Therapist: How *likely* is it that you would get sick from shaking hands with someone at your church and not washing your hands? What percent?
Susan: Maybe 70 or 80 percent.
Therapist: So it sounds like that reception line was scary for you because you were telling yourself that shaking people's hands, without washing your own, would probably result in you and your family becoming very sick.
Susan: Yes, that's right.

As the reader can identify, Susan's beliefs included overestimates of the probability, severity, and responsibility for preventing illness. Note that at this point the therapist does not question or challenge the patient's clearly unrealistic assumptions. Instead, the focus is on developing rapport and collecting information about the cognitive basis of obsessional fear.

Not all patients articulate the kinds of explicit fears of disastrous consequences just illustrated. Some report that obsessional cues evoke only a vague sense that "something bad will happen," and others say they would "just feel anxious." The downward-arrow method often reveals that the underlying catastrophic beliefs for such individuals are that their anxiety or distress will persist indefinitely, spiral to unmanageable levels, or lead to harmful consequences (e.g., "I will have a breakdown"). Research suggests that it is important to help patients clarify their feared consequences, even if they are merely that anxiety will persist indefinitely, so that such fears can be explicitly disconfirmed during exposure exercises (Foa et al., 1999).

Self-report questionnaires should be used to assist with ascertaining dysfunctional beliefs. Two excellent instruments developed by the OCCWG (2001, 2003, in press)—the Obsessive Beliefs Questionnaire (OBQ) and Interpretation of Intrusions Inventory (III)—assess many of the OCD-related cognitive distortions discussed in chapter 3. These two measures are reprinted in Appendix F. Other questionnaires, as described next, have been devised to identify cognitions associated with specific OCD symptom dimensions.

Contamination.   The cognitive basis of contamination symptoms is the belief that feared contaminants pose a significant threat to one's physical or mental well-being, or pose a significant social threat. Moreover, patients may believe they are especially vulnerable to harmful effects of contaminants, and that unsafe levels of contamination are easily transmitted to oneself or to others (Rachman & Hodgson, 1980). Many, but not all, individuals with contamination symptoms overestimate the probability and severity of becoming ill or spreading illnesses to others (Jones & Menzies, 1997a, 1997b). Other patients describe disgust (Tolin, Woods, & Abramowitz, in press) or imperfection associated with their contamination concerns and fear that the associated distress will persist indefinitely or increase to harmful levels if action is not taken to remove feared contaminants and restore a "perfect state of cleanliness." The responsibility–threat estimation subscale of the OBQ measures the tendency to overestimate the probability and severity of danger as well as responsibility for spreading illness to others. The Disgust Scale (Haidt, McCauley, & Rozin, 1994) assesses sensitivity to disgust-evoking stimuli.

Harming.   Intolerance of uncertainty regarding feared situations plays a role in nearly all OCD symptom dimensions, but is most prominent in obsessional thoughts and doubts about harm and mistakes. That is, people with this symptom presentation often fear that because harm could occur (no matter how slim the possibility), they must act to prevent it or face full responsibility for its cause (e.g., "I can't take the chance that the feared outcome will occur"). The probability and severity of feared negative outcomes are also overestimated. Sometimes, fear is associated with uncertainty regarding negative consequences that might occur in the distant future, or that can never be confirmed or disconfirmed (e.g., getting cancer in old age, going to hell when one dies). Several self-report measures can be used to assess the catastrophic cognitions associated with the harming dimension. The Responsibility Attitudes Questionnaire, which measures general beliefs about responsibility, and the Responsibility Interpretations Questionnaire, which measures specific interpretations of intrusive thoughts about harm, are extremely useful and can be found in an article by Salkovskis et al. (2000). For patients with scrupulous doubts, the Penn Inventory of Scrupulosity (reprinted in Abramowitz, Huppert, et al., 2002) assesses the fear of committing sins and catastrophic beliefs about divine punishment.

Incompleteness.   Obsessions involving the need for symmetry and order are often mediated by the need to have things perfect, balanced, or completely under control, or by what more recently have been termed *not just right experiences* (NJREs; Coles, Frost, Heimberg, & Rheaume, 2003). Some patients fear that the sense of uneasiness over having things incomplete will persist indefinitely or increase to unmanageable levels and result in psychological harm. Coles, Frost, Heimberg, and Rheaume (2003) developed the NJRE questionnaire, which assesses the presence of such experiences (e.g., "When hanging a picture on the wall I have had the sensation that it did not look just right"). For a minority of patients, responsibility cognitions and intolerance of uncertainty mediate incompleteness symptoms. Such individuals associate NJREs with an increased chance that disastrous consequences (e.g., bad luck, accidents, death) will befall themselves or their loved ones.

Unacceptable Thoughts and Covert Rituals. Intrusive blasphemous, violent, or sexual ideas, images, and impulses are often catastrophically appraised as personally significant and indicators of immorality, depravity, perversion, evil, dangerousness, or insanity. Cognitive distortions include "only cruel, maleficent people think about hurting loved ones," "If I think about what my grandparents look like naked, it means I am a depraved, perverted, 'freak,'" and "My blasphemous thoughts mean that I am an utter disgrace to God." Patients might also believe that their violent thoughts, if not kept in check, will lead to action: "Because I think about stabbing my wife in her sleep, I am likely to do it," or "If I don't control my sexual thoughts, I will become a rapist." The Importance/Control of Thoughts subscale of the OBQ, and the Thought–Action Fusion Scale (Shafran et al., 1996), are excellent self-report instruments for assessing the belief that thoughts are psychologically equivalent to the corresponding actions (moral TAF), and that thoughts about negative events increase the likelihood of such events and should therefore be controlled (likelihood TAF).

Identifying Responses to Obsessional Stimuli (Safety Behaviors)

Next, the focus shifts to assessing the deliberate responses that patients perform to reduce obsessional discomfort, or evade it altogether; namely avoidance, compulsive rituals, and other neutralizing strategies. These safety-seeking behaviors arise from the catastrophic beliefs and perceptions described in the preceding section. For example, avoidance of public bathrooms is motivated by the fear of illnesses. Urges to check the roadside for dead bodies are motivated by intolerance of uncertainty regarding culpability for hit-and-run accidents. Mental rituals to neutralize violent obsessions are motivated by the belief that violent thoughts are equivalent to violent behavior and must be controlled (i.e., TAF). As these examples illustrate, the patterns of thinking and behavior in OCD are meaningful and internally consistent to the patient (after all, who wouldn't try to dismiss thoughts of violence if they believed such thoughts lead to violent actions). Thus, from within the context of the patient's thinking, the therapist can often anticipate what safety-seeking behavior is used in a given situation (a rhetorical move that may increase the patient's confidence).

Therapist: When you park the car, do you always have to make sure the odometer ends in an even number?

Patient: Yeah. How did you know?

Therapist: Well, you said that you're afraid odd numbers will lead to bad luck. So, it makes sense that you would avoid them. Lots of people with OCD do this.

Patient: But I waste so much time doing that. I mean, it's not really logical, is it?

Therapist: That's what OCD is all about. It has its own logic that it tricks you into following.

Patient: Wow. I feel like you really understand my problem. I really think you're going to be able to help me.

Avoidance, rituals, and other neutralizing strategies are targeted in treatment not only because they are wasteful and interfere with daily functioning, but because they prevent extinction and hinder the correction of catastrophic beliefs (see chapter 4). Clinicians should inquire about how the patient interprets the outcome of his or her avoidance and safety-seeking maneuvers. Often, the lack of a disastrous outcome is perceived as a near miss, implying that safety seeking prevented the harm (e.g., "I would have become ill if I hadn't washed my hands," or "If I didn't stop on an even number, something bad would have happened"). Accordingly, to reduce obsessional fear, all of these responses must be eliminated in CBT (i.e., response prevention).

The initial consultation should yield information about the patient's main rituals and areas of avoidance. However, it is unusual for individuals to spontaneously describe their full array of safety-seeking behaviors during the initial assessment. Some avoidance, mental rituals, and neutralizing strategies might be so subtle or routine that they are not recognized as part of OCD. To facilitate reporting of these covert and surreptitious responses, the therapist should introduce the concepts of avoidance and safety seeking as protective responses to obsessional fear. Patients should be given examples of these strategies and encouraged throughout assessment and treatment to report any behaviors or mental strategies performed with the intent of alleviating obsessional distress. To this end, good assessment questions include the following:

- What else do you do when confronted with situations and thoughts that evoke obsessive fears?
- When you're feeling anxious about (fill in obsessional fear), how do you reduce your distress?

Passive Avoidance

Passive avoidance, which is defined as the intentional failure to engage in an objectively low-risk activity, can often be predicted from obsessional cues and catastrophic beliefs. For example, fears of corpses might lead to avoidance of funerals; fears of thoughts about molesting children might lead to staying away from playgrounds; fear of AIDS often leads to avoidance of anything red (which might be blood); fears of bad luck may result in avoidance of the number 13; and so on. Some patients ask others to engage in avoidance, such as in the case of a man who forbid his wife to shop in a certain "contaminated" food store. Good questions for patients include the following:

- What kinds of things do you not do because of your obsessional fears?
- Do you ask other people to avoid certain situations for you?

The clinician should feel free to ask about additional avoidance strategies if there is good reason to think they might be present; for example:

- I know you are afraid of touching the floor. Do you also avoid touching shoes because of this?

Contamination.   Common examples include avoidance of shoes, floors, unknown substances of particular colors (e.g., red spots), and particular surfaces (railings, door handles), people, and animals. This may include touching the "least used" part of the door handle, using a sleeve or tissue to push the elevator button, or squatting above the toilet seat. In more severe cases avoidance extends to secondary and tertiary (and so on) sources, leaving the patient with few "safe" or "clean" areas in which to function freely. One example is a man who feared being poisoned by lawn chemicals such as fertilizer. During spring he could not leave his home, and moreover, he worried that items brought into his house might contain traces of harmful lawn chemicals that were in the air. The patient had also established "safety zones" in his home where contaminated items (and people) from outside were not allowed unless they had been thoroughly washed (or had recently showered). All other "contaminated" parts of the home were avoided.

Harming.   Avoidance in this symptom presentation might involve situations and activities in which the person perceives that he or she could be responsible for causing or preventing for harm, or which evoke thoughts of feared consequences. The clinician should use knowledge of situational triggers and obsessional thoughts to guide assessment. Typical examples include driving, using the oven, writing bank checks, reading articles about disasters or illnesses, and being in charge of locking up the house (e.g., the last person to go to bed or to leave the house). Some avoidance is more subtle, such as not driving near school buses for fear of hitting children. One patient avoided listening to music or watching television while she wrote or typed on the computer because she was afraid that the distraction would lead to mistakenly writing obscenities. Another tried to avoid exposure to all obscene words or gestures for fear that he might use them at inappropriate times.

Incompleteness. The purpose of avoidance in the incompleteness dimension is often to reduce the need for rituals. Patients may avoid certain rooms knowing that entering them would evoke urges to rearrange objects, create "balance," or perform counting rituals. If perfectionism is the problem, one might avoid buying new items to prevent having to continually work on their upkeep. In a particularly severe case, a patient isolated himself as much as possible because of his persistent urges to mentally count letters in words, and words in sentences that he read or heard.

Unacceptable Thoughts and Covert Rituals. Patients with unacceptable, repugnant thoughts, images, or impulses often do what they can to avoid stimuli that trigger such thoughts. They may also avoid situations in which they fear acting on unwanted impulses. For violent or aggressive obsessions this includes potential weapons (knives, guns, baseball bats) and victims (babies, the elderly); police; words associated with violence (*blood, murder*); and places, pictures, shows or movies, or news articles associated with harm or violence. Depending on content, avoidance related to sexual thoughts might include hetero- or homoerotic material, gay bars, sexually provocative people (of either sex), gym locker rooms, changing diapers, noticing people's crotch or breasts, shows about pedophiles or rapists, or words like *rape* or *bestiality*. People with blasphemous obsessions may avoid places of worship for fear of committing blasphemy there, or religious objects for fear of offending God. Words such as *hell, devil, Satan,* or curse words may also be avoided.

Because of her contamination fears, Susan T. avoided touching most surfaces that other people often touch, including handrails, door handles, public telephones, and other people's writing implements. Public restrooms were a particular problem, as were gym locker rooms because of the sweat. This presented problems at school, where Susan suspected that a number of her students did not adequately wash themselves after using the bathroom or after their physical education class. Thus, items belonging to these children (and their close friends) were also avoided. In addition, Susan sometimes avoided holding or bathing her daughter, Jennifer, because of the fear of acting on intrusive violent thoughts.

Rituals

Most patients exhibit multiple types of rituals. Some of these could be described as compulsive—highly repetitive or performed according to strict rules (e.g., turning the light on and off 15 times), whereas others are brief and less rule-bound (e.g., using a "good image" to cancel a "bad image"). The clinician should obtain information about the frequency and duration of each ritual. Is the same ritual used each time a particular obsession arises? How does the patient know when it is safe to stop the ritual? Clinicians should also ask for a complete description of each ritual, including a demonstration (when practical) if the verbal description is unclear. Some rituals may be embarrassing to describe, such as excessive wiping after using the toilet. If this appears to be the case, the therapist should inquire in an understanding yet straightforward way; for example, "Many people with fears of bodily waste take a lot of time using the bathroom because they have to make sure they are entirely clean. Is that a problem for you? Would you feel comfortable describing what you do?"

Clinicians should also assess the functional relationship between rituals and obsessional fear. Recall that in general, rituals are deliberate attempts to escape from anxiety or prevent feared consequences. Inquiry might include questions such as these:

- How do you feel after you have checked?
- When you finish washing your hands, how do you feel about the risk of getting sick or making other people sick?
- How do you think canceling out the blasphemous thoughts affects your moral standing?

Contamination. Susan T.'s decontamination rituals were typical of patients with this symptom presentation: excessive hand washing, showering, and toilet routines; cleaning inanimate objects such as the shower stall, toilet, clothes, or items brought into the home; and using barriers when touching contaminated objects (this may be considered avoidance or ritualistic). Like many patients, Susan had a specific routine for washing herself in the shower and this included counting the number of times she washed various body parts. Some patients involve others in decontamination rituals, such as one woman who had her husband and children change their clothes when they entered the home. As mentioned previously, along with specifics of each ritual (time spent, frequency), it is important to assess stopping rules; that is, how does the patient know when he or she can stop washing or cleaning?

Harming. Checking is the chief method of relieving anxiety and uncertainty regarding obsessions of responsibility for causing or preventing harm. Susan often rechecked the grades she assigned to students for fear that she had made errors. Before leaving the house and going to bed, she repeatedly checked that appliances were off to prevent fires. Clinicians should clarify the frequency and duration of checking rituals; Susan's routine often took up to 30 minutes and she had to repeat these rituals if any intrusive doubts about mistakes occurred during this routine. Other common examples include checking that other people have not been hurt (e.g., looking for bodies on the roadside, watching the news for stories of hit-and-run accidents), checking for egregious oversights (e.g., "Did I put poison in the baby's food?" "Did I write 'f—- you' instead of 'thank you'?"), checking to prevent loss (e.g., of one's wallet), checking that one has been understood by others, and repeatedly asking others for reassurance or clarification. The involvement of others in checking rituals should be assessed. Susan, like many patients, often asked her husband to recheck that appliances were safely off. Other patients repeatedly telephone loved ones to make sure they are safe—thus the other person is involved by simply answering the phone.

Some individuals use repeating or ordering rituals to reduce doubts about responsibility for harm. For example, one man had to put his clothes on the "right way," otherwise he feared his parents would die in a car accident. Often he would dress and undress multiple times because he did not feel the ritual had been done properly. Unlike with checking, the link between repeating rituals and fears of disasters is not readily apparent and may seem magical. Other examples include having to tap a certain number of times or go through doorways the "correct" way to prevent some sort of harmful idea that comes to mind. In some instances, the number of times the ritual can (or cannot) be performed is determined by lucky or unlucky numbers (e.g., even numbers, multiples of 5). Thus, assessment should also include questions about the details of counting and numbers with special significance.

Incompleteness. In this symptom dimension, compulsions are performed primarily to achieve order, achieve perfection, and reduce NJREs; they might not be limited to manipulating objects. For example, one patient who heard or read the word *left* felt a strong urge to hear or read the word *right* (and vice versa). Other examples include the need to mentally count letters in words (or words in sentences), to look or stare at certain points in space to establish symmetry, and the urge to rewrite things until they look balanced or perfect.

Unacceptable Thoughts and Covert Rituals.   Identifying covert rituals requires careful inquiry because these phenomena are often subtle and may occur exclusively in the patient's mind. When Susan's violent obsessional thoughts of harming her daughter evoked anxiety, she resorted to "canceling out" these thoughts with another thought. Specifically, she repeated the following prayer to herself seven times: "Please God, I pray to thee, don't let me harm my daughter." It bears emphasizing here that clinicians must avoid labeling mental rituals as obsessions simply because they are cognitive events. Recall that whereas obsessions are involuntary thoughts that evoke distress, mental compulsions (like their behavioral counterparts) involve purposeful thinking (i.e., mental behavior) that is intended to reduce distress.

Mental rituals can be assessed straightforwardly by asking questions such as, "Sometimes people with OCD use mental strategies in response to their recurring unwanted distressing thoughts. Do you ever use any strategies like that?" Providing examples may elicit additional information: "A common mental ritual is to 'cancel out' obsessions by repeating special 'safe' words, phrases, or images to yourself. Do you ever do this?" Some patients mentally review their behavior or analyze particular events over and over to reassure themselves of the invalidity of intrusive thoughts (e.g., trying to reason through whether or not one's intrusive doubts really mean they do not believe in God). A variation is *testing*, wherein the person tries to collect some sort of evidence that feared consequences are improbable. For example, one man with intrusive doubts about the nature of his sexuality (he feared he was homosexual) repeatedly looked at other men's buttocks and focused attention on his internal state to determine whether he felt sexually aroused.

Patients with unacceptable thoughts may use overt rituals as well, such as checking for harm or asking for assurance. We have even observed patients who wash their unacceptable thoughts away as if feeling contaminated by them. This highlights the importance of assessing the idiosyncratic cognitive links between obsessions and rituals. Here, useful questions include the following:

- What else do you do when these unwanted thoughts come to mind?
- Why does doing that ritual make you feel better?

Covert Neutralizing

Most neutralization attempts are brief and unobservable; this inaccessibility makes them a challenge for many clinicians to recognize. Because neutralization is functionally similar to compulsive rituals—both produce short-term anxiety reduction yet reinforce obsessional beliefs in the long term—it must be a target of therapy. Freeston, Ladouceur, Provencher, and Blais (1995) have developed an interview to assess a variety of neutralization strategies used with obsessional thoughts, which is reprinted in Appendix G. The interview allows the clinician to obtain data on the context in which specific neutralizing strategies are used, as well as on the perceived effectiveness of each strategy.

Susan reported two of the most common neutralizing strategies: thought suppression and concealment. She attempted to suppress intrusive thoughts about harming her infant whenever they came to mind. Her reasons for suppression attempts included concern that she might act on the thought if it remained in her mind, and that she felt like a terrible mother for thinking such thoughts. In general, Susan said that her suppression attempts did not work well. Moreover, she reported feeling that her failure to dismiss "bad" thoughts meant she really was becoming a violent person. Susan concealed her obsessional thoughts about harm and mistakes from others because she was concerned that others would think she was a bad mother or an incompetent teacher if they knew the kinds of thoughts she had. She was also concerned that she was the only person who thought this way, and believed that verbalizing these thoughts might somehow bring her closer to acting on them (i.e., "If I talk about it, I am one step closer to doing it").

SELF-MONITORING OF SAFETY BEHAVIORS

Once information gathering is initiated, the patient is introduced to self-monitoring. Asking patients to keep a log of their symptoms is a standard procedure in virtually all forms of CBT. In the treatment of OCD, self-monitoring involves recording instances of obsessional fear, avoidance, and safety behaviors as they occur in real time. It is an important tool because it furnishes the patient and clinician with precise information about the situational cues, frequency, intensity, and duration of these symptoms. For patients with multiple symptom dimensions, one or two particularly prominent symptom themes can be chosen for self-monitoring. A model form for self-monitoring appears in Fig. 8.2. Clinicians can review the form with patients by having them record actual recent examples. Because it can be an arduous task, some patients have difficulty with adherence to self-monitoring. It is therefore essential to acknowledge that the exercise requires substantial effort. Nevertheless, it is an important component of treatment. A cogent rationale for self-monitoring should be presented that underscores the need for accurate and timely recording of symptoms. Patients should be instructed to keep the form with them at all

SELF-MONITORING FORM

Date	Time	Situation or intrusive thought (brief description)	Fear level (0-100)	Avoidance or safety behavior	Minutes (if ritual)

FIG. 8.2.   Example of a self-monitoring form.

times, rather than waiting until the end of the day (or immediately before the next session) to try to recall all instances of safety behaviors. Susan T.'s therapist gave the following explanation:

Therapist: I realize that doing self-monitoring might seem demanding. After all, you probably have never done this kind of exercise before. Let me give you three reasons why self-monitoring is an important part of treatment. First, it will give us accurate information about the problems you are having with OCD in your daily routine. In other words, it will tell us about the various triggers and thoughts that evoke compulsive rituals and how much time these problems take up. Second, it will help us assess your improvement. In other words, toward the end of therapy we can look back and examine how much less you are ritualizing. Finally, self-monitoring can actually help you reduce your OCD symptoms right away. That is, many people say that just knowing they have to write it down helps them resist doing rituals. So, I want you to do an honest job and I will be looking forward to seeing your completed forms at the beginning of the next session. In fact, the first thing we will do next time will be to review your forms.

When examining the completed self-monitoring form, the clinician should stop to ask the patient to review a few exemplary episodes in greater detail. Critical information for the clinician to acquire includes how obsessional fear is triggered (e.g., "What is it about driving that worries you?"), what situations are avoided (e.g., "Do you always avoid driving near school buses?"), and why ("What do you think might happen if you drove behind a school bus?"). Also, how does the patient respond to obsessional fear ("What else, besides checking, do you do to reduce your fears of molesting a child?"). Self-monitoring aids the clarification of internally consistent associations among the patient's fear, avoidance, and rituals. These associations should be clear to the therapist; if they are not, further examples should be reviewed until they are clarified. Situations and thoughts that trigger rituals should be considered for inclusion as exposure exercises (see chapter 10).

CASE FORMULATION

At the end of the functional assessment, the therapist should have the information necessary to construct an individualized model of the patient's specific OCD symptoms. This *case formulation* incorporates the content of obsessions, appraisals, and safety behaviors, as well as the processes that maintain these symptoms. The formulation must be credible to the patient and provide a rationale for using CBT procedures such as exposure, response prevention, and cognitive therapy to reverse the maintenance processes.

Constructing an Individualized Formulation

The case formulation is synthesized from information collected during the functional assessment. A straightforward approach is to begin by listing (a) the situations and thoughts that trigger obsessional fear, (b) the associated dysfunctional and catastrophic misinterpretations, and (c) safety-seeking behaviors. Next, based on the cognitive-behavioral model of OCD (see chapters 3 and 4), derive links between these content-related phenomena with arrows to indicate the influence of maintenance processes on the symptoms and cognitions. It is smart to involve the patient in developing the formulation to impart a collaborative ownership of the model. Sketching the model for the patient to see (e.g., on a whiteboard) and inviting his or her input conveys that conceptualization and treatment planning are open processes (as opposed to secretive). This is likely to foster buy-in to the model and the recommended treatment strategies.

A case formulation of Susan's main OCD symptoms appears in Fig. 8.3. Stimuli such as bathrooms and certain "dirty" students from her class triggered obsessional thoughts of contamination. Obsessional doubts about mistakes were evoked when grading students' papers and entering these grades into the computer. The sight of knives, other sharp objects, and situations such as giving Jennifer a bath precipitated intrusive violent ideas of harming this child. Susan reported perceiving trigger situations as overly dangerous and risky. On measures of OCD-related cognitive distortions (e.g., the III and OBQ), she endorsed the tendency to misinterpret the presence and meaning of her intrusive thoughts and impulses as overly significant and needing to be controlled. She also evidenced overestimates of threat, an inflated sense of responsibility for causing and preventing harm, and an intolerance of uncertainty.

For some patients it is possible to draw hypotheses about the origins of dysfunctional cognitions, although this is not a required element of the case formulation. The cognitive-behavioral model suggests that the ways in which Susan perceived obsessional situations and thoughts might have been influenced by early experiences that produced relatively stable beliefs about her self and the world (including her thoughts). For example, Susan said that when she was a child her mother had repeatedly warned her against wishing bad things on people because such wishes might come true. Perhaps such experiences fostered strong beliefs (i.e., core beliefs) that merely thinking about something could influence the outside world, or that thoughts about harmful circumstances are equivalent to the corresponding

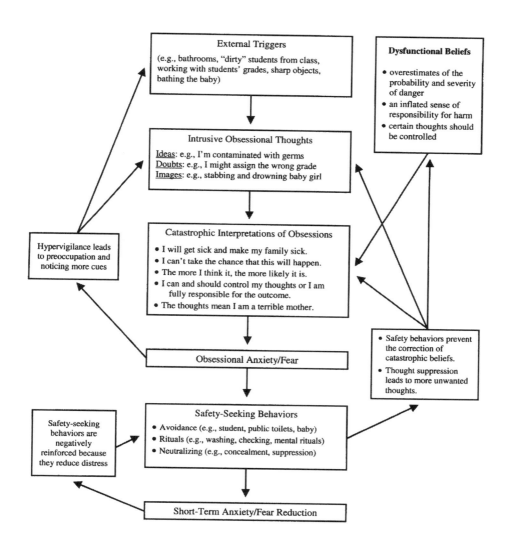

FIG. 8.3. Case formulation for Susan T.'s OCD symptoms.

events. This would explain, for example, why Susan feels highly responsible for preventing harmful consequences that she merely thinks about.

Although some patients might seem to gain fulfillment by speculating about the possible origins of their OCD symptoms, discussions of this nature should be kept to a minimum because such speculations can never be verified and contribute little in CBT. Moreover, the effectiveness of CBT techniques depends not on an awareness of causal factors, but instead, on an understanding of the processes that lead to the persistence of such symptoms. Another trap to avoid is that of speculating about what may have influenced the content of obsessional thoughts themselves; for example, whether traumatic childhood experiences, such as sexual abuse, led to obsessions about certain topics (e.g., sexual obsessions). Recall that cognitive-behavioral models assume that how one appraises and responds to obsessional thoughts is more important than the content of the intrusions themselves.

Assessment revealed a number of factors that contributed to the persistence of Susan's obsessional fears. First, safety-seeking responses to obsessional distress, such as avoidance, rituals, and other neutralizing behavior (e.g., concealment), prevented her anxiogenic beliefs and misperceptions from self-correcting. For example, Susan credited her compulsive hand washing, rather than a low probability of harm, with preventing her from becoming ill when exposed to feared contaminants. Similarly, she believed that her failure to stab her daughter was due to her ritualistic prayer and avoidance, rather than to the fact that she is a gentle person with good judgment. Because these safety behavior responses resulted in immediate (albeit temporary) anxiety reduction, their use was reinforced.

According to the cognitive-behavioral theory, Susan's anxious mood and attempts to suppress unwanted thoughts also contributed to the persistence of obsessions. As part of her body's normal anxiety response (i.e., the flight-or-flight response) she became hypervigilant and preoccupied with triggers and obsessional thoughts. Thought suppression habits led to a paradoxical increase in unwanted thoughts, which, in the context of beliefs about the necessity of controlling such thoughts, was misperceived as further evidence of danger (e.g., "When I try to dismiss the thoughts, they come back—there must really be something terribly wrong").

Deriving a Treatment Plan Based on the Formulation

Developing a patient-specific case formulation is important because it clarifies the targets of CBT and specifies an internally consistent relationship between the symptoms and treatment. Susan's case formulation, which is prototypical of individuals with OCD, suggests that effective treatment must accomplish a number of goals. First, Susan must be taught to understand her symptoms according to the formulation. If she accepts this conceptual model, it is likely that she will work with the therapist to more fully engage in office-based and homework treatment procedures. Second, Susan must be trained to distinguish between intrusive obsessional thoughts and the appraisals or interpretations of these stimuli. Third, Susan must learn to challenge the catastrophic beliefs and interpretations of obsessional stimuli that lead to anxiety, and develop more realistic and healthier ways of thinking. Fourth, avoidance and other maladaptive habitual responses to obsessional fear (i.e., compulsive rituals and neutralization) must be replaced with healthier responses that promote the correction of dysfunctional catastrophic thinking and the extinction of obsessional fear. The implementation of treatment procedures that are used to achieve these goals is described in the next several chapters.

9

Cognitive Therapy: Education and Encouragement

The first cognitive theorist, in a manner of speaking, was the Roman (Greek-born) slave and Stoic philosopher Epictetus (55–135 AD). He is credited with introducing the idea that although we do not always have control over the positive and negative circumstances and events that occur in our lives, we can control how we think about these situations. Furthermore, he proposed that negative emotional states such as depression and anxiety are caused not by situations themselves, but instead by overly negative or exaggerated (maladaptive) interpretations of situations. The implication here is that we can gain mastery over our emotions by learning to interpret events and situations—even negative ones—in adaptive (although not necessarily positive) ways. However, what to Epictetus and the Stoics was self-evident—and what has been demonstrated again and again by scientific study (e.g., Frost & Steketee, 2002)—is often overlooked by individuals with OCD who may seek to blame their troubles on things such as genetics, abnormal brain chemistry, bad parenting, and traumatic experiences. The reason for this oversight is obvious—interpretations are transient, nebulous, and not readily observable. They occur rapidly and with such subtlety that many people hardly notice them at all. Although it may be difficult for patients to see that the faint voice they hear in their heads is the real culprit, overcoming OCD ultimately requires changing how one interprets key internal (mental) and environmental stimuli.

Cognitive therapy (CT) techniques for OCD are concerned with the identification and correction of dysfunctional beliefs about obsessional stimuli that, according to the cognitive-behavioral model, lead to obsessional fear and maladaptive responses such as avoidance and safety behaviors. CT is educational. To a degree it assumes that if the patient knew the truth about the low probability of harm associated with obsessional stimuli, he or she would not have obsessional problems. Fear-evoking stimuli would be perceived as nonthreatening and safety-seeking behavior would be unnecessary—it would indeed be redundant.

What is the role of CT in CBT? As I reviewed in chapter 5, research indicates that cognitive techniques by themselves have limited efficacy in reducing OCD symptoms. The most powerful treatment procedures for reducing OCD are exposure and response prevention. However, this does not mean that CT elements do not contribute to treatment outcome. Indeed, cognitive techniques can play a substantial role in facilitating assessment, preventing premature discontinuation, and maximizing adherence with difficult ERP exercises (Kozak & Coles, 2005; Salkovskis & Warwick, 1985; Vogel et al., 2004). In particular, CT can help weaken dysfunctional catastrophic beliefs and appraisals to the point that the patient can more easily engage in and profit from exposure exercises. Additionally, CT helps with the development of a trusting therapeutic relationship, the importance of which is often underestimated in exposure therapy. Thus, clinicians should view the cognitive techniques described in this chapter as setting the table for therapeutic exposure.

This chapter begins with a description of general stylistic issues to be considered when using cognitive interventions. Next, several practical CT techniques for facilitating belief change and engagement in ERP are described. The chapter concludes with discussions about when it is appropriate to use these techniques.

STYLISTIC CONSIDERATIONS

Two general styles of CT are used in the treatment of OCD: didactic presentation of psychoeducational material and Socratic dialogue regarding mistaken beliefs. Often the therapist switches back and forth between the two styles as both are verbal methods and can easily be incorporated into discussion. I mentioned earlier that CT is educational; indeed, most patients hold an incomplete understanding of the intricacies of their OCD symptoms. They do not realize that intrusive senseless thoughts are normal, universal experiences; that beliefs cause anxiety; and that safety behaviors used to deal with obsessional anxiety are counterproductive. Patients undergoing CBT must be taught to view their problem according to this model because it is the conceptual basis of treatment. If the patient is not socialized to this model properly, he or she may reluctantly go along with some elements of therapy, but refuse to sufficiently engage in the more challenging components such as ERP. Helping patients to think about their own OCD symptoms along the lines of the cognitive-behavioral model also helps solidify a collaborative therapeutic relationship (i.e., the patient and therapist are working together as a team).

Psychoeducation

During the initial therapy sessions, psychoeducation should focus on the following points:

- Intrusive thoughts are normal experiences.
- Catastrophic thinking leads to obsessional anxiety and compulsive (neutralizing) behavior.
- Avoidance, compulsive rituals, and neutralizing strengthen obsessional fears
- Correcting faulty thinking and appraisals, and dropping safety-seeking behaviors, will lead to a reduction in obsessional fear.

The presentation of psychoeducational material should be preceded by a discussion of the patient's preexisting understanding of his or her problem. This allows the new information to be used to correct particular inaccuracies, rather than acting as general reassurance.

The Socratic Style

The Socratic style employs open-ended questions, reflective listening, and summary statements that are all aimed to help the patient gain greater perspective on his or her dysfunctional beliefs and to foster the consideration of suitable alternatives. As Wells (1997) has pointed out, appropriate open ended questions include those that:

- Open up a particular area of exploration (e.g., "What is it like for you when you have to use the bathroom?").
- Clarify a point of view (e.g., "When you say you 'think you will get sick,' what particular illnesses do you have in mind?")
- Probe for worst case scenarios (e.g., "What's the worst thing you image happening if you don't wash your hands after using the bathroom?").

In reflective listening, the therapist reflects what the patient has said with a slight degree of reframing or modification for the sake of clarifying the patient's point of view. This also communicates the therapist's respect for the patient and the therapeutic relationship, and can be used to selectively reinforce ideas that the patient expresses (Taylor & Asmundson, 2004). For example:

Patient: After I use the bathroom I spend 10 minutes washing my hands to make sure all the germs are washed away.
Therapist: So, after urinating, you feel you have to wash your hands to prevent illness.

and

Patient: If I think that maybe I hit someone with my car, I have to drive back and check the road to be sure nothing happened.
Therapist: So, the way you are responding when you have intrusive doubts is by checking—as if the doubts were really true.

Summary statements further facilitate reflection on the dialogue and incorporate a follow-up question:

- So, you avoid public bathrooms because you are afraid of catching diseases from toilet seats. I wonder how you think people who don't avoid public bathrooms feel about toilet seats?
- Have you ever actually hit someone with your car? Do you think you would know if it actually happened? What might that be like?

It is important for the therapist to demonstrate curiosity and a genuine interest in learning how the patient experiences his or her world. The patient should never feel interrogated or put in the position of wanting to defend his or her erroneous beliefs.

Individuals with OCD, particularly those with insight into the senselessness of their symptoms, are often ambivalent about their obsessional fears and compulsive urges. Although at times they are fearful of catastrophic consequences, they would also like to believe that such outcomes are improbable. The fact that most patients at one time or another have successfully resisted the urge to ritualize suggests that they have thought about the senselessness of their fears and necessity of safety behaviors (e.g., "Maybe I don't need to change my clothes every time after I use the bathroom"). It is helpful for the therapist to amplify the patient's ambivalence and elicit a sense of cognitive dissonance because this will foster open-mindedness and willingness to test (and change) dysfunctional beliefs. Importantly, instead of forcefully telling the patient that he or she is wrong about the probability of disastrous consequences or the meaning of obsessional thoughts, the therapist should carefully help the patient draw his or her own conclusions and generate more reasonable alternative beliefs based on any available evidence. Forcefully trying to convince the patient that he or she is wrong can backfire and cause the patient to defend his or her illogical position.

There is widespread agreement among cognitive-behavioral therapists concerning the importance of using Socratic methods whenever possible. Studies from the fields of clinical and social psychology demonstrate that people hold onto beliefs more strongly when the beliefs are self-generated as opposed to when they are spoon-fed to them didactically. Thus, although didactic psychoeducational procedures have their place in treatment, supplementary discussions of didactic material should be conducted by using Socratic questioning to lead the patient to the desirable conclusions. The examples in Table 9.1 illustrate the differences between a didactic style and a Socratic style.

NORMALIZING OBSESSIONAL THOUGHTS

As I have alluded to in previous chapters, numerous studies (e.g., Rachman & de Silva, 1978) show that intrusive thoughts are normal experiences: Over 90% of the general public reports them. In OCD, however, the presence and content of these thoughts is misinterpreted as significant and threatening. Patients often incorrectly feel they are mad, bad, or dangerous for having such thoughts. Therefore, time should be taken to describe the results from research on intrusive thoughts and present examples of "normal" intrusions. Therapists can review with patients Handout 9.1, which includes a list of intrusive thoughts reported by people without OCD. Patients who conceal their repugnant aggressive, sexual, or religious obsessions should be encouraged to discuss these thoughts without restraint in recognition that these are normal experiences. It may be helpful for the therapist to model this behavior by openly sharing some of his or her own intrusive thoughts.

Most patients are at once surprised and relieved to learn that everybody has intrusive thoughts. Many report that this gives them some reassurance that they are not "going crazy" or suffering from a chemical imbalance of the brain. Although the occasional patient rejects this explanation, most begin to challenge the dysfunctional ways they have been interpreting their obsessions and readily adopt a less threatening view. For those who are less eager to embrace this account, the therapist can show research articles documenting the frequency of normal intrusions (in Rachman & deSilva's [1978] article in the journal *Behaviour Research and Therapy,* similarities be-

TABLE 9.1
Examples of Didactic and Socratic Styles
of Conveying Therapeutic Information

Example 1: Obsessional thoughts are normal phenomena.

Didactic style

- Everyone has intrusive, upsetting, unwanted thoughts. In fact, people without OCD experience the same kinds of unwanted thoughts as do people with OCD. This is important because it means that people with OCD are not "abnormal"; their thoughts are no different than people without OCD. The difference is that people with OCD interpret unwanted upsetting thoughts as very significant.

Socratic style

- Are you abnormal because you have unwanted thoughts?
- Are unwanted thoughts always dangerous?
- Can you think of any upsetting thoughts you have had that did not cause problems for you?
- What do you tell yourself about the intrusive thoughts that might make them seem threatening?

Example 2: Doing safety behaviors prevents one from learning that his or her obsessional fears are irrational.

Didactic style

- When you unplug appliances, such as the toaster, and check that they remain unplugged, it prevents you from learning that your fears of starting fires are unrealistic.

Socratic style

- When you see that the appliances are unplugged, what do you think afterward?
- What does checking make you think about the fact that your house has not burned down?
- Do you attribute the fact that there has not been a fire to your keeping the toaster unplugged, or to the possibility that your thoughts about fires are not necessarily realistic?

tween normal and abnormal obsessions are spelled out with exceptional clarity). Another strategy is to suggest that the patient take a poll by asking 10 acquaintances whether they sometimes experience intrusive or upsetting thoughts.

One question that often arises from this discussion is, "Why do people have strange negative unwanted thoughts in the first place?" To address this issue it may be useful to explain that the human brain is highly devel-

Unwanted Thoughts

Intrusive thoughts are entirely normal experiences. We know this because virtually everyone, whether or not they have OCD, has these kinds of thoughts from time to time. Below are examples of intrusions reported by people **without** OCD.

Thought of jumping from a high place like a building
Thought of receiving the news that my husband has been killed
Image of the baby being thrown down stairs
Thought of having a terrible disease like cancer or AIDS
Thought of jumping in front of a fast-moving car
Impulse to jump on the train tracks as a train comes into station
Idea of attacking an elderly person that I love
Thought of leaving the cat in the fridge
Impulse to run over a pedestrian who walks too slow
Thought of harming someone who does not deserve it
Thought of wishing that a person would die
Thought that the baby will die in his crib
Image of taking a wine bottle and threatening someone in the family
Imagining what it would be like if my brother died
Thought of decapitating the baby with a butcher knife
Thought of catching diseases from various people or places
Thought of deliberately crashing the car into a tree or telephone pole
Thought of dropping the baby
Thought of putting the baby in the microwave
Thought that my hands are contaminated after using the bathroom
Thoughts that run contrary to my moral or religious beliefs
Thought of swearing rudely at someone I am not angry with
Idea that I could contaminate or poison my child's food
Thoughts of smashing a table full of crafts (at a market for e.g.) made of glass
Image of screaming harshly at my baby
Impulse to call my girlfriend and break up even though we are deeply in love
Thoughts of doing something embarrassing such as forgetting to wear a shirt
Thought to yell curse words loudly in a religious service
Thought that I left door unlocked
Thought that I left an appliance on and caused a fire
Thought about objects not arranged just right
Thought of my house getting broken into while I'm not home
Image of what someone's penis looks like
Image of my grandparents having sex
Sexual thought about someone other than my spouse
Thought of "unnatural" sexual acts
Impulse to inappropriately accost an obese person

Note: Compiled from Abramowitz et al. (2003); Rachman & deSilva (1978); and numerous personal communications with people who do not have OCD. Thanks to Sabine Wilhelm, PhD.

Handout 9.1. List of intrusive thoughts collected from nonpatients.

oped and capable of enormous creativity. Therefore we are able to imagine all kinds of scenarios—some pleasant, others unpleasant. Think of how often we daydream of winning the lottery or scoring the winning touchdown in the Super Bowl. Just as our "thought generator" produces positive thoughts that are unlikely to come true, it can also spawn senseless and unpleasant thoughts. A related point to be underscored is that the aim of therapy is not to eliminate obsessional thoughts altogether, but rather to reduce the amount of distress associated with these normally occurring experiences. Once intrusive thoughts are no longer perceived as threatening, it will not matter when or how frequently they occur.

Normalizing intrusive thoughts is useful for individuals with any symptom dimension, although its most straightforward application is in the case of unacceptable aggressive, blasphemous, and sexual obsessions, and with intrusive doubts about making terrible mistakes and being held responsible for harm. For patients with contamination symptoms this exercise can be used to normalize images of germs (e.g., the feeling of doubt over whether one has microscopic organisms on his or her hands or face). One patient in our clinic, for example, reported recurrent images and ideas about his favorite possessions covered in germs. He considered these thoughts senseless and bizarre and was concerned there was something wrong with him for repeatedly thinking about such things. Senseless thoughts and ideas concerning order, symmetry, and exactness, such as the preference for even numbers or left–right balance, can also be normalized in this way.

Patients may allude to the fact that although everyone has intrusive thoughts, their own intrusions are more frequent, more distressing, and more intense compared to those of nonsufferers. Indeed this is true, and it is therefore important for patients to understand how normal, innocent intrusive thoughts escalate into severe recurrent obsessional preoccupations. Methods for presenting this information are described next.

PRESENTING THE COGNITIVE MODEL OF EMOTION

Beliefs Create Anxiety

The idea that emotional and behavioral responses are determined by one's beliefs and perceptions about situations and events should be revisited throughout treatment. This is the A-B-C model, wherein A is an *activating event* (or *antecedent*), B is a set of *beliefs* about A, and C is the emotional or behavioral *consequence* of B. It is the causal relationship between catastrophic thinking and strong emotional responses such as anxiety (the *B–C connection*) that must be clearly understood to provide an explanation for how obsessional anxiety arises. In short, the patient must recognize that the real problem is his or her dysfunctional beliefs about obsessional triggers and intrusive thoughts, not the (objectively safe) triggers and intrusions themselves.

Dysfunctional thinking may occur on two levels: automatic thoughts and dysfunctional assumptions. *Automatic thoughts* are in-situation interpretations and appraisals that go through a person's mind and provoke an emotional response. For example, when Susan T. approached a doorknob she would think, "What if someone with sweaty hands just touched this door? I will get sick." *Dysfunctional assumptions*, on the other hand, are general underlying (core) beliefs that people hold about themselves and the world that make them inclined to interpret specific situations and stimuli in a catastrophic manner. For example, the beliefs "I am highly susceptible to illnesses" and "public surfaces contain lots of dangerous germs" would make someone like Susan fearful if he or she had to touch surfaces that are often touched by others. As another example, the dysfunctional assumption "thinking about violence can lead to violence" led Susan to interpret her intrusive thoughts about hurting her infant as threatening and needing to be controlled (e.g., "I can't let myself think about this. I might kill Jennifer if I don't stop these thoughts."). Unlike automatic thoughts, dysfunctional assumptions usually do not enter a person's consciousness while he or she is in the anxiety-evoking situation. Instead, dysfunctional assumptions are best elicited through detailed assessment (as described in chapter 8).

Susan T.'s therapist introduced the A-B-C model and helped Susan understand how her beliefs and interpretations dictate her emotional and behavioral responses as follows:

Therapist: When something happens, we don't usually take the time to consider how much our beliefs and thoughts influence our emotional and behavioral reactions. For example, if I get nervous when I have to take a test, I might tell myself that "tests make me nervous." But actually, if I feel nervous over taking a test it is not really because of the test itself. The test can't make me nervous—it's a piece of paper. The reason I become nervous is that I am telling myself something threatening about the test—something like "I'll probably fail." So, I actually *make myself* nervous over tests. Do you see that?

Susan: Yes.

Therapist: Let's take another example of how our thoughts and beliefs influence our emotions. Suppose you and a friend have planned to meet for dinner at 7:00, but it is now 7:30 and your friend still hasn't shown up. If you guess that your good friend may have been injured in a terrible accident on her way to meet you, how will you feel?

Susan: Worried.

Therapist: Right. And you might even want to call the police. How will you feel if you told yourself that she probably found someone more fun to have dinner with instead of you?

Susan: Sad or depressed, probably.

Therapist: Right again. How about if you believed your friend was being late on purpose just to jerk your chain?

Susan: Then I'd feel angry.

Therapist: Sure, and with good reason. So, what if instead of thinking those things, you thought to yourself that your friend is probably on her way and has some good reason for running behind that she'll tell you about when she arrives? What would you feel then?

Susan: I'd probably just feel normal—maybe a little hungry.

Therapist: Right. Do you see the importance of your interpretations?

Susan: Yeah. The situation is the same—my friend is late. But I could interpret it in different ways; and depending on how I interpret the situation, I will feel differently.

Therapist: That's exactly right. So, since the only thing that has changed is your interpretation of the situation, we can say that your interpretations cause your emotional responses. Your beliefs dictate how you feel.

After demonstrating the cognitive model with a situation that is not emotionally charged, the next step is to apply it to OCD-relevant situations.

Therapist: Now, let's see how this might apply to situations and thoughts that give you problems as part of OCD. You said that you become very anxious and feel like washing your hands for several minutes whenever you shake hands with someone. How must you be interpreting shaking hands that causes you to feel so anxious and like you have to do the washing ritual?

Susan: I'm telling myself that there are millions of germs on the person's hands and that they will make me sick if I don't wash.

Therapist: Exactly. So, your interpretation of what happens when you shake hands causes both anxiety and urges to do compulsive behaviors. How about your husband, Steve; does he worry about shaking people's hands?

Susan: No. And I don't understand why it doesn't bother him.

Therapist: Well, let's apply the cognitive model. What do you think he's telling himself about shaking hands that allows him not to feel so anxious?

Susan: Maybe that it's no big deal or that there aren't enough germs to hurt you. That's what he tells me when I worry about it.

Therapist: OK. So, do you see how it is your interpretation of the other people's hands as very dangerous that leads you to feel very anxious about shaking them? If you changed your thinking and considered that other people's hands might not be so dangerous, you could probably get yourself to feel more like the way Steve does.

Susan: I understand, but I can't just change my mind about the germs. I think there really is some danger.

Therapist: Right, and that's what therapy is going to help you with. We're going to work together to help you learn how to interpret these kinds of situations, and your obsessional thoughts, in ways that will be more helpful to you. For now, though, it is important that you see how your thinking affects your anxiety.

In OCD, the anxiety-evoking stimuli (the As in the A-B-C model) are sometimes intrusive thoughts. Because we typically think of As as external events or situations (e.g., a toilet, completing a form, the number 13, shaking hands), applying the cognitive model in the case of intrusive thoughts can be a bit tricky. That is, when both are cognitive events, some people have difficulty distinguishing between the intrusive obsessional thoughts (the As) and the automatic thoughts or appraisals of the intrusions (the Bs). Table 9.2 provides some examples from patients seen in our clinic. Susan's therapist helped Susan recognize this distinction and apply the cognitive model to her obsessional thoughts as follows:

Therapist: The same relationship occurs with your unwanted thoughts about harm, like the ones about hurting your baby. You said that when these kinds of thoughts come to mind you start to believe that you are a terrible mother and that you need to stop thinking this way. Can you see how you are interpreting your unwanted thoughts as very significant and even dangerous?

Susan: Yes, I see that.

Therapist: First you have the unwanted intrusive thought about harm but then you interpret it as meaning that you are a bad person or that you might act violently. How do you think that makes you feel? What does it make you do?

Susan: It makes me scared of those thoughts so I avoid the baby or try to get the thought out of my mind.

Therapist: That's right. So, the question is, are you correct in believing that your unwanted gruesome thoughts about harming your baby really mean you are a bad mother? Do you really need to avoid or suppress the thought in order not to do something terrible? Think back to what we discussed about those kinds of intrusive thoughts.

Susan: Well, if most people have strange thoughts as you said, even thoughts about hurting people they love, I guess there's nothing wrong with having the thoughts. But that seems so strange. I've been afraid of those thoughts for so long.

TABLE 9.2

Examples of Intrusive Thoughts, Dysfunctional Automatic Thoughts, and Consequences From Patients With OCDs

Intrusive Obsessional Thought	Dysfunctional Automatic Thoughts	Consequences
• (In the gym locker room) Unwanted homosexual image	• The thought means I am turning gay.	• Thought suppression, seeks reassurance of heterosexuality, avoids looking at other men
• (In the synagogue) Thoughts of desecrating the Torah	• I am an immoral person, I will be punished.	• Thought suppression, ritualistic praying for forgiveness, avoidance of the synagogue
• (Walking in the hospital) Impulse to push an unsuspecting elderly woman to the ground	• If I don't stop this thought, I will act on it.	• Thought suppression, puts hands in pockets, avoids elderly persons
• (After sealing an important letter in its envelope) Doubts that I wrote curse words in the letter	• I will be terribly embarrassed. I've got to make sure I didn't write anything inappropriate.	• Opens the envelope and ritualistically checks the letter
• Images of germs	• If I'm thinking about them, they must be there. I can't take the chance that I'll get sick.	• Avoidance, hand washing

201

Therapist: That's because you have believed for a long time that those thoughts are important or dangerous. You've even been *acting* as if they are. But as you just explained to me, they're really not. In fact, most new parents have them from time to time. So, lucky for you, the real problem is not that you have these thoughts, but rather how you misinterpret them as very significant and threatening. You can't change the fact that we all have upsetting thoughts, but you can change how you interpret these thoughts. In therapy, you will learn more healthy ways to think about these thoughts so that (like people without OCD) you can experience them without becoming alarmed.

Discussing and Challenging Cognitive Distortions

According to the cognitive theory each emotion is linked to a particular type of thinking. For example, thoughts about the likelihood of danger or harm lead to anxiety and thoughts of personal loss lead to depression. As reviewed in chapter 3, OCD is associated with systemtic aerrors in reasoning about responsibility for causing (and preventing) harm, the importance of intrusive thoughts, the need to control thoughts, the overestimation of threat, need for perfection, and intolerance for uncertainty among others (Frost & Steketee, 2002). Acquainting patients with the various types of thinking errors helps them become aware of when they are victims of such patterns. To this end, Handout 9.2 provides a list of cognitive errors in OCD. The handout, which can be reviewed in the session, can lead to a discussion of how various cognitive distortions play a role in the patient's particular OCD symptoms. Interview data collected during the information- gathering sessions and responses to the self-report measures of cognition administered during assessment (see chapter 8) may also be used to point out the patient's distinctive patterns of responding to obsessional triggers. Important points to convey to patients regarding each type of cognitive distortion are discussed next.

Intolerance of Uncertainty. At some level, most avoidance and compulsive behavior in OCD can be conceptualized as attempts to gain reassurance. Consider the woman who wears three layers of clothing fearing that mosquitoes carrying the West Nile virus will penetrate the first two layers, the man who locks his kitchen drawers and hides the key so that he does not stab his children with knives, the woman who rereads her letters (opening sealed envelopes again and again) to be completely certain she did not write anything obscene by mistake, the man who avoids looking at another man's rear end for fear of having homosexual thoughts and "turning gay," and the woman who keeps a journal of all her activities through the day so that she can reassure herself that she has not had an extramarital affair

Cognitive Distortions in Obsessive-Compulsive Disorder

1. **Intolerance of Uncertainty:** You feel as if you *must* have a 100% guarantee of safety or absolute certainty. Any hint of doubt, ambiguity, or the possibility of negative outcome (however small) is unacceptable. This is the core distortion of OCD.
2. **Overestimation of Threat:** You exaggerate the probability that a negative outcome will occur; or you exaggerate the seriousness of any negative consequences.
3. **Overestimation of Responsibility:** You believe that because you think about harmful consequences, you are therefore responsible for preventing harm from coming to yourself or others. Failure to prevent (or failure to try to prevent) harm is the same thing as causing harm.
4. **Significance of Thoughts:** You believe that your negative obsessional thoughts are overly important or very meaningful. For example, the idea that there is something seriously wrong with your brain because you have senseless thoughts.
   > **Moral Thought-Action Fusion:** You believe that your unwanted thoughts are morally equivalent to performing a terrible action. Therefore, you think you are an awful, immoral, or disgraceful person for thinking these thoughts.
   > **Likelihood Thought-Action Fusion:** You believe that thinking certain thoughts increases the chance that something terrible will happen. For example, "If I think about death, someone will die."
5. **Need to Control Thoughts**: Beliefs about the significance of thoughts lead you to feel the need to control your obsessional thoughts (and actions). You worry that if you don't control (or try to control) unwanted thoughts, something terrible could happen that you could have prevented. Some people worry they will act on their unwanted thoughts unless the thoughts are suppressed.
6. **Intolerance of Anxiety:** You feel that anxiety or discomfort will persist forever unless you do something to escape. Sometimes the fear is that the anxiety or emotional discomfort will spiral out of control or lead to "going crazy," losing control, or other harmful consequences.
7. **The "Just Right" Error (Perfectionism):** You feel that things must be "just right" or perfect in order to be comfortable. A related belief is the feeling that things need to be "evened out" or symmetrical or else you will always feel uncomfortable.
8. **Emotional reasoning:** You assume that danger is present based simply on the fact that you are feeling anxious.

Handout 9.2.   List of common cognitive distortions in OCD.

without realizing it. It is as if patients believe the absence of a complete guarantee of safety is evidence for a high risk of harm. Contrast this way of thinking with that of most non-OCD sufferers who are able to assume that a situation is safe simply by the absence of clear-cut danger cues. That is, people without OCD have the ability to feel certain about many things despite the fact that absolute certainty is more or less an illusion. At first it might appear as if people with OCD have a deficit in their ability to manage uncertainty or ambiguity. However, a closer look shows that they only have trouble with uncertainty in specific situations that are relevant to their obsessional fears. Susan T.'s therapist used the following demonstration to illustrate for Susan how she already knows how to live with uncertainty:

> Therapist: Your husband, Steve. Is he alive right now at this very moment?
>
> Susan: Sure. Why do you ask?
>
> Therapist: Well, I am interested in how you know for *sure* that he's alive.
>
> Susan: I talked with him on my cell phone while I was in the waiting room waiting for you.
>
> Therapist: How long ago was that?
>
> Susan: About half an hour ago.
>
> Therapist: So you know he was alive *then*. But isn't it possible that something terrible could have happened to him just in the last half-hour? You never know what could happen, do you?
>
> Susan: I guess that's true. So, I guess I don't know for certain that he's alive. But, I would bet that he is.

The therapist and Susan next discussed how it would be impossible for Susan to be certain that Steve is alive at this very moment (indeed meteors, accidents, and medical emergencies are possible). However, despite this, Susan coped in a healthy way, basing her judgment on a probability as opposed to a guarantee, and not making frantic attempts to check on Steve. This led to a further discussion about other low-probability events that the patient takes for granted on a regular basis such as when using scissors (a potential source of injury), electrical appliances (a potential source of shock), and crossing the street. Such a discussion can help teach patients that they already know how to manage uncertainties, and therefore can learn how to tolerate other low-risk uncertainties, such as those featured in obsessions. Indeed, to reduce obsessional fear and compulsive urges, patients must be willing to learn to live with acceptable levels of uncertainty.

Some patients describe obsessional fears of disastrous outcomes that will occur at some point in the distant future, such as getting cancer from long-term exposure to pesticides or eternal damnation because of the failure to control blasphemous or other immoral thoughts. They may be presently avoiding certain situations or performing compulsive rituals because they believe such precautions will guarantee that the feared disasters do not ever occur. It is of no use trying to convince the patient that these feared consequences will never happen—it is impossible for anyone to know such things. Moreover, such a strategy would merely be playing out the patient's ritualistic and maladaptive ways of coping with this normal uncertainty. Instead, the therapeutic discussion should focus on reaching a shared understanding of the way that OCD works (i.e., the cognitive-behavioral model) and a less threatening alternative interpretation of the ambiguity and uncertainty. The aim is to help the patient discover that he or she already accepts many uncertainties, and therefore can learn to become more comfortable with others. For example:

> Therapist: So, you don't know for sure whether Steve is alive, but you'd bet that he is. What kind of a bet are you making when you have intrusive doubts that maybe you assigned a student the wrong grade on their report card?
>
> Susan: I'm betting that I made a mistake.
>
> Therapist: Right; and where does that bet lead you?
>
> Susan: I see what you mean. I get anxious and have to check and re-check. I even called a student's parents once just to be sure.
>
> Therapist: And how often do you find that you've actually made such a mistake?
>
> Susan: Never. I have never caught any mistakes when computing or assigning grades on report cards. But it could happen.
>
> Therapist: You're right. It could. But, remember, Steve could be dead right now and you could be hit by a car the next time you cross the street. If you apply the same strategy you use in these cases, what could you tell yourself about assigning the wrong grade the next time you have the obsessional doubts?
>
> Susan: I could tell myself that I probably haven't made the mistakes I am worried about, that I'm only thinking about it.
>
> Therapist: Exactly. You have to be willing to live with some uncertainty. That means no longer trying to be 100% *sure* about your obsessional fears.

Once the patient accepts that he or she must learn to tolerate uncertainty, ERP exercises can be discussed as vehicles for promoting this change. By engaging in ERP, the patient will learn that uncertainty is manageable and that the negative outcomes he or she is concerned with are unlikely to materialize even if no safety-seeking behavior is performed.

Overestimation of Threat.   People with OCD tend to exaggerate the threat associated with obsessional situations. They predict that their worst fears will likely come to pass, even when the risk of negative outcomes is realistically quite low. Such predictions can take two forms: overestimation of the probability of harm (jumping to conclusions) and overestimation of severity (catastrophizing). These cognitive distortions fuel anxiety because they imply that danger is lurking. They also place the patient on high alert and put him or her at further risk of misinterpreting harmless situations or events as dangerous.

Socratic dialogue is the recommended format for discussing overestimates of threat. Recall that the aim of such discussions is not to provide a guarantee of safety, but to help the patient devise a more valid set of beliefs regarding the risk associated with obsessional situations. Once the patient understands the importance of evaluating his or her logic, the therapist can discuss how ERP techniques are designed to help gather additional evidence that obsessional fears are less likely to materialize than had been thought. An example of a Socratic dialogue between Susan and her therapist is presented here.

Therapist: So, you are having lots of trouble using the toilet at school where you work?

Susan: Yes. It seems like there are so many germs in the faculty bathroom. So many people use that toilet, it's probably not safe.

Therapist: Can you tell me specifically what you think might happen if you used the toilet?

Susan: I am afraid of catching something from the toilet seat.

Therapist: Like a disease or a cold?

Susan: Hmmm. I never thought about exactly what might happen. I suppose I would get very sick from the toilet germs and pass them to my family.

Therapist: Would you and your family die from the toilet germs?

Susan: Probably not, but we would be very, very sick.

Therapist: OK. How about the other teachers you work with. How do they feel about that particular toilet? Do they avoid it too?

Susan: Not really. I know most of them use the bathroom during school hours. I've seen them excuse themselves to go there sometimes.

Therapist: Hmm. So, then I guess these other teachers must get sick a lot, right?

Susan: (thinks) … Well, I don't think they get sick very often. In fact, one of them always wins the award for perfect attendance.

Therapist: Interesting. So what does that say about using the toilet in the faculty bathroom if other people use it routinely and don't seem to be getting sick all the time?

Susan: Well, maybe it's not as dangerous as I thought. I never thought about it that way before. But still, what if I am more susceptible to germs than other people are? Doesn't it make sense to avoid it just to be on the safe side?

Therapist: Well, I agree with you that the toilet is probably not as dangerous as you think. Otherwise the people who used it would be
getting sick all the time. As far as being more susceptible, I
don't know if you are or not. What makes you think that you
are more susceptible than someone else might be?

Susan: Nothing really. I guess I'm just afraid of the germs.

Therapist: Yes, I agree with you. There really is no good reason to think
you are more susceptible. It sounds like you are letting your
fear do the thinking for you (emotional reasoning). So, I'm
glad you recognize that you have been overestimating the
dangerousness of the toilet. That's probably what leads you to
be fearful and avoid. The exposure therapy exercises I will assist you with later on are going to help so that you will be able
to go to the bathroom, if you need to, and not be so fearful.

Therapists should be alert for two kinds of objections patients sometimes
raise when their overestimates of threat are challenged. First, some individuals reason that although feared outcomes may be unlikely, they still could occur. So, taking precautions such as avoidance and rituals seems prudent. For
example, one individual with contamination obsessions argued that it was
worthwhile for him to wash his hands periodically throughout the day because it was "better to be safe than sorry." Another explained that although
she knew the chances of her computer or television catching fire were "one in
a million," she could be that "one." Such thinking indicates that the patient is
still ignoring important evidence of low risk. Thus, such evidence should be
revisited. To counter the "one in a million" argument, therapists can direct
the conversation toward correcting the faulty beliefs that the patient's personal chances of being harmed are higher than that of other people in comparable positions (e.g., coworkers, family members) who do not have similar
fears. Where appropriate, it can also be pointed out that people routinely face
more "dangerous" situations without suffering the dreaded consequences;
such as nurses and doctors who are routinely exposed to blood or dead bodies; forensic pathologists and morticians who work with corpses; and waste
management workers, electricians, and fumigators who are routinely exposed to pesticides and other potentially dangerous substances.

The second kind of rebuttal is based on the belief that safety behaviors
have prevented disastrous outcomes from occurring. For example, a patient with unwanted impulses to harm her baby might say that she did not
act on the violent thought *because she canceled it out* (neutralized it) with a
"safe" thought. In such cases the therapist must help the patient understand the mechanism by which safety-seeking behaviors serve to reinforce
overestimates of threat. Specifically, safety-seeking behaviors are normal
responses when threat is perceived. Anyone who thinks they are likely to
murder their child, become sick, or be responsible for a terrible mistake

would do what they could to avoid such adversity. People leave a burning building as quickly as they can. However, if the perception of danger is based on a misinterpretation of the situation (or thought), then the avoidance or safety-seeking behavior prevents the person from finding out that his or her fear is groundless. So, following circumstances that should demonstrate that a feared consequence is unlikely, a person with OCD will believe that he or she narrowly escaped tragedy because he or she performed a ritual to make things safe. This can lead to a discussion of the use of ERP techniques to obtain a nonbiased perspective on the likelihood of feared outcomes and ultimately correct overestimates of threat.

Overestimation of Responsibility. On some level, concerns about being responsible for others' safety seem sensible, if not imperative. Yet patients sometimes have difficulty drawing the distinction between failing to do everything to prevent possible harm (e.g., rechecking the floor for wet spots and warning people about them) versus actually inflicting harm (e.g., deliberately causing someone to slip). Overestimation of responsibility actually consists of two types of distortions: First is an inflated sense of the amount of responsibility one has in the situation (e.g., "If a person slips on the floor it is completely my fault"). Second is an inflated sense of the consequences of being responsible (e.g., "If someone slips, I am liable for negligence").

The therapist can help the patient gain perspective on his or her own role in causing negative events by having the patient identify all possible contributing factors and then rate how much each factor contributes (what percentage) to the overall responsibility for the negative event. Van Oppen and Arntz (1994) recommended incorporating this information in a pie chart to visually illustrate the logical error. Figure 9.1 illustrates the use of this method for a female patient who was afraid that because of her carelessness, a child (not her own) would ingest her medications and die. This patient believed that she alone would be responsible if her pill container broke, some of her medication fell on the floor, and a child ate some of the pills. First, factors (other than herself) were listed that would contribute to such an event. The patient cited the bottle manufacturer, the child, and the child's parent for not keeping an eye on the child. Next, she rated the percentage of total responsibility attributable to each of these contributions (25%, 25%, and 40%, respectively) and drew these in as pieces of the pie on the whiteboard. Finally, the patient labeled the leftover part of the pie as her own contribution (10%) and was able to acknowledge that even by her own ratings, her responsibility for this imagined event was quite minimal.

Significance of Thoughts and TAF. The therapist should introduce to the patient the concept of TAF as a habit of lending undue (negative) signifi-

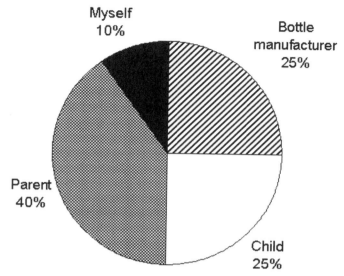

FIG. 9.1.   The pie chart method to illustrate factors that could contribute to a child's death by ingestion of medication that was accidentally dropped on the floor.

cance to otherwise inconsequential intrusive thoughts. Behavior such as avoidance, checking, and other safety-seeking strategies (e.g., neutralizing) would be expected if unwanted unacceptable thoughts are believed to be important or have disastrous consequences. Socratic dialogue can include questioning to help the patient develop more ambivalence about the importance of his or her thoughts; for example, "Are all of your thoughts important, or just those about your infant?" and "What makes some of your thoughts more important than others?" The aim of this conversation is to make it apparent that not all of our thoughts are significant just because we think them; and that the patient has many thoughts that (a) he or she would not consider particularly important and (b) do not have external consequences. The therapist can then ask the patient about more appropriate ways to interpret obsessional thoughts in light of knowing that such thoughts are normal and do not portend danger.

Individuals with unacceptable violent, blasphemous, or sexual obsessions may harbor the idea that thinking about dishonest, disgusting, and dreadful events is morally equivalent to carrying out the corresponding behaviors (moral TAF). Such beliefs indicate the need for additional discussion regarding the normalcy of intrusive upsetting thoughts. It might be useful to ask patients what they would think if they found out that someone they considered highly virtuous, ethical, or kind entertained a similar "bad" thought from time to time. If a double standard is present (e.g., "It's OK for someone else, but not for me, to think bad thoughts"), this should be pointed out and possible alternative explanations generated. The patient can be asked how he or she might explain that seemingly "good" people sometimes have "bad" thoughts.

If the patient believes that unwanted thoughts will lead to the corresponding event, the therapist can inquire about the mechanism by which this could occur:

- How do you think your thoughts of raping another man will lead you to commit this action?
- How will thinking about your mother getting cancer make her actually get cancer?

The goal here is not to put the patient on the spot, but rather to help him or her conscientiously reflect on beliefs and assumptions that might be taken for granted. Logical inconsistencies can be explored in a Socratic way to facilitate the correction of such beliefs:

- If thoughts lead to actions, how are people able to maintain control of themselves when they get angry or sexually aroused?
- Can you recall a time when you prayed, hoped, or wished for something and it didn't happen?

A related issue is the ecological validity of obsessions; that is, obsessions are incongruent with the patient's worldview. People intent on harming a baby would not be worried if they thought about the harm they were about to inflict. An atheist would not be concerned over blasphemous images. A gay person would not become upset over sexual images involving a same-sex partner. Thus, Socratic discussion can focus on the "kinds" of people who would and would not be concerned about violent, blasphemous, or sexual thoughts. Does the patient have a history of behavior or thoughts consistent with the obsessions? What evidence is there that the patient has acted or will act on the thought?

To help the patient recognize the faulty logic of TAF thinking, he or she can be given an object and asked to think about throwing it across the room. The patient might be asked to visualize throwing the object or even say out loud, "I want to throw the _____." The patient's restraint is then used as a basis for discussing the process by which one decides to act. Thoughts alone do not translate to impulsively engaging in improper behaviors. This and other similar exercises (e.g., going outside and "wishing" for car accidents, thinking of throwing a ball through the therapist's window, buying a lottery ticket and thinking of winning) provide a robust demonstration that thinking about an event has no direct or automatic causal influence. Moreover, it facilitates openness to engage in ERP exercises to reduce fears of intrusive thoughts.

Need to Control Thoughts.   The effects of thought suppression should take center stage in addressing the need to control obsessive thoughts. Patients should understand how their misinterpretations of obsessions as dangerous, morally unacceptable, or otherwise significant lead to desperate and intense attempts to resist or remove such thoughts from consciousness. In the short term, if successful, this might make the patient feel more in control of his or her thoughts. It may also reduce the perceived probability of feared consequences. However, patients must be taught how thought suppression attempts paradoxically exacerbate obsessional problems as explained in chapter 4. Moreover, for patients who are unaware that thought suppression attempts often fail, the occurrence of mental intrusions despite tenacious efforts to banish them may lead to further negative appraisals (e.g., "My mind is out of control"; Purdon et al., 2005) and intensified efforts to suppress. The result is a self-maintaining cycle of suppression attempts, increased intrusions, and anxious thinking that results in greater frequency and severity of the unwanted thought.

A robust way of demonstrating how attempts to suppress unwanted obsessional thoughts backfire is to engage the patient in a brief experiment as follows:

Therapist: Let's try an experiment. I'd like you to not think of a pink elephant for one minute. So, try to think of anything else in the world except for a pink elephant. OK?

Invariably, the patient will have pink elephant thoughts and agree that it is nearly impossible to fully suppress them (I have never had this experiment fail!). Next, the patient can be asked about how this phenomenon applies to OCD symptoms. Such a discussion should focus on how thought suppression attempts are unnecessary because obsessive thoughts are not inherently dangerous in the first place. However, attempts to suppress are doomed to fail and therefore they directly contribute to the escalation of normal intrusive thoughts into clinical obsessions. In addition, the more effort the patient invests in trying to control or suppress, the more the unwanted thoughts will surface. Thus, the patient should expect for intrusions to recur when efforts to suppress them are intensified.

This exercise, and the patient's newfound knowledge that intrusive thoughts occur normally and are not dangerous, leads nicely into presenting a rationale for the imaginal exposure techniques used in therapy. For example, the patient can be asked, "If trying to suppress obsessional thoughts only makes the problem worse, and if obsessional thoughts aren't dangerous in the first place, what do you think would be a more healthy way of dealing with your unwanted thoughts?" The answer is that learning to embrace such thoughts as a normal part of life, rather than trying to control them, will reduce obsessional fear. The problem is not that the thoughts are present, it is how they are appraised and dealt with. In imaginal exposure, the patient will practice confronting his or her intrusions and refraining from safety behaviors to gain evidence that such thoughts do not portend negative consequences.

Intolerance of Anxiety. Some people with OCD believe that feeling anxious is dangerous because it will prevent them from functioning, make them "lose control," or that it will persist forever and spiral to unmanageable levels. Such beliefs understandably present a barrier to successful ERP and should be addressed prior to beginning such exercises. When intolerance of anxiety is identified, therapists can adopt materials from cognitive-behavioral treatment manuals for panic disorder (e.g., Craske & Barlow, 2001) that aim to educate patients about the physiology of the anxiety response. In particular, patients are taught that anxiety is a normal emotion designed by nature to protect the organism from danger. Anxious (sympathetic) arousal, often called the fight-or-flight response, involves the onset of numerous somatic symptoms that may seem uncomfortable or scary (e.g., racing heart, dizziness, numbness and tingling, sweating), but that are not at all dangerous (indeed the response is designed to protect the organism). Myths and misinterpretations about the harmful effects of anxiety symptoms can be addressed by assessing catastrophic beliefs about harm from long-term anxiety (e.g., "My nerves will get fried out") and by providing corrective information about the feared somatic sensations and their actual functions. Therapists can also have the patient describe previous experiences with anxiety to illustrate how such sensations subside over time and do not result in marked functional disability or loss of control.

If the patient experiences panic attacks and agoraphobic avoidance, it is worthwhile spending as much time as is needed to normalize the anxiety response. Doing so will increase compliance with ERP because these procedures require tolerance of prolonged anxious arousal. Exposure to obsessional cues might even be preceded by interoceptive exposure that involves direct confrontation, in a systematic and controlled way, with feared somatic sensations. This exposure format, which is well described in panic disorder treatment manuals (e.g., Craske & Barlow, 2001) is designed to demonstrate that anxiety-related sensations are transient and harmless.

The "Just Right" Error. Perfectionism in OCD is characterized by beliefs that minor flaws, or even the sense of imbalance or imperfection, can have serious negative consequences including that associated distress will persist forever. In discussing such beliefs, the therapist can help the patient recognize disadvantages of an "all-or-nothing" approach, including its futility given that absolute perfection can be rarely attained. Other instances (that are unrelated to OCD) in which the patient does not demand perfection, and yet there is no associated distress, can also be discussed. Thus, the patient may "know" how to manage imperfection and must learn to apply this skill to his or her OCD concerns. Sometimes perfectionism interferes with the patient's ability to complete therapy assignments; that is, in trying to do them perfectly, patients fail to benefit from them. In such instances the patient should be encouraged (or assigned) to complete such tasks imperfectly and observe whether this leads to feared outcomes (e.g., failure to benefit from treatment, unremitting anxiety).

Emotional Reasoning. In emotional reasoning the patient uses his or her feelings of anxiety as evidence to support catastrophic thinking. In other words, "If I am anxious, there must be danger." For example, an individual has the intrusive doubt that she may have left the oven on at home, and that her house will burn down. If she misinterprets this thought as highly significant and requiring action, she will develop obsessional anxiety. She might then fall prey to emotional reasoning by thinking along these lines: "I'm nervous. I'm afraid. There must be a good chance that something terrible will happen. If not, why would I feel so afraid? I'd better go back and check that the oven is off."

The problem with emotional reasoning is that feeling anxious is not firm evidence of danger. Obsessional fear is the result of a misinterpretation of low risk situations and stimuli as threatening. Because emotional reasoning can prevent one from realizing the difference between feelings and facts, the patient should be taught to recognize when emotions are being used to validate fears and urges to perform compulsive rituals. Some patients articulate that they "know" their obsessional fears are senseless, but that when very anxious, they cannot resist performing compulsive rituals. To this end, the therapist can use Socratic dialogue to help the patient recognize that the probability of a feared outcome (e.g., sickness, fires) remains the same regardless of whether or not one is feeling anxious.

DISCUSSING HOW SAFETY BEHAVIORS MAINTAIN OBSESSIONAL FEAR

The counterproductive effects of safety behaviors should be thoughtfully discussed to promote adherence with response prevention instructions. Handout 9.3, which succinctly summarizes this information, can be reviewed by the patient between sessions and subsequently discussed with the therapist. Susan T.'s therapist began by quizzing Susan on the functional relationship between obsessions and compulsions. Using impromptu oral

UNDERSTANDING HOW OCD WORKS

Obsessive-compulsive disorder (OCD) is an anxiety disorder, meaning that it involves excessive, irrational, or unreasonable fear and anxiety. Anxiety is typically associated with the anticipation of future negative events; for example, *"What if ___ happens?"* Other anxiety disorders include phobias (e.g., fears of thunderstorms or heights); panic attacks, and generalized anxiety disorder, which involves uncontrollable worries about situations such as work, health, or finances. In OCD, people have unwanted or senseless thoughts (obsessions), and urges to perform behavioral or mental rituals (compulsions).

Researchers have been interested in understanding the causes and symptoms of OCD, and thus have conducted numerous studies on this topic beginning in the middle of the 1960s. This research has confirmed two important facts about OCD: (a) obsessions evoke anxiety and (b) compulsive rituals (for the most part) reduce anxiety. This handout explains these important relationships in more detail. The explanations can be divided into two parts: (a) how obsessional fears develop, and (b) why obsessional fears persist.

OBSESSIONS

Obsessions are unwanted intrusive thoughts, ideas, or images that evoke anxiety, worry, or discomfort. Their content is usually senseless or bizarre— and the person often (but not always) recognizes this. People with OCD try to resist their obsessions, meaning that they try to stop the thoughts, often unsuccessfully. Broadly speaking, obsessions usually concern the possibility of danger, harm, or responsibility for danger or harm. Their specific content may focus on aggressive actions, contamination, sex, religion, mistakes, physical appearance, diseases, and need for symmetry or perfection, among other topics.

PART 1: WHAT CAUSES OBSESSIONS?

You may be surprised to learn that just about everyone, whether or not they have OCD, experiences intrusive, upsetting, unwanted thoughts from time to time. Indeed, human beings have many, many thoughts while awake and during sleep—some are positive thoughts and others are negative ones. This is entirely normal. What is also normal is that sometimes our brains focus on *bizarre* or *senseless* thoughts or ideas. In one research study, groups of people with OCD and without OCD were asked to list some of their unpleasant, bizarre, or senseless unwanted thoughts (people with OCD were asked to list their obsessions). The researchers then gave the lists of thoughts to psychologists and psychiatrists and asked them to try to distinguish between the thoughts of people with and without OCD. The results might be surprising: Even these mental health professionals did a poor job of determining whether the thought was from someone with OCD or someone without OCD. Again, this confirms that people with OCD and those without all have upsetting, unwanted thoughts. On the next page are listed several examples of intrusive thoughts reported by people <u>without</u> OCD:

Handout 9.3. Understanding how OCD works. *(continued)*

- The impulse to harm a loved one
- Thoughts of accidents involving loved ones
- Thought of harm coming to one's children
- Impulse to jump in front of an oncoming vehicle
- Impulse to shout rude or inappropriate things during a performance
- Thought about harm from asbestos
- Impulse to shout at someone or abuse them

- Doubts about having committed a sin
- Thought of being punished by God
- Impulse to curse in church
- Thoughts of accidents or mishaps
- Thoughts of children getting sick
- Thought of "unnatural" sex acts
- Thought about molesting children
- Images of germs festering on one's skin
- Sense that something is not perfect
- Bad thoughts about God

The fact that everyone experiences intrusive, distressing, or senseless thoughts means that people with OCD do not have something terribly wrong with their brains that cause them to have these kinds of thoughts. And, this is good news because it suggests that people with OCD are not suffering from a "brain abnormality." Their thoughts are no different than the thoughts of people without OCD. Of course, there is no question that people with OCD do experience their upsetting thoughts more frequently and as more distressing compared to people without OCD. The reasons why this is so are explained below.

You might also be wondering why these strange but completely normal negative intrusive thoughts exist in the first place. This is probably due to the fact human beings have highly developed and creative minds. We are able to imagine all kinds of scenarios—some more pleasant than others. The "thought generator" in our brains sometimes generates thoughts we would rather not think about. Sometimes, the generator produces thoughts about harm, immorality, or danger even though there may not be any real threat present.

DIFFERENCES BETWEEN PEOPLE WITH AND WITHOUT OCD

If intrusive distressing thoughts are a normal part of life for everyone, every day, why do some people develop OCD and others do not? It turns out that scientists have discovered differences in how people with and without OCD interpret their unwanted negative thoughts. First, let's consider what people without OCD do with their unwanted thoughts. Research shows that people without OCD typically dismiss their intrusive, unwanted thoughts as insignificant, meaningless, and not worthy of any further attention. In response to such a thought, they might automatically say to themselves, "That's a silly thought, I would never do that," or "That thought doesn't make sense—time to think about something else." When this happens, the person doesn't pay any more attention to the thought, and the thought soon passes.

But things go much differently for people with OCD. Studies have found that people with OCD misinterpret their intrusive thoughts as highly meaningful or significant in one way or another. In fact, many people with OCD view their intrusive thoughts as threatening or immoral. When this happens, it activates the body's automatic danger detection system (the "fight–flight" system), which causes us to pay more attention to the perceived threat. But, as we learned above, the thoughts are not actually dangerous—they're normal. So, the danger detection system doesn't actually need to be activated (there is no actual threat to be protected from). The result is that the person feels as if

Handout 9.3.   *(continued)*

215

there is a tiger lurking around the corner, when there is really only a kitten. So, it is not surprising that people with OCD pay lots of attention to their upsetting unwanted negative thoughts. This obsessional preoccupation occurs because the thought is perceived as threatening and paying attention to threat serves a protective mechanism.

So, as you can see the main difference between people with and without OCD is in the importance that they attach to their intrusive thoughts—not the thoughts themselves. It is no coincidence that we typically see contamination obsessions among clean people, harming obsessions among nice people, sacrilegious or sexual obsessions among strictly religious or moral people, and thoughts about mistakes among careful people. The more important something is, the worse it seems to have a bad thought about it.

THINKING PATTERNS IN OCD

It turns out that most people with OCD have similar problematic patterns of thinking that lead them to misinterpret their intrusive thoughts in ways that lead to feeling threatened. Below, we will explore some of these thinking patterns.

Inflated Sense of Responsibility

People with OCD often feel overly responsible for harm or danger associated with their obsessions. They may feel as if they have a special responsibility to reduce the chances of something terrible happening. But they do not stop to evaluate the realistic probability of danger—which is usually extremely low. So, people with OCD often act on the blind assumption that their intrusive obsessional thoughts are true (which, as we have seen, is not the case). In addition, whereas people without OCD typically assume a situation is safe if there is no recognizable sign of danger, people with OCD assume obsessional situations are dangerous and require excessive assurance that they are, in fact, safe. Thus people with OCD have an "intolerance of uncertainty."

Oversignificance of Thoughts

Another error that people with OCD sometimes make is to believe that it is bad to have "bad thoughts." As we have seen above, this is simply not true. As human beings, we are fortunate to have the capacity to think about anything we want. We can plan ahead, remember, and create fantasies about both positive and negative events. Everyone at times has unpleasant thoughts about things we might consider inappropriate or immoral. Whereas there might be consequences for acting on these thoughts, we are completely free to imagine such events without consequences. Indeed, most movies, shows, books, artwork, and science are the result of this wonderful ability to think creatively.

"Bad" Thoughts Lead to Bad Behavior

Some people with OCD fear they will automatically "lose control" and act on their obsessional thoughts without thinking. So, having a "bad" thought is perceived as dangerous because it will lead to a terrible action. However, this is not true. Our thoughts are not the only determinant of our actions. Indeed, we have the free will to pick and choose which thoughts we will act on and which we will not. Thoughts about inappropriate or harmful actions (that you don't want to act on) cannot actually cause you to act against your will.

Handout 9.3. (*continued*)

Magical Thinking and Emotional Reasoning

Another problematic thinking pattern is "magical thinking"—believing that if you have a thought about an event, it makes the event more likely to happen. But, just because we think of something does not make it more likely to occur. Think of how many times you think about something and it doesn't happen. Another mistake is <u>emotional reasoning</u>—the tendency for people with OCD to base their beliefs on what they *feel*, rather than on what other kinds of valid *evidence* tells them. An example is the following: *If I feel anxious, I must really be in danger*. But this is backward logic. Just because you *feel* a certain way doesn't make it true.

The Need to Control Thoughts

Another common mistake is to believe that you can, and should, *control* your thoughts. This is also not true. In fact, human beings are poor at controlling their thoughts. You might know this firsthand if you have ever tried to stop yourself from having a specific thought—this is called thought suppression. Most likely you found that attempts to suppress your unwanted thoughts resulted in the thought coming back. Researchers have studied thought suppression extensively, finding that people cannot stop their thoughts by simply telling themselves not to think them. So, using this strategy with obsessions is doomed to fail also. In fact, one of the ways obsessions can develop is by habitually trying to suppress thoughts. If you believe a thought is dangerous and try to suppress it, but can't, you will start to feel more and more anxious. However, if you believed 100% that your unwanted thoughts are not threatening, you would not have the need to control or suppress them, and the thoughts would actually occur less frequently.

A MODEL OF THE DEVELOPMENT OF OBSESSIONS

What we have described so far helps to explain how obsessional thoughts develop. A simple model of the development of obsessions would look like the following:

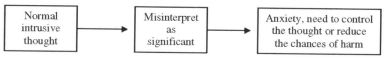

PART 2: WHY DO OBSESSIONAL FEARS CONTINUE?

This brings us to the second part of our explanation: how obsessions continue. Once a fear or obsession is established, people naturally seek to reduce their discomfort. If a person feels threatened, he or she will act to remove the threat. People with OCD generally use two strategies for removing threat caused by unwanted thoughts. The first strategy is to <u>avoid</u> threatening situations or thoughts in the first place. The second is to <u>escape</u> from unavoidable situations or thoughts. As we will see, both have the same eventual outcome—they actually strengthen obsessional fears. We will focus on avoidance first.

AVOIDANCE

People with OCD spend a lot of energy avoiding situations that provoke obsessional anxiety. This is understandable because no one wants to feel anxious or

Handout 9.3.   *(continued)*

threatened. Avoidance may be subtle, such as turning the channel on the television or not touching a certain surface; or it may be overt, such as driving out of your way to avoid passing a certain landmark. Thus, avoidance tends to be one of the more devastating aspects of OCD because it can severely restrict people from their normal functioning. The purpose of avoidance in OCD is to dodge confrontation with feared situations featured in obsessional thoughts and reduce the likelihood of anxiety and harm. So, there is a relationship between obsessional thoughts and situations that are avoided. However, as we have seen above, obsessional fears are unrealistic. Thus, avoidance is an exaggerated response to situations that pose little if any real threat.

Not only is avoidance an excessive response to obsessions, it also <u>strengthens</u> obsessional fears in three ways. First, because it requires effort, avoidance calls greater attention to the obsessional thought. You start to believe "If I have to go to so much effort to avoid, it must be important" (this is a form of *emotional reasoning*). Second, avoidance leads to being overly watchful, or "hypervigilant," for possible things you must avoid. This results in paying more and more attention to the fearful things you must avoid, which leads to noticing more obsessions. Third, avoidance prevents you from learning that your obsessional fear is not valid. That is, by avoiding, you never give yourself the opportunity to enter a feared situation and see that (a) harm is unlikely to occur, and (b) you can handle temporary anxiety and discomfort that eventually goes away. Thus, avoidance contributes to the continuance of obsessional fears.

COMPULSIVE RITUALS AND SAFETY BEHAVIORS

If a threatening situation cannot be avoided, people with OCD try to *escape* from their obsessions using certain strategies called "rituals" or "safety behaviors." These behaviors often take the form of repeated washing, checking, praying, arranging, mentally neutralizing, repeating, and asking for assurance. They are all performed with the aim of reducing obsessional anxiety, uncertainty, and the perceived possibility of danger. For example, people with obsessional fears of contamination from floors might avoid touching floors. But if they happen to come into contact with the floor, they might wash their hands to remove the feared contamination. After the washing is completed, the people feel less anxious.

It is important to consider that it is perfectly natural to want to escape from potential harm—people try to leave a burning building as quickly as they can! So, safety behaviors in OCD are understandable. The problem, however, is that they are based on a mistaken belief about danger. That is, if there is a very slim probability of harm from touching the floor, then hand washing is unnecessary. This is the main problem with compulsive rituals and other kinds of safety behaviors—they are excessive and unnecessary.

As with avoidance, compulsive rituals and safety behaviors serve to strengthen obsessional fears. First, you may have come to believe that "something worth ritualizing about must really be dangerous" (*emotional reasoning*). Second, if compulsive rituals serve as an escape from perceived danger, by performing rituals you never give yourself the opportunity to see that the obsessional situations are not dangerous. Third, people with OCD often come to believe that their rituals really prevent the disastrous consequences they fear. In the example above, the person might believe, "I

Handout 9.3. (*continued*)

did not get sick because I washed my hands." This is a dangerous trap because not only is it a false belief (the floor probably wasn't going to make you sick in the first place), but it leads to strong feelings that the ritual is important for keeping safe. Thus, safety behaviors are maladaptive because they reinforce obsessional fears.

A final point about compulsive rituals is that they seem to be effective for reducing anxiety in the short term. That is, after performing a ritual, you might feel a sense of relief or completion. When this occurs, it means you have tricked yourself into believing that you have just averted catastrophe. As we have seen, there was no threat to avoid in the first place, so this feeling is superstitious. However, the feeling of relief is important because it quickly leads to more urges to complete this ritual the next time you feel threatened. That is, because the ritual made you feel better, you learn to do it again to escape threat under similar circumstances in the future. Psychologists call this "negative reinforcement." This is how rituals become a strong habit. In the long term, however, rituals are wasteful because they teach you to use excessive, time-consuming, and meaningless tactics to reduce fear and distress.

So, you can see how avoidance and compulsive rituals, by virtue of their ability to reduce fear and distress, help to strengthen OCD symptoms of obses- sional fear. If we think of a model of OCD that incorporates rituals and avoidance, we have the following:
Misinterpretations of normal, harmless intrusive thoughts lead to increased fear and urges to reduce the fear by ritualizing or avoiding. Rituals reduce the fear in the short term, but reinforce the misinterpretation of obsessional fears and situations as dangerous. Thus, opportunities to learn that your fears are unfounded never occur. Obviously, then, once you believe that obsessional situations and thoughts do not represent a high risk of harm, you will feel fewer urges to avoid situations or perform compulsive rituals.

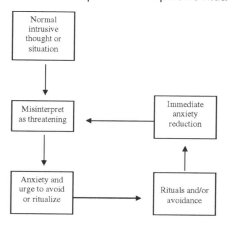

Cognitive-behavior therapy (CBT) is a treatment based on this idea and will help you to (a) correct faulty beliefs that lead to obsessions, (b) weaken the pattern of becoming anxious when you experience certain thoughts, and (c) weaken the pattern of avoidance and performing compulsive rituals in response to obsessional fear.

Handout 9.3.   (*continued*)

examinations helps impart to the patient the importance of understanding the conceptual model.

> Therapist: Remember when we developed the model of your OCD symptoms and we talked about the relationship between obsessions and compulsions? Can you tell me the relationship between obsessions, compulsions, and anxiety?
>
> Susan: Sure. My obsessions increase my anxiety and my compulsions decrease it temporarily. But the compulsions don't work because after a while I get more obsessive fears.
>
> Therapist: Very good. Also, there are other strategies you use that have the same effect as compulsive rituals. These include avoidance, like how you avoid contact with the "dirty" child in your class, and subtle rituals we call neutralizing, such as when you try to force out of your mind the unwanted thoughts of hurting baby Jennifer. Collectively, we call these behaviors safety behaviors because they make you feel safer—like you have narrowly averted catastrophe. It is this sense of safety that decreases your anxiety.

Many patients view their avoidance and compulsions as bizarre, automatic, and uncontrollable behaviors. Thus, the therapist next helped Susan to see that such behaviors are actually understandable and predictable for someone who believes himself or herself to be in serious danger. Of course, the problem is that objective danger does not exist in the first place. Thus, these responses are redundant.

> Therapist: At various times you might have thought that your avoidance and rituals seemed so strange as to defy logic, or that they are out of your control. However, these are actually very normal responses for someone who feels as if they are in danger, or as if they hold the responsibility for preventing something terrible. No one likes feeling anxious, so we do whatever we can to avoid threatening situations, and if we can't avoid them, we do whatever we think will make us feel better or safer. For example, if you are afraid you will make your family ill by bringing home germs from the "dirty" child in your class, it is sensible that you avoid him. Similarly, if you are afraid that you have assigned a student the wrong grade, checking that this hasn't happened seems like a good idea. Do you see what I mean?
>
> Susan: Yeah, but why do I do these things to such extremes?
>
> Therapist: That's a good question. Let's talk about avoidance first. When you avoid situations that are not as really dangerous as

they seem, it tricks you into thinking that you averted a catastrophe. So it makes you feel less anxious. For example, you think the faculty bathroom at work is likely to make you sick. So, if you avoid it and then you don't get sick, you will think that you didn't get sick because you avoided the bathroom. So, you continue to avoid the bathroom, as well as other things that you connect with the bathroom. The problem with so much avoidance is that it keeps you from ever finding out whether or not the bathroom is really as dangerous as you think. In other words, when you avoid, you never have the chance to disprove your fears. You also never have the chance to see that your anxiety about the bathroom, and other situations, would eventually go away on its own if you didn't avoid. So, you keep avoiding and it becomes a habit.

Next, the therapist helped Susan to understand the effects of performing compulsive rituals and how rituals develop their repetitive nature.

Therapist: If you could, you would probably avoid all of the things that trigger your obsessional fears. However, it is hard to completely avoid obsessions because sometimes they are triggered by situations that are not convenient for you to avoid. A good example is grading papers, which as a teacher, you can't avoid. So, the next best solution is to search for a way to relieve the anxiety as quickly as possible. For you, that means rechecking grades or calling students' parents to get reassurance that their grade is correct.

Now, if, at some point, these checking strategies make you less anxious, or make you feel as if you have dodged a bullet, then you become more likely to use them over and over when faced with the same obsessional doubt. And, each time you use the strategy and your anxiety goes down, you strengthen this pattern.

It is important to draw attention to subtle neutralizing strategies because they are functionally equivalent to compulsive rituals in their ability to propagate obsessive fear.

Therapist: Neutralizing strategies are another kind of maladaptive response to obsessions that provide an escape from distress in the short term, but that make things worse in the long run. Neutralizing involves doing something to remove an unwanted thought, to control the thought, or get reassurance that nothing bad will happen as a result of having the thought. You said that when you get thoughts of harming Jennifer you try to force them out of your mind or ask for reassurance from others that you will not hurt the baby. Again, these behaviors seem like a good idea because you have the fear that you will act on your violent thoughts. However, neutralization strategies are maladaptive for a number of reasons. First, as we discussed before, trying to suppress thoughts doesn't work. So, then, you start to worry that there is something terribly wrong since the bad thoughts don't go away even when you try to force them out. Worse, each time you neutralize, you lend more attention and importance to a thought that is really less important than you fear. Finally, neutralizing prevents you from learning to examine your thoughts closely and finding out that the obsessional anxiety will eventually decrease on its own.

Once the patient understands the antecedents and consequences of avoidance, rituals, and neutralizing, the therapist can help him or her think of these behaviors as patterns that can be weakened with practice. This is a critical point because response prevention will entail refraining from all of these behaviors to learn that obsessional fears are unfounded. To this end, it is useful to reframe avoidance, compulsive rituals, and neutralization strategies as ill-advised choices the patient makes when faced with obsessional triggers. Thus, by choosing not to avoid, ritualize, or neutralize, the patient would create opportunities to confront feared situations and thoughts and learn that these stimuli are not as dangerous as he or she thinks. This issue is discussed in greater detail in the chapters describing the use of ERP techniques.

WHEN TO USE COGNITIVE TECHNIQUES

As shown in Table 9.3, the cognitive techniques described previously can and should be used throughout the course of therapy. Socialization to the cognitive-behavioral model should occur during the assessment and conceptualization phase via discussions about the normalcy of thoughts and how mistaken interpretations evoke obsessional fear and compulsive urges. Because of the importance of rapport building during the initial sessions it is probably best to refrain from strongly challenging the patient's dysfunctional beliefs early on in treatment. Instead, Socratic dialogue should be used to amplify the patient's ambivalence and help him or her to recognize the inconsistencies in his or her thinking ("I am a murderer because of my terrible impulses" vs. "I have never acted on unwanted impulses to harm people"). This helps to induce a sense of cognitive dissonance that the patient can later be helped to resolve through Socratic discussions and ERP. Along these lines, patients should be informed that

TABLE 9.3
Opportunities to Use Cognitive Therapy Techniques
During the Psychological Treatment of OCD

Phase of Treatment	Purpose of Cognitive Techniques
Assessment/information gathering/formulation	Socialize the patient to the cognitive-behavioral model, build rapport
Treatment planning	Prepare the patient for confronting feared situations during exposure and response prevention
Exposure therapy sessions	Facilitate cognitive change during and after exposure
Reviewing homework assignments	Identify and correct cognitive distortions
Follow-up/maintenance	Consolidate and reinforce information learned during the active phase of treatment

therapy is an open, collaborative process that requires a shared understanding of the problem and how it can be reduced. Psychoeducational discussions serve to reinforce this focus.

Exposure therapy sessions also afford numerous opportunities for informal discussions about mistaken cognitions. Cognitive change can be maximized during exposure by having the patient process, in cognitive terms, his or her experience of confronting the feared situation and the evidence that is being collected by performing the exercise. For example, the normalcy of intrusive thoughts, futility of trying to achieve a guarantee of safety, importance of risk taking, and the costs of avoidance and compulsive rituals can be discussed within this context. Socratic dialogue is best used to help the patient articulate corrected beliefs about exposure stimuli he or she once feared or avoided. Strong affect during exposure, whether about the present exercise or the assigned homework practice, can also be seen as an opportunity to use cognitive techniques. The emotional patient should be asked to identify the thoughts and images running through his or her mind at that moment. Next, a Socratic dialogue addressing mistaken beliefs, assumptions, or interpretations can ensue. The therapist can also point out and summarize changes in beliefs during and after the completion of an exposure exercise. Once the patient is well socialized to the cognitive-behavioral model, he or she can be asked to provide such summaries. I discuss in more detail the integration of cognitive techniques with exposure exercises in the chapters on exposure therapy.

Reviewing self-monitoring forms at the beginning of each session presents another opportunity to use CT. In particular, the performance of rituals indicates the presence of mistaken cognitions and should be discussed within the context of the cognitive-behavioral model; for example, "What were you telling yourself about sitting on the sofa that made you decide to change your clothes?" "How did you interpret the doubts about your faith that led you to complete the prayer ritual?" or "What were the short- and long-term consequences of your ritualizing?" Mistaken beliefs can be challenged using the available evidence and Socratic questioning.

Although not the primary focus of therapy, events outside the context of treatment and issues related to the therapeutic relationship may also evoke strong emotional responses. Here again, the therapist can help the patient identify specific activating events (e.g., breakup of a romantic relationship, nearing the end of therapy) and related thoughts, beliefs, and assumptions. Socratic techniques can be used to help the patient challenge identified thinking errors and generate more healthy alternatives.

10

Treatment Planning I: Rationale and Hierarchy Development

Exposure therapy refers to a set of behavior therapy procedures in which patients confront fear-evoking stimuli in real life (situational or in vivo exposure), in imagination (imaginal exposure), or by other media (e.g., in virtual reality, interoceptively [exposure to internal body sensations]) until the associated fear is reduced. Response prevention, in which the patient refrains from safety-seeking behaviors such as rituals and neutralizing, is a necessary accessory to exposure, as it prolongs confrontation with the feared stimulus and teaches the patient that anxiety declines even if safety behaviors are not performed. Chapters 10 and 11 present the procedures for planning a successful course of ERP treatment. In this chapter, I describe how to provide a coherent rationale for ERP and develop with the patient a fear hierarchy of situations to be confronted during exposure sessions. Chapter 11 covers how to devise a plan for response prevention, enlist a support person to help the patient between sessions, and finalize the treatment plan. Typically about 3 to 5 hours (therefore multiple treatment sessions) is needed when planning for ERP. Here again, the case of Susan T. is used to illustrate the techniques.

PRESENTING THE RATIONALE FOR ERP

The therapist should begin treatment planning with a review of the conceptual model of OCD. To gauge how well the patient understands this model it may be useful to ask questions such as these:

- What are your obsessions and what happens to your anxiety level when they are triggered?
- What are your rituals (safety behaviors) and what do they do to your anxiety level?
- Why aren't your avoidance and safety behaviors helpful in the long term?

When satisfied that the patient has a working understanding of the model, the rationale for using ERP procedures to reduce obsessions and compulsions can be presented. The rationale includes elements of both the behavioral (habituation) and cognitive explanations for how exposure reduces fear: By remaining in the feared situation and resisting rituals, the patient learns that obsessional anxiety diminishes on its own, that feared consequences are unlikely, and that an acceptable degree of uncertainty is manageable. This rationale is a crucial part of the psychoeducational process because it helps patients understand why they should engage in a therapy that involves facing their worst fears while dropping their safety nets. The rationale must therefore enumerate logical links between the patient's OCD symptoms, the treatment procedures, and the anticipated outcome. It should also be individualized according to the patient's idiosyncratic symptoms.

Note that the purpose of exposure is not to reassure the patient that feared consequences would never happen. Rather, it helps the patient learn that the risks associated with obsessions are acceptably low. Therefore, safety strategies such as avoidance, rituals, reassurance seeking, and neutralizing are redundant and unnecessary. That the patient must learn to tolerate acceptable levels of risk and uncertainty should be reiterated throughout therapy. Susan T.'s therapist provided the following treatment rationale.

Therapist: The main treatment techniques we will use are called exposure and response prevention and they are designed to weaken the two patterns in OCD. The first pattern is the one of becoming very anxious when you have obsessional thoughts. We will weaken this pattern using exposure, which means that you will practice gradually confronting the situations and thoughts that evoke anxiety until they no longer make you feel so anxious. The second pattern is that of using avoidance and rituals to reduce your anxiety. We will weaken this pattern by implementing response prevention, which means helping you practice resisting the urge to do anything to get rid of the obsessional anxiety except staying exposed to the situation.

So, for example, I will help you to practice confronting things like bathroom germs and the student in your class who you have been avoiding. At the same time, you will practice resisting your urges to decontaminate yourself by washing or showering. We will also practice working with students' grades to help you refrain from checking, and we will help you confront thoughts about harming your daughter.

The basic idea of exposure therapy is simple. Exposure helps you learn three things. First, you will learn that your anxiety does not stay at high levels forever or spiral "out of control." In fact, your anxiety will actually subside as you repeatedly confront a feared situation and remain exposed for an extended period of time. This process is called habituation. You probably have never discovered this on your own because you usually avoid or ritualize as quickly as possible. In other words, you usually escape from the obsessional situation before you have the chance to see that your fear would naturally decrease anyway.

The second thing you will learn is that the consequences you fear as a result of exposure are much less likely to happen than you have been thinking. So, you will see that you probably don't get sick from bathrooms as easily as you had thought, that you need not worry so much about assigning the wrong grades, and that you are unlikely to harm your baby despite your violent thoughts. This new learning is what reduces obsessions, and doing exposure and response prevention exercises will provide the opportunities for this learning to take place.

The third thing you will learn during exposure is how to manage uncertainty and doubt. Instead of needing a guarantee of safety, this therapy will teach you how to live more comfortably with acceptably low levels of risk that most people take for granted.

At this point it is useful to draw a graph for the patient (or present him or her with a handout) depicting the expected habituation curves over the course of several sessions of exposure. Using a whiteboard, Susan's therapist drew and briefly explained the graph in Fig. 7.1 (p. 160).

Therapist: Exposure and response prevention are very helpful for reducing OCD if they are done correctly. But this treatment is hard work and you should expect to feel anxious at times, especially when starting to confront the feared situations. Fortunately, this anxiety is temporary. This graph shows what we expect to happen when you repeatedly expose yourself to obsessional situations. As you begin exposure for the first time you will probably feel uncomfortable. It is at this point that you typically perform a ritual to reduce your anxiety, but over the course of an exposure session your anxiety level will decline as habituation occurs. At the next session you will initially feel uncomfortable, but your anxiety will subside more quickly because you have learned that habituation occurs. By the time you have practiced exposure several times and in different situations, your beginning anxiety level will be lower and it will subside even more quickly because you have learned that the situation is not as dangerous as you thought. With repeated practice, the feared situations will no longer provoke anxiety. Of course, this only happens if you remain exposed and do not perform rituals or neutralizing behaviors to escape from the anxiety prematurely. So, for exposure to work, you must remain in the situation long enough for anxiety to subside on its own. As I like to tell people, you must invest anxiety now to have a calmer future.

There are two types of exposure that we will use. One type, called situational or in vivo exposure, means confronting actual feared situations. We will do situational exposure exercises both in the office and on field trips to places like public bathrooms. I will also ask you to practice situational exposures between sessions. When it is not possible to conduct situational exposure, I will help you to confront obsessional situations and thoughts in imagination using imaginal exposure.

Of course, I will do what I can to make the exposure exercises as easy for you as possible without compromising the effectiveness of the therapy. My job is to help you to succeed. One way I will help minimize the unpleasantness is by developing with you a list of exposure situations that begins with less anxiety-provoking situations and gradually works up to those that are more difficult. Exposure will begin with situations that evoke less distress. In fact, you will have a large say in when we conduct each exposure and I will always obtain your permission before beginning each exercise. We will plan these exercises together ahead of time so that there are no surprises. I will also be there to support and coach you through each in-session exposure. Nevertheless, you will still have to tolerate some anxiety, at least initially, as you learn to weaken your OCD patterns. Do you have any questions?

The therapist then described the nature of the therapeutic relationship so that Susan knew what she could expect from her therapist:

Therapist: You can think of me as your coach and your cheerleader. As a coach, my job is similar to that of a trainer or teacher. Did you ever take lessons to learn how to play a sport or a musical instrument?

Susan: Yes. I took golf lessons for a long time.

Therapist: Excellent. Do you play golf now?

Susan: Yes. I've become pretty good at it.

Therapist: So, when you were learning how to play, your instructor, who was probably an expert golfer, probably analyzed your swing to look for things that needed to be corrected and then gave you instructions for how to improve. He or she probably also had you practice certain exercises over and over on the driving range or the putting green to help you learn to hit the ball well. Now, if you didn't practice the exercises the way the teacher told you to, you would not have improved your golf game. Also, your teacher probably never forced you to practice. You made up your mind to practice on your own because you wanted to become a good golfer.

Therapy for OCD works the same way. As your coach or teacher, I know the kinds of exercises you must do to reduce your symptoms. We will build a program that is tailored to your specific symptoms. If you follow the program the way that I show you, chances are you will see improvement, but if you decide not to practice the exercises in the correct way, the chances are you will not improve as much as you would like. I will never force you to do the exercises—this is *your* therapy and the decision has to come from you. However, I might try to help you see that your feared situations are not as dangerous as you think, and that it is in your best interests to approach, rather than avoid these situations.

At some point during treatment I might ask you to do things that seem especially risky or that people don't typically do in their daily lives. For example, sometimes I ask people not to shower for an entire day or not to wash their hands before they eat. I might also ask you to purposely think distressing obsessional thoughts. It is important for you to understand that the purpose of exposure and response prevention is not just to practice doing what is *normal* or what *most people* do. The purpose of these exercises, which are designed especially for you, is to weaken your OCD patterns.

I said that you could think of me as both a coach and a cheerleader. In my role as cheerleader I will be behind you every step of the way as you complete this challenging therapy. We are a team and I will give you my support and do whatever I can to help you complete the exercises in a therapeutic way. If you feel very scared, or if you feel like you are having difficulty, I want you to let me know so that I can help you. Similarly, if I think you are having a difficult time, I will step in and help you out. What questions do you have for me?

DEVELOPING THE FEAR HIERARCHY

In planning for ERP, the therapist must engineer experiences in which the patient confronts stimuli that evoke obsessional fears of disastrous consequences, but where the feared outcomes do not materialize and the only explanation is that the stimuli are not as dangerous as was thought. The exposure treatment plan, or *fear hierarchy*, is a list of specific situations, stimuli, and thoughts the patient will confront during therapy. Prolonged exposure to each hierarchy item, one at a time, is conducted repeatedly (without safety behaviors) until distress levels are reduced to the point that the patient can manage adaptively with the situation. It is critical that hierarchy items match the specific situational and cognitive elements of the patient's obsessional fears. For example, an individual with obsessions of hitting pedestrians with his car must expose himself to driving on crowded streets or parking lots. If he believes such accidents are especially likely after dark, he must practice this after nightfall. Practicing driving during the day will not be effective in completely modifying the patient's fear because if no one is injured he might attribute this to the daylight, rather than recognizing that he was unlikely to hit someone. The importance of closely matching hierarchy items to the patient's fear cannot be emphasized enough; and this highlights the importance of careful ongoing assessment. Hierarchy items are also ranked according to the level of distress that the patient expects to encounter during exposure to that particular item. So, for the patient just described, exposure to driving near pedestrians during the day would be less anxiety provoking than the same situation practiced at night.

Susan T.'s therapist introduced the concept of the fear hierarchy in the following way:

Therapist: Our goal for today's session is to begin planning for exposure. To do this we need to make a list of the specific situations and thoughts that you avoid, or that make you feel like doing rituals. These will be the situations that you will practice exposing yourself to during treatment. I'll need your help in making this list because you know best what kinds of situations and stimuli evoke your symptoms. Once we have our list I'll ask you to rank each situation according to how uncomfortable you think it will make you. Then we can arrange the situations in the order that you will practice them. You can choose when you confront each situation, although I might make certain recommendations to ensure that we get the best possible results. Usually, the best approach is to begin with easier situations and work up to the more difficult ones. This list of situations is called a fear hierarchy and you can think of working through the hierarchy as climbing up a ladder. During each session you will take another step up the ladder until you reach the top. I will also ask you to continue practicing exposures between sessions. Treatment will be most effective if we plan to go gradually, yet steadily, up the ladder. Remember that I will help you at each step.

Situational (In Vivo) Exposure

Deciding on Hierarchy Items

Thoughtful and creative planning are the cornerstones of an effective ERP program. Therefore, developing the in vivo exposure hierarchy requires careful inquiry. Informed by the detailed information collected during the assessment and information gathering phases (e.g., obsessional fears, situational cues, catastrophic cognitions, and avoidance; see chapter 8), the therapist generates a list of between 10 and 20 situations that evoke obsessional fear, which will be confronted during ERP sessions. Situations that evoke rituals as noted on the patient's self-monitoring forms should also be considered for exposure. The Fear Hierarchy Form, which appears in Fig. 10.1, provides space for recording hierarchy items slated for situational (SIT) exposure. Some general considerations for the hierarchy development process appear in Table 10.1 and are discussed next. Recommendations for generating hierarchies for fears characteristic of each OCD symptom dimension appear later in this chapter.

Specificity.   The specificity of hierarchy items is subject to the therapist's discretion. Although it is necessary to include items that match core elements of the patient's obsessional fears, it is not essential that the hierarchy include every potential fear cue or possible exposure variation. As an example, consider the patient discussed earlier that feared injuring pedestrians with his automobile. In this case, driving might be a single hierarchy item. Alternatively, this might be broken down into multiple items of varied difficulty: driving on a deserted street, driving where pedestrians are walking (e.g., a crowded parking lot), and driving where pedestrians are

Description of the Exposure	SUDS	Session
1. SIT: IMAG:		
2. SIT: IMAG:		
3. SIT: IMAG:		
4. SIT: IMAG:		
5. SIT: IMAG:		
6. SIT: IMAG:		
7. SIT: IMAG:		
8. SIT: IMAG:		
9. SIT: IMAG:		
10. SIT: IMAG:		
11. SIT: IMAG:		
12. SIT: IMAG:		
13. SIT: IMAG:		
14. SIT: IMAG:		
15. SIT: IMAG:		

FIG. 10.1.   Fear Hierarchy Form.

walking at night. Kozak and Foa (1997) suggested that it is best to develop an initial hierarchy with enough detail to advise the patient (and therapist) of the nature and difficulty of the exposure exercises, but general enough to leave open the option to modify the specific task(s) in accord with the patient's idiosyncratic concerns. This allows greater flexibility in developing exposure tasks of varying degrees of difficulty if needed, some of which might not be contrived until the particular exposure is begun.

TABLE 10.1
General Considerations for Preparing the Fear Hierarchy

In vivo exposure

- Specificity of hierarchy items should be at the therapist's discretion.
- Each hierarchy item should have an identified rationale.
- Each hierarchy item should target a dysfunctional or catastrophic cognition.
- Consider exposure "field trips" for confrontation with stimuli outside of the office.
- Choose items that represent an acceptable level of risk.
- Begin exposure with moderately distressing items and progress to highly distressing stimuli (i.e., graded exposure).
- The worst fear must be included in the hierarchy and scheduled for the middle of treatment.

Imaginal exposure

- Primary imaginal exposure—exposure to fear-evoking thoughts aided by written or tape recorded material.
- Secondary imaginal exposure—visualizing feared consequences of not performing rituals.
- Preliminary exposure—imagining the confrontation with feared stimuli before engaging in actual exposure.

To further illustrate, Susan described a fear of garbage cans, but said that whereas some garbage cans posed little difficulty (e.g., those in offices), others were extremely frightening (e.g., those in bathrooms and other public places). Dumpsters were also completely avoided. Thus, garbage cans was included as a hierarchy item, which allowed the therapist to help Susan begin with easier garbage cans and gradually work her way up to confronting more difficult ones within the treatment session. This also permitted the therapist to vary the way Susan confronted the garbage cans according to her specific fear. Each new situation began with touching the outside of the can, discarding an item, touching the inside, and then removing an item from the can. The specifics of conducting exposure sessions are discussed in chapter 12.

Rationale. The patient and therapist must both understand how each exposure task is designed to modify expectancies of danger. This ensures that rather than something the therapist makes the patient do, each exposure is a mutually agreed on undertaking. During the treatment planning process, the reasons for selecting each hierarchy item should be made clear to the patient as in the following example.

Therapist: What is it about shaking people's hands that is so distressing for you?

Susan: I am worried that other people's germs will contaminate me and my family, and make us all sick.

Therapist: So, you either avoid hand shaking or you wash immediately afterwards.

Susan: Right.

Therapist: I see. So, it sounds like a helpful exposure practice for you would be to shake people's hands and then touch your husband and children.

Susan: But that's crazy. I mean, I couldn't do that.

Therapist: Well, I understand that it's difficult for you to think about doing that right now because you see it as very risky. But remember that one of the goals of exposure is to help you learn that the probability of your fears coming true is much lower than you think. By doing exercises like this you will learn that you don't need to fear shaking hands. By refraining from ritualizing you will also learn that you don't need to spend so much time doing cleaning rituals because they're unnecessary. Do you see what I mean?

Susan: Well, that will be a tough one, but I need to get over this problem.

Targeting Cognitions.   As the preceding exchange illustrates, hierarchy items should be chosen with one or more particular dysfunctional beliefs or catastrophic misinterpretations in mind. In this case the belief was Susan's overestimation of the threat of illness from contact with other people's hands. Therapists should think of exposures as experiments in which patients test their catastrophic beliefs and assumptions as if they were experimental hypotheses. This again highlights the importance of assessing patients' feared consequences of exposure and of not performing rituals.

Feared consequences that involve the possibility of disasters in the distant future (e.g., "I will get cancer in 40 years," or "I will go to hell when I die") are not subject to immediate disconfirmation via exposure because it is impossible to be 100% certain of whether such events will occur. Yet, people with such fears fruitlessly seek to reduce the probability of feared disasters and gain assurances of safety with their safety-seeking behaviors. In these instances, the patient's problem is how he or she responds to doubt and uncertainty, not that the feared disasters could one day occur (indeed they could). Thus, exposure should focus on evoking uncertainty so that the patient can learn to better manage such doubts.

Pushing the Envelope: Where to Draw the Line?   Although people with OCD grossly overestimate the probability and severity of potential danger associated with their obsessions, the situations they fear often hold some element of risk. This raises the issue of where to draw the line in exposing patients to "risky" situations. As a general rule of thumb, situations should be chosen that represent "acceptable levels of risk" within the confines of the therapist's (or an expert's) judgment (Steketee, 1993). For example, the risks associated with incidental contact with urine are sufficiently low that the therapeutic benefits of putting a few drops on the skin outweighs the risk of harm to someone fearful of becoming ill in this way (in fact, most urine is sterile). Conversely, immersing one's hand in a dirty toilet would be unnecessarily excessive. Scrupulous obsessions represent another level of concern and later in this chapter I address the delicate issue of how far to urge patients toward completing exposures in which they must act unscrupulously (e.g., by breaking religious laws).

When therapists I am working with become concerned that a particular hierarchy item is too dangerous for exposure therapy, I suggest they ask themselves the following question: Are there ways in which people without OCD inadvertently perform this exposure (perhaps without even realizing it)? As a general rule, if the answer is "yes," then the exposure is probably safe. Consider, for example, that many people do not wash their hands after activities such as handling money, using the bathroom, picking up items that have fallen on the floor, and casually making contact with garbage cans. Stepping in dog feces is common. People also leave appliances plugged in and lights and ovens on for hours at a time. It is even routine to leave appliances such as computers and furnaces running for lengthy periods when no one is home. Similarly, errors in paperwork, accidentally dropping potentially harmful items such as pins or thumbtacks, using knives, and encounters with "unlucky" numbers (e.g., 13 and 666) occur routinely in day-to-day life. Thus, purposeful confrontation with such situations is very instructive for patients who feel they must go to great lengths to reduce the potential risks associated with such things. In contrast, people do not eat pest control products, leave their doors unlocked overnight, leave very young children unattended with dangerous items, or purposely smear dog feces on their clothing; so these would be inappropriate exposure tasks.

Incorporating the Worst Fear. Although research suggests the order in which hierarchy items are confronted does not influence treatment outcome (Hodgson et al., 1972), from a purely practical standpoint patients are most receptive to initially approaching less threatening items and progressing gradually to more disturbing ones (i.e., graded exposure). Importantly, situations or stimuli that evoke the patient's worst obsessional fears *must* be included on the hierarchy and confronted during therapy. Failure to do so leaves critical dysfunctional cognitions firmly entrenched; for example, the belief that some obsessional fears really are extremely dangerous and should be avoided. To explain to patients the importance of confronting highly distressing situations, we often use the metaphor that in therapy "we must bulldoze OCD over, or else, like weeds in a garden, the symptoms will grow back." Most patients understand this and, although they may initially resist, can usually be encouraged to keep an open mind. It might also be useful to point out that for most patients, success with less frightening exposures often makes the more anxiety-evoking situations much less difficult.

Using the Subjective Units of Discomfort Scale

Once an initial list of exposure situations and stimuli has been generated, a scaling system called the Subjective Units of Discomfort Scale (SUDS) is applied. The patient assigns a SUDS score to each item on the Fear Hierarchy Form so that the items can be ranked according to how much subjective distress the patient anticipates during exposure. The therapist can introduce this concept using Handout 10.1 as follows:

Therapist: Now that we have a list of exposure situations, the next step is to rank the situations according to how much anxiety they would evoke. To do this, we will use the SUDS scale—SUDS stands for subjective units of discomfort [therapist gives the patient Handout 10.1 or draws a similar scale on the whiteboard]. As you can see, the SUDS goes from 0 to 100 and it helps you tell me how anxious you feel. It is your own personal interpretation of your anxiety. If your SUDS level is 0, then you are not anxious at all—like you're asleep. If your SUDS is about 20 or 30, it means you have a mild degree of anxiety or distress. If your SUDS is 50, you are moderately distressed. A rating of 70 to 80 SUDS means a high degree of distress. And 100 SUDS is like experiencing the worst possible anxiety you could think of—like you are tied to the railroad tracks and the train is coming around the bend. Usually when people have a high SUDS rating they also experience physical reactions like a pounding heart, shortness of breath, sweating, or feelings of dizziness.

The **SUBJECTIVE UNITS OF DISCOMFORT** *Scale (SUDs)*

0	10	20	30	40	50	60	70	80	90	100
Not at all distressing		**Mildly distressing**			**Somewhat Distressing**		**Highly Distressing**			**Extremely distressing**

Handout 10.1.   Introduction to SUDS.

The therapist should help the patient calibrate his or her SUDS ratings by giving and asking for examples.

Therapist: It might take a little practice to get the hang of SUDS ratings. Don't worry if at first it feels like you aren't doing it right— it's meant to be your own personal rating system. So, a 65 for you is different than a 65 for someone else.

Right now, my SUDS is about 15. Overall I feel relaxed, yet I know some of the things we are discussing are probably making you feel anxious. Tomorrow, however, I have to give a lecture to a large group of students. When I think about doing that, my SUDS goes up to about 30 because I'm a little uneasy about speaking to large groups of people that I don't know. How about you? What is your SUDS right now? What kinds of situations might make that higher or lower?

At any point, if necessary, the therapist should help the patient make adjustments in SUDS by pointing out when numerical ratings do not seem to correlate with other variables (e.g., "You don't look as anxious as I would expect you to look with a SUDS of 80. I wonder if you are overestimating your SUDS"). Once the patient is able to provide reliable and valid SUDS ratings, the situations and stimuli on the exposure hierarchy are ranked. Susan's therapist initiated this process as shown here:

Therapist: Now, I'd like you to give each item on the hierarchy a SUDS rating so we can see which situations are more and less distressing for you. Let's start with touching public surfaces such as pay phones, railings, elevator buttons, and door handles. What would your SUDS be if you were to touch these things and not wash your hands afterward.

Susan: That would make me fairly anxious. I guess my SUDS would be about 50.

Therapist: Good. How about using a public bathroom, like the faculty restroom at your school?

Susan: And I couldn't wash afterwards, right?

Therapist: Right. You'd have to go without washing; so you'd be feeling contaminated.

Susan: That would make me very, very anxious. I feel my heart racing just thinking about it. So, I guess my SUDS would be about an 85.

Therapist: Good job. How about if you had to hand out graded papers to your students without rechecking for any mistakes?

Susan: That would be a little easier—like about 65.

Imaginal Exposure

Why Imaginal Exposure?

Recall that for individuals with OCD, fear is evoked not only by environmental triggers such as bathrooms and knives, but also by internal stimuli such as intrusive thoughts, impulses, doubts, and images. Whereas situational exposure is designed to reduce fearful responses to external situations and stimuli, the aim of imaginal exposure is to foster habituation to fear-evoking obsessional thoughts, and to help patients correct how they misinterpret the presence and significance of such thoughts. To illustrate, consider the case of Jill, who was obsessed with the idea that she might mistakenly poison her family's food with lye-based household cleaning agents. To ensure against any harm, Jill kept all poisonous substances locked in a basement closet. Although she frequently checked that the closet remained locked, Jill continued to have upsetting thoughts and doubts about whether her family was truly safe from what she believed were her "unconscious evil tendencies." To reduce her doubts, Jill ritualistically asked her relatives for assurance that they were feeling OK. Treatment included situational exposures in which Jill prepared food for her family in the presence of open bottles of cleaning solution. For imaginal exposure, she purposely visualized a scene in which she had mistakenly poisoned her family because she was not careful enough about toxic materials. Repetition of the scene continued, and Jill refrained from seeking reassurance, until her anxiety habituated.

In contrast to situational fear cues, which are often concrete, internal fear cues are covert and highly elusive, and therefore can be precarious targets for exposure. Although in vivo exposure often implicitly evokes obsessional thoughts, imaginal exposure provides a more systematic approach for exposing the patient to the key fear-evoking elements of his or her obsessions. The recommended methods for conducting imaginal exposure include (a) using audiocassette tapes (endless loop tapes work especially well) or (b) written scripts containing the anxiety-evoking material (Freeston & Ladouceur, 1999). Both of these media allow the therapist to prolong the patient's confrontation with an otherwise intangible stimulus and, if necessary, manipulate its content. Moreover, the repetition of fear-evoking material (i.e., via loop tape) is incompatible with engaging in mental rituals or covert neutralization; thus it assists with response prevention. The use of an audiotape further ensures that self-supervised (homework) exposure will incorporate confrontation with the correct stimuli.

Types of Imaginal Exposure

Imaginal exposure is an essential treatment component for most, but not all, individuals with OCD. However, this technique may be used in three different ways depending on the specifics of the patient's symptoms (the techniques are illustrated later).

- *Primary imaginal exposure* is essentially situational exposure to unwanted thoughts. It involves directly confronting repugnant thoughts, images, and urges (i.e., violent, sexual, or blasphemous obsessions) via methods such as loop tapes. If situational triggers do not evoke these obsessions, primary imaginal exposure might be the only available means of direct exposure to these mental stimuli.

- *Secondary imaginal exposure* is used to augment situational exposure when confrontation with actual situations evokes fears of disastrous consequences (e.g., in Jill's case described earlier). In such instances, imaginal exposure is begun during or after situational exposure, and should involve visualizing the feared outcomes or focusing on uncertainty associated with the risk of feared outcomes.

- *Preliminary imaginal exposure* entails imagining confronting a feared stimulus as a preliminary step in preparing for situational exposures. For example, a patient might vividly imagine touching the bathroom floor before actually engaging in situational exposure to the bathroom floor.

Susan's therapist gave the following introduction to imaginal exposure:

Therapist: I mentioned that in addition to practicing exposure to real-life situations, we would conduct exposure in imagination. Imagery exposure is used to reduce fear associated with certain thoughts, such as your unwanted thoughts of harming your daughter. The process is very similar to situational exposure in that you will practice thinking the anxiety-provoking thoughts over and over, and without ritualizing, until your distress reduces on its own. Eventually you will find that you can think the obsessional thought without experiencing so much distress. We will do imaginal exposure using endless loop tapes. That is, we will make recordings of the anxiety-evoking thoughts and then you will practice listening to the tape until habituation of anxiety occurs.

Imaginal Exposure and the Fear Hierarchy

Scenes and scenarios for imaginal exposure are chosen from the list of obsessional thoughts and feared consequences generated during assessment and information gathering (see chapter 8). Brief descriptions of these scenes are entered onto the Fear Hierarchy Form (IMAG) along with the corresponding situational exposures where applicable. For example, a situational exposure to driving at night might be followed by a corresponding imaginal exposure to doubts about possibly having hit a pedestrian. Because the imaginal exposure stimuli also must match the patient's fear, it is important for the therapist to know the specific cognitive elements the patient finds distressing; for example, the idea that "the police are probably looking for me," and how "my family will be terribly upset when they learn that I killed someone."

Primary Imaginal Exposure.   Primary imaginal exposure items might have their own place on the fear hierarchy, especially if the particular thought will not be addressed with situational exposure. Items will include articulations of the distressing thought, such as an explicit narrative of an unacceptable sexual encounter, description of a horrible accident, or repetition of an upsetting phrase. The thoughts can be articulated in written form or verbally recorded onto an audiotape (i.e., loop tape). The therapist and patient should outline the content of each imaginal item before beginning each exposure so that both are aware of the desired content and expected distress level.

The following example illustrates a primary imaginal exposure for a man with unacceptable homosexual obsessions. When conducting loop tape exposures, it is up to the therapist to decide whose voice is heard on the tape (therapist or patient). This particular patient remarked that hearing himself verbalize the obsessional thought would evoke more anxiety than listening to the therapist's voice. Therefore, after the following text was collaboratively drafted and edited, the patient read it aloud (in an appropriately funereal tone) into the tape recorder.

> I am in the locker room at gym after a long hard workout. I decide to take a shower even though I am afraid that I will see other men in the nude. There are several other guys in the locker room in various states of undress. I can see their butts as they bend over, and I can see their penises. I look at their bodies and find myself admiring their muscles and the size of their penises. Then I feel the urge to kiss one of them and to touch him. I don't know if this means I am gay or not. I think about what it would feel like to kiss another man and touch his penis. Instead of trying to push the thought away, I let it just stay in my mind. He is a young, muscular guy, about my height. I think about his pubic hair and what his penis must look like when it is erect. It is probably very long and has a large circumference. I think about kissing it and putting it in my mouth …

Patients' apprehension over merely uttering their seemingly horrific, immoral, or obscene obsessional thoughts can interfere with the planning of imaginal exposure (the concealment of obsessions is discussed in previous chapters). However, this is equivalent to avoidance and will prevent the therapist from being able to match the exposure stimuli to the patient's actual fear. To manage concealment, the therapist should assess how patients are interpreting their obsessional thought that leads them to feel they cannot describe it out loud. Next, cognitive techniques can be used to help the patient think differently about the obsession (i.e., normalizing). The therapist should also empathetically reiterate that the purpose of treatment is to help the patient confront, rather than avoid, feared thoughts.

On a related note, therapists should be aware that obsessional thoughts can be extremely offensive, unsettling, and graphic. It behooves one to prepare for this and to regulate his or her response to hearing a patient describe these intrusions. Recognize that the patient probably harbors the concern that "even the therapist will be 'freaked out' by my horrible thoughts." Thus, even a hint of alarm, horror, or disgust on the part of the therapist could reinforce such maladaptive beliefs. The appropriate response to an admittedly repugnant obsession is to acknowledge in a nonjudgmental way that it is understandable how the patient could assume that such a thought is significant, but that nevertheless, even highly disturbing intrusive thoughts are neither harmful nor especially important. The therapist might even take the opportunity to one-up the patient by describing one of his or her own distressing intrusions. As a final point, there is no evidence that repeated exposure to patients' descriptions of their horrific thoughts causes traumatization to either the patient or the therapist, as has been espoused by some in the traumatic stress studies field (e.g., Stamm, 1999).

Secondary Imaginal Exposure.   Secondary imaginal exposures are conducted in conjunction with the corresponding situational exposures. Here, the most practical way of presenting the fear-evoking material is via a scripted narrative, spoken by the patient or therapist. As described previously, the narrative contains the most distressing feared consequences associated with situational exposure (and failure to perform safety behaviors). It should be presented in the aftermath of situational exposure to the corresponding external trigger. An example of a secondary imaginal exposure scene for a patient with fears of unlucky numbers and prayer rituals is presented here. The patient, whose dysfunctional beliefs included an inflated sense of responsibility for preventing harm, had just completed situational exposure to the number 13:

> You are thinking about how you have exposed yourself to the number 13 today. You wrote "13" over and over on a piece of paper, on the whiteboard in my office, and you even wrote it on your hand and on the back of your father's picture. You have never dared to do such things because you think it will bring bad luck. Now, you wish you could pray to God to prevent bad things from happening to your father. But you know that for treatment to work, you must refrain from praying. So, you don't allow yourself to pray. Just then, the phone rings. It is your sister calling from the hospital. She is crying and is barely able to tell you that Dad has just been killed in a terrible car crash. A large truck that ran through a red light hit his compact car. He didn't stand a chance. You tell yourself that it's your fault. You know why Dad is dead. If only you hadn't acted so irresponsibly with the number 13. If only you'd prayed. Now Dad is gone and you could have prevented it.

Preliminary Imaginal Exposure.   In most cases, preliminary imaginal exposures are not specifically proposed during the treatment planning phase. Instead, they are used as needed when conducting situational exposure. For example, if a patient is extremely anxious about walking through tall grass for fear of stepping in dog feces, he or she might agree to imagine doing this as a precursor to the actual exercise. Importantly, studies indicate that all things being equal, situational exposure is more potent than imaginal exposure for reducing fears of external obsessional triggers (e.g., Rabavilas et al., 1976). Thus, preliminary imaginal exposure should be undertaken with the patient's understanding that actual exposure will follow.

EXPOSURE STIMULI FOR DIFFERENT SYMPTOM DIMENSIONS

We now turn to a discussion of the issues involved with developing fear hierarchies and arranging exposure exercises for each of the OCD symptom dimensions. The actual implementation of exposure procedures is described in chapter 12.

Harming

Exposure for harming symptoms must entail (a) confronting situations in which the patient fears that he or she will be responsible for harm, and (b) imagining the feared consequences. For Susan's fear of assigning incorrect grades, the therapist suggested exposures involving grading papers quickly, recording the grades hastily, and returning the assignments without compulsively checking for accuracy; then imaginally confronting doubts about mistakes and thoughts that her carelessness might have cost some students successful careers. From the behavioral perspective, such exposures promote habituation to feared situations and doubts about feared disastrous outcomes. From a cognitive point of view, these techniques modify overestimates of threat and responsibility, as well as the intolerance of uncertainty. Patients learn that their feared consequences are unlikely enough that they need not be concerned that the absence of an absolute guarantee indicates a strong probability of disaster. The imaginal exposure component also serves to modify beliefs about the importance of thoughts. Informal cognitive interventions can be incorporated into exposure sessions to facilitate the correction of faulty cognitions.

Additional examples of exposure exercises for patients with harming obsessions include the following: If patients are afraid of fires, exposure can involve leaving lights and appliances on while leaving the home. Switches or knobs can be turned off rapidly and without checking. If the fear of burglary is present, the patient can lock the door in a "careless" way and leave home quickly without double-checking. Fears that one will cause bad luck can be addressed by having the patient do whatever he or she fears might cause bad luck; for example, writing phrases such as "I wish Mom would get cancer." If patients are afraid of harming pedestrians or causing traffic accidents, they can drive in crowded places (e.g., parking lots) without checking the rearview mirror. If patients are concerned about being distracted while they drive, the radio volume can be turned up. For fears of causing injury in other ways, situational exposure might involve placing items such as glass or pins on the ground or handling sharp objects in the presence of others. Obsessions about making mistakes with paperwork can be confronted by working very quickly without rechecking for accuracy (perhaps with distractions as well). Fears of mistakenly discarding items (e.g., notes, money) can be addressed by throwing away trash without carefully checking. Each of these situational exposures should be followed by secondary imaginal exposure to being responsible for the feared consequences (or not knowing for sure whether the consequences will occur). This prolongs the exposure, facilitates habituation to the feeling of uncertainty, and helps the patient learn that he or she can manage uncertainty.

An exemplary fear hierarchy for Kristi, a patient who feared she might blurt out insults and obscenities (or write them in letters and e-mails) at inopportune times (e.g., when speaking with her boss), is presented below. Kristi's therapist arranged in vivo exposure to different situations that Kristi was afraid might lead her to use curse words. Imaginal exposures involved thinking about the feared consequences of these situations.

- (Situational) Think the word *bastard* while talking with the therapist (45 SUDS).
- (Situational) Think the word *bastard* while writing e-mail or letters to friends (55).
- (Imaginal) What if I wrote *bastard* by mistake and will lose my friends (60)?
- (Situational) Think the word *shithead* while sending e-mail to the boss (70).
- (Imaginal) What if I accidentally wrote *shithead*, boss is offended, I lose my job (75)?
- (Situational) Type the word *shithead* before typing e-mail to the boss (80).
- (Imaginal) What if I typed *shithead* in the wrong place by mistake, boss is offended, I get fired (85)?

Before moving on, let us consider some practical tips regarding exposures for harming symptoms. First, the therapist's presence sometimes invalidates exposure because the patient can easily transfer responsibility for any negative outcomes onto the therapist (e.g., "The therapist wouldn't let anything terrible happen"). If this is the case (and patients should be asked about this directly), the exposure must be performed without close supervision. For example, In Kristi's case, the therapist left the room so that she could not see what Kristi wrote or typed. This ensured that Kristi would learn that the only explanation for her failure to write curse words was that thinking curse words does not directly cause one to write them. Second, many situational exposures for harming concerns are brief and exclude the repetition of the same task within a single session. For example, locking the door and leaving the house takes only a few seconds and repeating this activity (or prolonging it) would essentially be checking and attaining reassurance that the door is locked. Thus, instead of repeating such exercises multiple times during the session, the situational exposure is followed by procedures to help the patient confront obsessional thoughts and uncertainty associated with not checking (recall that intolerance of uncertainty is a primary cognitive feature of this symptom dimension). Imaginal exposure to the feared consequences is the best way to accomplish this goal.

Finally, for patients with fears of harm that could occur in the distant future, exposure exercises should be designed to weaken associations between uncertainty and high levels of anxiety. In vivo exercises can incorporate situations that arouse feelings of uncertainty, and imaginal exposure should focus on not knowing for sure whether the feared consequence will happen (Abramowitz, 2001). From the behavioral perspective, such exercises facilitate habituation to feelings of uncertainty. From the cognitive point of view, such exercises "decatastrophize" uncertainty and help patients to better manage obsessional doubt.

Contamination

Exposures for this subtype must include confrontation with feared contaminants that evoke avoidance or urges to perform decontamination rituals. Recall the discussion of primary and secondary sources of contamination in previous chapters. Whereas direct exposure to the primary source of contamination is usually essential, confronting every secondary source may not be necessary. The patient and therapist should agree to practice with those stimuli that are associated with functional impairment. Common exposure stimuli include floors, toilets, hospitals, public surfaces (e.g., elevator buttons, waiting room chairs, sink or shower faucets), body parts (e.g., anus), bodily fluids (e.g., urine), chemicals (e.g., pesticides), certain people (e.g., homosexuals), and specific places (e.g., cemeteries). Some patients have highly idiosyncratic fears of contamination from certain clothes, geographic locations (e.g., Canada), or colors (e.g., red), which might represent earlier events or relationships that are distressing (e.g., there was an outbreak of SARS in Canada). During exposure, patients must learn that contamination is ubiquitous. Therefore they should become thoroughly immersed in the feared stimulus. If patients try to avoid contaminating special items (e.g., favorite keepsakes), people (one's children), or places (e.g., certain rooms), exposure must entail tainting these things as well. If obsessional ideas or images of germs or illness are prominent or are misappraised as very significant, secondary imaginal exposure to such mental stimuli should accompany situational exposures. Next I present a typical fear hierarchy for a patient with contamination fears. The patient in this example, Jim, was fearful of contamination from dog feces.

- (Situational) Newspaper from front lawn (35 SUDS).
- (Imaginal) Feces might have been on lawn, and now might spread all over the apartment.
- (Situational) Shoes (45).
- (Imaginal) Might have stepped in dog feces without realizing it (60).
- (Situational) Walk in park where dogs go to the bathroom (65).
- (Situational) Step in dog feces and wipe off with tissue (75).
- (Imaginal) I am contaminated with germs from feces (75).
- (Situation) Walk in others' homes with shoes that had been in the park (80).
- (Imaginal) What if I make others sick from feces germs (80).
- (Situational) Contaminate self, car, and apartment with shoes from the park (95).

From a behavioral perspective, contamination exposures cultivate habituation to feared contaminants and weaken anxiety responses associated with such stimuli. From a cognitive standpoint, these exercises might address a number of faulty cognitions. If patients have fears of illnesses that will ensue if exposure is not terminated by washing or cleaning, exposure corrects overestimates of the threat of illness. If there is a fear of contaminating others and making them ill, exposure also addresses the inflated sense of responsibility. For patients with no specific fears of illnesses, exposure targets the intolerance of imperfection and anxiety so that they learn that affective discomfort does not persist indefinitely.

As discussed previously, patients' fears occasionally necessitate exposure to things that can pose actual danger or that evoke disgust for most people. Examples include chemical pesticides and bodily fluids or wastes. When it comes to such contaminants, people with OCD usually fear that they *might* have been exposed, and their decontamination rituals are therefore designed to remove such contaminants *just in case* (this is the intolerance of uncertainty component). Therefore, exposure need not involve bathing in pesticides or putting one's hand in a dirty toilet. Evoking the sense of uncertainty is often sufficient (e.g., when walking in the park, you *might* have stepped in dog feces). Some suggestions for how to expose patients to such items follow: For the fear of pesticides, the patient can visit a hardware store, touch bottles of pesticides, and practice applying the chemical as directed on the label (without taking extra precautions). For fears of feces (as in Jim's case earlier), harmless spots or stains can be obtained on a paper towel, which may be carried around in the patient's pocket or used to contaminate other "safe" areas.

Incompleteness

Situational exposure tasks for patients with this presentation of OCD will be those that evoke discomfort associated with imbalance, disorder, and asymmetry (i.e., NJREs). Hierarchy items often need to be highly patient specific, but might include the following: tilting pictures unevenly; putting items in the "wrong" place or arranging them asymmetrically; using poor handwriting; arranging bookshelves or drawers out of order; and putting smudges on tables, windows, or the computer screen. For patients with obsessions with certain lucky numbers, the "wrong" number can be chosen wherever possible, counting can be done out of order, to the "wrong" number, or routine activities performed the "wrong" number of times. For those with the need for left–right balance, left–right asymmetry can be achieved by physical (e.g., brushing against the right side only) or visual means (e.g., look only at the right side). For some patients, it will be important that exposure be consistent. Thus, for example, desks at home and at work must be rearranged, and friends or relatives may be enlisted to help with such tasks.

Imaginal exposure is typically not used for patients with incompleteness symptoms who fear only that their distress will persist indefinitely. However, as with exposure for harming symptoms, if the not just right feeling is associated with magical thinking concerning responsibility for harm (e.g., "I must put my shoes on in the right order or else my father will die"), secondary imaginal exposure to such disasters should be incorporated. So, from a behavioral standpoint, exposure for this symptom dimension fosters habituation to feeling uncertain or not just right. From the cognitive perspective, such exercises modify beliefs about the intolerability of distress, NJREs, and uncertainty. An example of a fear hierarchy for Tiffany, who had incompleteness symptoms, is provided here.

- (Situational) Place books out of order on the bookshelf (45 SUDS).
- (Situational) Leave the bed unmade (50).
- (Situational) Write a note to boyfriend with sloppy handwriting (55).
- (Situational) Tilt the pictures on office and bedroom walls (55).
- (Situational) Write bank checks with "sloppy" handwriting (55).
- (Situational) Leave the dresser drawers and closets with clothes "out of order" (60).
- (Situational) write work memos and forms with "sloppy" handwriting (80).

Unacceptable Thoughts

It is helpful for therapists to think of this symptom dimension as a phobia of thoughts. Thus, the fear hierarchy must incorporate primary imaginal exposures in which the patient repeatedly thinks the unacceptable intrusive obsessional thoughts (ideas, images, impulses), as well as in vivo exposure to any key situations and stimuli that evoke such obsessions. For example, an individual afraid of losing control and acting on impulse should be exposed to the situation in which the impulse occurs. If the unwanted urge to yell curse words is evoked by attending religious services, the patient should attend a religious service and experience the urge without engaging in avoidance or any safety behaviors. The aim of this exercise is not to desensitize patients to the idea of acting inappropriately. Instead, this particular exposure would help the sufferer learn that thinking about acting inappropriately is not what causes inappropriate behavior, and therefore, avoidance and safety behaviors are unnecessary.

As I have discussed earlier, written narratives and loop tapes describing anxiety-evoking scenes are the best methods of systematically exposing patients to their feared thoughts. From the behavioral point of view, exposure exercises for unacceptable thoughts promote habituation to these unwanted disturbing intrusions and extinguish classically conditioned fear. From the cognitive point of view, this type of ERP modifies erroneous beliefs about the importance of, and need to control, unwanted thoughts (e.g., TAF), as well as overestimates of threat and responsibility. Imaginal exposures for violent obsessions will be highly idiosyncratic and based on the patient's specific unacceptable thoughts. Examples include describing images of stabbing loved ones and thoughts of children dying. Situational exposures could include handling potential weapons (perhaps beside a sleeping baby or spouse), standing on a subway platform, watching the news, viewing violent movies, reading books about violence, or saying and writing words associated with violence (e.g., *murder, stab*), or whatever triggers the unwanted idea, image, or urge.

For patients with unacceptable thoughts or doubts regarding homosexuality, imaginal exposure might include confronting images of oneself engaged in homosexual behavior or thoughts that evoke uncertainty over sexual preference (e.g., "Maybe the rush you felt when you were in the gym locker room was really a sign of latent homosexuality"). In vivo exposure might involve viewing homoerotic stimuli (e.g., gay literature or pornography), visiting gym locker rooms or gay bars, and words such as *gay* or *lesbian* (which might entail writing the word repeatedly on a piece of paper and keeping the paper in a pocket or wallet). Similarly, for someone with unwanted sexual thoughts about children or incest, imaginal exposure should involve thoughts of such activities. Ideas for situational exposure include watching children on playgrounds; seeing one's child naked;

glancing at relatives' crotches or looking at pictures and focusing on these areas; and words such as *molest, pedophile,* and *incest.* An example fear hierarchy for Danielle, who suffered with unacceptable violent obsessions about harming her newborn baby, is presented here.

- (Situational) Burp the baby after giving him a bottle (45 SUDS).
- (Imaginal) Ideas of beating the baby very hard on his back (50).
- (Situational) Hold baby while near a flight of stairs (50).
- (Imaginal) Images of throwing the baby down the stairs (75).
- (Situational) Take the baby to the train station and stand on the platform (65).
- (Imaginal) Images of throwing the baby in front of an approaching train (85).
- (Situational) Give the baby a bath (80).
- (Imaginal) Thoughts of drowning the baby in the tub (85).
- (Imaginal) Images of shaking the baby very hard.
- (Imaginal) Images of the baby lying dead in her crib.
- (Situational) Using a knife while the baby is nearby.
- (Imaginal) Thoughts of stabbing the baby.
- (Situational) Hold blunt end of knife to the baby's skin.
- (Imaginal) Thoughts of stabbing the baby.

One patient who was evaluated and treated in our clinic described a less common presentation of unacceptable thoughts. His main fear was that the mere presence of senseless intrusive thoughts (many of which he appraised as unacceptable and therefore took great pains to try to control) indicated that he had a serious cognitive deficit. He spent hours on end fighting his (normal) senseless thoughts, trying to figure out why these thoughts were occurring and what they meant about his cognitive functioning. He even noticed that he was having difficulty attending to conversations and reading material (likely due to the fact that he was deploying inordinate attention to battling intrusive thoughts), and was convinced this was evidence of a serious cognitive dysfunction. It was somewhat difficult to arrange an exposure hierarchy for this individual because there were few particular recurring intrusions—distress could literally be evoked by any unwanted or senseless cognitive intrusion (e.g., images of people he did not like, "Could I be cloned?"). The only consistently recurrent obsessional intrusion was the doubt about his cognitive well-being. Thus, cognitive techniques were used to help him correct how he was interpreting his senseless thoughts, and imaginal exposure involved purposely evoking doubts and uncertainty about whether he had a serious cognitive disorder.

Religious obsessions present challenges to the hierarchy development process because patients with such symptoms often believe they have committed sins (and will suffer serious consequences) when, in fact, they have not. Moreover, the patient's religious and social environment reinforces such beliefs, at least on an intermittent basis. Exposure items for such obsessions, which can often be derived directly from avoidance patterns and descriptions of anxiety-evoking stimuli, involve deliberately engaging in behavior (including thinking unacceptable thoughts) that the patient perceives as blasphemous or immoral, but which are not necessarily condemned by religious authorities. For example, a person who is afraid of experiencing blasphemous thoughts while reading the Bible should read the Bible for situational exposure. Other examples of possible exposures include houses of worship, books about atheism, and other religious icons that evoke unwanted intrusions. Potential imaginal exposures include images of Jesus masturbating on the cross, doubts about God's existence, and ideas of desecrating religious artifacts or places of worship. The nature of these tasks requires that the rationale for ERP be clearly explicated to the patient. If this is misunderstood, or the therapist is perceived as insensitive, the patient may view therapy as an assault on his or her religion. Some suggestions for helping patients with religious obsessions (i.e., scrupulosity) embrace ERP are provided in the text that follows.

Patients with religious obsessions often hold catastrophic views of God and sin that are inconsistent with even their own religious doctrine (Abramowitz, Huppert, et al., 2002). Whereas most modern religions teach that God loves all people unconditionally and that one may repent for sins and be forgiven, those with religious obsessions often view God as petulant, easily angered, and vengeful. Naturally, such beliefs lead to practicing religion out of fear rather than out of love and faith. It is worth pointing out this distinction to patients so that they may see how their extremely fearful view of God departs from what other members of their denomination (e.g., family and clergy) believe. An important message is that according to most religions, patients will not lose God's love unless they (a) intentionally decide to do things they know are evil (e.g., murder someone) and (b) remain remorseless. Therefore, unwanted thoughts, ideas, or images do not count as violations. The therapist can also point out to believers that if God created the human mind, then God surely understands that people sometimes have thoughts that are contrary to their true beliefs. The case should be made that doing ERP will help the patient become a more faithful follower of his or her religion because it will help him or her to trust God, rather than being fearful.

People with religious obsessions are often narrowly focused on trivial violations of religious doctrine, often overlooking more important religious commandments (Greenberg, 1984). For example, one devout Catholic patient was extremely fearful that he would be punished if his relatives decided not go to Mass (Catholics are not to deliberately interfere with others' plans to go to Mass). However, he thought nothing of cursing at his parents (a violation of the Fifth Commandment to honor thy mother and father) in his attempt to convince them to go. Moreover, his history of sampling fruit and candy for sale at the grocery store when no one was looking, and taking magazines from the dentist's waiting room without asking (Thou shalt not steal) did not seem to concern him. The patient benefited from a discussion of his lack of concern with minor infractions, and learned that the purpose of ERP was to teach him how to manage his obsessional fears in a similar way.

Informing patients that for centuries, theologians have prescribed strategies similar to ERP for people with religious obsessions is another way to encourage individuals with such symptoms to undertake treatment (Ciarrocchi, 1995). From a theological perspective, scrupulosity and obsessional fear puts one in danger of sin by pride, self-will, and disobedience. The Jewish Talmud (written law) also considers religious acts performed out of the fear of punishment to be antithetical (*Sotah*, 22b). Training manuals for pastoral counselors recommend that people with scrupulosity purposely act contrary to their scruples. Specific guidelines include (a) emulating conscientious people even if doing so might violate the rule in question, (b) allowing oneself to purposely evoke "impure" thoughts, and (c) disavowing oneself of repetitive confessions and redundant prayer (Jones & Aldeman, 1959). Note the similarities between these guidelines and the components of CBT. Ciarrocchi's (1995) self-help book on scrupulosity presents an excellent discussion of this topic and is a useful resource for helping strictly religious patients who are ambivalent about beginning ERP.

As a last resort the patient may be permitted to consult with a religious authority (e.g., a priest, rabbi, or pastor) regarding what is appropriate to do for exposure. The hierarchy may then be assembled according to this guidance. If at all possible, the therapist should see that such advice is obtained from a more liberal authority as to avoid misunderstandings and reinforcement of the patient's fears. It should also be agreed that the authority's suggestions (no matter how vague) would be followed without the pursuit of further advice or second opinions (as this would constitute reassurance seeking). If ERP can be conducted by relying on what religious authorities have previously told the patient (i.e., without consultation during treatment), this is ideal.

FINALIZING THE EXPOSURE PLAN

Scheduling Exposures

The final step in planning for exposure is deciding on when (i.e., which session) each hierarchy item will be confronted. Typically, the therapist suggests that exposure begin with moderately anxiety-provoking situations

(situations that produce only *minimal* anxiety do not provide therapeutic benefit) and progress, in order of difficulty (i.e., SUDS level), to more distressing stimuli. Beginning with less difficult tasks increases the likelihood of a successful initiation to exposure. This will raise the patient's confidence and motivate him or her to stay engaged during more difficult exercises. If the patient reports that all hierarchy items evoke similar levels of distress, it may be left up to the patient to decide on the order of items. Progression up the hierarchy should occur as rapidly as possible so items with the highest SUDS ratings can be confronted sooner rather than later, perhaps as early as during the sixth exposure session (Kozak & Foa, 1997). Scheduling the most distressing exposures for relatively early in treatment buys the therapist more time to help the patient confront these difficult situations should intermediate steps be required. On the other hand, delaying exposure to the worst fears until late in therapy reinforces the patient's avoidance habits. Worse, not confronting the worst fear at all during treatment sends the message that such situations are dangerous and really should not be confronted. Procrastination and avoidance undermine the aim of treatment and are likely to lead to relapse because they propagate mistaken beliefs about obsessional stimuli. After the greatest fear has been faced, treatment sessions are used for extending exposure practice to multiple contexts (including in the patient's home). Susan's initial exposure hierarchy, complete with SUDS ratings and session assignments, appears in Fig. 10.2. Implementation of this treatment plan is described in chapter 12.

Description of the exposure		SUDS	Session
1.	SIT: Public surfaces IMAG: Germs on self, contamination of family	50	1
2.	SIT: Grading papers and recording grades IMAG: Possibility of mistakes, ruining students' career	55	2
3.	SIT: Leave applicances plugged in/on IMAG: Responsibility for causing fires	65	2
4.	SIT: Hand papers back to students (no checking) IMAG: Uncertainty over mistakes in assigning grades	65	
5.	SIT: Use knife while Jennifer is nearby IMAG: Thoughts of stabbing Jennifer with a knife	65	3
6.	SIT: Give Jennifer a bath IMAG: Thoughts of drowning Jennifer in the bathtub	70	
7.	SIT: Shaking hands IMAG: Germs possibly on self, passing germs to family	65	4
8.	SIT: Sweat IMAG: Germs possibly on self, passing germs to family	65	4
9.	SIT: Saliva IMAG: Germs possibly on self, passing germs to family	65	4
10	SIT: "Contaminated" student from class IMAG: Germs possibly on self, passing germs to family	70	5
11	SIT: Garbage cans, dumpsters IMAG: Germs possibly on self, passing germs to family	75	6
12	SIT: Public bathrooms IMAG: Germs possibly on self, passing germs to family	80	7
13	SIT: Faculty bathroom at school IMAG: Germs possibly on self, passing germs to family	85	
14	SIT: Urine IMAG: Germs possibly on self, passing germs to family	90	8
15	SIT: Contaminate family members with urine IMAG: Responsibility for illness	90	

FIG. 10.2.   Susan T.'s fear hierarchy.

11

Treatment Planning II: Response Prevention, Support, and Clarification of the Plan

Chapter 10 described the procedures for explaining ERP and developing the fear hierarchy. This chapter opens with a discussion of guidelines for forming a response prevention plan. Specific techniques for stopping rituals across the various OCD symptom dimensions are presented. Next, the chapter focuses on how to help the patient's family (or cohabitants) end their participation in avoidance and rituals. Inclusion of one or more relatives or close friends in therapy as support persons is suggested, especially if the therapist is concerned that adherence to treatment is anticipated to be a problem. The chapter ends with an illustration of how to summarize the treatment plan and review what is expected of the patient during treatment. It is crucial that the patient, therapist, and anyone else involved in the treatment program align together in a collaborative effort to reduce the patient's OCD symptoms.

RATIONALE FOR RESPONSE PREVENTION

Simply put, response prevention is the termination of all safety-seeking behavior performed in response to obsessional fear.[1] This procedure prolongs

---

[1]Some authors use the term *ritual prevention* to describe this procedure (e.g., Kozak & Foa, 1997). However, I prefer *response prevention* because it implies a broad *(continued)*

253

exposure and ensures that habituation and cognitive change occur, and is therefore a critically important component of therapy. To illustrate, if Susan T. took a 20-minute shower to decontaminate herself after situational exposure to "garbage can germs," her distress would immediately be reduced; however, she would prevent herself from learning that her distress would have declined naturally anyway (i.e., habituation) even without the shower ritual. In addition, she is likely to attribute the nonoccurrence of an illness to the fact that she showered. This leaves unchanged her mistaken belief that garbage cans are dangerous ("If I had not showered, I would have become ill from the trash can"). Similarly, if she completes a prayer ritual each time she experiences unacceptable thoughts of harm to her daughter, she will never learn that intrusive thoughts do not automatically lead to taking action. Instead, she would continue to believe that one must take precautions to prevent acting impulsively on unwanted violent thoughts. The rationale for response prevention should be explicated during treatment planning and reiterated throughout the course of therapy. Susan's therapist introduced response prevention in the following way:

> Therapist: I said before that in addition to exposure, treatment will involve practicing changing your patterns of responding to obsessional fear. To do this it will be important for you to stop the habits you have been using, such as compulsive rituals, mental rituals, and attempts to suppress and neutralize upsetting thoughts. Collectively, we call these habits *rituals* or *safety behaviors*, because you do them to make yourself feel safer when you have obsessional thoughts about danger. Practicing stopping rituals and other safety behaviors is called response prevention, and there are three reasons why this is an important part of treatment. First, it will help you learn that your anxiety declines even if you remain exposed to your fears. Second, it will teach you that your rituals are unnecessary and that you don't need to do them to reduce obsessional fear or prevent disasters. That's because the things you are afraid of are unlikely to happen whether or not you ritualize. However, the only way you can learn this is by not ritualizing and observing what happens. Finally, by not ritualizing, you allow yourself to learn better strategies for coping with obsessional fear. Each time you ritualize, you

---

[1](continued) cessation of all safety-seeking responses to obsessional fear (i.e., avoidance, neutralization, rituals, reassurance seeking), whereas ritual prevention implies that only compulsive rituals are to be terminated.

strengthen your OCD patterns of using avoidance for dealing with obsessional distress. By resisting your rituals, you will develop healthy thinking and behavior patterns that won't interfere with your life or cost you so much time and energy.

DESIGNING THE RESPONSE PREVENTION PLAN

General Considerations

Preparation for response prevention parallels the planning of exposure tasks. The patient's compulsive rituals, subtle neutralizing strategies, and covert attempts to seek reassurance are described in detail and targeted for cessation. The optimal strategy is complete abstinence from all safety behaviors; however, some patients will require a gradual approach in which instructions to stop rituals correspond to progress up the exposure hierarchy (use of gradual response prevention is further discussed later). Table 11.1 lists important considerations for planning response prevention.

Attend to Subtle Safety Behaviors.   It is essential that the therapist train the patient to understand that rituals and safety behaviors are not defined by the complexity or repetitiveness of the action, but instead by their effects on obsessional fear. Anything done to deal with obsessional thoughts, reduce anxiety, or prevent feared consequences is a potential safety behavior. Because popular descriptions of OCD typically highlight classic compulsions such as prolonged washing or elaborate checking, patients (and therapists) sometimes overlook brief or subtle safety maneuvers that are equally anxiety reducing and therefore play an equally important

TABLE 11.1
General Considerations for Planning Response Prevention

- Be aware that patients may not always realize that certain behaviors (e.g., subtle mental rituals) are violations of response prevention.
- Target efforts to seek assurances.
- Help the patient *choose* to refrain from rituals.
- Limit response prevention to the taking of acceptable risks.
- Arrange for relatives to stop assisting with rituals.
- Complete abstinence from all rituals, neutralizing, and reassurance seeking is the goal.
- Some patients require that response prevention be applied gradually.

role in the maintenance of OCD. Even subtle rituals and safety behaviors must be targeted in response prevention. For example, one patient with fears of losing things would tap his pocket as a subtle check that he had not left his keys somewhere. Another wiped her hand on her pants to decontaminate. Further examples include visually inspecting people's facial expressions, opening doors with a barrier (sleeve, tissue), and mentally reviewing (or keeping a record of) one's behavior through the day to make certain that no awful mistakes were made. These more or less fleeting efforts to reduce discomfort are often not reported to the therapist because patients do not realize they constitute escape from obsessional fear. However, if they persist, treatment outcome can be attenuated. Patients must therefore recognize and report even "little actions" performed to reduce obsessional distress.

Target Efforts to Seek Assurance. Some patients have an especially difficult time not being reassured of safety and, to reduce their anxiety, engage in incessant subtle and not-so-subtle strategies to attain reassurance. One individual who feared contamination from pesticides insisted that he and the therapist meet with a pesticides expert to define a safe level of exposure. When it was agreed that the instructions included with particular products would be used to guide ERP tasks, he excessively reread safety instructions, continued to ask frequently for assurances from the therapist (e.g., "Are you sure this is safe?" "Would you hold your child this close?" "Would you eat without washing your hands after doing this?"), and even made extraneous visits to gardening stores to speak with additional "experts." Further, he engaged in subtle forms of reassurance seeking during exposure, such as performing crude risk analyses and trying to recall the percentage of bug spray (parts per 100) that contained the active ingredient. These behaviors interfere with progress in ERP because they prevent direct exposure to the feared situation, which involves being uncertain about the consequences. Because overcoming OCD means learning to live with everyday uncertainties, attempts to gain reassurance should be identified and eliminated as part of the response prevention plan. Of course, compulsive reassurance seeking must be handled with caution because miscommunications can derail the collaborative therapeutic relationship. In chapter 14, I describe some helpful ways to address these problems.

Present Abstinence as a Choice. Because response prevention is generally conducted between sessions by the patient, he or she must be encouraged to choose not to perform safety behaviors when the urge to do so mounts. No one will be looking over the individual's shoulder to make sure that every safety behavior is resisted (indeed this is impossible for mental safety behaviors). However, some patients believe their rituals are involuntary and cannot be controlled voluntarily. It is important to empathize with such a position, but also to point out that there have probably been times when a ritual was delayed or postponed. This suggests that with hard work and perseverance, such behaviors can be regulated. Therapists are encouraged to repeatedly remind patients of the importance of refraining from safety-seeking behavior, but also to caution them against excessive self-criticism founded on unrealistic perfectionism, as at least some violations of response prevention are inevitable.

Therapist: I realize that just stopping your rituals and other safety behaviors cold turkey is going to be difficult for you. You might even feel like you can't do it. Doing response prevention can be very hard, but it is not impossible. Think of the times when you delayed your rituals for a little while for one reason or another—last time you mentioned that you sometimes resist washing your hands until you are alone. So, although it may not seem like it, performing rituals is very much a choice that you make. And in order to reduce your OCD symptoms, you have to choose not to ritualize and instead choose to let yourself be anxious for a while. Although this is a difficult choice, it is within your power and I will expect you to try. Remember that once you get some practice and see that your anxiety is temporary, you will also see that it becomes easier and easier to resist rituals, and the compulsive urges will become weaker and weaker.

Kozak and Foa (1997) pointed out that the very term *response prevention* can imply that somebody actively stops the patient from performing rituals. Of course, as a rule, this is not the case—and the therapist must make it very clear that the decision to adhere to ERP instructions is ultimately the patient's. At most, the therapist might gently cajole, distract, or redirect the patient to help him or her resist ritualistic urges, but no physical force is ever used.

Define the Limits of Response Prevention. As with exposure, the response prevention plan should involve taking only acceptable risks. If broad instructions such as "no checking mirrors while driving" or "no contact with water" are imposed, provisions or adjustments should be made where actual health, hygiene, and safety concerns exist. For example, it is important to check the rearview mirror when backing up in the car; thus patients fearful of injuring others can be limited to one brief check. Similarly, denying a daily wash or toothbrushing violates cultural hygiene norms; thus one daily 10-minute shower can be permitted as long as the shower does not involve the completion of rituals and the patient re-exposes himself or herself to feared contaminants immediately afterward.

Engage Relatives in Response Prevention. As I have discussed, patients' friends or relatives sometimes become entangled in compulsive rituals, avoidance, and other efforts to gain reassurance. One patient required his family to carry out elaborate decontamination rituals before entering the home. Another gained reassurance by merely mentioning to her husband when she perceived potential danger (e.g., pins, glass on the street). She believed that his acknowledgment of these warnings absolved her of responsibility for any harm that might ensue. A good rule of thumb is that the patient is to refrain from asking others for the following: (a) assurances, (b) to engage in any avoidance behavior, and (c) to perform any rituals. If such appeals are made, others should be instructed not to provide assistance or assurance. It is wise to have at least one family member attend the treatment planning sessions to be given the rationale and specific instructions for helping the patient with response prevention. The specifics involved with preparing an appropriate support person for this role (e.g., teaching them how best to respond to requests for assurance) are discussed later in this chapter.

Abrupt Versus Gradual Response Prevention. The expectation that patients cease *all* safety behaviors is sometimes difficult to reconcile with the use of a graduated exposure hierarchy. That is, patients may have unplanned encounters with feared stimuli that evoke very strong urges to ritualize, but that have not yet been practiced in session. Thus, the patient may not have practiced resisting his or her ritualistic behavior in response to such stimuli. As an alternative to starting complete response prevention from the first session, therapists might consider a gradual approach in which instructions to stop safety behaviors parallel progress up the exposure hierarchy (with the goal being complete abstinence midway through treatment). Summerfeldt (2004) advocated a stepwise approach in which the patient initially practices delaying the ritual, and where the delay interval (i.e., between exposure and safety behavior use) is gradually increased until compulsive urges subside and complete abstinence can be attained. The following text illustrates the use of a gradual approach for a patient with severe contamination concerns.

> Andrea's main fear was that she would contaminate others with her "negative essence" that was especially concentrated in her genital area. She worked as a physician's assistant and had ready access to Betadine, an abrasive cleanser that she used with high frequency both at home and at work. While at work, she managed to function by wearing three layers of gloves, which went unchallenged by coworkers. As a medical professional, she acknowledged that her concern was irrational, yet she was so fearful of the possibility

of harming others that she was engaging in extensive avoidance and safety behaviors. For example, at her initial consultation, Andrea reported that she had not touched the lower half of her body in 5 years without using a barrier (e.g., glove) to prevent direct contact with her skin.

The most fear-evoking item on Andrea's exposure hierarchy was touching her genital area with her bare hand. However, when Andrea's therapist described the rationale for complete response prevention, Andrea said she would discontinue treatment if it meant eliminating barriers when touching herself. The therapist assured Andrea that many patients feel the way she did, and that gradual exposure to her feared situations would make refraining from her safety behaviors easier. However, Andrea asserted that once her use of barriers was eliminated, she would be forced to confront her worst fear almost immediately, because she would have to wipe herself after urinating and defecating without any protection. Even at home, she was using abrasive cleaners, triple gloves, and engaging in an extensive laundry ritual that reduced her fears of becoming contaminated by her genitals and spreading the contamination with her hands.

The therapist acknowledged that it would be overwhelming for Andrea to give up all rituals and safety behaviors from the start of treatment, and thus a gradual response prevention plan was created. Andrea would progressively eliminate each set of gloves as she practiced exposure to certain stimuli, until she was wearing no gloves and doing no washing in her home or work environment. For example, it was acceptable for her to use single gloves after defecating and urinating until such time that these items were confronted on the fear hierarchy. Only after she had refrained from rituals for 2 consecutive days were exposures to directly contacting skin on the lower half of her body implemented. This graded response prevention plan allowed Andrea to avoid confronting her greatest fears until it was time to conduct exposure to these stimuli.

Handout 11.1 provides space for recording patient-specific response prevention instructions. After agreeing on the specifics of which behaviors will be stopped and when, these details should be written down on the form and given to the patient.

SPECIFIC RESPONSE PREVENTION GUIDELINES FOR OCD SYMPTOM DIMENSIONS

Harming

Patients with harming symptoms must refrain from all checking rituals, as well as other efforts to prevent feared consequences or to gain assurance that negative outcomes will not occur (e.g., picking up objects from the ground, counting, reporting potential hazards to others, retracing steps, making lists). In addition, family members may not perform these behaviors by proxy. If checking involves simply looking at something (e.g., at a lightswitch or lock), such objects can be covered or masked (e.g., with a piece of paper) to obscure them from view. For patients afraid of mistakes, paperwork may be checked once (briefly), but without the use of spelling or

Help with Response Prevention

- Specific response prevention Instructions:

- **Choose not to ritualize**-- even small rituals interfere with your progress.

- If you are having trouble resisting the urge to ritualize:

➤ Remember that the urge is based on a mistaken belief or assumption. You don't *really* need to ritualize to feel better or reduce the chances of harm or danger.

➤ Find someone to talk to and ask them to stay with you until the urge passes.

➤ Leave the situation for a while (if possible) to get away from reminders.

➤ If you perform any rituals, immediately record the ritual on a self-monitoring form and discuss it with your therapist.

➤ Deliberately re-expose yourself to the situation that evoked the ritual.

Handout 11.1.   Help with Response Prevention form.

grammar-checking software. Reviewing mathematical calculations is not permitted. Mentally reviewing past behavior or conversations, and seeking information or advice that has already been given (e.g., questioning for re-assurance) also constitute rituals and must be halted. When ritualistic prayers or other mental neutralizing strategies are difficult to stop completely, the patient can, as a preliminary step, be instructed to purposely perform these safety behaviors incorrectly, or in a way that leads to feeling uncertain about feared consequences. Examples include counting to the wrong number, praying incompletely or for the wrong outcome, and re-membering actions incorrectly. Family and friends should be instructed not to respond to requests for assurance, but instead to engage the patient in another activity as a temporary distraction (e.g., "I know you feel like you need me to reassure you, but Dr. ____ said it is best if I don't answer that question. So, how else can I help you feel less anxious?"). For gradual response prevention, seeking assurances may be permitted only if the corresponding situation has not yet been addressed in exposure.

Contamination

Bodily contact with water should be limited to one daily 10-minute shower (which should be timed). The shower should be ineffective as a decontamination ritual and serve merely to maintain minimal standards of hygiene (specific rules will vary from patient to patient). Hand washing after activities such as using the bathroom and taking out the garbage, and before handling food, is prohibited. Toothbrushing is allowed, yet shaving should be done with an electric razor to minimize water use. Other methods to remove or prevent contamination, such as hand wiping and the use of sanitizing gels, are not permitted. Cleaning inanimate objects (e.g., doing extra laundry loads, wiping furniture) is also not allowed and patients should not use barriers (e.g., tissues, gloves, shirt sleeves) when touching surfaces. Finally, friends and family members are not to be asked to follow any rules for avoidance or decontamination. Of course, cleaning or washing is allowed in extenuating circumstances, such as if grease is visible on one's hands or clothes. However, after any washing or cleaning, the patient should recontaminate with items from the fear hier-archy to maintain exposure.

Incompleteness

Patients with incompleteness symptoms must refrain from rituals performed in response to a sense of inexactness, unevenness, imbalance, and general imperfection. Objects may not be reordered, cleaned, or rearranged. Efforts to balance things out (e.g., counting to an even number, touching the left side if only the right side was touched) must be resisted.

For some patients, counting is performed mentally and feelings of symmetry or order are achieved visually (e.g., by looking or staring in specified ways) or with special bodily movements (e.g., tapping) or vocalizations (e.g., repeating words or phrases). Because of their pervasiveness, abruptness, and subtlety, such rituals might seem automatic and difficult to stop. A strategy that is often helpful in such cases is for the patient to initially keep track of these rituals (e.g., using a handheld counter). Next, he or she should practice performing the ritual incorrectly (e.g., counting to the wrong number, staring the wrong way, saying the wrong words), so that it does not relieve distress. This intermediate step eases the eventual complete stoppage of the ritual.

Recall that some incompleteness rituals are performed to magically prevent negative consequences such as bad luck or death. One man seen in our clinic described the need to look at people's facial features in a certain order to reduce intrusive distressing images of having his genitals "lopped off." In such cases, any behavior that reduces distress about encountering feared outcomes (including having unwanted images) must be stopped. This example illustrates the overlap in symptom dimensions that can sometimes occur between incompleteness and unacceptable thoughts, as described next.

Unacceptable Thoughts

Response prevention for this symptom dimension targets all behavioral and mental acts performed to neutralize or "put right" unwanted thoughts. Of special concern are mental rituals. Specifically, patients must resist urges to mentally cancel, replace, neutralize, analyze the meaning of, or otherwise suppress their obsessions. Special prayers and confessions for blasphemous obsessions are not permitted. Patients with sexual thoughts and doubts must not review their sexual history or monitor their body for signs of sexual arousal (a covert form of reassurance seeking). Resisting and stopping such mental maneuvers is challenging if the patient is not properly socialized to the cognitive-behavioral model of OCD and rationale for CBT, hence the importance of psychoeducation. One common mistake is to confuse mental rituals with obsessions. The therapist should frequently assess success with response prevention because the persistence of mental rituals can reduce therapy effectiveness by impeding habituation to obsessions and preventing cognitive change. Because thinking obsessional thoughts is incompatible with neutralizing them with mental rituals, the best form of response prevention for mental rituals is continual *exposure* to the obsessional thought. Loop tape exposure (as described in chapter 10) can therefore be used as both exposure and response prevention. As a backup plan, mental rituals that cannot be resisted may be performed incorrectly as described earlier.

When Patients Use Religious Rituals.   Very religious patients who suffer from unacceptable thoughts often need help differentiating between healthy religious behavior on the one hand, and religious strategies that they use expressly in response to obsessional thoughts on the other. Whereas the former need not be targeted in response prevention, if the latter persist, they reinforce dysfunctional beliefs such as "Praying keeps me from acting on unwanted sexual impulses." In addressing this dilemma, the therapist should show respect and understanding for the patient's religious beliefs, yet help the patient see that some of his or her "religious" behavior is actually safety seeking and counterproductive. Whereas directly confronting the patient with this fact might appear as an assault on his or her religion, a suggested solution is to engage in a Socratic dialogue that induces the patient into elaborating this point, as in the following example:

Therapist: It sounds like you often turn to prayers for managing your obsessions; like to get rid of your unwanted sexual thoughts.

Patient: Yes. God is the only one who can save me from all my immoral thoughts and make them go away.

Therapist: And what effects do the prayers have on the obsessions? Does praying make the thoughts go away?

Patient: Well, if they worked, I wouldn't be here.

Therapist: What do you mean? Tell me more about that.

Patient: Even though I'm always praying to stop the thoughts, I'm still having them as much as ever. I think that lately they've even become worse, if anything.

Therapist: Interesting. So what you're saying is that despite all your prayers, the obsessions have intensified. What do you think that says about praying as a strategy for managing obsessional thoughts?

Patient: Hmm [thinks to himself]. I never looked at it that way before.

Therapist: I know that prayer is important for you, and that it makes you feel closer to God. But since you are telling me that praying about the obsessions hasn't worked very well, would you consider learning a different strategy when it comes to dealing with these thoughts?

Patient: Well, my pastor did say that I pray too much about the wrong things. Maybe he was right.

Allowing the patient to take the lead in sorting out which religious behaviors could be labeled as part of OCD and which as part of routine religious practice may be helpful. Religious behavior motivated by obsessional thoughts is not technically religious. Such behavior is fear based rather than faith based. Therefore, effective treatment will help the patient practice his or her religion in a healthier way (without obsessive fear). The assistance of family members and religious authorities who can reinforce the distinction between healthy and unhealthy religious practice may be necessary for implementing response prevention for such patients.

INCLUDING FAMILY MEMBERS
AND FRIENDS IN TREATMENT

For many patients, assessment will reveal that family and friends have become involved with OCD symptoms. Patients with checking rituals often ask cohabitants to conduct a final examination of the doors and windows before coming to bed. Those with contamination fears might require family members to avoid certain areas of the house or engage in washing or cleaning rituals. Other patients repeatedly query relatives and friends for reassurance. Because treatment cannot be successful if such behavior is occurring, it is important that family and close friends curb their participation in these symptoms. In addition, a particular support person can be identified who will help the patient complete homework tasks and refrain from rituals between sessions. In the following sections, I describe how to prepare significant others for involvement in treatment.

Ending Family Involvement in Symptoms

Friends and relatives of the patient must agree to no longer respond in ways that sustain OCD symptoms, and it is a good idea to stipulate with family members or close friends some specific guidelines for ending such behavior. First, family members must stop assisting the patient with avoidance behavior. For example, parents are no longer to restrict what they touch or who or what they bring into the house; and friends should no longer avoid feared numbers or words (e.g., *cancer*). A second guideline is that relatives must agree to refrain from helping the patient perform compulsive rituals. For example, extra soap or wipes should no longer be stocked in the house and spouses should refuse to check doors and appliances or call poison control. Finally, those close to the patient must stop responding to requests for reassurance. When asked questions such as "Do you think this will poison me?" "Did I pick up all of the pieces of broken glass?" or "Should I confess about my bad thoughts?" relatives should remind the patient that they have agreed not to answer such questions any longer.

Certain challenges may arise when asking family members to end their participation in OCD symptoms. For example, relatives may be concerned that if they stop helping, the patient will be subjected to harmful levels of anxiety. This underscores the importance of reviewing how anxiety is not dangerous and how it subsides naturally even if rituals are not performed. Another reservation concerns the prospect of hostility if the patient's requests for help are not met. Some patients manipulate others using tantrums and threats such as "If you don't flush the toilet for me, I will go berserk!" In such instances the therapist should acknowledge that it is difficult to change such behaviors, but that if treatment is to be successful, family members must not help with OCD symptoms, and the patient must agree not to act in hostile or otherwise manipulative ways. Reaching an agreement before treatment begins regarding how such conduct will be handled is often a good way to sidestep such problems.

The Designated Support Person

Choosing a Support Person. Help from a relative or close friend who understands the symptoms of OCD and the demands of treatment is likely to make the distress experienced during ERP easier for the patient to endure. In chapter 7, I discussed certain characteristics to look for in a potential support person. Briefly, the patient should choose someone who is considerate, sensitive, and optimistic that treatment will be helpful. The support person should also be warm, thoughtful, and willing to challenge or confront the patient constructively and in a nonjudgmental way when difficulties arise. Family members who appear overbearing, pessimistic, sarcastic, highly critical, or antagonistic should not be selected because greater harm might be done than progress made. On the other hand, someone who is smothering or eager to become overly involved in treatment is equally undesirable because he or she might inadvertently act in ways that absolve the patient of his or her responsibility for getting well. For this reason, it is recommended that the therapist meet and briefly evaluate the patient's rapport with the support person before agreeing to their coming on board.

Preparing the Support Person. It is helpful for the designated support person to be present intermittently during the treatment planning phase so that he or she may be socialized to the cognitive-behavioral model of OCD and the treatment rationale. For two reasons, I find it useful to ask the patient to take the lead in teaching the support person(s) about this material. First, this provides a guarantee that the patient has consolidated this material well enough to explain it coherently to someone else (the therapist can fill in gaps as needed). Second, it reinforces the patient's role as taking responsibility for his or her own treatment. It is helpful to also have the support person present during the initial exposure sessions so that he or she gets a sense of how treatment is implemented and what is expected of the patient.

The support person's role should be precisely clarified: It is to function as an advisor to the patient. He or she should provide encouragement and make suggestions and recommendations, typically when the patient requests help or needs guidance. No threats or physical force are to be used to change the patient's behavior. The support person should not be "on the patient's back." Examples of useful comments that support persons can make at various junctures during treatment are presented in Table 11.2. These might be reviewed, and role plays conducted, to ensure that such comments are given appropriately. Patients should be instructed to call on the support person when they feel they need help. My colleague Dr. David Tolin has developed a useful handout for reviewing these arrangements and agreeing on a specific plan (see Handout 11.2). The handout, which is to be reviewed during treatment planning, includes a contract defining the roles of the patient and support person. It also reinforces a team approach to overcoming OCD.

> Susan elected to have her husband, Steve, serve as her support person. Steve and Susan appeared to have a sound marriage and seemed to communicate well with each other. After discussing how Susan and Steve interacted regarding Susan's problems with OCD, the therapist agreed that Steve would be a fine source of support for Susan. Although Steve was also interested in helping his wife, he understood that his role was not to scrutinize her behavior, but instead to be there for her when she needed him. When not physically in the same place, he agreed to be available by cellular phone as much as possible. Handout 11.2 was then reviewed and Steve was invited to attend the first exposure session.

CLARIFYING THE TREATMENT PLAN

When completed, the fear hierarchy and response prevention plans represent a contract that must be explicitly endorsed by both the patient and therapist. Mutual agreement on how exposure sessions will proceed helps build the patient's trust that there will be no surprises. It also gives the therapist leverage if the patient refuses to engage in certain exposures. Nevertheless, flexibility is important because unanticipated factors that are beyond the patient's or therapist's control inevitably influence the course of treatment. For example, the initial fear hierarchy is subject to alteration if it becomes clear that the patient is having difficulty managing associated distress. In such cases the planned exposure may be temporarily tabled in favor of intermediate situations that evoke less distress.

Before beginning ERP, Susan's therapist reiterated key points about the treatment plan and what would be expected of Susan during treatment. Steve was present for this discussion.

> Therapist: Over our last few meetings we have exchanged a great deal of information. You have taught me about the particulars of your OCD symptoms and I have taught you how to think about these symptoms in a way that will help us to reduce them. We have also put together a plan for reducing your

TABLE 11.2
Comments for Support Persons to Use
When Assisting Patients with OCD Treatment

During homework exposure practices

- I know this must be hard for you, but you're doing a good job so far.
- Remember that the anxiety is temporary. Think of how good you'll feel when you're finished.
- Remember what Dr. _____ said … you have to make yourself anxious to get better.
- Let's talk about the realistic chances that harm will actually occur.
- If you stop now, you'll only be making OCD worse. It's worth deciding to be anxious.
- We can take a break as long as we decide now when we are going to try again.
- I'm sorry that you have decided not to do the exposure. We'll have to let Dr. _____ know.

If the patient is having difficulty resisting urges to ritualize or seek reassurance

- Let's go for a little walk and maybe that will help.
- Remember that your urge will go down, but only if you keep resisting. Remember, the anxiety is temporary.
- It sounds like you want reassurance, but we all agreed that it is not helpful for me to answer that question.
- Do you really think _____ will happen if you don't ritualize? Let's talk about that.
- I know it's hard to resist doing rituals. What can I do to help you get through this tough time?
- I don't think you're making a good choice here, but I realize it's hard for you. Make sure you write down that you did a ritual so that we can talk about it with Dr. _____. There will be other chances for you to practice more.

If the patient is avoiding fear-evoking situations that have already been addressed in exposure sessions

- By avoiding you are just making OCD stronger. I think you're making a bad choice.
- I know it's a challenge, but you can do it. Confronting will help you overcome OCD.
- What evidence is there that this is dangerous? Let's look at the realistic probability of harm.
- Remember what happened when you confronted this situation before? You eventually felt much less anxious. There is every reason to think the same thing will happen if you face your fear again.

267

PLEASE HELP ME WITH MY OCD!

I am working on overcoming OCD. The purpose of this handout is to ask for your help with my therapy.

OCD consists of *obsessions*, which are upsetting thoughts, images, or impulses; and *compulsive rituals*, which are repeated behaviors that I do to try to cope with the obsessions or make me feel safer. Some common rituals are: washing or cleaning, checking, arranging, praying, repeating actions, or asking for reassurance. Some common "compulsive reassurance-seeking" questions are: "Will I get sick if I touch this?" "Are you sure I turned the stove off?" "Are you sure nothing bad is going to happen?"

The problem is that even though my rituals make me feel a little bit better for a short while, they prevent me from getting better in the long run. How does this happen? Rituals prevent me from learning that a situation is safe and that I can handle obsessional fear. They teach me that the only way to cope with my anxiety is to do *more rituals*!

So obsessions and rituals are related to each other in a cycle, like the drawing on the right. Obsessions lead to rituals, but rituals also keep me from overcoming my obsessions. I'm trapped!

I need help to break out of this cycle. Obsessions are involuntary, meaning I don't have them on purpose and can't just make them go away. But compulsive rituals are voluntary; I do have control over them (even though I don't always feel like I have control). So the best way for me to break the OCD cycle is to *stop doing rituals*

Here's how I'd like you to help:

1. I need your encouragement not to do rituals. If you see me doing any of my rituals, please remind me *gently* that I'm not supposed to do them any more. Don't use force, threats, yelling, or nagging—those just make me feel more anxious. Instead, please give me support and show me that you care about me and want me to get better by stopping my ritualizing. Remember that OCD is the enemy, not me!

2. I might slip up and ask you to cooperate with my rituals, or even do them for me. But, this is very bad for me! *Please do not cooperate with my rituals, even if I ask you to.* I promise to try not to ask you to, but if I do, please respond with: "*We agreed that I would not cooperate with your rituals. Because I care about you and want you to get better, I'm not going to... (do that for you, answer that question, etc.).*"

When you stop cooperating with my rituals, I might try even <u>harder</u> to get you to cooperate with the rituals. I will try my best not to do this, but if I do, it's important that you not give in to my OCD.

I understand that overcoming OCD is *my* responsibility, not yours. But I would like your help if I need it. This letter signifies my commitment to overcoming OCD, and my serious desire for you to help me in the ways described in this letter.

_____

Signatures

Date

Handout 11.2. "Please Help Me With My OCD." Developed by David F. Tolin, PhD, The Institute of Living, Hartford, CT. Adapted with the permission of David F. Tolin, PhD.

symptoms in which you will practice confronting the situations and thoughts that evoke obsessional fear while refraining from maladaptive behaviors such as washing and checking rituals. Before we start, I want us to review this treatment plan one last time to be sure we are on the same page about how therapy will progress from here.

The therapist then showed Susan a copy of the fear hierarchy (see Fig. 10.2).

Therapist: As we have talked about, when you avoid situations that evoke obsessional fear, like public bathrooms, you are able to hide from your OCD symptoms. However, avoidance is not a good long-term solution because it prevents you from being able to tell whether your obsessional fears are unfounded. So, avoidance prevents you from getting over OCD. Beginning with the next session, I will help you to practice confronting the items listed on the fear hierarchy that we developed together. You will start with exposure to situations that evoke moderate levels of anxiety and work up to facing more difficult situations that you perceive as highly risky or dangerous. Of course, the exposure tasks will more than likely produce feelings of anxiety, especially in the beginning. After all, you have been trying to avoid these situations as much as you can. However, it is important for you to remember that your anxiety will diminish during the exposure session by the process of habituation. Each time you practice an exposure, your symptoms will decline further and further. Exposure exercises will also help you to correct mistaken beliefs about risk and danger associated with your obsessional thoughts and situations. For example, by repeatedly touching the toilet, you will find out that toilets do not usually make people sick.

As a result of habituation and the correction of mistaken beliefs, exposure situations will become easier and easier to face. This is how your obsessional fear will be weakened. I will also be giving you exposure tasks to complete between sessions and I expect that you will devote ample time and effort to these practices. To get better you will need to consistently practice confronting, rather than avoiding, situations that evoke obsessional fear. If you have trouble with doing these exposures, you should ask Steve to help you.

Next, the therapist addressed response prevention and the seemingly strict guidelines for curtailing all rituals. It is important that the patient understand the reason for putting these rules into place. Susan's response prevention plan is shown in Fig. 11.1.

> Therapist: Exposure will probably also make you want to do rituals and other safety behaviors to relieve your anxiety; after all, that has been your pattern of responding to obsessions for a long time. However, while rituals might make you feel better in the short term, they are not a good long-term solution because they prevent you from getting over OCD. For example, how can you ever learn that trash cans aren't dangerous if you always wash your hands immediately after throwing

---

Help with Response Prevention

- Specific response prevention Instructions:

  1. No contact with water except for one 10-minute shower each morning.
  2. No cleaning of objects (including the toilet seat).
  3. No rechecking for mistakes in working with students' papers/grades.
  4. No checking applicances (or asking others to check).
  5. No cancelling out or suppressing unwanted thoughts.
  6. No praying in response to unwanted thoughts.

- **Choose not to ritualize--** even small rituals interfere with your progress.
- If you are having trouble resisting the urge to ritualize:
- ➤ Remember that the urge is based on a mistaken belief or assumption. You don't *really* need to ritualize to feel better or reduce the chances of harm or danger.
- ➤ Find someone to talk to and ask them to stay with you until the urge passes.
- ➤ Leave the situation for a while (if possible) to get away from reminders.
- ➤ If you perform any rituals, immediately record the ritual on a self-monitoring form and discuss it with your therapist.
- ➤ Deliberately re-expose yourself to the situation that evoked the ritual.

FIG. 11.1. Susan T.'s response prevention plan.

something away? So, starting at our next session, you must also agree to work very hard on stopping all of your compulsive rituals and other strategies to neutralize obsessional fear. In addition, you are not to ask other people to ritualize for you or to do anything else to help you cope with obsessional fear by avoidance. This is the response prevention component of CBT. Only when all rituals are stopped can you learn that these behaviors are not necessary to keep you safe. If you continue to do rituals like washing and checking, it will undermine exposure. There is no point in exposing you to touching toilets if you are going to take a long shower afterward since you would never learn that toilets are not as threatening as you fear.

You can expect that at times, resisting the urge to wash, check, and dismiss intrusive thoughts will be difficult for you. If you feel you cannot resist doing a ritual, you should find Steve and ask for his help; he has agreed to assist by distracting you or by helping you think more clearly about your fears. If you are still unable to resist doing a ritual, or even if you do one without thinking about it, you need to let me know by recording what happened on your self-monitoring forms. I will not be upset with you if you ritualize, but instead we will use the opportunity to problem solve about ways to help you better resist these compulsions. Also, any rituals should be followed by immediate re-exposure to the situation or thought that triggered the rituals.

This handout (referring to Fig. 11.1) contains your goals for response prevention. I know that some of the rules we have set up go beyond what people ordinarily do. I know that while most people are encouraged to wash their hands after using the bathroom or before they eat, you are not supposed to do these things during treatment. The reason for restricting your washing and cleaning is to help you change your beliefs about danger. That is, by not washing, you will give yourself the opportunity to find out that all of the extensive washing you were doing was unnecessary and that even if you resist urges to wash, you are unlikely to get sick or make others sick. Do you have any questions about this plan?

Next, the therapist reiterated his own role in the therapy program. Active treatments such as CBT are collaborative efforts between the therapist and patient. This means that the patient, therapist, and any support persons agree to form an alliance against OCD. The therapist is viewed as an expert, teacher, or coach, and the patient as apprentice or pupil. The therapist's job is to listen to the patient's concerns, teach skills, and encourage. The patient's job is to express his or her difficulties, practice, learn, and implement what he or she is learning.

> Therapist: As I have said before, you can think of me as your coach and your cheerleader. As your coach, my job is to help you learn and practice techniques that will reduce your OCD symptoms. These techniques help many people with OCD, but only when they are used in the right way. So, your job will be to practice these techniques in the exact way that I coach you so that you can get the most out of them. If you don't practice them correctly, you will reduce the chances of getting over OCD. This means that the responsibility falls on you to let me know when you are having trouble, need my help, or if you are upset with me or do not want to follow my instructions. It is important that we openly discuss and try to resolve any concerns that you have. If you do not bring these problems to my attention, you might end up missing out on opportunities to take advantage of my coaching. As a coach, it is not my job to *force* you to practice the techniques I teach you, and so I will not try to do this.
>
> In my role as cheerleader, I will be supporting you every step of the way as you implement your new skills. I will help you troubleshoot and encourage you to work your hardest. I will also give you a pat on the back when you do a nice job and try to motivate you to stick with it if the going gets tough. So, do you agree to this treatment plan?

The treatment planning phase concludes with a discussion of any questions or concerns raised by the patient or any others who have joined the session. When the patient indicates acceptance of the treatment plan, the initial exposure session can begin.

12

Conducting Exposure Therapy Sessions

Exposure and response prevention are the essential component of CBT for anxiety disorders. In the case of OCD, successful long-term improvement requires that the patient repeatedly confront obsessional stimuli directly and without engaging in safety behaviors such as compulsive rituals, neutralization, or reassurance seeking. Therapeutic exposure elicits obsessional fear, which is then allowed to decline while the patient remains exposed to the obsessional stimuli. Cognitive techniques are also used to facilitate the correction of catastrophic beliefs that underlie OCD symptoms. This chapter discusses how to conduct exposure therapy sessions for OCD. It covers procedures for acclimating patients to the treatment procedures, assisting them with gradually confronting stimuli of greater and greater difficulty, and assigning and reviewing homework exposure practice. The integration of cognitive techniques with exposure is highlighted throughout the chapter. As in previous chapters, Susan T.'s case is used to illustrate how exposure procedures are commonly implemented.

GETTING THE MOST OUT OF EXPOSURE: CAPITALIZING ON COGNITIVE AND BEHAVIORAL MECHANISMS OF CHANGE

The initial explanations for how exposure procedures reduce anxiety were couched in behavioral terms: With repeated and prolonged exposure, classically conditioned fear responses gradually diminish by the process of habituation or desensitization (Stampfl & Levis, 1967; Wolpe, 1958). Later theories proposed a cognitive mechanism: Confrontation with fear-evoking stimuli, in the absence of the expected feared consequences, provides the patient with corrective information that disconfirms catastrophic beliefs that cause obsessional anxiety (Foa & Kozak, 1986). Although CT is also proposed to reduce anxiety by correcting irrational beliefs, exposure procedures are actually more persuasive vehicles of cognitive change than are verbal CT techniques. In acknowledgment of this, some authors include exposure techniques (renamed behavioral experiments) as core components of CT (e.g., Van Oppen & Arntz, 1994). Used in this way, the conditioning or habituation explanation is dropped and exposure is used expressly to test predictions about the dangerousness of situations and the need for safety behaviors.

However, using exposure therapy with the intention of modifying faulty cognitions does not rob this technique of its behavioral effects (i.e., habituation). In fact, habituation itself provides a major source of cognitive change: Patients learn that their anxiety remains manageable and subsides over time even if safety behaviors are not performed. In addition to providing ideal conditions for modifying cognitions, exposure therapy affects the patient's self-concept. By facing feared situations and developing healthy coping strategies, the individual is forced to modify negative representations of the self, leading to a sense of confidence that he or she can manage the situation (Tallis, 1995). Such changes probably contribute to the patient's decision to persist with intrinsically difficult treatments such as ERP. Therefore it is most beneficial for therapists to capitalize on the fact that ERP can produce change through both cognitive and behavioral mechanisms. Accordingly, the exposure procedures described in this chapter include systematic repeated and prolonged confrontation with feared stimuli in the absence of safety behaviors (to promote the habituation of fear). These exercises are framed in terms of their effects on cognitions (to promote the correction of faulty beliefs).

Unfortunately, the dialogue that takes place between patient and therapist during the implementation of exposure often receives short shrift in descriptions of ERP. Nevertheless, the use of CT techniques (as described in chapter 9) to assist patients with examining and modifying their thinking in the context of exposure likely contributes to exposure's effectiveness. As I illustrate in this chapter, cognitive interventions can be utilized at various points during exposure sessions to promote adherence and facilitate symptom reduction. When preparing for each exposure exercise, cognitive techniques are used to help identify the key mistaken cognitions and feared consequences. The importance of learning to take risks and manage acceptable levels of uncertainty should also be discussed. During exposure exercises, cognitive interventions can be used to develop healthy psychological responses to obsessional fear (e.g., "I must confront my fear to prove to myself that harm is unlikely," or "Even if I initially feel anxious, these feelings subside if I do not do any rituals"). After completing an exposure task, cognitive techniques are used to help the patient review the outcome of the exercise, examine evidence for and against catastrophic beliefs, and develop more realistic beliefs about obsessional stimuli.

THE STRUCTURE OF EXPOSURE SESSIONS

Optimally, 90 minutes should be allotted for each exposure session. This is usually sufficient time to allow patients to experience habituation of anxiety. Each appointment should begin with a 5- to 10-minute check-in and review of the past session's homework assignment, which includes examination of self-monitoring forms and exposure practice forms (discussed later in this chapter). Next, the prearranged exposure task is introduced and the patient confronts the feared stimuli in vivo or in imagination. The actual duration of exposure is determined by the patient's anxiety level. As described later, exposure is terminated when the patient's anxiety level (i.e., SUDS) has decreased to at least 50% to 60% of its initial (or peak) level. Ideally, the patient should remain in the feared situation until he or she experiences only a mild sense of subjective distress. About 15 minutes at the end of each session should be allocated for debriefing, assigning homework practice, and discussing the next session's exposure task.

EARLY EXPOSURE SESSIONS

On an organizational note, because Susan T.'s first exposure targeted contamination fears (see Fig. 10.2), this section simultaneously illustrates how to conduct early exposure sessions, as well as how to implement exposure for contamination symptoms. Later sections of this chapter illustrate the implementation of exposure for the harming, incompleteness, and unacceptable thoughts symptom dimensions.

Preparing the Patient

Early exposure sessions should begin with a brief review of the cognitive-behavioral model of OCD and rationale for ERP. The therapist might "quiz" the patient on this information by asking questions such as, "Why will purposely facing the situations you are afraid of help you reduce OCD symptoms?" Some patients are skeptical about exposure therapy on the basis of previous attempts at confronting obsessional stimuli that failed to reduce fear. If this point is raised, the therapist should draw a distinction between typical exposure and therapeutic exposure. Whether deliberately or by accident, most patients at some point encounter their feared stimuli. However, in most cases, they manage to avoid direct or prolonged exposure and are inclined to ritualize as soon as possible after the encounter. This is referred to as *typical exposure* because it is characteristic of how the patient has used maladaptive OCD habits to handle confrontation with obsessional stimuli. In contrast, *therapeutic exposure* is well planned, involves rational thinking, is performed without avoidance or safety behaviors, and lasts until anxiety subsides on its own. If the patient experiences a sense of relief on terminating exposure, it will reinforce avoidance habits as well as the belief that feared consequences are likely. Only systematic, prolonged, and well-controlled exposure practices are sufficient to reduce obsessional fears at the gut level. Such practices must be repeated until they no longer evoke distress. Handout 12.1, "Guidelines for Effective Exposure Practice," helps to clarify expectations for how exposure sessions should proceed. The handout should be reviewed with patients before getting started.

Managing "Cold Feet"

Therapists should be prepared to offer comfort and encouragement if the patient reports apprehension before beginning the first exposure. Susan's initial exposure involved touching communal surfaces such as door handles, stairway railings, elevator buttons, and public telephones. However, she expressed trepidation at the prospect of beginning this task. The therapist understood her concerns and explained how the session would proceed.

Therapist: You look apprehensive. What are your thoughts about doing this exposure?

Susan: I'm a little scared. I don't know what to expect and I don't like feeling anxious.

Guidelines for Effective Exposure Practice

1. **Prepare to feel anxious.** It is normal to feel uncomfortable during exposure practice. In fact, if you feel anxious it means you are doing exposure correctly. The object is to provoke obsessional fear and urges to ritualize, which you will practice resisting. Your job is to remain in the situation until your anxiety subsides on its own.

2. **Try not to fight your fear.** Fighting the anxiety during exposure will make you even more anxious. Instead, just let yourself be uncomfortable. Remember that the worst thing that will happen is *temporary* distress.

3. **Do not use avoidance, rituals, or reassurance seeking during exposure.** In order to reduce your fears, exposure practices must be completed without compulsive rituals, reassurance seeking, avoidance, distraction, medications, alcohol, or other strategies that make you feel safer or that prevent you from becoming anxious.

4. **Test out negative beliefs about the consequences of facing your fear.** Before beginning an exposure, ask yourself what you are afraid might happen if you confront this situation. Then, like a scientist, test out whether your fearful prediction is true by doing the exposure. Afterwards, consider what the experience has taught you. What evidence did you gain? What do you now think about the exposure situation?

5. **Keep track of your SUDS.** During exposure practices it is important to monitor how distressed you are feeling using the SUDS scale from 0 (calm) to 100 (extremely anxious). Pay attention to whether your level of fearfulness changes as time goes by.

6. **Each exposure practice should continue until you feel a significant reduction in anxiety.** Remain exposed to the feared situation until your anxiety subsides, no matter how long this takes. If you leave the situation when you are still very anxious, you are convincing yourself that the situation is dangerous and you will not reduce your fear.

7. **Repeat exposures until they no longer make you very anxious.** The more an exposure is practiced, the more your feelings of anxiety will decrease and the easier it will be to feel comfortable with the feared situation.

8. **Practice exposure in different settings.** Confronting your fears in new and different settings helps to solidify your improvement. Practice exposure with your therapist, with family members (if applicable), on your own, and in various places that trigger obsessions.

Handout 12.1.   Guidelines for effective exposure practice.

Therapist: I understand. Would it help if I told you how I think we should proceed?

Susan: Sure.

Therapist: First, you will be in the driver's seat. My job is only to help you get the most benefit from the exercise. So, we will go around touching door handles, railings, and elevator buttons that you are afraid will produce illness. I will be monitoring your level of distress, but you should also feel free to let me know how you are doing. I will also be helping you resist any urges to ritualize. At first, I expect that you will feel uncomfortable. But you will see that your distress subsides over time. We will stop the exposure when your anxiety has decreased considerably from the starting level. Then, we will discuss what you learned from doing the exercise, and come up with some situations for you to practice on your own before the next session. How does that sound?

Susan: Scary, but I know it's what I have to do. Let's get started.

Introducing the Exercise

The therapist begins by describing how the feared stimulus will be confronted, for how long, and what kinds of behaviors are not permitted. A brief description of the exercise can be entered on the Exposure Practice Form (Fig. 12.1), which is used to keep a record of beliefs and SUDS levels during the exposure session. Susan's therapist introduced Susan's first exposure as follows:

Therapist: We'll begin the exposure gradually so that you ease yourself into it, but my goal is for you to "contaminate" yourself with "germs" from surfaces other people often touch. So, first we'll walk around the clinic, then we can go to some nearby places; and your job will be to practice touching things. I will be asking you to rate your SUDS level every 5 minutes, so have a number between 1 and 100 in mind.

Eliciting Dysfunctional Beliefs

The therapist should be able to anticipate the patient's dysfunctional beliefs about the feared consequences of exposure to the selected hierarchy item(s). Typical examples include an exaggerated fear of harm as well as the fear that anxiety will persist if safety behaviors are not performed. If such negative predictions cannot readily be identified, the therapist should specifically inquire about fear of anxiety or discomfort ("Do you worry that you would never be

Exposure Practice Form

Name: Date: Time: Session #:

1. Description of the exposure practice:

2. Feared outcome of exposure:

3. What is the chance that the feared outcome will occur? (0-100%): _____ %

4. If the feared outcome occurred, how severe would it be? (0-100%): _____ %

5. Every _____ minutes during the exposure, rate SUDS from 0 to 100:

6. SUDS when beginning exposure (0-100) _____

SUDS	SUDS	SUDS	SUDS	SUDS
1. _____	7. _____	13. _____	19. _____	25. _____
2. _____	8. _____	14. _____	20. _____	26. _____
3. _____	9. _____	15. _____	21. _____	27. _____
4. _____	10. _____	16. _____	22. _____	28. _____
5. _____	11. _____	17. _____	23. _____	29. _____
6. _____	12. _____	18. _____	24. _____	30. _____

6. What was the outcome of the exposure? What was learned?

7. Revised likelihood estimate: (0-100%): _____ %

8. Revised threat severity estimate: (0-100%): _____ %

FIG. 12.1. Exposure Practice Form for use with in-session exposure tasks.

able to feel comfortable if you were exposed to this situation without doing rituals?"). The feared consequence should be clarified as specifically as possible because it is this belief that the exposure task needs to disconfirm. Once identified, the belief is recorded on the Exposure Practice Form. Susan's therapist explained the cognitive aspects of exposure as follows:

Therapist: During exposure, we will be putting your fears to the test. So, before we start, what are you afraid might happen if you touch things like door handles and public telephones, knowing that washing your hands is off limits?

Susan: I could get sick or spread germs and make other people sick. You never know who put their hands there last.

Therapist: [writes these beliefs on the Exposure Practice Form] So, how likely is it (what percent) that you will get sick if you touch door handles without washing?

Susan: Not too likely … maybe about 30%. [Therapist writes the probability estimate on the form.]

Therapist: And how severe would it be if your fears came true?

Susan: About 75%. [Therapist records severity rating on the form.]

Introducing the Feared Stimulus

After obtaining a baseline SUDS rating (Susan's was 50) the feared item is presented. It is a good idea to begin contamination exposures gradually and observe how the patient responds. If he or she eagerly "jumps in," reinforce this and follow the lead. If things are progressing very slowly, some encouragement might be needed to pick up the pace. If necessary, the therapist can model initial contact with the feared stimulus. Patients are encouraged to focus on, rather than distract themselves from, the exposure stimulus (Grayson, Foa, & Steketee, 1982, 1986). Regularly asking questions such as "How are you feeling now?" "What are you telling yourself?" or "What's your SUDS?" is a good way to maintain this focus and to continually assess thoughts and feelings during the exercise.

Susan and her therapist walked to the door of another office in the clinic. The therapist first modeled exposure by grabbing hold of the door handle and instructing Susan that she would be expected to do the same when it was her turn. It is important for patients to fully confront feared contaminants. Briefly touching items with fingertips does not make for adequate exposure. Patients must feel thoroughly contaminated.

Therapist: Now, I'd like you to do what I'm doing.

Susan: [hesitates] … OK. [holds on to the door handle] There, I'm doing it.

Therapist: Great … Make sure you have good firm contact … So, how does it feel?

Susan: My head is spinning a little. I'm nervous. I don't know who else has touched this or where they had their hands.

Therapist: Well, that's true. I don't know who has touched this either. But most likely, it's safe enough. After all, people use door handles all the time. What's your SUDS now?

Susan: About 60.

Therapist: How strong is your urge to wash right now?

Susan: Pretty strong. I would definitely like to wash my hands.

Therapist: You're doing a great job. Keep holding on.

Note how the therapist amplified Susan's sense of uncertainty regarding who else had touched the door handle, yet also modeled a noncatastrophic response to this uncertainty. This maneuver helps the patient learn alternative ways to view acceptable levels of risk and uncertainty (i.e., as nonthreatening). Note also the use of praise for following through with exposure tasks. This is an important rhetorical strategy for encouraging adherence.

The therapist then gave Susan two paper towels and asked her to contaminate them with "door handle germs" by touching the paper towels to the door handle. Next, the exercise was repeated with several other door handles, a hand railing, a public telephone, and elevator call buttons. At each step, the paper towels were used to collect "germs." Every 5 minutes the therapist inquired about Susan's SUDS ratings. After about 10 minutes of touching these surfaces, Susan's SUDS had decreased to 50. At that point they returned to the office to continue the exposure using the contaminated paper towels. Sitting in a chair, Susan spread the paper towels out in her lap and placed her hand on top of them. She acknowledged feeling quite contaminated. Over the next 10 minutes, though, her SUDS decreased to 40.

Amplifying the Exposure

Amplifying refers to purposely increasing the difficulty of an exposure to address a particular aspect of avoidance or a specific dysfunctional belief. For contamination exposures, amplification usually involves contaminating the parts of one's body or inanimate objects that the patient would otherwise try to avoid tainting. Common examples include the face, hair, purses, wallets, lipsticks, and so on. Once Susan appeared less distressed with the paper towels in her lap, the therapist encouraged her to spread the contamination to other parts of her body:

Therapist: What's your SUDS now?
Susan: I'm at about 40. I'm doing OK.
Therapist: Good. You look more at ease than you did a little while ago. I'd like you to touch the paper towels to the rest of your body … your arms, face, and hair.
Susan: Oh, I don't know if I can do that.
Therapist: Would you like me to show you what I mean?
Susan: Sure.
Therapist: [Confidently takes one of the paper towels and rubs it on his arms, legs, face, and hair]. There, now I'm all contaminated.

Now, you try it. Spread the contamination all over and let yourself feel totally tainted.

Susan: That looks really hard.

Therapist: Just take a deep breath and go for it. It will only get easier from here.

Susan: [Takes the paper towel and thoroughly touches it to various body parts including her face and hair.] There, I did it. Look at that. I did it.

Therapist: Yes you did. Great going! That's pretty brave. What's your SUDS?

Susan: 55.

About 5 minutes later, the therapist asked Susan to repeat this amplification exercise. By this time, her SUDS had decreased back to 40. Exposures should be reamplified every 5 to 10 minutes during the session until little or no distress is evoked. Further discussion revealed that Susan was worried contamination would spread to her purse, its contents, and various other personal items such as her wallet, lipstick, and water bottle. She also feared this could increase the chances of becoming sick. Therefore, subsequent amplification involved tainting these items. After about 30 minutes of exposure, Susan's SUDS level was 30.

The therapist then reminded Susan that she would have to go the rest of the day without washing or cleaning and asked if she could think of any obstacles to adhering with the response prevention plan. Susan remarked that eating would be particularly troublesome because she was concerned that germs from her hands would be transferred to food. To address this concern, the therapist suggested that Susan eat a snack (peanuts) off the contaminated paper towels using her hands (contamination exposures can often be amplified by having the patient handle and eat food during the session). At first, Susan was reluctant. Yet after a discussion about her mistaken beliefs concerning danger, and the fact that her anxiety had subsided, she agreed to give it a try. After the therapist modeled eating several peanuts that had been placed on the paper towels, Susan followed suit. Although her SUDS initially increased with this exercise, after about 10 minutes, it had decreased back to 30. She said she felt more comfortable about eating without washing. After 45 minutes of exposure, Susan's SUDS was 20 and the exercise was stopped. Susan was instructed to place one of the tainted paper towels in her pants pocket and the other in her purse to ensure that she remained contaminated for the rest of the day. She was instructed to refrain from ritualizing, but that if she did violate response prevention, she must record the violation on the self-monitoring forms and recontaminate herself by either touching more public surfaces or using the paper towels.

Careful Observation and Ongoing Assessment

The therapist should continually be on the lookout for subtle safety behaviors such as wiping one's hands on one's pants, opening doors with one's feet, or any other curious maneuvers that most individuals under similar circumstances probably would not do. Patients who appear to "space out" during exposure should be asked whether they are engaging in mental strategies such as praying, reassurance seeking, distracting, or analyzing. These safety behaviors limit the effectiveness of therapy because they protect the patient from direct exposure to feared stimuli and thereby prevent the natural habituation of anxiety. These behaviors might also have become so habitual that they occur without the patient's awareness. Accordingly, they should be brought to the patient's attention whenever they are observed, and strongly discouraged.

The therapist should be on the lookout for additional situations that need to be incorporated into the present exposure or targeted in homework practices. Patients often make impromptu remarks about aspects of the feared stimulus that they find especially fearful or distressing. These comments reflect catastrophic cognitions. Susan, for example, mentioned during the session that she would feel especially fearful if she contaminated her children's belongings with germs from public surfaces. In other words, she believed that she was likely to make her children sick. The therapist must be attentive to such comments (and encourage the patient to be open in reporting them) so that exposures can be designed to target as specifically as possible the patient's obsessional fears. Accordingly, Susan was encouraged to contaminate her children's bedrooms with the paper towels from the session (see the discussion of homework exposure later in this chapter).

Incorporating Imaginal Exposure to Feared Consequences

Secondary imaginal exposure to feared consequences (see chapter 10) is often useful with contamination exposures. If not knowing whether feared consequences will happen (or have already happened; e.g., "I could have poisoned someone without realizing it") is a source of anxiety, the scene should focus on uncertainty (i.e., not knowing the outcome). Because Susan described images of germs and fears of contaminating her children, an imaginal exposure was conducted to these obsessional stimuli. The therapist introduced the procedure as follows:

Therapist: You told me about certain thoughts you were having, such as images of germs and doubts about making your family sick. When these obsessional thoughts occur, you are in the habit of responding as if they are true just *because you think them*. This leads to anxiety and makes you do rituals like washing and cleaning just in case the thoughts are true. To help you change the way you manage these obsessional thoughts, we're going to have you practice thinking about obsessional thoughts without responding as you usually do. By practicing this technique, you will see that your distress subsides just like with situational exposure.

We will do this using a loop tape on which we will record your obsessional thoughts. You will then listen to the tape until it no longer evokes significant anxiety or urges to wash or clean. Every now and then I will ask for your SUDS rating.

Susan was instructed to write a lengthy description of her images of germs and of a scene in which she finds out that her children have become sick because she inadvertently contaminated them. The scene was then edited with the therapist's help and recorded onto a 2-minute loop tape. The therapist read the scenario into the tape recorder slowly to allow Susan time to visualize the scene's distressing content. Susan practiced listening to the tape and visualizing the scene while seated in a comfortable chair in the therapist's office with her eyes closed. The exposure continued until her SUDS declined from 45 to 15 (about 15 minutes). The scene that Susan confronted during her first exposure was as follows:

> You think about how you have touched all sorts of things that the general public puts their hands on. You don't know who touched the railings, elevator buttons, public telephones, and doorknobs that you touched. Now you are concerned about germs from these things. You can't see or feel the germs, but something tells you they're there. You can just imagine the germs crawling up your hands, your arms, your face, hair, and just spreading themselves all over you. You feel like going to the bathroom and washing, or taking a nice shower to make yourself feel better, but you don't. You decide to just go with the germy feeling. Now your thoughts turn to your family. You might bring home some awful sickness because you touched surfaces today and didn't wash or clean. You could infect your family. You can just picture Brian and little Jennifer becoming sick because of all the ill-advised things you did. Now, because you didn't wash, your family might become sick.

Some guidelines for implementing imaginal exposure are presented next. First, the patient should be instructed to put himself or herself "in the scene," rather than be an observer. That is, the scene should be imagined as if it were happening to them. Second, the scenes should include response prevention. For example, Susan imagined herself resisting the urge to decontaminate. Just as in situational exposures, there should be no relief (including imagined relief) from obsessive fear during imaginal exposure. Similarly, the urge to distract or disengage from the induction (e.g., "I know this isn't really happening. I'm just listening to a tape") must be resisted. The therapist might continually assess the vividness of the scene to ensure against cognitive avoidance. Finally, therapists might consider imagery training if the patient is a "poor imager." Imagery training involves instructing the patient to practice imagining scenes that tap into all five senses; for example, imagining sitting by an open window through which the sun is shining and a gentle breeze blowing. The patient is asked to feel the warmth of the sun on his or her face, the breeze gently blowing across his or her forehead, and to hear the sounds of birds and of cars passing by. Out the window, a man can be seen cutting the grass, which smells of the fragrance of cut grass. The patient then imagines taking a sip of apple juice and is struck by the taste of the cool drink. Imagery training continues until the patient reports imagining the scene vividly.

Augmenting Exposure with Cognitive Interventions

The therapist takes an active role in facilitating cognitive change during exposure. In other words, one does not simply sit and wait passively for habituation to occur. Instead, cognitive interventions should be used to help the patient challenge problematic beliefs about the feared consequences relevant to the current exposure task. The therapist should be sure to reinforce the patient's decision to face feared stimuli and the importance of adopting habits of confronting rather than avoiding such situations. This can lead into a discussion about risk taking and embracing acceptable, everyday levels of uncertainty. Therapists should emphasize that the practicalities of taking such low-level risks outweigh the consequences of trying to eliminate all risk to procure an absolute guarantee of safety (which is not feasible). In other words, the aim of treatment is not to provide an absolute guarantee of safety, but to teach the patient how to live comfortably with acceptable levels of uncertainty. Informal Socratic questioning and discussions of the evidence for and against mistaken beliefs (as described in chapter 9) are two of the most useful cognitive interventions to be deployed in the context of exposure. Toward the end of Susan's first exposure session, the therapist engaged her in a Socratic discussion about changes in her anxiety level and dysfunctional beliefs.

> Therapist: Let's examine what you've done in the last hour. You touched things that you had been avoiding because of your fear of germs and sickness. You contaminated your face, hair, and your personal items. You even ate food off of a contaminated paper towel with contaminated hands. You did all of this with-

out washing even once. So, you would expect your SUDS to be very high right now, but it's only 25 and you haven't gotten sick. What's going on? How did that happen?

Susan: I guess I got used to it; and I found out this isn't as dangerous as I had thought.

Therapist: Exactly. Now, how would you have ever learned that if you never did exposure?

Susan: I probably wouldn't have learned it. I would just go on avoiding and thinking they were harmful.

Therapist: That's exactly right. When you face your obsessional fears head on, and you resist ritualizing, your SUDS eventually goes down and you realize your fears are probably unrealistic.

Therapists should avoid trying to convince the patient that exposure situations are "not dangerous." This is for the patient to discover for himself or herself through experience. Risk levels are best described as "acceptably low" rather than "zero." Occasionally, patients will appear as if they are straining to obtain a guarantee of safety. This might take the form of subtle reassurance-seeking strategies (e.g., watching the therapist's facial expression closely). As a general rule, questions about risk in a given situation should be answered only once. Dealing with patients who persistently request reassurance is discussed in chapter 14.

Debriefing

At the conclusion of each exposure, the initial feared consequences and estimates of probability and severity are revisited and revised based on the outcome of the exercise. Was doing the exposure as awful as had been anticipated? Did the feared consequences come true? If not, how come? Susan was surprised that her anxiety declined during ERP. She also remarked that her fear of becoming ill from touching public surfaces had decreased. She estimated that the likelihood of becoming ill was 10% and the severity, 25%. These ratings were recorded on the Exposure Practice Form and discussed in terms of the redundancy of safety-seeking rituals (i.e., if the probability of illness is so low, rituals are unnecessary).

Sometimes anxiety does not decrease during the exposure, or the patient becomes so uncomfortable that he or she chooses to leave the situation before anxiety habituates. In such instances cognitive techniques can be used to closely examine the patient's thoughts and experiences. For example, overly negative beliefs such as "treatment isn't working" can be processed and modified into more realistic self-statements such as "I can't expect to get rid of such a strong habit in one day," or "I have to give therapy a chance to work. This time my anxiety didn't decrease, but if I keep working at it, I am likely to succeed." The therapist can also point out that the patient made an effort to confront a situation or stimulus that he or she had been avoiding, and that this is a good first step. Thus, even if the exercise is unsuccessful, the patient should feel as if something was gained by attempting exposure.

HOMEWORK EXPOSURE

Assigning Homework Practice

Just as learning to be a good musician or athlete requires practice between lessons, a person with OCD must practice exposure and response prevention between treatment sessions to achieve lasting improvement. Even if the in-session exposure goes extremely well, it must be followed by repeated practice in the natural environment until the feared situation poses no difficulty. Therefore, at the end of each exposure session, a homework task is assigned (I often substitute the term *practice* in place of *homework* because many patients struggle through school and do not feel inspired by having to complete more homework assignments). The arrangement of practice assignments should be deliberate (as opposed to haphazardly chosen) and collaborative. Early in treatment, assignments should merely include repetition of in-session exposure exercises. Later on, homework can involve exposure to situations and stimuli not confronted during the session.

The rationale for each practice assignment should be clearly specified. This increases the patient's ability to consolidate information learned during the task. It also promotes adherence—patients are more likely to complete exposure tasks when they understand the reasons for which they are assigned (Abramowitz, Franklin, Zoellner, & DiBernardo, 2002). To ensure the rationale is clear, the therapist might ask the patient to describe it in his or her own words (Taylor & Asmundson, 2004). As treatment progresses, the patient should be encouraged to take a more active role in designing homework exposures (any initiative on the part of the patient should be reinforced). As a rule of thumb, at least 1 or 2 hours of homework exposure practice should be prescribed per day. Patients should also be reminded to adhere to the response prevention rules and to record any violations of the rules on the Self-Monitoring Form (see Fig. 8.2).

Homework exposure practice is conducted in the same manner as in-session exposure. The main differences are that the therapist is absent and exposure is taking place in one's typical surroundings. Patients should therefore review the Guidelines for Effective Exposure Form (Handout 12.1) before beginning each assignment. Instructions for each exercise must be clearly described, including how the specific task is to be performed, where, when, and for how long. Recording this information on a copy of the Exposure Practice Form (Fig. 12.1) that is given to the patient also promotes adherence (multiple copies will be necessary if multiple assignments are given). The therapist then carefully reviews how the patient is to complete the remainder of the form (e.g., identification of feared consequences, probability and severity ratings, outcome, etc.). The patient is also to keep track of SUDS during the homework exposure and is told to discontinue the exercise after a specified amount of time or when the SUDS level declines greater than 50% or 60% from baseline. Susan's therapist presented the following homework instructions at the end of the first session. Note how Susan was involved in the planning of the assignment:

> Therapist: The next step is for you to practice doing exposure on your own and in familiar settings. So, each day between now and our next session, I would like you to contaminate yourself by touching railings, door handles, and the like—just as we did in today's session. I also want you to practice contaminating your home with these germs. You can use paper towels to collect the contamination; then, you should bring the paper towels home and contaminate things that you would normally avoid. So, tell me, where should you spread the germs in your house?
>
> Susan: I guess I should get them in my car, the bedrooms, the furniture, and the kitchen. That's where I'd be most concerned about having germs.
>
> Therapist: Good. I want you to repeat this practice every day until our next session. You should also keep the contaminated paper towels with you at all times to show yourself that you don't need to avoid contamination to feel OK. Also, you must refrain from washing and cleaning, except for the one shower as we agreed. Your job is to practice feeling contaminated all the time so that you eventually realize that you don't have to be concerned with these thoughts and feelings. That means if you slip up and wash or clean, you must recontaminate with your paper towels immediately afterwards. You must also record the ritual on your self-monitoring form. Remember that you have Steve to help you out if you have trouble resisting urges to ritualize. Do you have any questions about your practice?
>
> Susan: No. I know what I have to do.

After the first exposure session, the therapist gave Susan several copies of the Exposure Practice Form with the following specific assignment written in Item 1: "Contaminate yourself and your home with germs from public surfaces; listen to tape about germs and illness." Instructions for completing the rest of the form were reviewed. Imaginal exposure practice should be conducted in a quiet atmosphere and when alone and alert. Bedtime is not a good time for imaginal exposure because of the risk of falling asleep. Susan was also taught how to complete the various items on the form and instructed to monitor and record her SUDS every 10 minutes during each day's exposure practice. To reinforce the importance of completing the assignments, the therapist said that the next session would begin with a review of the completed practice forms. The session ended with Susan and the therapist looking at the fear hierarchy and agreeing on the situation to be confronted for exposure during the next session.

Checking Homework Assignments

It is imperative that the therapist makes a point of reviewing the patient's self-monitoring record and homework exposure practice forms at the beginning of each session. This verifies that these important assignments have been completed and sends the message that working on OCD between sessions is a significant part of treatment that the therapist takes seriously. Reviewing the self-monitoring form also allows the therapist access to information about difficult situations in which the patient was unable to resist safety-seeking behaviors. Such situations can be incorporated in subsequent exposure sessions. Particular attention should be paid to making sure that adequate habituation occurred during homework exposure, and that the patient was able to consolidate new information about the feared stimulus and about the usefulness (or uselessness) of safety behaviors. Verbal reinforcement (appropriate praise) for successfully completed homework should be given liberally. Instances in which homework was attempted but habituation did not occur can be labeled as common (but temporary) outcomes when trying to change long-standing habits. Normalizing the failure to habituate places the blame on technical factors rather than on the patient or the therapy itself. A detailed analysis of failed exposures should be undertaken to determine whether or not the exercise was performed correctly. If the patient did not attempt the assigned practice at all, the therapist should problem solve and help the patient complete the task before moving on to more difficult hierarchy items. The management of chronic adherence problems is discussed in chapter 14.

CONDUCTING EXPOSURE
FOR DIFFERENT SYMPTOM DIMENSIONS

Using the treatment session just described as a general outline, this section describes the nuances of tailoring exposure for each of the OCD symptom dimensions. Stylistic issues and common procedural variations, such as conducting exposure outside the office, are discussed in later sections of this chapter.

Contamination

The preceding section illustrates exposure for contamination symptoms where the patient articulates feared consequences such as becoming ill or causing others to become ill. The exposure session proceeds similarly to one that would be conducted for specific phobia. For individuals who are fearful of spreading contamination, we might have them shake hands with "innocent victims," or surreptitiously taint objects in other people's offices. For those concerned with floor germs, we conduct entire sessions seated on the floor (in an office or perhaps in a bathroom, depending on the patient's idiosyncratic concerns). For those fearful of bodily waste and secretions, we supervise direct confrontation with such substances (or situations in which the substances might be present; e.g., using the toilet without washing afterward, dirty towels at the gym locker-room). The aim of helping patients to repeatedly practice taking such "risks" is not to permanently alter their hygiene practices. Instead, the desired goal is belief change. Through these exercises the patient learns that the feared consequences (i.e., illness) are far less likely than he or she had anticipated. Patients also discover that precautions such as excessive ritualized washing, cleaning, and other safety behaviors to prevent or remove contact with feared contaminants are unnecessary. On occasion, patients ask whether they must continue ERP indefinitely. We typically explain that when treatment is successful, patients feel at greater liberty to decide how to lead their lives without their choices being governed by obsessive fear. That is, there will eventually be less riding on the decision to wash or not wash one's hands.

For the group of patients with contamination obsessions but no specific concerns about germs or sickness, the main feared outcome of exposure is that the sense of distress or uncleanness will persist indefinitely or become unmanageable unless decontamination rituals are performed. For such patients, exposure exercises should be framed as helping to demonstrate that the sense of discomfort associated with contamination does not persist indefinitely. This can employ both the habituation model and the cognitive perspective. Indeed, habituation during ERP sessions provides compelling evidence against the patient's belief that distress will persist indefinitely. This outcome is discussed to facilitate changes in expectations when contaminants are encountered in the future. Typically, imaginal exposure is not a necessary component of treatment for patients with this presentation of contamination symptoms.

Harming

Exposure for harming symptoms is often more complex than for contamination symptoms. First, the situations and stimuli that trigger obsessions about responsibility for harm or mistakes vary tremendously and are highly patient specific. The therapist therefore has a greater challenge in matching exposure tasks to the exact nature of the patient's fear. Second, obsessional fear is typically associated with uncertainty and thoughts of disastrous consequences that are evoked by certain situations, rather than by palpable external stimuli such as urine or pesticides as in contamination symptoms. This necessitates the use of secondary imaginal exposure (along with situational exposure) to promote habituation to, and modification of beliefs about, the salient obsessional thoughts and doubts.

Often, evocation of harming obsessions can be achieved in the clinic, such as by having the patient write unlucky numbers or complete important paperwork while being distracted. In other cases, it is necessary to conduct situational exposure outside the office. Examples include accompanying the patient to his or her home to practice leaving appliances plugged in, driving to confront fears of hitting pedestrians, and going to public places to put "dangerous" objects (e.g., glass, pins) where people walk. Whether conducted in or out of the office, it is essential to systematically expose the patient to his or her thoughts and doubts of being responsible for harm (or uncertainty regarding whether such harm will occur) as evoked by the situational exposure. Cognitive interventions are used in the context of exposure to help the patient think differently about risk and uncertainty, and to correct dysfunctional and catastrophic interpretations of the presence and meaning of obsessive doubts about feared consequences.

When arranging situational exposures for harming obsessions, the therapist must ensure that the patient feels responsible for any possible negative consequences of exposure. For example, someone with fears of hitting pedestrians while driving might feel more comfortable when accompanied by the therapist on a driving exposure because, in the words of one patient, the therapist "would never let a hit-and-run accident happen." The therapist should be attentive to such details and ask whether conducting the driving exposure unsupervised would evoke more distress than if the task was supervised. On a related note, some exposures to situations in which there is a fear of harm could be compromised if the patient remains for an extended period of time. For example, staying in the house after plugging in the television or turning on the stove is inherently a check that no fire has started. Therefore, when situational exposure evokes uncertainty about negative outcomes, necessary precautions should be taken to ensure that no de facto reassurance seeking occurs. Secondary imaginal exposure to the feared outcomes (including not knowing

for sure if they will occur [or already have occurred]) should be com-
menced to prolong the exposure exercise.

Susan's main harming symptoms included the fear of assigning incorrect grades to her students, which she feared would ruin their academic careers. In response to these obsessions, she excessively checked that her
grading was "fair and accurate" and that she had correctly recorded her assigned grades into her computer spreadsheet. Susan and the therapist had
planned for Susan to grade papers during the second exposure session. After reviewing Susan's self-monitoring forms and her progress with between-session (homework) exposure practice, the therapist described how
the session would proceed:

Therapist: I see that you brought in some papers to grade for our exposure today as we had planned. Tell me all about what happens when you try to grade papers.

Susan: I brought in spelling tests to grade. They are one of the biggest
problems. First, it has to be absolutely quiet or else I'm afraid
I will mess up. If I'm distracted, I have to start over. Then, I
have to carefully go over each student's paper and compare
his or her answers to the answer key. I usually review the paper two or three times to be sure I didn't grade anything incorrectly. Sometimes, I'll wonder whether I made a mistake
on a certain student's paper and have to go back through the
pile to check again. When it's really bad, I get Steve to recheck
my grading just to make sure there are no mistakes. Then, entering the grades into the computer is another story. I have to
check and recheck to make sure I didn't switch students'
grades by accident, and sometimes have to re-enter all the
grades to be sure there are no mistakes. Sometimes I have to
do this a few times until I feel satisfied that it's correct. The
whole thing can take a few hours when I only have about 25
students in the class.

Therapist: Well, we're going to help you with overcoming your urge to
check. How long should it take you to grade each test?

Susan: About a minute each.

Therapist: And I'm curious about how often you find that you've actually made a mistake.

Susan: I never find mistakes; but I *could* make them. And they would
have terrible effects.

Therapist: Interesting that you never find errors, though. What does that
tell you?

Susan: That I probably won't make any mistakes.

Therapist: I suppose you're right ... *probably* not. So, today, I'd like you to sit at my desk and grade these papers without checking. You're allowed to spend 1 minute on each paper, and I'll be timing you. After you're finished each paper, you must put them back into your bag and not recheck them. Then, you will enter the grades into the spreadsheet and put the laptop computer away without checking. The other thing is that I'm going to turn on this radio and sit in the corner reading some journal articles. So, I won't be there to catch any mistakes. OK?

Susan: I don't know. I think we should do it without the radio. I'm afraid I'll get distracted and make a mistake.

Therapist: Well, if we leave the radio *off* and you start to feel more and more comfortable with grading the papers, will you think that's because you're unlikely to make mistakes, or because you're not being distracted?

Susan: Probably because I'm not being distracted.

Therapist: That's right. But in order to reduce your fear, you need to learn that it's not the lack of distraction that keeps you from making mistakes; it's that you're less likely to make them than you think. So, I'm afraid the exercise wouldn't be as helpful of we kept the radio off. Do you see what I mean? How about giving it a try my way?

Susan: OK, I'll try it.

After discussing feared consequences (making mistakes in grading, ruining academic careers) and the initial probability and severity estimates (80% and 65%, respectively), Susan gave an initial SUDS rating (78) and began grading each spelling test while the radio played fairly loud rock music. She graded each test within the 1 minute allotted to her. Every 5 minutes the therapist asked for a SUDS rating. After 20 minutes, when all tests had been graded, Susan's SUDS was 40 and she was visibly less distraught as compared to when the exercise began. Next, she was instructed to enter the test grades into her spreadsheet program on her laptop computer without double-checking for accuracy. Her SUDS increased noticeably (75), as did her urges to check. The therapist employed cognitive strategies to help Susan manage her strong ritualistic urges.

Susan: I really need to recheck the computer grades. I know it's a ritual but that's the only permanent record of the test grades once I hand them back to the students. If it's wrong, something terrible could happen when I have to turn in final grades for report cards.

Therapist: I suppose you are right about that. There is a possibility of error. However, what do you think you would find if you went back and checked? What do you usually find when you do checking rituals?

Susan: That everything is OK. There are no mistakes.

Therapist: Right … you know what you'd find if you checked. So, checking is merely a habit to give you reassurance. We need to break this habit because it only leads to a vicious cycle as we have talked about. Think back to our discussion of intrusive thoughts and how people with OCD react to them. If someone had intrusive thoughts about making unlikely mistakes but interprets those thoughts as very significant and meaningful, how would the person feel and what would they probably do?

Susan: They'd feel anxious and check to make sure there is no mistake.

Therapist: Right. Do you see how you're doing this? [Susan nods in agreement] Now, what is a more helpful way of dealing with these intrusive thoughts? What's a more realistic interpretation that leads to less checking?

Susan: That the thoughts are just thoughts. They don't mean anything.

This dialogue led to a secondary imaginal exposure that was introduced as a way of weakening the pattern of becoming anxious and checking in response to senseless obsessional doubts. Susan was instructed to describe a scene in which she makes a grading error, resulting in a student failing and eventually not being accepted to college. The patient and therapist derived an imaginal exposure script together and made it as generic as possible (this way, the scene could be used along with multiple exposures to similar situations). The final product was as follows:

In rushing through grading the papers, I might have mistakenly marked three answers as incorrect on a particular student's paper, when he or she actually had them correct. The radio was playing, I was distracted, and I was grading quickly. I didn't check the papers either. So, if I made this mistake, I didn't catch it. Then, I entered all the grades into the computer. So, if I did make a grading mistake, the students' final average for the year could be bumped down from what they really deserved. And it's my fault. I could have checked and avoided this problem. As a result, some of my students might be placed in a lower level English class next year and might not do well because the less demanding teachers usually teach the lower level classes in middle school. They might end up not doing well in English all through middle and high school and then not get into any good colleges because of this. It would be entirely my fault. If I could just check the papers again … if I could just be sure that all the papers are graded correctly I would know that everyone would be OK. Because I am not going to check, it is possible that my students' future is up in the air, and it could be my fault if they end up failures in life. I'll never know because I am resisting checking this time.

Susan recorded the scene onto a loop tape by reading it aloud. Then, the tape was replayed with instructions for Susan not to check, neutralize, or do anything else to gain reassurance. Instead, she was encouraged to allow the thoughts and uncertainty to linger in her mind and consider the thoughts as normal, senseless intrusions. Susan's SUDS decreased after about 20 minutes of listening to the tape. A discussion about Susan's ability to manage uncertainty and her tendency to misinterpret intrusive thoughts followed the exposure. For homework practice, she was instructed to grade another set of papers and enter them into the computer while listening to the radio or television, and then to complete imaginal exposure to the loop tape until her anxiety habituated. No checking was permitted and Susan was reminded to record any instance of checking on her self-monitoring form. She was also instructed to hand back the papers to students without any checking. Throughout the rest of treatment, Susan was instructed to grade all papers using the techniques practiced in the session. She was also informed that in-session time could be used for additional practice if she experienced difficulty grading on her own.

Unacceptable Thoughts and Covert Rituals

The aim of exposure for this dimension is to weaken the connection between repugnant obsessional thoughts and anxiety. This occurs through habituation and by helping the patient develop a new, nonthreatening understanding of intrusive obsessional thoughts, impulses, images, and ideas (e.g., as "brain farts"). Therefore, the main exposure technique is primary imaginal exposure wherein the patient repeatedly practices thinking the intrusive, unwanted thought. As discussed in chapter 10, this technique is akin to situational exposure, except that the stimuli are thoughts rather than external cues. Loop tapes provide an excellent means of prolonging confrontation with thoughts because the stimulus is presented without giving the patient an opportunity to neutralize or suppress. Naturally, if there are particular situations or stimuli in the environment that the patient avoids, these should be incorporated as situational exposures as well. For example, a female patient who avoids looking at attractive women for fear of thinking lesbian thoughts might practice looking though fashion magazines (situational exposure) and purposely thinking about lesbianism. If necessary, secondary imaginal exposure to feared consequences should also be incorporated into the loop tape. For example, if the fear exists, this patient should also be exposed to uncertainty regarding whether she will become a lesbian because of all the thoughts she has.

During the third exposure session, Susan confronted unwanted thoughts of stabbing her baby girl, Jennifer. Jennifer was brought to the appointment, as had been prearranged. The session began with the therapist eliciting the details of the obsessional thought, Susan's appraisals of the thought, and her responses. Note how the therapist helped Susan to see how her appraisals of her obsessions influence her use of safety behaviors:

Therapist: Can you describe the details of the thoughts you have about stabbing Jennifer?

Susan: It's difficult to say ... If I'm using any sharp object ... a kitchen knife, the scissors, I get the thought of stabbing her. I think about how easy it would be. She's just a baby and wouldn't know how to stop me. I feel so bad for thinking about how easily I could kill her.

Therapist: I realize those are upsetting images for you. When they come to mind, how do you interpret them? What do you think they mean?

Susan: I must be a terrible person for having those thoughts. I mean, what kind of person thinks about killing their own child? I feel very guilty.

Therapist: How much do you worry about acting on the thoughts?

Susan: I don't want to—I love her with all my heart. But I sometimes wonder whether I might just snap and do something terrible since I think about it so much. You hear those stories of people who snap and kill their kids from time to time. What if I'm next?

Therapist: Yes, I am aware of those stories. That's very tragic. One of the things we should do is look more closely at the evidence regarding how likely *you* are to hurt Jennifer. But first, let's examine your interpretations of these thoughts. If you're telling yourself the thoughts mean you're a terrible person and that they could make you do terrible things, how are you going to feel?

Susan: Scared.

Therapist: That's right. And how will you respond to the thoughts?

Susan: I would try to make them go away, which is basically what I do.

Therapist: That's right. As we have talked about before, your interpretations dictate your responses. But how well do your strategies for dealing with the thoughts work?

Susan: Not too well, I guess. I mean, I keep having the thoughts.

Therapist: That's right. Remember when we talked about trying to suppress thoughts of a white bear? People are not very good at stopping their own thoughts. [pauses] The real question is,

"Do the thoughts about harming Jennifer really mean what you think they do?" Maybe you don't need to spend all of this time and energy worrying and trying to suppress them. What did we learn a few sessions ago when we were talking about who has senseless nasty thoughts?

Susan: Well, everyone has them from time to time. You said they're normal. You said you even have bad thoughts sometimes.

Therapist: That's right, I sure do. Real bad ones, sometimes ... as do most people. But I don't get worried when those thoughts come up. Why do you think that is?

Susan: Because you know they are just normal thoughts.

Therapist: So, if you interpreted your nasty thoughts about Jennifer as normal thoughts that everyone has, how would you feel when they come to mind, and what would you do?

Susan: I guess I'd feel less afraid. I wouldn't have to avoid situations where they came up, and I wouldn't feel like I always have to try to push them out of my mind.

Therapist: Yeah, that's right. If you knew in your gut that the thoughts are meaningless, insignificant, and not at all dangerous, you wouldn't worry whether they come to mind or not. It wouldn't be an issue. And you'd be less preoccupied with them, so you would probably notice them less often. The exercises we will do today are designed to help you change your perception of these thoughts and help you develop more helpful ways of responding to them.

The therapist then introduced the exposure task that had been planned for the third session and asked Susan to generate evidence for and against her belief that she would act on her intrusive thoughts to stab Jennifer. The evidence for and against this belief was recorded in tabular format on a whiteboard as shown in Fig. 12.2. After a discussion that involved a review of the cognitive-behavioral model of obsessions and a closer look at the differences between people with OCD and those with antisocial personality or psychosis, Susan was able to recognize that she was unlikely to do any harm (her likelihood rating was 10%).

Susan was told the exposure exercise would begin by working with the therapist to compose a loop tape containing a vivid description of the unacceptable stabbing thought. Next, she would listen to the tape while holding Jennifer. Then, a knife would be placed next to Susan as she held the child and listened to the tape. Finally, Susan would hold the knife and use it to slice food while continuing to think about stabbing Jennifer. Susan was instructed to refrain from any forms of thought suppression or neutralizing. Instead, she was told to "go with" the unwanted thoughts, and let them

My thoughts of stabbing Jennifer will cause me to stab Jennifer

Evidence for	Evidence against
• Some parents kill their children	• Thoughts alone can't make me act
• I could stab her	• I have no history of hurting people
	• I am even afraid to *think* about hurting people
	• I love Jennifer and don't devalue her
	• I have thought about hurting her many times before but never acted on the thoughts
	• Everyone thinks about doing bad things from time to time
	• Parents that kill their children have other problems
	• I don't want to hurt Jennifer
	• The therapist seems confident that I am not dangerous

FIG. 12.2. Evidence for and against Susan's belief..

"hang out in her brain." She was also permitted to consider the evidence generated from the CT exercise (which remained for her to see on the whiteboard). Susan was told this exposure task would help her in two ways: First, it would help her test (and disconfirm) the validity of her belief that thinking about stabbing Jennifer would lead to losing control and acting violently. Second, it would help her see that she can think this unwanted thought without remaining highly anxious.

Initially, Susan, like many patients, balked at purposely inducing her upsetting obsessional thoughts:

Susan: I don't know if I should make myself think about stabbing Jennifer. It's really not a good idea to think those kinds of things just for the sake of doing it.

Therapist: But I think there's a good reason for doing this exercise. It will reduce your fear of the thoughts. Just like with the exposures you've done over the last few sessions, this will help you see that your violent thoughts are not as dangerous as you think.

Remember how we talked about changing your interpretation of these thoughts? This exercise is designed to help you do just that. We need to correct your pattern of responding maladaptively to this thought.

Susan: I'm not sure I can do it.

Therapist: Actually, I *know* you can do it. I know this because you say that you spend hours thinking these very thoughts every day. So, I'm not asking you to think about anything you're not already thinking about, right? The difference is that you are going to practice using more helpful strategies for dealing with the thoughts. When you confront the thoughts today, you will give yourself the chance to see how harmless they really are. Remember, these are normal thoughts; the exposure task is a way of helping you prove to yourself that you don't have to worry so much. So, what do you say?

After this discussion, Susan agreed to begin the exposure. Her initial SUDS rating was 80. The content of the imaginal exposure loop tape, as generated by Susan and the therapist, was as follows:

> You are thinking about your 3-month-old baby, Jennifer, who you love so much. She's so sweet and innocent. She's small and cuddly. You and Steve are so careful not to let anything happen to her. She's a wonderful little baby. Now, you are thinking about stabbing her ... What an awful thing that would be. You have an image of losing self-control and just slicing her neck with a knife. Or, you could stab her in the stomach, over and over. There would be blood gushing out of her body ... she'd be kicking and screaming with pain ... you can just hear it ... she would probably die of the wounds you inflicted. And she never had a chance ... you're just too strong for a helpless infant to defend herself against. As you look at her cute little face, you think about how there's really nothing stopping you from doing this ... just your own judgment ... You allow yourself to think about stabbing Jennifer. You imagine vividly what it would feel like ... You try to picture how would it feel ...? How would it look ...? What would your husband say ...? And what would happen afterwards with the police ...? You let yourself just dwell on these thoughts of stabbing Jennifer. Keep the images in your mind as vividly as you can. Stabbing Jennifer ...

Susan successfully listened to the tape while holding Jennifer, and after 15 minutes her SUDS was reduced to 30. In fact, she reported becoming "bored" with the thought—which is exactly the intention (boredom is incompatible with feeling anxious). At that point, the knife was introduced. At first, it was placed next to Susan on a table. Then Susan held the knife while also holding Jennifer. The therapist periodically praised Susan for her bravery and reminded her not to do any mental rituals or thought suppression. After an initial increase to 70, her SUDS dropped back to 45. At the

40-minute mark of the session, the therapist took out an apple and a cutting board. Susan was asked to put Jennifer on the floor and slowly slice the apple right next to her, while continuing to listen to the loop tape. Susan successfully completed the task without an increase in SUDS. The therapist inquired whether his leaving the room would increase Susan's fear of acting on the intrusive thoughts. Susan said she had considered that the therapist would intervene if she had started to stab her daughter. Therefore, the therapist left the office. From another extension, he telephoned Susan every 5 minutes to obtain a SUDS rating and reinforce Susan's hard work. After 60 minutes, Susan's SUDS had decreased to 25 and she appeared visibly more comfortable. At that point, the exercise was terminated.

Debriefing followed along the lines of previous exposures. Using a Socratic style, the therapist asked Susan what she had learned from the exercise. Susan reported believing quite strongly that she was unlikely to act on her thoughts. She was quite surprised that her distress had decreased so dramatically even without safety behaviors. The therapist reminded Susan to use the same approach when unwanted intrusive thoughts came to mind at home. Accordingly, she was instructed to practice the same exercise at least once each day between appointments and to record her progress using the appropriate forms.

It is vital that the therapist exudes confidence in the cognitive-behavioral model when discussing objectionable thoughts and when suggesting (and implementing) exposure exercises. Demonstrating conviction that such thoughts are ordinary and innocuous, and that exposure is likely to be helpful, probably increases the odds that the patient will agree to confront these stimuli. After completing the exposure exercise, Susan mentioned that the therapist's very eagerness to have her think violent thoughts while holding a knife in one hand and Jennifer in the other arm helped to convince her that her fears were unrealistic.

Incompleteness

Although Susan did not display obsessions and rituals associated with incompleteness, a discussion of how to conduct exposure sessions for these types of symptoms is essential because many patients present with such concerns. As with the contamination subtype, patients with incompleteness OCD symptoms may or may not articulate explicit fears of harm. When the sense of inexactness, disorder, imperfection, or asymmetry evokes obsessional fears of responsibility for disasters (e.g., "Mother will be injured if I do not put on my clothes the 'correct' way"), situational exposure to external cues should be conducted, accompanied by secondary imaginal exposure to the feared consequences. In practice, such exposures are similar to those typically conducted for the harming symptom dimension discussed previously. Cognitive interventions are used to modify intolerance of uncertainty, excessive responsibility, and the misinterpretations of intrusive thoughts about disasters. Patients must, of course, be reminded to refrain from safety-seeking behaviors such as checking and repeating rituals, and reassurance seeking. As an example, one patient, concerned that stepping on sidewalk cracks would cause harm to his relatives, practiced purposely stepping on cracks and confronting thoughts of his parents being horribly injured. Another patient, who feared bad luck from odd numbers, practiced confronting odd numbers wherever possible (e.g., ordering food that cost $7.00, choosing to be the fifth person in the line) and wishing for bad luck to occur.

Exposure for incompleteness symptoms without fears of causing harm is focused on desensitizing the patient to the subjective sense of incompleteness (i.e., habituation). From a cognitive perspective, repeated and prolonged exposure helps the patient develop a more realistic appraisal of these feelings. Instead of requiring an immediate response to prevent ever-increasing subjective distress, the patient learns that the distress associated with these feelings fades over time, thereby rendering compulsive rituals unnecessary. Verbal cognitive techniques can be used to highlight patients' mistaken appraisal of "not just right" feelings as dangerous or likely to persist indefinitely if rituals are not completed. Imaginal exposure is typically not included in the treatment of such symptoms.

CONFRONTING THE GREATEST FEARS

Some words are in order regarding helping patients (across symptom dimensions) to confront their most feared stimuli. First, exposures to the most difficult hierarchy items should be conducted during the middle third of the treatment program. This way, plenty of therapy time remains to sort out any unforeseen difficulties that arise while working up the hierarchy or when attempting to confront the most difficult stimuli. Second, although for many patients success with early exercises translates to relatively straightforward high- level exposures, for some individuals the process is anything but routine. Such patients require no small dose of encouragement and praise for their efforts. The therapist should, on the one hand, take a firm stand that such exposures are a necessary part of therapy as agreed to during treatment planning, yet on the other hand, convey sensitivity and understanding that these tasks are likely to evoke high SUDS levels. Patients can be reminded that distress during exposure is a temporary side effect. It might be motivational for the therapist to model difficult exposures before they are attempted by the patient. A third, and related, point is to encourage the liberal use of cognitive interventions. Informal discussions of evidence collected from previous exposure exercises, acceptable versus unacceptable risks, and learning to tolerate uncertainty are often quite useful.

Another benefit of having the patient face the most difficult exposure situations relatively early in therapy is that this affords ample time for confronting the most feared stimuli in varied contexts and independently. Experimental research (e.g., Bouton, 2002) suggests that fear reduction tends to be most complete and long-lasting if the patient conducts exposure (situational and imaginal) in different settings. For example, suppose a patient with blasphemous obsessional thoughts has become relatively comfortable facing such thoughts in the therapist's office. He might next practice evoking these obsessions in situations that he has been avoiding, but that regularly trigger the obsession, such as in a place of worship or cemetery. A different patient who fears responsibility for car accidents might practice driving on roads she has been avoiding, and with greater distractions (e.g., loud music, talking on a cell phone) in the car. The assessment of each patient's idiosyncratic beliefs and avoidance patterns will be especially important for determining in what specific contexts exposure needs to be done.

LATER EXPOSURE SESSIONS

As a rule, each hierarchy item is repeatedly confronted (e.g., at least daily) until it evokes a minimal level of distress or urge to ritualize. After exposure to the most distressing hierarchy items evoke minimal distress, the remaining therapy sessions and homework assignments involve confrontation with various items in a range of contexts where they might be avoided or still cause difficulty. This serves to generalize the effects of treatment. For example, one patient—a real estate agent—was afraid of leaving lights and appliances on that might cause a fire. One of his exposures had involved turning the lights and appliances in his home on and off quickly, and then leaving the premises and imagining the possibility of a fire. During later sessions, this patient practiced similar exercises in the homes he was showing for sale. Another patient with obsessional fears of yelling obscenities and insults practiced "tempting himself" to verbalize (e.g., by thinking of or whispering to himself) such epithets during later sessions in various places he was still avoiding (e.g., libraries, places of worship, among people of different races). Home (or workplace) visits can also occur during the later treatment sessions. For patients with contamination symptoms who are fearful of soiling their personal living or work spaces, the therapist can oversee the spreading of contaminants already confronted during earlier sessions into these hallowed areas.

STYLISTIC CONSIDERATIONS

Conducting exposure-based therapy is at once a science and an art. As discussed previously, the treatment is based firmly on well-understood principles of normal human cognition and behavior. Moreover, substantial (and consistent) research evidence indicates that therapeutic exposure causes significant reductions in pathological fear. Less well studied, but probably equally important, are the technical aspects of implementing exposure therapy. I have already discussed how cognitive interventions can be used to "tenderize" strongly held dysfunctional beliefs and encourage patients to persist with treatment. In this section, I describe a number of additional tactics therapists can employ to help patients get the most out of the treatment program.

Building on Early Successes

Many patients experience higher levels of anticipatory anxiety as the difficulty level of exposures increases. To encourage patients to confront more challenging situations, therapists should heed, rather than disregard, the patient's distress, yet affirm the importance of choosing to persist with these exercises. One strategy the therapist can use is to remind patients of the outcomes of previous successful exposure tasks. The following is an example of how Socratic questioning was used to guide Susan toward the conclusion that conducting a higher level exposure task would likely have the same consequences as previous tasks.

Susan: I'm not sure I'm ready to touch garbage cans yet. It seems like it's going to be very hard to do this knowing I can't wash my hands afterwards.

Therapist: I see. Is there something in particular that you're worried about?

Susan: I'm just very scared to do it. I almost didn't come today because I knew we were going to do this.

Therapist: Well, I'm glad you came. It sounds like this is an especially tough one for you. Hmmm. I remember how anxious you were before you practiced getting your hands contaminated from public door handles. But what happened once you got started?

Susan: My SUDS went down after a little while.

Therapist: Right. It took some time, but you stuck it out and saw that you felt better after a while. And how sick did you become, or make your family?

Susan: No one got sick. That's true.

Therapist: Right. Actually, all of the exposures you've done have reduced your anxiety, and none have resulted in the negative consequences that you worried about. So, what makes you think this one will be any different?

Susan: I don't know. I guess I should give it a try and see.

Refining the Fear Hierarchy

When the therapist adheres to the collaboratively developed exposure plan, it reinforces the systematic nature of the therapy and places clear expectations on the patient. This consistency probably helps to cultivate trust and confidence in the therapist and favors a continued commitment to the therapy. Nevertheless, important details of the patient's obsessional fears are sometimes not revealed until well into the exposure phase of treatment. Therefore, in addition to progression up the fear hierarchy as planned, exposure sessions should involve continued assessment and course correction depending on the phenomenology that is unearthed as treatment progresses (Kozak & Foa, 1997).

One circumstance in which it becomes necessary to adjust the exposure hierarchy is when the patient refuses to confront a particular stimulus because of extreme anxiety. For example, Susan and her therapist had planned for Susan to be exposed to a public bathroom during the seventh exposure session. However, when the therapist suggested that the exercise take place in a local fast food restaurant's bathroom, Susan expressed profound anxiety and put her foot down, saying she would not do this task. Instead of demanding that Susan confront this bathroom, the therapist suggested that she spend the seventh session confronting an "easier" public bathroom to help her prepare for eventually facing the fast food bathroom during a later session. This use of *transitional exposure* is described here.

Susan: I can't do it. I can't make myself go into a fast food bathroom.
Therapist: I understand this is a difficult exposure for you, but we did agree to practice this today. What in particular would be so bad for you about going to a fast food bathroom?
Susan: I know I agreed to do this, but fast food bathrooms are so dirty. No one ever cleans them and all kinds of people use them. That would be the worst possible bathroom for me.
Therapist: I see. If going to a fast food bathroom is the most difficult perhaps you could pick a less difficult public restroom where you would be willing to practice today. Do you have any suggestions?
Susan: I guess I could try going to a hotel lobby bathroom.
Therapist: OK. And why would that be easier for you?
Susan: Well, they're usually better cleaned. I guess I won't be as grossed out.
Therapist: Well, it's not exactly what we had planned, but it is a public restroom. So, I think that's a good choice for today. But we

need to agree that next session you will expose yourself to a bathroom in a fast food restaurant. What we're doing today will help to prepare you for doing that. OK?

Susan: OK. Thanks for taking it easy on me today.

Therapist: Well, the most important thing is that you face your fears. If it takes a little longer than we had originally planned, it's OK.

Conducting Exposures Outside of the Office

The idiosyncratic obsessional fears and avoidance patterns of OCD patients often require that exposure practice be conducted outside the therapist's office. Examples include visiting public bathrooms, funeral homes, the pesticide aisle in grocery stores, areas of town where "contaminated" people might be found, churches or synagogues, driving on highways or parking ramps, and walking through parks where dog feces may be found. Some patients' symptoms require that exposure be conducted in their own home due to fears of contamination from certain rooms or concerns about causing fires. It is therefore advantageous for therapists to have the flexibility of being able to leave the office to accompany patients on such field trips.

For the most part, exposures in public places such as restaurants, stores, and cemeteries can be conducted surreptitiously and with anonymity. Plans for how the exercise will be proceed should be discussed in private beforehand so that overt directives can be kept to a minimum during the task. Necessary behaviors such as touching or rearranging items, or leaving them on the floor, should be performed discreetly so as not to draw undue attention. Prolonged exposure and amplification can be accomplished by holding an item (e.g., a bottle of pesticide) while continuing to browse or by placing it in a shopping cart and picking it up periodically. Unforeseen difficulties such as unexpectedly high anxiety or persistent sales clerks can be managed by leaving the scene, regrouping, and returning at a later time (Steketee, 1993).

In other situations where there might be less anonymity it is wise to ask permission and provide advance warning when contemplating out-of-the-office exposure. On occasion, the other party will want an explanation of the therapeutic activity, and as a rule (as long as the patient consents), honesty is the best policy. For example, one patient treated in our clinic was afraid of contamination from dead bodies and required exposure to a funeral home. When planning this exercise, the therapist telephoned a local funeral home to inquire about a visit. The director, perhaps thinking he was getting a new client, asked about the purpose of the appointment. Fortunately, the patient had given the therapist consent to disclose the actual nature of the proposed visit. After a brief description of the purpose and procedures of exposure therapy, the director was happy to give the therapist and patient a tour of the funeral home.

We find that many patients are willing to go out in public with their therapist. Still, it is important to discuss and plan for all possible contingencies, including a cover story and strategy for expeditiously handling awkward encounters with friends, relatives, or others while out in public places. Liability issues are also a reality in today's world, adding another dimension of precaution for the therapist. For example, in our clinic, therapists are not permitted to drive patients to exposure destinations. Thus, plans for meeting at specific destinations are arranged ahead of time.

Teaching the Patient to Be His or Her Own Therapist

An early study by Emmelkamp and Kraanen (1977) found that OCD patients who completed all exposure tasks under the close supervision of their therapist showed a slight relapse of their symptoms after ending treatment, whereas those who had confronted feared stimuli on their own (i.e., self-controlled exposure) continued to improve. Self-controlled exposure probably promotes autonomy and helps the patient gain confidence in his or her ability to combat OCD symptoms whether or not the therapist is present. Thus, after formal treatment ends, patients who have learned to implement these skills on their own are likely to be better off than those patients who have not learned how to do this. These results highlight the importance of homework exposure practice. They also insinuate that it is therapeutic to use a fading procedure across treatment sessions. That is, although close management of the initial exposure exercises is imperative, the therapist should consider stepping back and encouraging patients to become "their own therapist" when it is clear they have learned to effectively implement the treatment techniques. This entails allowing the patient to choose (from equally fear-evoking stimuli), design, and implement exposure tasks. The therapist, of course, maintains the role of coach and lends his or her expert guidance during each exercise. Decisions to confront highly anxiety-evoking stimuli are reinforced with praise, whereas avoidance is followed up with questioning to assess the nature of the fear and address the causes of avoidance.

Programmed and Lifestyle Exposure

Most people with OCD have a chronic problem, and chronic problems require constant attention over the long term. Therefore, instead of a quick fix, CBT promotes permanent lifestyle change by helping patients make sustainable modifications to their thinking and behavior. This involves the patient working hard to incorporate ERP as part of day-to-day life, rather than something to be done only when directed by the therapist. New habits of confronting obsessional fear must be practiced in diverse situations to promote generalization of treatment effects.

Whereas patients usually understand that response prevention entails across-the-board abstinence from safety behaviors such as rituals, neutralization, and assurance seeking, it may be less clear that they must also practice *avoidance prevention*. That is, some patients complete their assigned exposures and then proceed to use avoidance strategies between sessions. For example, one patient with fears of contamination from homosexuals diligently completed the assigned homework task to visit a gay bar and subsequently refrained from his typical decontamination routines. However, he also avoided wearing certain clothes and sleeping in his bed (he took to sleeping on the couch after exposures) because of his fear of spreading contamination from the bar. As a result, his contamination concerns remained intact.

From the first exposure session, the patient should be taught to think of ERP as a new lifestyle that is conducive to gaining control over, rather than being controlled by, OCD. To promote this new set of healthy habits, we find it useful to differentiate between programmed and lifestyle exposure. *Programmed exposure* includes carefully developed, hierarchy-driven exercises that the patient agrees to conduct in session and under specified circumstances, at predetermined times, and in particular locations between sessions. *Lifestyle exposure,* on the other hand, refers to making choices to take advantage of additional opportunities to practice confronting rather than avoiding obsessional fears (i.e., focus on choosing to be anxious). The patent is encouraged to be opportunistic and to view spontaneously arising obsessional triggers as occasions to practice ERP techniques and work on further reducing OCD symptoms, not as situations to be avoided or endured with great distress. Patients should often be reminded that every choice they make regarding whether to confront or avoid an obsessional cue carries weight. Each time they choose to confront such a situation without using avoidance or safety behaviors, they are weakening the OCD patterns. Alternatively, each time a decision is made to avoid, the OCD patterns are strengthened. For some patients, for whom obsessional stimuli are truly ubiquitous and rituals dominate the day, embracing ERP as a new lifestyle may be the difference between treatment success and failure.

Using Humor

The use of humorous comments or modest laughter to lighten the mood during awkward exposures, or to help the patient's anxiety to habituate, is often appropriate and can even be beneficial. Nevertheless, it is not advised if the patient appears highly distressed. In such instances, the therapist should convey understanding of how difficult exposure can be, and that with time and persistence, the exercises will ultimately become more manageable. The therapist must be a keen judge of when the use of humor is befitting. A good rule of thumb is to follow the patient's lead and ensure that he or she understands the therapist is laughing *with*, and not *at* him or her. Remarks should remain relevant to the exposure situation and should not serve to distract the patient from the task. Susan, for example, began chuckling during one exposure session in which she and the therapist were eating M&Ms off of paper towels that had touched various surfaces in public bathrooms: "It's like we're eating at a buffet of contamination," Susan said. The therapist then quipped, "Yes, and please don't miss out on the toilet-flavored M&Ms over here … they're the catch of the day … mmmm!"

13

Wrapping Up and Following Up

The first part of this chapter addresses the sensitive issue of terminating therapy for OCD. The therapist should begin to prepare the patient for the end of treatment before the final therapy session. This involves a review of the patient's progress as well as deciding on whether additional follow-up sessions will be scheduled. The second part describes a brief follow-up program for patients who complete the active phase of therapy, yet remain at risk for significant relapse. This program consists of several interventions, including the didactic presentation of information about anxiety, a discussion about the issue of lapse versus relapse, additional cognitive interventions, planning for self-controlled ERP, and arranging for the continued involvement of a support person.

ENDING TREATMENT

As a result of the collaboration and intense emotional experiences that accompany CBT for OCD, it is common for strong therapeutic (working) relationships to develop between the therapist and patient. Thus, it should not be surprising that the end of therapy frequently evokes apprehensiveness on the part of the patient. Thinking of continuing without the therapist's consistent support might be somewhat like considering the prospect of removing the training wheels from a bicycle. The patient may wonder how he or she will persist in the fight against OCD. During the closing treatment sessions, time should be taken to discuss this and other issues related to the conclusion of therapy. These topics include:

- Ending response prevention.
- Assessing the patient's outcome.
- Reviewing how helpful the patient has found the various procedures used in therapy.
- Deciding on the need for follow-up sessions or a referral for ongoing care.
- Considering the patient's posttreatment social and occupational plans.
- Obtaining information about anticipated stressors and developing strategies for managing them.

Ending Response Prevention

As formal treatment draws to a close, the return to ordinary behavior should be discussed with patients who have been practicing complete response prevention. When is it appropriate to perform behaviors such as washing, cleaning, arranging, or praying? When should such behavior be considered as residual OCD symptoms? Although the level of oversight regarding rituals can be eased, patients must remain aware of the antecedents of their behaviors. As a general rule, if such behaviors are performed out of fear, or seem uncontrolled, they are likely rituals and should be curtailed. Thus, patients often must decide whether urges to check, wash, and so on, are based on necessity or fear. The patient is often able to determine this on his or her own, yet Kozak and Foa (1997) suggested developing specific guidelines for "normal" behavior. To illustrate, for a patient who prior to treatment checked that the door was locked by jiggling the door handle while counting to 20, these might be suitable guidelines:

- Once the door is closed, you are allowed to turn the handle once to make sure it is firmly locked. If the door does not open, you are to walk away from the door.
- Returning in the middle of the day to check that the door is locked is not allowed, even if persistent doubts and uncomfortable images arise.

For someone who took full showers multiple times each day to avoid sickness from germs, the following might be appropriate:

- Showers may be taken only once per day—in the morning before getting dressed—and should not exceed 10 minutes in length. Exceptions to this rule include after vigorous exercise (i.e., if there is extreme perspiration and body odor) and before getting dressed if going out for the evening. During any shower, each body part may be washed only once.

• Even after having a particularly messy bowel movement or changing an especially messy diaper, there is to be no extra showering.

Sometimes, the new rules will not conform to "typical" or "normal" standards. For, example, someone who formerly engaged in religious rituals, such as excessive prayer to prevent bad luck, might be asked to consider greatly limiting his praying, as in the following guideline:

• You are permitted to pray once each day: before going to bed. The only exception is if you attend a religious service. You are only to pray about general things, such as the "family's" health or the "children's" good fortune. Prayers about specific people or events constitute compulsive rituals. Do not repeat any prayers.

Of course, the terms of such guidelines will rely on what is clinically necessary and what the patient agrees to do. Thus, it is important to include the patient in developing such rules. The use of Socratic dialogue to help the patient establish such guidelines based on his or her own experiences in therapy is likely to enhance adherence because individuals are more likely to follow rules they have helped to arrange, rather than those that have been imposed on them.

Assessing Outcome and Benefit
From Specific Treatment Procedures

Although progress should be informally assessed on a continual basis throughout treatment, a more rigorous evaluation of treatment outcome—using objective and subjective methods—should occur during the final therapy sessions. We typically send a packet of self-report questionnaires home with the patient during the penultimate session to be completed and brought in for review during the last appointment. This packet contains the Obsessive Compulsive Inventory–Revised, Beck Depression Inventory, Beck Anxiety Inventory, Sheehan Disability Scale, Obsessive Beliefs Questionnaire, and the Interpretation of Intrusions Inventory. The subjective component of the posttreatment assessment might include a discussion facilitated by questions such as the following:

• What have you noticed about your obsessional fears and avoidance strategies?
• Tell me about your urges to ritualize and how you feel you can manage them now.

- Which of the things we did in therapy did you find most helpful in managing your obsessions and compulsive urges?
- What symptoms or other problems are you still concerned about?

After discussing these issues, the Y–BOCS severity scale, Brown Assessment of Beliefs Scale, and Hamilton Depression Scale should be administered to quantify the patient's degree of improvement from baseline and current symptom severity. Although it is perfectly fine for the therapist to assess his or her own patient, rater bias can be reduced by having someone else who is familiar with the assessment measures, yet uninvolved in the patient's treatment, administer these measures. Finally, it is important to give the patient feedback regarding his or her degree of change on the various symptom measures. Susan T.'s therapist discussed Susan's progress in the following way:

Therapist: So, let's look at the results of your posttreatment assessment. On the Y–BOCS, your score is now 11. When you came for your initial consultation, it was 27. So, this is about a 60% improvement in OCD symptoms. That's right on par with what we'd expect from CBT. Your score on the Hamilton Depression Scale went from 10 at your initial assessment to 3, which is also what we'd expect. So, this is telling us that, at least according to the numbers, therapy has been very helpful. How does that fit with your own experience?

Susan: I feel so much better now. There are so many things I can do more easily, like use the bathroom, give Jennifer a bath, leave the house, and grade papers for work. I don't worry nearly as much as I used to about those things. You've really helped me.

Therapist: That's great. But, really, you're the one who did all the hard work. I was just your coach.

Some patients raise the issue of their residual symptoms, and whether the remaining obsessions and ritualistic urges will ever completely disappear. In discussing this issue, it is important to emphasize that "normal" obsessions and rituals are a part of everyday life for just about everyone. So, these experiences will never completely be absent. However, treatment has changed the way the patient *responds* to obsessional stimuli. Therefore, even if (or more aptly, *when*) obsessional thoughts and stimuli appear, the patient will be able to manage them in healthy ways that do not lead to problems with anxiety, fear, or wasteful avoidance and rituals. Further, the more one practices self-controlled exposure and implements cognitive interventions, the less these situations will arise. An excellent analogy to illustrate this point is the following:

> Therapist: Let's suppose you decide to change your name from Susan to Tammy. You tell everyone you know about this change and all agree to call you Tammy from now on. At first, if someone slips up and calls you Susan, you might still respond to them because you had the name Susan for many years. But, as the months and years go by, if you heard someone say Susan, you would probably respond less and less. Nevertheless, you would still remember that Susan used to be your name. Even 10 or 20 years later, when you heard someone say Susan, you might still think about how that used to be your name, but you probably wouldn't pay much attention because you have become well practiced at using the name Tammy. Your recovery from OCD will be much the same way. You will still have intrusive thoughts and encounter obsessional situations from time to time. After all, everyone does. However, as you practice your new responses to these situations—the ones you learned in therapy—those thoughts and situations will become less and less significant in your life and you will pay less and less attention to them.

Discussing the Continuation of Care: Where to From Here?

If the issue has not yet been raised, a discussion of the patient's plans for after treatment is in order. The patient should be encouraged to keep in mind the lessons learned in therapy and understand that the therapist is available for follow-up if needed. In addition, it is important to stress the continued review of educational materials and the continued practicing of the ERP and cognitive interventions. The patient might feel the need for additional formal or informal treatment. If so, what are the remaining problems that need to be addressed? Is a referral to another provider in order? As a general rule, patients who have made little progress after 16 to 20 sessions of CBT for OCD are unlikely to benefit further by adding additional sessions. Such individuals might be referred for supportive psychotherapy to help manage existing OCD symptoms and the stress associated with them. Attending a support group run by a local affiliate of the Obsessive Compulsive Foundation (www.ocfoundation.org), if available, is an excellent suggestion. If residual OCD symptoms are minimal, yet there is concern about possible relapse, a formal follow-up program, such as that described later in this chapter, can be offered. Alternatively, a less formal strategy can be assumed that would involve telephone calls and less frequent (perhaps monthly) appointments.

Considering Future Plans

It may be important to address the patient's social and occupational plans for after treatment. If he or she has stopped working, is there a game plan for restarting? Are there potential stressors and other barriers to assuming a "normal" life, such as family turmoil, lack of social support, or residual disability from OCD? In some cases, successful treatment leaves formerly debilitated patients with exorbitant amounts of "downtime" that used to be taken up with compulsive rituals. The final sessions should involve discussions of how such time can be managed, including the possible referral to social service agencies or an occupational therapist. Volunteer work is often an excellent suggestion for easing the patient into a workday schedule. The volunteer work, which should be carefully chosen so that it is a rewarding activity for the patient, can be increased gradually as necessary until the goal of a full day is reached.

Preparing for Stressors

Patients should be informed that even in the best case scenario, they can expect to experience bumps in the road with residual OCD symptoms. Most often, these will occur during times of increased life stress, such as in the midst of occupational or family conflict, following a death or serious illness in the family, job changes, and around the time of childbirth. Thus, patients can be assisted with identifying "high risk" periods during which they should be ready to apply the techniques learned in therapy, if obsessions or safety behaviors become more numerous or distressing. Therapists should also refer to the section on lapse versus relapse.

MAINTAINING TREATMENT GAINS

Although most patients have some residual OCD symptoms at the end of treatment, they now have the tools to manage such problems and keep them under control. This section describes the topics to be included in a brief follow-up program for OCD patients who have completed an adequate trial of exposure-based CBT. The curriculum presented here is based on programs described previously by Öst (1989), Hiss, Foa, and

Kozak (1994), and McKay (1997). In general, the program emphasizes practicing the skills learned during the active therapy period; namely exposure, response prevention, and cognitive techniques. Follow-up sessions can be initiated directly on completion of the standard CBT protocol described in the previous chapters (i.e., as a maintenance program). Alternatively, these procedures can be incorporated into booster sessions for patients who, after completing a course of CBT, begin to experience a return of symptoms at some later point. In either instance, follow-up sessions should occur no more frequently than once per week to allow ample time for the patient to practice by himself or herself. In our clinic, no more than six weekly follow-up sessions are scheduled at one time. The follow-up program should incorporate the following components:

- Identifying high-risk situations and the relationship between OCD and stress.
- Practicing a lifestyle of confronting, rather than avoiding, obsessional stimuli.
- Preventing lapses from becoming relapses.
- Practicing evidence-based thinking.
- Maintaining social support.

High-Risk Situations

Even following successful treatment, most patients report that certain situations or thoughts occasionally still evoke ritualistic urges. These stimuli can be viewed as *high-risk situations*. It is important for patients to be aware of these stimuli and plan ahead if confrontation with them is anticipated. This allows the patient to plan in advance the kinds of appropriate coping strategies (i.e., cognitive techniques) that can be put to use. If the patient can anticipate high-risk situations, he or she will be better prepared for them. Times of increased life stress might themselves be high-risk situations. It is important to review with patients that OCD symptoms wax and wane, often related to the degree of stress in a person's life. When stress is high, patients need to prepare themselves for the possibility of increased obsessions and ritualistic urges. Self-monitoring (as was done during regular treatment) is a useful tool to help patients identify changes in the frequency of their symptoms.

Often, high-risk situations involve stimuli or the use of safety behaviors that were not identified or adequately addressed during therapy, and therefore continue to be associated with dysfunctional beliefs. If this is the case, it should be pointed out that unless such situations are now properly addressed, the patient can expect continued difficulty. For example, one patient treated in our clinic worked as a funeral director. Although this man successfully confronted many obsessional situations and stimuli, and refrained from most of his washing rituals during treatment, he chose to continue wearing extra gloves to protect himself against "dead body germs" he thought would cause him and his family to become seriously ill. Unfortunately, a few months after the conclusion of treatment (which was generally successful), some "contaminated" materials came into contact with his shoes, which ignited avoidance and cleaning rituals that snowballed until he was again showering in the middle of the day and asking his children to wash and clean themselves excessively. High-risk situations, such as this patient's contaminated shoes, become the exposure targets during the follow-up phase.

Practically speaking, once a set of high-risk situations is identified, a brief exposure hierarchy is developed. Because the patient is already accustomed to the treatment procedures, there is no need to begin with less anxiety-evoking stimuli. However, before beginning, it is important to ensure that the patient has retained a complete understanding of the rationale for exposure. Because only a handful of follow-up sessions are typically scheduled, situations and stimuli that cause the most distress or interference in functioning should be confronted immediately. The patient is also assigned daily programmed exposure practice for homework. The following analogy of someone learning to play the piano can be used to convey the importance of continued programmed and lifestyle exposure practice even after formal therapy has ended.

> Therapist: Let's say you wanted to learn to play the piano. So, you decide to take lessons for 6 months. After completing 6 months of lessons, you would still only know the basics of how to play the piano, and by no means would you be an expert musician. To become a skilled pianist, you must continue to practice, learn more and more songs to understand different styles of playing, improve your coordination, and progressively refine your playing ability. If you were to stop playing, even after finishing the lessons, your skill level would gradually deteriorate until you would be back to square one. Then if you tried to play, you would find that you didn't know how to any more. The same is true for the skills you learned during treatment of OCD. If you continue to practice confronting rather than avoiding situations that make you distressed, and if you continue to practice resisting urges to ritualize, you

will continue to improve your use of these skills, and you would be able to use them no matter what challenging situations came your way. On the other hand, if you return to your old habits of avoidance and rituals, you will find that OCD symptoms gradually return. It's a case of "use it or lose it."

Maintaining a Lifestyle of Exposure

By the end of treatment, patients have learned a variety of behavioral and cognitive techniques for keeping OCD symptoms in check. As I discussed in chapter 12, patients must incorporate lifestyle exposure as a daily habit, in addition to practicing programmed exposure exercises. One important topic to be discussed during follow-up is how to remain motivated to persist with exposure efforts. It is useful to think of motivation in terms of rewards. In other words, what reward does exposure bring for the patient? What does he or she stand to gain from deciding to face, rather than avoid, his or her fears? Avoidance and rituals have reward value as well: They bring about an immediate reduction in obsessional distress. However, in the long run, these safety behaviors preserve dysfunctional cognitions and contribute to the persistence of OCD. Although exposure reduces obsessional problems in the long term, it results in short-term anxiety. The hurdle here is that humans are more sensitive to short-term than long-term effects. Thus, safety seeking seems (on the surface) like the best decision.

Increasing Motivation

To increase patients' motivation for long-term maintenance, the therapist can help the patient arrange contingencies so that exposure and abstinence from safety behaviors have short-term reward value, and engaging in avoidance and rituals has negative consequences. Some specific suggestions are described here:

- Patients can make contracts with themselves such that enjoyable activities (e.g., television shows, gifts, special meals, trips) can only be done if no safety behaviors are performed for a specific amount of time. Of course, goals should be set collaboratively, and they should be realistic. The idea is for the patient to reinforce himself or herself frequently and not fail very often.
- Patients can make their self-monitoring forms available for public viewing, for example, on the refrigerator door at home. Family members will see this and congratulate (reward) the patient on his or her

progress. Posting of such forms can also serve as a reminder to the patient to keep up his or her hard work. In addition, because violations of the response prevention rules would become public, this might help the patient think twice about engaging in safety behaviors.

Neither of these techniques is completely painless, but this is part of the reason they work. If avoidance and safety behaviors interfere with improvement, it is better to feel the "pain" now and do something about it than to wait until it is too late. Such strategies also require patients to be honest with themselves about their behavior. If they cheat to attain rewards for ritual abstinence, they are only fooling themselves in the long run. Other techniques for increasing motivation include the following:

- Making a list of the benefits of reducing OCD symptoms and the benefits of working hard to prevent them from returning. For example, how will it affect academic or job performance, social or dating activities, self-perception?
- Listing things that the patient does differently now than at the start of the treatment program. This encourages him or her to reflect on personal progress.
- Selecting a specific short-term goal to work on, and identifying a short-term reward for accomplishing this goal. As mentioned earlier, the goal should be reasonable and likely to be obtained. The reward should fit the accomplishment—perhaps something fun that the patient will do or purchase if and only if the goal is reached.

The Abstinence Violation Effect.   We sometimes observe individuals with OCD who run into trouble because they attempt to change their behavior by setting very rigid or absolute goals; for example, by stating that they will *never* ritualize again. Inevitably, when a ritual is performed, the person then berates himself or herself for violating a self-imposed, yet unrealistically obtainable, standard. At that point, the person decides that because he or she has already spoiled the plan for complete abstinence, he or she might as well continue to ritualize. This process is called the *abstinence violation effect* and it is a common phenomenon among those attempting to stop any habit such as smoking, substance abuse, and overeating. To avoid falling prey to the abstinence violation effect, patients must avoid "black-and-white" or "all-or-none" styles of thinking. One way to counter this type of rigid thinking is to allow for compromises. Patients can be helped to view their life as a continuum wherein most of the time they will be able to manage obsessional anxiety and resist ritualistic urges. However, on occasion, they (as would anyone) will have their difficulties. Luckily, if rituals are performed, patients can recover quite easily. The steps for doing so include analyzing the situation (i.e., self-monitoring) and re-exposing themselves to the situation or stimulus that evoked the ritual.

Lapse Versus Relapse

As the preceding discussion implies, patients should not be concerned with periodic slips—such lapses are inevitable. A *lapse* can be considered a temporary setback that is identified and dealt with effectively. However, concern is warranted if lapses progress toward relapse. *Relapse* is defined as a return to baseline of obsessional fear, avoidance, and safety behavior. It involves thinking that all the work during therapy was for naught. The distinction between lapse and relapse is an important one for patients. If they can identify a lapse, self-monitor, and implement ERP, they are halfway to overcoming the lapse and avoiding relapse.

The therapist and patient should work collaboratively to develop a list of specific strategies for managing lapses. Such strategies should draw on what has been learned during treatment. Socratic questioning can be used to help the patient arrive at his or her own solutions. Some useful strategies include the following:

- Consider the difference between lapse and relapse. Expect lapses from time to time ("not a matter of *if*, but *when*").
- Take action to prevent the lapse from becoming a relapse.
- Determine the stimulus that evoked the fear or safety behaviors, as well as the relevant cognitive distortions.
- Repeatedly confront the situation that evoked the lapse and refrain from safety behaviors.
- Remain exposed to the situation until anxiety subsides naturally.
- Ask for help from a support person or call the therapist.

Logical Thinking

Although CT interventions play an important role in the treatment of OCD, not all patients require instruction in formal cognitive restructuring techniques such as those described by Beck (1976) or Burns (1980). However, follow-up sessions present an opportunity to introduce patients to the use of such strategies for modifying beliefs and assumptions that continue to produce obsessional anxiety as well as other negative emotional consequences. As the review of such strategies is outside the scope of this book, the reader is referred to excellent sources of information on cognitive therapy, including Beck's (1976) text and Burns's (1980) self-help book.

Continued Social Support

Two types of social support might be important for helping patients maintain their treatment gains: informational support and practical support.

Informational Support. *Informational support* is the provision of information required to solve a problem. For example, if you are trying to be on time for an appointment but cannot find the street address, you stop and ask someone for directions. This exchange of information (or informational support) occurs informally each day in the form of childrearing or household hints, for example. Individuals with OCD require informational support from experts on OCD and its treatment, such as their therapist. This is why it is important that patients raise questions or concerns they have during treatment. However, once therapy has ended, patients need to find additional sources of accurate informational support. The therapist should play a role in identifying such resources. Although indiscriminant use of the World Wide Web can present patients with plentiful misinformation about OCD, certain sites do furnish a wealth of helpful information on OCD. An annotated list of suggested Web sites is presented in Table 13.1

Practical Support. *Practical support* involves help and encouragement from understanding and sympathetic family members or friends. On an emotional level, this kind of support helps to enhance patients' feeling of self-worth and belonging because they feel cared for and understood. On a practical level, such support helps the patient manage difficult situations (i.e., lapses) by being reminded and assisted with implementing skills learned during therapy. Whereas some patients have ready access to practical support, others are not so lucky. For those who require help with asking for support, the following parameters should be discussed:

- What could the patient's friends and family members do to support efforts in fighting OCD?
- How should the patient ask others for their support?
- Who are good people to ask and who are not the best people to ask for support?
- Who would be the easiest (and who the most difficult) to ask?

Requests for support should be assertive and specific. It is also important for the patient to let others know he or she appreciates their interest and support, and how their support was helpful. This recognition increases the chances of receiving additional support. Role playing such interactions during the therapy session might help hesitant patients to gain confidence in asking for help.

TABLE 13.1

Annotated List of Helpful World Wide Web Sites on OCD and Anxiety Disorders

Resource and Internet Address	Summary
Obsessive Compulsive Foundation (OCF) www.ocfoundation.org	The Web site for the OCF offers information about OCD and related problems, including an "Ask the Experts" page. The Foundation is an excellent resource for OCD sufferers and their families, and it sponsors an annual conference.
Anxiety Disorders Association of America (ADAA) www.adaa.org	The site for the ADAA includes information about OCD as well as other anxiety disorders. There is a "How to Get Help" link that can help individuals find treatment providers that specialize in anxiety disorders. The ADAA's annual conference also offers resources for patients and their families.
The OCD Source www.ocdsource.com	The OCD Source Web site is run by individuals with OCD and contains a multitude of helpful resources, such as chat and message boards.
National Institute of Mental Health (NIMH) www.nimh.nih.gov/HealthInformation/ocdmenu.cfm	The NIMH OCD site includes authoritative information about OCD including printable booklets and links to other Web sites pertaining to research on OCD.

14

Addressing Obstacles in Treatment

In many instances the course of treatment for OCD proceeds smoothly and without complications. However, rough waters are occasionally encountered. The therapist might have difficulty conceptualizing a particularly complicated symptom presentation; the patient might fail to adhere to treatment instructions; or improvement might be slow despite apparent compliance with all of the therapy procedures. This final chapter addresses common barriers to successful treatment that I have not covered in earlier chapters. By and large, such complications arise from two general sources: (a) patient factors, and (b) factors related to treatment delivery. Obstacles associated with the patient's behavior include rejection of the treatment rationale, adherence difficulties, extreme difficulty refraining from reassurance seeking, and the presence of undetected safety-seeking behavior. Obstacles related to the treatment program itself include contradictory information obtained from outside sources, the inclination to challenge the obsession using cognitive techniques, the misuse of cognitive techniques as reassurance rituals, problems with the planning and implementation of exposure, and therapist trepidation with fully implementing the treatment techniques. Strategies for overcoming these challenges are also presented.

PATIENT-RELATED OBSTACLES

Negative Reactions to the Cognitive-Behavioral Explanation

Whereas most patients are open to conceptualizing their OCD symptoms in terms of cognitive and behavioral processes, some maintain a strong belief that obsessions and compulsions are caused by a chemical imbalance and therefore talk therapy will not be much help. Because such beliefs can lead to premature discontinuation of therapy, they are best addressed early in treatment. The therapist should openly discuss any doubts the patient has about the cognitive-behavioral model and indicate that this model was developed to explain the *symptoms* of OCD (i.e., how thinking and behavior are related), not necessarily what causes the problem in the first place. Treatment based on this model, therefore, does not require us to know about the causes of OCD. The therapist might also point out to the patient that studies have shown that CBT has effects on brain functioning (e.g., Baxter et al., 1992).

Nonadherence

The most common obstacle encountered in CBT for OCD is the patient's failure to follow treatment instructions as directed by the therapist. Patients might refuse to engage in supervised or homework exposure exercises, balk at response prevention rules, or refuse to self-monitor their rituals. Because these interventions represent the active ingredients in therapy, noncompliance must be dealt with early in treatment. Luckily, many problems with adherence can be circumvented if the therapist is proactive. First, it is critical to make sure that patients grasp the cognitive-behavioral model of OCD and understand how their own symptoms are maintained according to the conceptualization outlined in chapter 4. Second, the rationale for CBT must be clear—patients should understand how engaging in difficult and frightening therapy exercises will reduce their OCD symptoms in the long term. These two points underscore the importance of CBT's psychoeducational component. A third strategy for avoiding adherence problems is to ensure that the patient feels involved in the selection and planning of exposure exercises and response prevention rules.

If a patient is not following through with completing exposure tasks, the therapist should first inquire as to why. Sometimes noncompliance with homework can be addressed with problem solving (e.g., making more time available for practicing). It is also important to make sure that the exposure task itself is a good match to the patient's obsessional fears and dysfunctional beliefs. If not, the patient might perceive the exercise as irrelevant. If high levels of anxiety prompt refusal or "shortcuts" (e.g., subtle avoidance or safety strategies) during exposure, the therapist should review the importance of confronting obsessional fears and the role of avoidance in maintaining obsessions. Cognitive strategies (e.g., Socratic dialogue) can then be used to identify and address the patient's catastrophic predictions about danger that underlie the reluctance to fully confront the feared stimulus. With an understanding of the purpose of the exercise, and the expectation that anxiety will temporarily increase before habituation occurs, it is often possible to successfully encourage patients to invest anxiety now in a calmer future.

Sometimes, therapists are tempted to suspend or postpone the scheduled exposure due to the patient's high anxiety. Refining the exposure hierarchy and adding intermediate items (as discussed in previous chapters) are sometimes appropriate therapeutic maneuvers; for example, if the patient threatens to discontinue treatment. However, therapists are discouraged from the liberal use of these tactics, even when patients appear quite scared. Habituation *will* occur at some point, and postponing exposures only reinforces avoidance patterns and unrealistic beliefs about the dangerousness of objectively low-risk situations. Instead, the therapist should emphasize the patient's control over exposures—it is ultimately his or her choice to perform the tasks. However, this choice has important consequences: Choosing not to complete the exercise as directed is essentially the decision to strengthen OCD symptoms. The therapist can use motivational interviewing techniques to create and amplify, from the patient's point of view, the discrepancy between nonadherence and his or her broader goals and values. When nonadherence is perceived as conflicting with important personal goals (e.g., self-image, happiness, success), change becomes more likely (Miller & Rollnick, 2002).

Dealing With Argumentative Patients

During interventions such as exposure and CT, patients sometimes become contentious and look for flaws in the psychoeducational information they are given, rather than processing this information in a helpful way. This can be avoided by using a less didactic style and increasing the use of Socratic dialogue so that the belief-altering information is generated by the patient himself or herself. If discussions about mistaken beliefs take an argumentative or combative turn, the therapist should summarize the discussion and reach a conclusion that the patient *could* be correct in his or her assertions, but that rather than taking anything for granted, it is important to closely examine the facts or test them out. For example, if a patient strongly states that speaking once more with the rabbi would permanently quell his need for reassurance about fears of violating Jewish dietary laws, this should be honestly considered. However, the ensuing dialogue should include questions about past experiences. For example, has the patient ever made the "just one more time" promise before? If so, what was the outcome? What could be done to find out whether the reassurance seeking is really necessary? What have rabbis told him in the past, and what does he expect to hear this time? Would it be more helpful to learn how to manage with such situations without reassurance? This highlights the importance of maintaining a collaborative relationship.

Therapists are strongly advised to refrain from protracted debates with patients over the potential risks involved with doing exposure exercises and stopping rituals. Not only are such arguments fruitless; they also reinforce the patient's OCD habits of spending too much time worrying about risk and uncertainty. Essentially, arguments of this type are nothing more than an acting out of the patient's mental analyzing rituals. Moreover, when patients perceive that the therapist is frustrated, angry, or trying to coerce them into compliance (e.g., "You can't make me do this."), they tend to lose motivation. When a reluctant patient attempts to engage in rational argument about risk and danger, the best course of action for the therapist is to step back and recognize that the decision to engage in treatment is a difficult one. Motivational statements, such as the following, are often persuasive:

- Remember that we both agreed on a plan for the exposures that you would practice. I hope you will hold up your end of the agreement.
- You're right. There is risk involved, but it is not high risk. The goal of treatment is to weaken your anxiety about situations where it is impossible to have a complete guarantee of safety.
- It looks like you are having a lot of difficulty with deciding to do this exposure, but if you are going to get over OCD, you have to confront your uncertainty and find out that the risk is low.
- I realize most people wouldn't do what I am asking you to do. However, the therapy isn't about what *most people* do. It's about helping you overcome OCD. Stopping these rituals is designed to help you learn to better manage acceptable levels of risk and uncertainty.
- You are here in treatment for yourself—not for me. So, I won't argue or debate with you. This is entirely your choice. However, I will point out that you stand to gain relief from your symptoms by trying these exercises and enduring the short-term anxiety. On the other hand, you are the one who has to live with the OCD symptoms if you choose not to do the therapy.

Deciding to Terminate Therapy

If, despite much effort to repair such problems, the patient persists in refusing to cooperate with treatment instructions, it may be suitable to suspend therapy. For some clinicians, this might mean shifting the focus of treatment to some other problem (or working on identifying where the patient's motivation for change *does* lie). For others, this might mean ending therapy altogether. If this becomes inevitable, it should be done in a sensitive (as opposed to a punitive) way, and the door should be left open for the patient to return at some point in the future. My colleagues and I have found that discussing nonadherence as indicative of "bad timing" often works well, as in the following monologue:

> Therapist: It seems to me that for whatever reasons, we are not getting very far with therapy. I know that this treatment can be very difficult, and you are clearly having a hard time doing the exercises that will help you overcome OCD. And so treatment cannot be as effective for you as it should be. When this happens it means that now is not the right time for you to be in this kind of therapy. So it is best that we stop at this point. Maybe at some point in the future it will be a better time for you, and you will be able to do the exercises you need to do to benefit. I would be happy to work with you at that point.

Excessive Reassurance Seeking

Some OCD sufferers approach therapy believing the goal is to obtain the "ultimate guarantee" of safety, which they can then apply whenever and wherever they feel anxious. Such patients may try to hijack cognitive interventions by using them to hear from an "expert" (i.e., the therapist) that, for example, one cannot get sick from using a public bathroom or that one will never act on unacceptable violent, aggressive, or sexual impulses. Whereas efforts to gain assurances are usually straightforward and easily identified (most patients will ask the same questions again and again—perhaps in different ways), some patients are more subtle. Keen judgment is sometimes needed to assess whether the function of questioning truly is reassurance seeking. Once patients understand the problems associated with reassurance seeking, it is appropriate to ask about the purpose of suspected questions (e.g., "You've asked me that question a few times today; are you trying to get me to reassure you about this?"). In my own work, when I hear myself repeating the same information to a patient more than once or twice, it is a signal to consider whether I am unintentionally helping the patient to ritualize.

The problem with providing assurances, of course, is that the patient learns nothing about the process of evaluating his or her dysfunctional beliefs. Moreover, during exposure, reassurance seeking prevents prolonged confrontation (and habituation) to the feared situation, which involves being uncertain about the feared consequences. It is therefore important for the therapist to recognize the patient's attempts to seek reassurance and avoid the temptation to ease the patient's distress by providing guarantees. Some patients have difficulty resisting urges to seek reassurance even when given instructions not to do so. Excessive and persistent reassurance seeking must be handled with caution because miscommunications can derail therapy. Next I describe some useful ways my colleagues and I have addressed these problems (Abramowitz, Franklin, & Cahill, 2003).

Appeals to Authority. In some instances patients desire a consultation with an expert on the feared situation or stimuli. For example, individuals with religious obsessions often seek reassurance from clergy. One man, who feared that he was becoming schizophrenic, persistently e-mailed and telephoned various OCD experts to ask questions on the relationship between OCD and schizophrenia. Requests for such consultations should be considered and discussed in light of whether or not they will be helpful for moving the patient toward overcoming his or her need for certainty. In some instances, a single consultation with an expert might be appropriate, especially if this would prevent the patient from discontinuing treatment. However, the aim of such a consultation is to establish guidelines about safety—not to inquire about every possible situation that could arise. Patients must learn to apply judgment about risk rather than know for sure about the probability of harm in specific feared situations. In preparation for meeting with an expert, the patient and therapist should agree on certain broad questions that will be addressed, and the therapist should be present to ensure that excessive ritualizing (i.e., reassurance seeking) does not occur.

A similar situation arises when patients turn to the Internet or other "authorities" (e.g., medical references) for reassurance. Such behavior often leads to obtaining incorrect or contradictory information that augments uncertainty and strengthens inaccurate beliefs. For example, patients might read about and misinterpret statistics regarding the relationship between hand washing and illness. Individuals with the habit of searching Web sites for information about each situation in which obsessional fear is evoked should be persuaded to cease and desist from such behavior during treatment (i.e., as part of response prevention) because the aim of therapy is to learn to rely on judgments about risk that are derived from real-world evidence.

Asking for Reassurance During Exposure. When patients desire a guarantee of safety during exposure exercises (e.g., "Are you sure I'm not going to get sick if I touch the toilet seat?"), the first inclination may be to put them at ease by reassuring them they are not in any danger. However, this undermines the goal of living with acceptable levels of risk and uncertainty (indeed, people routinely touch toilet seats). On the other hand, the patient should not be made to feel as if he or she is at high risk for negative consequences. Thus, the ideal response uses empathy, focusing on how exposures are designed to evoke uncertainty and how there can never be an absolute guarantee of safety. A general rule to keep in mind is that questions about risk in a given situation should be answered only once. Additional queries should be pointed out for the patient and addressed in the following way:

> Therapist: I can tell you're feeling uncomfortable and are searching for a guarantee right now—that's your obsessional doubting. Because I already answered that question, it would not be helpful for you if I answered it again. The best way to stop the obsessional doubts is for you to practice tolerating the distress and uncertainty. How can I help you to do that?

The therapist must also be alert for more subtle attempts to seek reassurance. As an example, one patient would make strategic statements (e.g., "Now that we've touched the toilet, I'm going to go home and play with my 6-month-old") and then scrutinize the therapist's facial expression for signs of concern. If such assurance seeking is suspected, this should be confirmed and discussed with the patient. The rationale for not seeking such assurances should also be revisited.

My colleagues and I have worked with some individuals who were completely unable (or unwilling) to resist persistent urges to seek reassurance both within and between therapy sessions. The uncertainty evoked by their OCD symptoms, which was intensified by doing exposures, was too much for them to bear. Because the persistence of assurance-seeking rituals inevitably compromises treatment outcome, therapy had to be suspended in these cases. As addressed earlier, suspension is the last resort when patients refuse to comply with treatment procedures and it is imperative that the therapist convey in a caring and sensitive way that discontinuation is recommended when patients are unable to carry out the treatment procedures in ways that would be beneficial.

Presence of Subtle Safety-Seeking Behaviors

Sometimes, patients fail to show a reduction in fear even after repeated trials of well-executed prolonged situational or imaginal exposure. If this occurs, it may be the result of subtle, undetected safety maneuvers (e.g., undetected mental rituals) that the patient continues to use to avoid feared consequences. Although some individuals blatantly use safety behaviors to avoid distress during exposure, others might use them quite innocently and are not aware that they are doing anything to disrupt treatment. Nevertheless, use of any safety behaviors during exposure snarls the process of habituation and cognitive change as I have described. In such cases, the therapist should inquire carefully about any sorts of strategies (behavioral or mental) the patient is using to reduce anxiety or prevent harm during exposure. Any identified safety maneuvers must, of course, be dropped in subsequent exposures.

OBSTACLES RELATED TO TREATMENT DELIVERY

Contradictory Information From Other Sources

Unfortunately, patients are often exposed to information that conflicts with what is taught in CBT for OCD. Misleading data may be gleaned from sources such as another treatment provider or paraprofessional (e.g., a pastoral counselor), radio and television advertisements for pharmaceutical products, and educational materials (print or Internet-based) about OCD. For example, one popular mental health Web site suggests incorrectly that thought stopping and aversive conditioning are effective interventions for OCD:

> Through thought-stopping, the individual learns how to halt obsessive thoughts through proper identification of the obsessional thoughts, and then averting it by doing an opposite, incompatible response. A common incompatible response to an obsessive thought is simply by yelling the word "Stop!" loudly. The client can be encouraged to practice this in therapy (with the clinician's help and modeling, if necessary), and then encouraged to transplant this behavior to the privacy of their home. They can also often use other incompatible stimuli, such as tweaking a rubber-band which is around their wrist whenever they have a thought. The latter technique would be more effective in public, for example. (PsychCentral, 2004)

Of course, the use of thought stopping contrasts with one of the chief principles of CBT for OCD: that intrusive obsessional thoughts are entirely normal and therefore not something to be avoided or suppressed. In fact, CBT helps patients *confront* their obsessional thoughts (precisely the *opposite* of thought stopping) as a way of learning to view the intrusions as harmless. It is also well known that aversive conditioning is not an effective way to manage obsessions (the only result is a sore wrist).

If a patient is receiving CBT from one provider, and another psychosocial intervention (e.g., religious counseling) from a different provider, it is critical that the clinicians support one another in terms of the kind of advice they give. This may be best accomplished through periodic communication between the treatment providers (Taylor, 2000). Receiving contradictory advice from two or more "authorities" can lead to confusion, or worse, cause the already anxious patient to worry further about satisfying two providers who are giving them incompatible directives (as in the case of exposure vs. thought stopping). In such cases, the best option is sometimes to suspend CBT until the patient has completed treatment with the other provider.

Inclination to Challenge the Obsession

It is tempting for therapists to fall into the trap of challenging the logic of obsessional thoughts per se (e.g., "the impulse to attack a child") rather than challenging the patient's faulty beliefs and interpretations of the thoughts (e.g., "The thought means I am a very dangerous person who is unfit to be a parent"). Intuitively, the obsession itself seems like a good target for cognitive interventions because it is both a cognition and foremost on the patient's list of complaints. It is also usually illogical. Yet, recall that the obsession is considered the "A" in the A-B-C model of cognitive therapy. It is the normally occurring (uncontrollable) activating event about which the patient has dysfunctional beliefs (Bs). It is the Bs that require modification if treatment is to be successful. Because most patients already recognize their obsessions as irrational, directly challenging the validity of these thoughts will likely have only a transient therapeutic effect. Moreover, such challenges could turn into reassurance-seeking rituals or maladaptive neutralization strategies used in response to the particular obsession (Salkovskis, 1985).

The best way to avoid challenging obsessions is to ensure that intrusive thoughts are differentiated from catastrophic interpretations and appraisals of obsessions (i.e., automatic thoughts and dysfunctional assumptions). Because both are cognitive events, disentangling them can be tricky. However, this can be clarified if the therapist considers the ego-dystonic intrusive thought not as the cognitive basis of distress itself, but rather as a stimulus about which the person has automatic thoughts and interpretations. Chapter 8 provides specific suggestions to help the therapist assess appraisals and interpretations of obsessions across the various OCD symptom dimensions. Table 9.2 also illustrates differences between obsessional stimuli and automatic thoughts about these stimuli.

When Cognitive Challenges Become Rituals

As mentioned previously, it is possible for psychoeducational material and information learned through Socratic dialogue to be converted into reassurance-seeking rituals or neutralization strategies. For example, after learning about the CBT model, one patient ritualistically repeated the phrase "obsessional thoughts are normal" to reduce anxiety associated with her intrusive thoughts of harming her baby. Moreover, this phrase had to be repeated three times "perfectly" before she could stop the ritual. Other patients become preoccupied with finding the single "best" way of challenging their obsession or identifying the phrase that "most completely" reassures them that feared consequences are impossible. The therapist can reduce the chances that CT techniques will become rituals by avoiding the provision of guarantees during CT. For example, rather than telling patents that they "probably won't get sick," it is better to explicitly say that the probability of becoming sick, although acceptably low, is *not zero*.

Freeston and Ladouceur (1999) suggested that if the patient repeats the same cognitive analysis, uses it in a stereotypic way, or requires increasing efforts to reduce distress, it means such material is being used for the purposes of neutralizing. In contrast, healthy use of CT techniques allows the patient to generate new interpretations of obsessional stimuli that lead to acting appropriately during exposure (managing distress, taking "risks"). For example, Susan T. was taught how to use her cognitive challenges to think less catastrophically about her intrusive thoughts, and then to engage in an exercise (e.g., holding or bathing the baby) to demonstrate that her feared consequences were unlikely.

Unbearable Anxiety Levels During Exposure

If the patient has difficulty tolerating an exposure—if he or she becomes extremely anxious and emotionally reactive, or fails to habituate—it probably means the task chosen for that particular session is too difficult. In such cases, the exercise should be stopped and the therapist should assess the cognitions underlying the intense anxiety. If the patient becomes concerned that treatment is not working because anxiety did not subside, the therapist should emphasize that therapy is a process that requires continued practice. Moreover, it can be pointed out that the patient took an important step simply by choosing to enter the feared situation at all (something he or she had been avoiding). If the patient refuses to tolerate high levels of anxiety, even after an appropriate intermediate exposure task has been identified, an alternative consideration is that depressive symptoms are interfering with habituation (e.g., Foa, 1979; Foa et al., 1983). In such cases, strategies to help manage depression might be undertaken before attempting exposure for OCD.

Absence of Anxiety During Exposure

At the other extreme, a patient might report that the planned exposure task evokes little or no discomfort. On the one hand, this could be an encouraging sign—the once-feared situation may no longer evoke distress because the patient's expectations about danger have been modified in some other way. This is most likely to be the case toward the end of treatment, once the patient has gained confidence with conducting exposures. If early exposures evoke little or no anxiety, it is wise to troubleshoot rather than assume that the patient has improved very rapidly. Absence of anxiety during exposure could result if the key anxiety-evoking aspects of the feared situation have not been incorporated into the exposure. This can be assessed and resolved by directly asking the patient why the exposure did not evoke anxiety, or how the situation could be made more anxiety evoking. The planning of subsequent exposures must then take this information into account.

A second possibility is that the patient has in some way nullified the exposure with cognitive avoidance or safety-seeking behavior. For example, before undertaking exposure to contaminating her son with "floor germs," one very religious patient ritualistically reminded herself that her son's health was entirely in God's hands. This maneuver functioned to absolve her of the responsibility for harm and therefore she did not become anxious even when feeding her son candy that had touched the floor. If avoidance and safety-seeking behavior is suspected, the therapist should carefully assess for its presence (e.g., "Is there anything you are doing, or anything you are telling yourself, that might make the exposure less distressing?"). The use of such strategies may indicate a problem understanding or accepting the rationale for exposure. If the patient does not see how exposure will be helpful, there will be little motivation to purposely subject himself or herself to additional anxiety. Additional time spent with psychoeducation might be necessary. Alternatively, the selected exposure task may simply be too frightening and a less distressing one should be considered.

When Exposure Exercises Go Amiss

Although the therapist aims to arrange exposure tasks that involve minimal risk, minimal risk is not the same as no risk. It is therefore possible for exposure to result in negative outcomes. Some examples from my, and my colleagues', experience include the following:

- A woman who was afraid of making mistakes while paying bills (she thought this would result in her utilities being turned off) conducted an exposure in which she wrote bank checks and completed her statements rapidly and without double-checking to ensure accuracy. However, she made an actual mathematical error during one assignment and sent the incorrect amount (too little) to the electric company.
- A patient with fears of contamination from fruit ate a fairly large quantity of berries and melon for an exposure. That evening he encountered problems with diarrhea that he believed resulted from contaminated fruit.
- A man conducting exposure to driving while speaking on his cell phone—he had obsessions about hitting pedestrians without realiz-

ing it—accidentally made a wrong turn onto a one-way street. Fortunately, there were no oncoming cars.
- A woman with obsessional fears of contamination from public bathrooms, and her therapist, both came down with colds the day after exposure to touching door handles from public bathrooms.

Initially, such occurrences might seem like setbacks. Exposure is supposed to *disconfirm* such fears. However, this is not necessarily the case. Recall that patients overestimate both the *probability* and *severity* of negative outcomes. Thus, if an exposure exercise goes wrong, the therapist can salvage some benefit from the experience by helping the patient modify cognitions about the "awfulness" of the "dreaded" outcome, acknowledging that sometimes negative events do happen. That is, the therapist can point out that although something negative occurred as a result of exposure, (a) the result was probably not as bad as the patient would have anticipated, and (b) the patient was able to deal appropriately with the situation. Such experiences probably build the patient's self-efficacy because they draw attention to his or her underestimated ability to cope with adversity. Next, I explain how each of the problematic exposures just described were resolved:

- The woman who underpaid her electric bill received a notice from the electric company informing her of the error and asking that she please pay the balance of last month's bill along with next month's bill. She learned that even if she made a mistake, she would have other chances before her utilities were shut off.
- The patient who experienced diarrhea after eating fruit told his wife that he believed the fruit he ate during exposure was contaminated and that now he was ill. His wife, who happened to be a dietitian, perceptively pointed out that the diarrhea was probably a normal gastrointestinal response to the sudden change in diet (increase in fiber). The patient had been avoiding eating fruit for a long time.
- The man who turned the wrong way down a one-way street quickly corrected his mistake and, although distressed at making the wrong turn, learned that he was able to recognize such errors. He concluded that if he was able to notice such a mistake so quickly, he would probably also realize if he had hit a pedestrian.
- The woman who, along with her therapist, caught a cold after the bathroom exposure made the following comment: "I'm not happy to have a sore throat and a cold, but if this is the worst thing that happens if you touch a bathroom door, then I shouldn't worry about it as much as I do."

Therapist Discomfort With Exposure Exercises

Finally, it is normal for beginner therapists, or those new to the use of exposure-based therapy for anxiety, to feel trepidation in asking patients with OCD to purposely confront stimuli that evoke obsessional anxiety and then resist safety-seeking behaviors. Perhaps the exercises seem unnecessarily painful. One might consider the following points if such consternation sets in.

- We know from a solid foundation of research that exposure-based therapy is the treatment of choice for OCD, and that without it, patients have less hope of improving. Ultimately reducing pathological anxiety, avoidance, and rituals requires temporarily evoking anxiety and urges to perform the unwanted behaviors.
- Exposure therapy does not demand anything of the patient that he or she is not already doing. That is, patients are already thinking their distressing thoughts repeatedly—this is the definition of an obsession. Exposure simply asks that the patient evoke the obsessional thought in a systematic and therapeutic fashion to practice more healthy ways of managing such situations. Further, there is no evidence that it is dangerous or harmful to interrupt a person who is engaged in compulsive rituals. At worst, interruption evokes temporary discomfort (e.g., Rachman & Hodgson, 1980).
- It is clear that the patient's habitual responses of attempting to avoid, resist, and control obsessional stimuli are maladaptive and serve only to maintain the associated distress and impairment. The cognitive-behavioral model posits that a much healthier strategy for dealing with obsessions is to consider them as normal mental stimuli that need not be resisted or controlled. Thus, exposure helps the patient experience his or her feared situations and intrusive thoughts in a way that leads to the development of more adaptive responses to these stimuli. Moreover, the new responses have the added benefit of being rational.
- The distress evoked during therapeutic exposure is temporary. When it decreases, patients are left with important knowledge about situations and thoughts they once believed were dangerous, and about their own ability to manage their own subjective distress.
- Amelioration of certain fears by exposure will not cause "symptom substitution" of additional problems. There is no evidence that obsessional fears and rituals are caused by unconscious conflicts that persist until they are resolved.
- Although exposure requires that the therapist purposely help the patient become anxious, I have found that when the rationale for these procedures is clear, and the treatment plan has been established collaboratively, the intervention engenders a warm and supportive working relationship that further authenticates the patient's courage and progress.

Appendix A:
OCD Treatment History Form for Assessing the Adequacy of Previous Cognitive-Behavioral Therapy Trials

Cognitive-Behavioral Treatment History Form

> **Instructions**: This form is designed to help assess whether a patient has received an "adequate trial" of cognitive-behavioral therapy (CBT) for obsessive-compulsive disorder. Use a separate form for each separate therapy "trial" the patient underwent for treatment of OCD. The questions in *italics* are to be asked to the patient.

Patient: _____ Dates of therapy: _____ to _____

Where did your therapy for OCD occur?

Location: _____
             Facility   city & state

What type of setting did this treatment occur in (prompt with the options below)

Check one...
- ❑ Inpatient facility
- ❑ Outpatient CMHC
- ❑ Outpatient medical center
- ❑ OCD/Anxiety specialty clinic
- ❑ Private practice
- ❑ Research trial

What was the name of the therapist you worked most closely with? What was his/her degree?

Name and degree of primary therapist _____

Were you also taking medicine for OCD while undergoing this therapy?
Did CBT occur while this patient was undergoing an adequate SSRI trial?   Yes   No

---

PART I. EXPOSURE

During the therapy were you instructed to confront situations, people, or places that you typically avoided because of your OCD? (Note: allow patient to describe exposure procedures, but use the prompts below to inquire about specific components)

a. *Did the therapist discuss with you why exposure helps to reduce obsessional anxiety?*
   Rationale for exposure provided   Yes   No

b. *During exposure practices, did you become anxious or uncomfortable?*
   Exposure to anxiety-evoking situations   Yes   No

c. *Did the therapist keep track of how anxious you were during exposure (such as by asking you to rate your anxiety level, or SUDS)?*
   Monitoring of anxiety levels in exposure   Yes   No

d. *Did you conduct this exposure with the therapist or only by yourself?*
   In-session, therapist-assisted exposure   Yes   No

e. *Did the therapist routinely assign "homework" exposure for you to practice on your own?*
   Routine homework exposure   Yes   No

f. *Did the therapist review the homework assignments you had done (collect forms, etc.)?*
   Homework review   Yes   No

g. *Did you come up with a list of all fearful situations and gradually confront more difficult ones?*
    Graduated, hierarchy-based exposure   Yes   No

h. *Did the therapist ask you to remain in exposure situations until your anxiety decreased?*
    Prolonged exposure   Yes   No

i. *Did the therapist ask you to repeat the exposures until the situations were less anxiety-provoking?*
    Repeated exposure   Yes   No

j. *Were there times when the therapist asked you to imagine distressing or anxiety-provoking scenes, thoughts, or images?* (i.e., using audio tapes?)
    Imaginal exposure   Yes   No

k. *Did the therapist help a family member or relative to assist you with difficult exposure practices (especially homework practices?)*
    Support person   Yes   No

WAS EXPOSURE ADEQUATE (b, d, e, h, & i MUST be answered "yes")?   YES   NO

PART II.   RESPONSE PREVENTION

Did the therapist ask you to reduce or stop your compulsive rituals? What kinds of instructions did they give you?
(Note: allow patient to describe response prevention procedures, but use the prompts below to inquire about specific components)

a. *Did the therapist discuss with you why stopping rituals would be helpful in reducing your compulsions?*
    Rationale for response prevention provided Yes   No

b. *Did the therapist ask you to make an effort to refrain from your compulsive rituals and provide a specific plan or guidelines to help you reduce your compulsions?*
    Response prevention with guidelines   Yes   No

c. *Did the therapist ask you to keep track of rituals you did perform during therapy (i.e., on record forms)?*
    Self-monitoring   Yes   No

WAS RESPONSE PREVENTION ADEQUATE (b MUST be answered "yes")?   YES   NO

PART III.   NONSPECIFIC VARIABLES

a. *How long did you continue this therapy?*
    At least 15 sessions   Yes   No

b. *How regularly did you meet with the therapist?*
    Sessions occurred at least once per week   Yes   No

c. *Did the therapist (and/or their supervisor) have specialized training/background in the treatment of OCD?*
    Therapist/supervisor had experience with treating OCD   Yes   No

d. *Why did this therapy end?*
    ❑   Patient got better
    ❑   Patient had too much difficulty with completing exposure/response prevention
    ❑   Patient completed exposure/response prevention, but was not getting better
    ❑   Other (explain):

WAS THIS AN ADEQUATE CBT TRIAL?
(adequate exposure and response prevention plus a & b in Part IV answered "yes")?   YES   NO

Appendix B:
The OCD Section
of the Mini International
Neuropsychiatric Interview
(MINI)

Note. Reprinted with permission from David V. Sheehan, MD, MBA.

H. OBSESSIVE-COMPULSIVE DISORDER

(➡ ABOVE A NO MEANS: GO TO THE DIAGNOSTIC BOX, CIRCLE NO AND MOVE TO THE NEXT MODULE)

H1	In the past month, have you been bothered by recurrent thoughts, impulses, or images that were unwanted, distasteful, inappropriate, intrusive, or distressing? (For example, the idea that you were dirty, contaminated or had germs, or fear of contaminating others, or fear of harming someone even though you didn't want to, or fearing you would act on some impulse, or fear or superstitions that you would be responsible for things going wrong, or obsessions with sexual thoughts, images or impulses, or hoarding, collecting, or religious obsessions.) (DO NOT INCLUDE SIMPLY EXCESSIVE WORRIES ABOUT REAL LIFE PROBLEMS. DO NOT INCLUDE OBSESSIONS DIRECTLY RELATED TO EATING DISORDERS, SEXUAL DEVIATIONS, PATHOLOGICAL GAMBLING, OR ALCOHOL OR DRUG ABUSE BECAUSE THE PATIENT MAY DERIVE PLEASURE FROM THE ACTIVITY AND MAY WANT TO RESIST IT ONLY BECAUSE OF ITS NEGATIVE CONSEQUENCES.)	NO ➡ to H4	YES

H2	Did they keep coming back into your mind even when you tried to ignore or get rid of them?	NO ➡ to H4	YES
H3	Do you think that these obsessions are the product of your own mind and that they are not imposed from the outside?	NO	YES obsessions
H4	In the past month, did you do something repeatedly without being able to resist doing it, like washing or cleaning excessively, counting or checking things over and over, or repeating, collecting, arranging things, or other superstitious rituals?	NO	YES compulsions
	IS H3 OR H4 CODED YES?	➡ NO ➡	YES
H5	Did you recognize that either these obsessive thoughts or these compulsive behaviors were excessive or unreasonable?	NO	YES

H6	Did these obsessive thoughts and/or compulsive behaviors significantly interfere with your normal routine, occupational functioning, usual social activities, or relationships, or did they take more than one hour a day?	NO YES O.C.D. CURRENT

Appendix C:
Yale–Brown Obsessive Compulsive Scale Symptom Checklist and Severity Scale

Note.   Reprinted with permission from Wayne K. Goodman, MD.

Yale-Brown Obsessive Compulsive Symptom Checklist (Y-BOCS)

current	past only	**AGGRESSIVE OBSESSIONS**
□	□	Fear might harm self
□	□	Fear might harm others
□	□	Violent or horrific images
□	□	Fear of blurting out obscenities or insults
□	□	Fear of doing something else embarrassing
□	□	Fear will act on unwanted impulses (e.g., to stab friend)
□	□	Fear will steal things
□	□	Fear will harm others because not careful enough (e.g., hit/run MVA)
□	□	Fear of being responsible for something else terrible happening (e.g., fire, burglary)
□	□	Other _____

current	past only	**CONTAMINATION OBSESSIONS**
□	□	Concerns or disgust with bodily waste or secretions (e.g., urine, feces, saliva)
□	□	Concern with dirt or germs
□	□	Excessive concern with environmental contaminants (e.g., asbestos, radiation, toxic waste)
□	□	Excessive concern with household items (e.g., cleansers, solvents)
□	□	Excessive concern with animals (e.g., insects)
□	□	Bothered by sticky substances or residues
□	□	Concerned will get ill because of contaminant
□	□	Concerned will get others ill by spreading contamination
□	□	No concern with consequences of contamination other than how it might feel
□	□	Other _____

current	past only	**SEXUAL OBSESSIONS**
□	□	Forbidden or unacceptable sexual thoughts/images/impulses
□	□	Content involves children or incest
□	□	Content involves homosexuality
□	□	Sexual behavior toward others (Aggressive)
□	□	Other _____

current	past only	**HOARDING/SAVING OBSESSIONS**
□	□	[distinguish from hobbies and concern with objects with monetary or sentimental value]
□	□	Fears of mistakenly discarding important things along with unimportant items

current	past only	**RELIGIOUS OBSESSIONS (SCRUPULOSITY)**
□	□	Excessive concern with sacrilege or blasphemy
□	□	Excessive concern with right/wrong, morality
□	□	Other _____

current	past only	**OBSESSION WITH NEED FOR SYMMETRY/EXACTNESS**
□	□	Accompanied by magical thinking (e.g., concerned that mother will have accident unless things are in the right place)
□	□	Not accompanied by magical thinking (just feels uncomfortable)

current	past only	**SOMATIC OBSESSIONS**
□	□	Concern with illness or disease
□	□	Excessive concern with body part or aspect of appearance (e.g., body dysmorphic disorder)
□	□	Other _____

	past	
current	only	**MISCELLANEOUS OBSESSIONS**
☐	☐	Need to know or remember
☐	☐	Fear of saying certain things
☐	☐	Fear of not saying just the right thing
☐	☐	Fear of losing things
☐	☐	Intrusive non-violent images
☐	☐	Intrusive nonsense sounds, words, or music
☐	☐	Bothered by certain sounds/noises
☐	☐	Lucky/unlucky numbers
☐	☐	Colors with special significance
☐	☐	Superstitious fears
☐	☐	Other _____

	past	
current	only	**WASHING/CLEANING COMPULSIONS**
☐	☐	Excessive or ritualized handwashing
☐	☐	Excessive or ritualized showering, bathing, tooth brushing, grooming, or toilet routine
☐	☐	Excessive cleaning of household items or other inanimate objects
☐	☐	Other measures to prevent or remove contact with contaminants
☐	☐	Other _____

	past	
current	only	**CHECKING COMPULSIONS**
☐	☐	Checking locks, stoves, appliances, etc.
☐	☐	Checking that did/will not harm others
☐	☐	Checking that did/will not harm self
☐	☐	Checking that nothing terrible did/will happen
☐	☐	Checking that did not make mistakes
☐	☐	Checking tied to somatic obsessions
☐	☐	Other _____

	past	
current	only	**REPEATING RITUALS**
☐	☐	Re-reading or re-writing
☐	☐	Need to repeat routine activities (in/out door, up/down chair)
☐	☐	Other _____

	past	
current	only	**COUNTING COMPULSIONS**
☐	☐	_____

	past	
current	only	**ORDERING/ARRANGING COMPULSIONS**
☐	☐	_____

	past	
current	only	**MENTAL COMPULSIONS**
☐	☐	Special words, images, numbers, repeated mentally to neutralize (e.g., lucky numbers)
☐	☐	Special prayers (short and long) repeated in a set manner (e.g., "God is good")
☐	☐	Mental counting
☐	☐	Mentally listmaking
☐	☐	Mental reviewing (e.g., reviewing conversations)
☐	☐	Other _____

342

	past	
current	only	**MISCELLANEOUS COMPULSIONS**
☐	☐	Excessive listmaking (writing or verbalizing aloud)
☐	☐	Urges to ask, tell, or confess
☐	☐	Urges to touch, tap, or rub
☐	☐	Rituals involving blinking or staring
☐	☐	Other measures (not checking) to prevent harm to self or others, or to prevent terrible consequences
☐	☐	Ritualized eating behaviors
☐	☐	Superstitious behaviors
☐	☐	Trichotillomania (hair pulling)
☐	☐	Other self-damaging or self-mutilating behaviors (skin picking)
☐	☐	Other _____

Yale-Brown Obsessive Compulsive Severity Scale (Y-BOCS)

Y-BOCS TOTAL SCORE (add 1-10) ☐

OBSESSIONS

	None / 0	< 1 hr./ rarely / 1	1-3 hr./ occasionally / 2	3-8 hr./ frequently / 3	> 8 hr./ constantly / 4
Time: how much time do obsessions occupy per day; how frequently do they occur	None — 0	< 1 hr./ rarely — 1	1-3 hr./ occasionally — 2	3-8 hr./ frequently — 3	> 8 hr./ constantly — 4
Interference: How much do obsessions keep you from doing activities (e.g., work/school, social)	None — 0	slight interference — 1	definite, but manageable — 2	substantial interference — 3	Incapacitating — 4
Distress: How much distress do the obsessive thoughts cause you?	None — 0	mild — 1	disturbing but manageable — 2	very disturbing — 3	disabling — 4
Resistance: How much effort do you make to resist thoughts? How often do you try to turn focus away?	always (100%) — 0	usually — 1	sometimes — 2	rarely — 3	never (0%) — 4
Control: How successful are you in stopping obsessive thoughts? How often can you beat the thought vs. the thought beating you?	always (100%) — 0	usually — 1	sometimes — 2	rarely — 3	never (100%) — 4

Obsessions Total _____

COMPULSIONS

	none / 0	< 1 hr./ rarely / 1	1-3 hr./ occasionally / 2	3-8 hr./ frequently / 3	> 8 hr./ constantly / 4
Time: how much time do you spend performing compulsions per day; how frequently?	none — 0	< 1 hr./ rarely — 1	1-3 hr./ occasionally — 2	3-8 hr./ frequently — 3	> 8 hr./ constantly — 4
Interference: How much do compulsions keep you from doing activities (e.g., work/school, social)	none — 0	slight interference — 1	definite, but manageable — 2	substantial interference — 3	unmanageable — 4
Distress: If you were prevented from performing compulsive rituals, how distressed would you become?	none — 0	mild — 1	disturbing but manageable — 2	very disturbing — 3	disabling — 4
Resistance: How much effort do you make to resist performing rituals? How hard do you try?	always (100%) — 0	usually — 1	sometimes — 2	rarely — 3	never (0%) — 4
Control: How successful are you in stopping rituals yourself?	always (100%) — 0	usually — 1	sometimes — 2	rarely — 3	never (100%) — 4

Compulsions Total _____

Appendix D:
The Brown Assessment
of Beliefs Scale

Note. Reprinted with permission from Jane Eisen, MD.

Brown Assessment of Beliefs Scale

1) Are there certain ideas or beliefs you have that are of significant concern to you **over the past week?** Which one would you rate as being of most concern? (principle belief):

_____

2) Do you have other ideas (thoughts/beliefs) that you are preoccupied with? _____

_____

For each item, circle the number identifying the response which best characterizes the patient **over the past week**. The patient's specific beliefs can be incorporated into the questions--for example, "How convinced are you of this belief--that touching doorknobs will make you ill?" Optional questions are indicated in parentheses; instructions to the interviewer are italicized.

1. Conviction

How convinced are you of these ideas/beliefs? Are you certain your ideas/beliefs are accurate? (What do you base your certainty on?)

0. – Completely convinced beliefs are false (0% certainty).
1. – Beliefs are probably not true, or substantial doubt exists.
2. – Beliefs may or may not be true, or unable to decide whether beliefs are true.
3. – Fairly convinced that beliefs are true, but an element of doubt exists.
4. – Completely convinced about the reality of held beliefs (100% certainty).

2. Perception of others' views of beliefs

What do you think other people (would) think of your beliefs? [PAUSE] How certain are you that <u>most</u> people think your beliefs make sense?

(Interviewer should clarify if necessary that the patient answers this question assuming that others are giving their <u>honest</u> opinion.)

0. – Completely certain that most people think these beliefs are unrealistic.
1. – Fairly certain that most people think these beliefs are unrealistic.
2. – Others may or may not think the beliefs are unrealistic, or uncertain about others' views concerning these beliefs.
3. – Fairly certain that most people think these beliefs are realistic.
4. – Completely certain that most people think these beliefs are realistic.

3. Explanation of differing views

You said that (*fill in response to item 1*) but that (*fill in response to item 2*). [PAUSE] How do you explain the difference between what you think and what others think about the accuracy of your beliefs? (Who's more likely to be right?)

(Interviewer should not ask this question if responses on item 1 and 2 are the same. <u>In that case, give the same score as in items 1 and 2.</u>)

0. – Completely certain that beliefs are unrealistic or absurd (e.g., "my mind is playing tricks on me").
1. – Fairly certain that beliefs are unrealistic.
2. – Uncertain about why others don't agree-- beliefs may be unrealistic <u>or</u> others may be wrong.
3. – Fairly certain that beliefs are true; view of others is less accurate.
4. – Completely certain that beliefs are true; beliefs of others is not accurate.

4. Fixity of ideas

If I were to question (or challenge) the accuracy of your beliefs, what would your reaction be? [PAUSE] Could I convince you that you're wrong?

(If necessary, supply a nonconfrontational example.)

(Rate on the basis of whether the patient could be convinced, not whether she wishes she could be convinced.)

0. – Eager to consider the possibility that the beliefs may be false; demonstrates no reluctance to entertain this possibility.
1. – Easily willing to consider the possibility that beliefs may be false; reluctance to do so is minimal.
2. – Somewhat willing to consider the possibility that beliefs may be false; but moderate resistance is present.
3. – Clearly reluctant to consider the possibility that beliefs may be false; reluctance is significant.
4. – Absolutely refuses to consider the possibility that beliefs may be false-- i.e., beliefs are fixed.

5. Attempts to disprove ideas

How actively do you try to disprove or reject your beliefs? How much effort do you make to convince yourself that your beliefs are false?

(Interviewer should rate attempts patient makes to talk him or herself out of the belief, not attempts to push the thoughts/ideas out of his/her mind or think about something else.)

0. – Always involved in trying to disprove beliefs, or not necessary to disprove because beliefs are not true.
1. – Usually tries to disprove beliefs.
2. – Sometimes tries to disprove beliefs.
3. – Occasionally attempts to disprove beliefs.
4. – Makes no attempt to disprove beliefs.

6. Insight

What do you think has caused you to have these beliefs? [PAUSE] Do they have a psychiatric or psychological cause or are they actually true?

(Interviewer should determine what the patient actually believes, not what she has been told or hopes is true. Psychological etiology should be considered equivalent to psychiatric illness.)

(recognition that the thoughts are excessive – i.e., taking up too much time—or causing problems for the patient should not be considered equivalent to psychiatric/psychological etiology. Instead, rate patient's awareness that the source/cause of the beliefs is psychiatric/psychological.)

0. – Beliefs definitely have a psychiatric/psychological cause.
1. – Beliefs probably have a psychiatric/psychological cause.
2. – Beliefs possibly have a psychiatric/psychological cause.
3. – Beliefs probably do not have a psychiatric/psychological cause.
4. – Beliefs definitely do not have a psychiatric/psychological cause.

TOTAL BABS SCORE _____ = SUM OF QUESTIONS 1 THROUGH 6

ADDITIONAL ITEM *(do not include in total score)*
7. Ideas/delusions of reference

Does it ever seem that people are talking about you or taking special notice of you because of *(fill in belief)*.
OPTIONAL: What about receiving special messages from your environment because of *(fill in belief)*.
(How certain are you of this?)

(This question pertains only to the beliefs being assessed by the BABS interviewer- not if the patient thinks s/he is noticed for a reason unrelated to the beliefs being assessed. Interviewer should NOT base answer on observable actions or compulsions; instead, rate core belief.)

0. – No, others definitely do not take special notice of me.
1. – Others probably do not take special notice of me.
2. – Others may or may not take special notice of me.
3. – Others probably do take special notice of me.
4. – Others definitely do take special notice of me.

Appendix E:
The Obsessive–Compulsive Inventory–Revised Version (OCI-R)

Note. Reprinted with permission from Edna B. Foa, PhD.

OCI-R

The following statements refer to experiences that many people have in their everyday lives. Circle the number that best describes **HOW MUCH** that experience has **DISTRESSED or BOTHERED you during the PAST MONTH**. The numbers refer to the following verbal labels:

0	1	2	3	4
Not at all	A little	Moderately	A lot	Extremely

1. I have saved up so many things that they get in the way.   0   1   2   3   4

2. I check things more often than necessary.   0   1   2   3   4

3. I get upset if objects are not arranged properly.   0   1   2   3   4

4. I feel compelled to count while I am doing things.   0   1   2   3   4

5. I find it difficult to touch an object when I know it has been touched by strangers or certain people.   0   1   2   3   4

6. I find it difficult to control my own thoughts.   0   1   2   3   4

7. I collect things I don't need.   0   1   2   3   4

8. I repeatedly check doors, windows, drawers, etc.   0   1   2   3   4

9. I get upset if others change the way I have arranged things.   0   1   2   3   4

10. I feel I have to repeat certain numbers.   0   1   2   3   4

11. I sometimes have to wash or clean myself simply because I feel contaminated.   0   1   2   3   4

12. I am upset by unpleasant thoughts that come into my mind against my will.   0   1   2   3   4

13. I avoid throwing things away because I am afraid I might need them later.   0   1   2   3   4

14. I repeatedly check gas and water taps and light switches after turning them off.   0   1   2   3   4

15. I need things to be arranged in a particular order.   0   1   2   3   4

16. I feel that there are good and bad numbers.   0   1   2   3   4

17. I wash my hands more often and longer than necessary.   0   1   2   3   4

18. I frequently get nasty thoughts and have difficulty in getting rid of them.   0   1   2   3   4

Scoring key: Checking: 2, 8, 14; Hoarding: 1, 7, 13; Neutralizing: 4, 10, 16; Obsessing: 6, 12, 18; Ordering: 3, 9, 15; Washing: 5, 11, 17

Appendix F:
The Obsessive Beliefs
Questionnaire and Interpretation
of Intrusions Inventory

Obsessional Beliefs Questionnaire (OBQ-44)

This scale lists different attitudes or beliefs that people sometimes hold. Read each statement carefully and decide how much you agree or disagree with it. For each statement, choose the number matching the answer that *best describes how you think.* There are no right or wrong answers. Simply keep in mind what you are like *most of the time.*

Use the following scale:

1	2	3	4	5	6	7
Disagree very much	Disagree moderately	Disagree a little	Neither agree nor disagree	Agree a little	Agree moderately	Agree very much

In making your ratings, try to avoid using the middle point of the scale (4), but rather indicate whether you usually disagree or agree with the statements about your own beliefs and attitudes.

1. I often think things around me are unsafe.   1 2 3 4 5 6 7

2. If I'm not absolutely sure of something, I'm bound to make a mistake.   1 2 3 4 5 6 7

3. Things should be perfect according to my own standards.   1 2 3 4 5 6 7

4. In order to be a worthwhile person, I must be perfect at everything I do.   1 2 3 4 5 6 7

5. When I see any opportunity to do so, I must act to prevent bad things from happening.   1 2 3 4 5 6 7

6. Even if harm is very unlikely, I should try to prevent it at any cost.   1 2 3 4 5 6 7

7. For me, having bad urges is as bad as actually carrying them out.   1 2 3 4 5 6 7

8. If I don't act when I foresee danger, then I am to blame for any consequences.   1 2 3 4 5 6 7

9. If I can't do something perfectly, I shouldn't do it at all.   1 2 3 4 5 6 7

10. I must work to my full potential at all times.   1 2 3 4 5 6 7

11. It is essential for me to consider all possible outcomes of a situation.   1 2 3 4 5 6 7

12. Even minor mistakes mean a job is not complete.   1 2 3 4 5 6 7

13. If I have aggressive thoughts or impulses about my loved ones, this means I may secretly want to hurt them.   1 2 3 4 5 6 7

14. I must be certain of my decisions.   1 2 3 4 5 6 7

15. In all kinds of daily situations, failing to prevent harm is just as bad as deliberately causing harm.   1 2 3 4 5 6 7

16. Avoiding serious problems (for example, illness or accidents) requires constant effort on my part.   1 2 3 4 5 6 7

17. For me, not preventing harm is as bad as causing harm.   1 2 3 4 5 6 7

18. I should be upset if I make a mistake.   1 2 3 4 5 6 7

19. I should make sure others are protected from any negative consequences of my decisions or actions.   1 2 3 4 5 6 7

20. For me, things are not right if they are not perfect.　1 2 3 4 5 6 7

21. Having nasty thoughts means I am a terrible person.　1 2 3 4 5 6 7

22. If I do not take extra precautions, I am more likely than others to have or cause a serious disaster.　1 2 3 4 5 6 7

23. In order to feel safe, I have to be as prepared as possible for anything that could go wrong.　1 2 3 4 5 6 7

24. I should not have bizarre or disgusting thoughts.　1 2 3 4 5 6 7

25. For me, making a mistake is as bad as failing completely.　1 2 3 4 5 6 7

26. It is essential for everything to be clear cut, even in minor matters.　1 2 3 4 5 6 7

27. Having a blasphemous thought is as sinful as committing a sacrilegious act.　1 2 3 4 5 6 7

28. I should be able to rid my mind of unwanted thoughts.　1 2 3 4 5 6 7

29. I am more likely than other people to accidentally cause harm to myself or to others.　1 2 3 4 5 6 7

30. Having bad thoughts means I am weird or abnormal.　1 2 3 4 5 6 7

31. I must be the best at things that are important to me.　1 2 3 4 5 6 7

32. Having an unwanted sexual thought or image means I really want to do it.　1 2 3 4 5 6 7

33. If my actions could have even a small effect on a potential misfortune, I am responsible for the outcome.　1 2 3 4 5 6 7

34. Even when I am careful, I often think that bad things will happen.　1 2 3 4 5 6 7

35. Having intrusive thoughts means I'm out of control.　1 2 3 4 5 6 7

36. Harmful events will happen unless I am very careful.　1 2 3 4 5 6 7

37. I must keep working at something until it's done exactly right.　1 2 3 4 5 6 7

38. Having violent thoughts means I will lose control and become violent.　1 2 3 4 5 6 7

39. To me, failing to prevent a disaster is as bad as causing it.　1 2 3 4 5 6 7

40. If I don't do a job perfectly, people won't respect me.　1 2 3 4 5 6 7

41. Even ordinary experiences in my life are full of risk.　1 2 3 4 5 6 7

42. Having a bad thought is morally no different than doing a bad deed.　1 2 3 4 5 6 7

43. No matter what I do, it won't be good enough.　1 2 3 4 5 6 7

44. If I don't control my thoughts, I'll be punished.　1 2 3 4 5 6 7

Responsibility/Threat estimation: items 1, 5, 6, 8, 15, 16, 17, 19, 22, 23, 29, 33, 34, 36, 39, 41; Perfectionism/Certainty: items 2, 3, 4, 9, 10, 11, 12, 14, 18, 20, 25, 26, 31, 37, 40, 43; Importance/Control of Thoughts: items 7, 13, 21, 24, 27, 28, 30, 32, 35, 38, 42, 44.

Interpretations of Intrusions Inventory (III-31)

We are interested in your experiences with unpleasant and unwanted thoughts or images or impulses that pop into your mind unexpectedly. Nearly everyone has such experiences, but people vary in how frequently these occur and how distressing they are. Some examples of the many possible negative intrusions are given below:

- an impulse to do something shameful or terrible
- the idea or image of harming someone you don't want to hurt
- the idea that something terrible will occur because you were not careful enough
- an unwanted sexual urge or image
- the thought that you or someone else will become dirty or contaminated by a substance that may cause harm
- the thought that you left an appliance on that might cause a fire
- an image of a loved one having an accident
- the thought that objects are not arranged perfectly
- a thought or image that is contrary to your religious or moral beliefs
- an impulse to say something rude or embarassing
- the thought of running the car off the road or into oncoming traffic
- the thought that you didn't lock the door and someone may break in

Please note that we are NOT talking about daydreams or pleasant fantasies. Nor are we interested in general worries about health or finances or other family matters. Also, we are NOT talking about the sort of thoughts that accompany depression or low self-confidence. Rather, we ARE interested in thoughts, mental images or impulses that pop into your mind and that you experience as intrusive and inappropriate.

In the spaces below please write down two unwanted mental intrusions that you have experienced:

(1) _____

(2) _____

Using the rating scales provided below, please answer the following questions ABOUT THE INTRUSIVE THOUGHTS YOU LISTED ABOVE or other similar intrusions. Please circle the appropriate number for the following questions:

A. When did you last experience an intrusion of this kind?

Within the last year	Within last 6 months	Within last 4 weeks	Within last 2 weeks	Within last week	Within last 24 hours
1	2	3	4	5	6

B. In the last 6 months, how frequently did you experience an intrusion of this kind?

less than once a month	about once a month	about once a week	a few times per week	about once a day	several times per day
1	2	3	4	5	6

C. On average, how much distress do you usually experience when you have an intrusion of this kind?

none	minimal	a little	moderate	great	extreme
0	1	2	3	4	5

When you were bothered by intrusive thoughts like the ones you described on the previous page, rate how much you believed each of the ideas listed below. Circle the number that best represents your belief when an intrusion is occurring.

Use the following scale:

	0	10	20	30	40	50	60	70	80	90	100	
I did not believe this idea at all					I was moderately convinced this idea was true				I was completely convinced this idea was true			

1. I must regain control of this thought. 0 10 20 30 40 50 60 70 80 90 100

2. Having this unwanted thought means I will act on it. 0 10 20 30 40 50 60 70 80 90 100

3. Because I've thought of bad things that might happen, I must act to prevent them. 0 10 20 30 40 50 60 70 80 90 100

4. Because I have this thought, it must be important. 0 10 20 30 40 50 60 70 80 90 100

5. I should be able to rid my mind of this thought. 0 10 20 30 40 50 60 70 80 90 100

6. Thinking this thought could make it happen. 0 10 20 30 40 50 60 70 80 90 100

7. This intrusive thought could be an omen. 0 10 20 30 40 50 60 70 80 90 100

8. Because I've had this intrusive thought, what I'm doing will be ruined. 0 10 20 30 40 50 60 70 80 90 100

9. If I don't do something about this intrusive thought, it will be my fault if something terrible happens. 0 10 20 30 40 50 60 70 80 90 100

10. I am irresponsible if I don't resist this unwanted thought. 0 10 20 30 40 50 60 70 80 90 100

11. Because this thought comes from my mind, I must want to have it. 0 10 20 30 40 50 60 70 80 90 100

12. It's wrong to ignore this unwanted thought. 0 10 20 30 40 50 60 70 80 90 100

13. Because I can't control this thought, I am a weak person. 0 10 20 30 40 50 60 70 80 90 100

14. I cannot take the risk that this thought will come true. 0 10 20 30 40 50 60 70 80 90 100

15. Now that I've thought of something bad that could go wrong, I have a responsibility to make sure it doesn't happen. 0 10 20 30 40 50 60 70 80 90 100

16. Because I've had this thought, I must want it to happen. 0 10 20 30 40 50 60 70 80 90 100

17. Having this intrusive thought means that I could lose control of my mind. 0 10 20 30 40 50 60 70 80 90 100

18. I would be a better person if I gained more control over this thought. 0 10 20 30 40 50 60 70 80 90 100

354

19. I need to be certain something awful won't happen as a result of this thought.	0	10	20	30	40	50	60	70	80	90	100
20. This thought could harm people.	0	10	20	30	40	50	60	70	80	90	100
21. Having this intrusive thought means I'm out of control.	0	10	20	30	40	50	60	70	80	90	100
22. Having this thought means I am weird or abnormal.	0	10	20	30	40	50	60	70	80	90	100
23. I would be irresponsible if I ignored this intrusive thought.	0	10	20	30	40	50	60	70	80	90	100
24. Having this intrusive thought means I am a terrible person.	0	10	20	30	40	50	60	70	80	90	100
25. If I don't control this unwanted thought, something bad is bound to happen.	0	10	20	30	40	50	60	70	80	90	100
26. I must have control over this thought.	0	10	20	30	40	50	60	70	80	90	100
27. The more I think about these things, the greater the risk they will come true.	0	10	20	30	40	50	60	70	80	90	100
28. I'll feel guilty unless I do something about this thought.	0	10	20	30	40	50	60	70	80	90	100
29. I should not be thinking this kind of thing.	0	10	20	30	40	50	60	70	80	90	100
30. If I don't control this thought, I'll be punished.	0	10	20	30	40	50	60	70	80	90	100
31. If I ignore this thought, I could be responsible for serious harm.	0	10	20	30	40	50	60	70	80	90	100

Scoring key:

Control of thoughts: items 1, 5, 8, 13, 17, 18, 21, 25, 26, 29, 30
Importance of thoughts: items 2, 4, 6, 7, 11, 16, 20, 22, 24, 27
Responsibility: items 3, 9, 10, 12, 14, 15, 19, 23, 28, 31

Appendix G:
Interview on Neutralization

Probe questions:

When you have this thought …

- Do you reassure yourself by talking to yourself? What did you say? What else might you say?
- Do you seek reassurance by talking to someone? Who do you talk to? Do you talk to anyone else?
- Do you perform some type of mental or observable action to remove the thought?
- Do you try to think it through?
- Do you replace the thought with another?
- Do you distract yourself with the things around you?
- Do you throw yourself into an activity?
- Do you say "stop" or something else?
- Do you sometimes do nothing with the thought?
- Do you do anything else that hasn't been covered? What do you do?

Follow-up questions for each strategy identified:

- Do you use this strategy in a particular situation or context?
- How intense is the thought just before you use this strategy? (0–4)
- How probable does the thought seem just before you use this strategy? (0–4)
- Do you generally use this strategy in a particular sequence, for example when one strategy hasn't worked, or before trying another?
- What are the emotions you feel just before you use this strategy?
- How intense is the emotion at this point? (0–4)
- How effective is the strategy in removing the thought immediately after you use it? (0–4)

Rating scale:

0	1	2	3	4
Not at all	A little	Moderately	Veru	Extremely

References

Abbruzzese, M., Bellodi, L., Ferri, S., & Scarone, S. (1993). Memory functioning in obsessive-compulsive disorder. *Behavioural Neurology, 6,* 119–122.

Abramowitz, J. S. (1996). Variants of exposure and response prevention in the treatment of obsessive-compulsive disorder: A meta-analysis. *Behavior Therapy, 27,* 583–600.

Abramowitz, J. S. (1997). Effectiveness of psychological and pharmacological treatments for obsessive-compulsive disorder: A quantitative review. *Journal of Consulting and Clinical Psychology, 65,* 44–52.

Abramowitz, J. S. (2001). Treatment of scrupulous obsessions and compulsions using exposure and response prevention: A case report. *Cognitive and Behavioral Practice, 8,* 79–85.

Abramowitz, J. S., Brigidi, B. D., & Foa, E. B. (1999). Health concerns in patients with obsessive-compulsive disorder. *Journal of Anxiety Disorders, 13,* 529–539.

Abramowitz, J. S., Deacon, B. J., Woods, C. M., & Tolin, D. F. (2004). Association between protestant religiosity and obsessive-compulsive symptoms and cognitions. *Depression and Anxiety, 20,* 70–76.

Abramowitz, J. S., & Foa, E. B. (1998). Worries and obsessions in individuals with obsessive-compulsive disorder with and without comorbid generalized anxiety disorder. *Behaviour Research and Therapy, 36,* 695–700.

Abramowitz, J. S., & Foa, E. (2000). Does comorbid major depressive disorder influence outcome of exposure and response prevention for OCD? *Behavior Therapy, 31,* 795–800.

Abramowitz, J. S., Foa, E. B., & Franklin, M. E. (2003). Exposure and ritual prevention for obsessive-compulsive disorder: Effects of intensive versus twice-weekly sessions. *Journal of Consulting and Clinical Psychology, 71,* 394–398.

Abramowitz, J. S., Franklin, M. E., & Cahill, S. P. (2003). Approaches to common obstacles in the exposure-based treatment of obsessive-compulsive disorder. *Cognitive and Behavioral Practice, 10,* 14–22.

Abramowitz, J. S., Franklin, M. E., & Foa, E. B. (2002). Empirical status of cognitive-behavioral therapy for obsessive-compulsive disorder: A meta-analytic review. *Romanian Journal of Cognitive and Behavioral Psychotherapies, 2,* 89–104.

Abramowitz, J. S., Franklin, M. E., Schwartz, S. A., & Furr, J. M. (2003). Symptom presentation and outcome of cognitive-behavioral therapy for obsessive-compulsive disorder. *Journal of Consulting and Clinical Psychology, 71,* 1049–1057.

Abramowitz, J. S., Franklin, M. E., Street, G. P., Kozak, M. J., & Foa, E. B. (2000). Effects of comorbid depression on response to treatment for obsessive-compulsive disorder. *Behavior Therapy, 31,* 517–528.

Abramowitz, J. S., Franklin, M., Zoellner, L., & DiBernardo, C. (2002). Treatment compliance and outcome in obsessive-compulsive disorder. *Behavior Modification, 26,* 447–463.

Abramowitz, J. S., Huppert, J. D., Cohen, A. B., Tolin, D. F., & Cahill, S. P. (2002). Religious obsessions and compulsions in a non-clinical sample: The Penn Inventory of Scrupulosity (PIOS). *Behaviour Research and Therapy, 40,* 825–838.

Abramowitz, J. S., Moore, K., Carmin, C., Wiegartz, P. S., & Purdon, C. (2001). Acute onset of obsessive-compulsive disorder in males following childbirth. *Psychosomatics, 42,* 429–431.

Abramowitz, J. S., Schwartz, S. A., & Moore, K. M. (2003). Obsessional thoughts in postpartum females and their partners: Content, severity, and relationship with depression. *Journal of Clinical Psychology in Medical Settings, 10,* 157–164.

Abramowitz, J. S., Schwartz, S. A., Moore, K. M., & Luenzmann, K. R. (2003). Obsessive-compulsive symptoms in pregnancy and the puerperium: A review of the literature. *Journal of Anxiety Disorders, 17,* 461–478.

Abramowitz, J. S., Schwartz, S. A., & Whiteside, S. P. (2002). A contemporary conceptual model of hypochondriasis. *Mayo Clinic Proceedings, 77,* 1323–1330.

Abramowitz, J. S., Tolin, D. F., & Diefenbach, G. (in press). Measuring change in OCD: Sensitivity of the Obsessive-Compulsive Inventory–Revised. *Journal of Psychopathology and Behavioral Assessment.*

Abramowitz, J. S., Tolin, D. F., & Street, G. P. (2001). Paradoxical effects of thought suppression: A meta-analysis of controlled studies. *Clinical Psychology Review, 21,* 683–703.

Abramowitz, J. S., Whiteside, S., Kalsy, S. A., & Tolin, D. F. (2003). Thought control strategies in obsessive-compulsive disorder: A replication and extension. *Behaviour Research and Therapy, 41,* 529–540.

Abramowitz, J. S., Whiteside, S. P., Lynam, D., & Kalsy, S. (2003). Is thought-action fusion specific to obsessive-compulsive disorder?: A mediating role of negative affect. *Behavior Research and Therapy, 41,* 1063–1079.

Abramowitz, J. S., & Zoellner, L. A. (2002). Cognitive-behavior therapy as an adjunct to medication for obsessive-compulsive disorder with mental rituals: A pilot study. *Romanian Journal of Cognitive and Behavioral Psychotherapies, 2,* 11–22.

Adams, P. L. (1973). *Obsessive children.* New York: Brunner/Mazel.

Akhtar, S., Wig, N. N., Varma, V. K., Pershad, D., & Verma, S. K. (1975). A phenomenological analysis of symptoms in obsessive-compulsive neurosis. *British Journal of Psychiatry, 127,* 342–348.

Alarcon, R. D., Libb, J. W., & Boll, T. J. (1994). Neuropsychological testing in obsessive-compulsive disorder: A clinical review. *Journal of Neuropsychiatry & Clinical Neurosciences, 6,* 217–228.

Alonso, P., Menchon, J. M., Mataix-Cols, D., Pifarre, J., Urretavizcaya, M., Crespo, M., et al. (2004). Perceived parental rearing style in obsessive-compulsive disorder: Relation to symptom dimensions. *Psychiatry Research, 127,* 267–278.

American Psychiatric Association (2000). *Diagnostic and statistical manual of mental disorders* (4th ed., Text revision). Washington, DC: Author.

Antony, M. M., Downie, F., & Swinson, R. P. (1998). Diagnostic issues and epidemiology in obsessive-compulsive disorder. In R. P. Swinson, M. Antony, S. Rachman, & M. Richter (Eds.), *Obsessive-compulsive disorder: Theory, research, and treatment* (pp. 3–32). New York: Guilford.

Arntz, A., Rauner, M., & van den Hout, M. (1995). "If I feel anxious, there must be danger": Ex-consequentia reasoning in inferring danger in anxiety disorders. *Behaviour Research and Therapy, 33,* 917–925.

Baer, L. (1994). Factor analysis of symptom subtypes of obsessive compulsive disorder and their relation to personality and tic disorders. *Journal of Clinical Psychiatry, 55,* 18–23.

Barlow, D. H. (2002). *Anxiety and its disorders.* New York: Guilford.

Baxter, L. R., Phelps, M. E., Mazziotta, J. C., Guze, B. H., Schwartz, J. M., & Selin, C. E. (1987). Local cerebral glucose metabolic rates in obsessive-compulsive disorder: A comparison with rates in unipolar depression and in normal controls. *Archives of General Psychiatry, 44,* 211–218.

Baxter, L. R., Schwartz, J. M., Bergman, K. S., Szuba, M. P., Guze, B. H., Mazziotta, J. C., et al. (1992). Caudate glucose metabolic rate changes with both drug and behavior therapy for obsessive-compulsive disorder. *Archives of General Psychiatry, 49,* 681–689.

Baxter, L. R., Jr., Schwartz, J. M., Mazziotta, J. C., Phelps, M. E., Pahl, J. J., Guze, B. H., et al. (1988). Cerebral glucose metabolic rates in nondepressed patients with obsessive-compulsive disorder. *American Journal of Psychiatry, 145,* 1560–1563.

Beck, A. T. (1976). *Cognitive therapy of the emotional disorders.* New York: International Universities Press.

Beck, A. T., & Emery, G. (1985). *Anxiety disorders and phobias: A cognitive perspective.* New York: Basic Books.

Beck, A. T., Epstein, N., Brown, G., & Steer, R. A. (1988). An inventory for measuring clinical anxiety: Psychometric properties. *Journal of Consulting and Clinical Psychology, 56,* 893–897.

Beck, A. T., Ward, C. H., Mendelsohn, M., Mock, J., & Erlbaugh, J. (1961). An inventory for measuring depression. *Archives of General Psychiatry, 4,* 561–571.

Black, D. W., Gaffney, G., Schlosser, S., & Gabel, J. (1998). The impact of obsessive-compulsive disorder on the family: Preliminary findings. *Journal of Nervous and Mental Disease, 186,* 440–442.

Black, D. W., Noyes, R., Pfohl, B., Goldstein, R. B., & Blum, N. (1993). Personality disorder in obsessive-compulsive volunteers, well comparison subjects, and their first-degree relatives. *American Journal of Psychiatry, 150,* 1226–1232.

Bouton, M. E. (2002). Context, ambiguity, and unlearning: Sources of relapse after behavioral extinction. *Biological Psychiatry, 52,* 976–986.

Brown, D., Pryzwansky, W. B., & Schulte, A. C. (2001). *Psychological consultation: Introduction to theory and practice.* New York: Allyn & Bacon.

Brown, H. D., Kosslyn, S., Breiter, H., Baer, L., & Jenike, M. (1994). Can patients with obsessive-compulsive disorder discriminate between percepts and mental images? A signal detection analysis. *Journal of Abnormal Psychology, 103,* 445–454.

Burns, D. (1980). *Feeling good.* New York: Avon.

Bystritsky, A., Ackerman, D. L., Rosen, R. M., Vapnik, T., Gorbis, E., Maidment, K. M., et al. (2004). Augmentation of serotonin reuptake inhibitors in refractory obsessive-compulsive disorder using adjunctive olanzapine: A placebo-controlled trial. *Journal of Clinical Psychiatry, 65,* 565–568.

Calamari, J. E., & Cassiday, K. L. (1999). Treating obsessive-compulsive disorder in older adults: A review of strategies. In M. Duffy (Ed.), *Handbook of counseling and psychotherapy with older adults* (pp. 526–538). New York: Wiley.

Calamari, J. E., Weigartz, P., & Janeck, A. (1999). Obsessive-compulsive disorder subgroups: A symptom-based clustering approach. *Behaviour Research and Therapy, 37,* 113–125.

Calvocoressi, L., Lewis, B., Harris, M., Trufan, S., Goodman, W., McDougle, C., et al. (1995). Family accommodation in obsessive-compulsive disorder. *American Journal of Psychiatry, 152,* 441–443.

Chambless, D. L., & Steketee, G. (1999). Expressed emotion and behavior therapy outcome: A prospective study with obsessive-compulsive and agoraphobic outpatients. *Journal of Consulting and Clinical Psychology, 67,* 658–665.

Christensen, G., Ristvedt, S., & Mackenzie, T. (1993). Identification of trichotillomania cue profiles. *Behaviour Research and Therapy, 31,* 315–320.

Ciarrocchi, J. W. (1995). *The doubting disease: Help for scrupulosity and religious compulsions.* Mahwah, NJ: Paulist Press.

Clark, D. A. (2004). *Cognitive-behavioral therapy for OCD.* New York: Guilford.

Clark, D. M. (1986). A cognitive approach to panic. *Behaviour Research and Therapy, 24,* 461–470.

Clayton, I., Richards, J., & Edwards, C. (1999). Selective attention in obsessive-compulsive disorder. *Journal of Abnormal Psychology, 108,* 171–175.

Coles, M. E., Frost, R. O., Heimberg, R. G., & Rheaume, J. (2003). "Not just right experiences": Perfectionism, obsessive-compulsive features and general psychopathology. *Behaviour Research and Therapy, 41,* 681–700.

Coles, M. E., Frost, R. O., Heimberg, R. G., & Steketee, G. (2003). Hoarding behaviors in a large college sample. *Behaviour Research and Therapy, 41,* 179–194.

Constans, J., Foa, E., Franklin, M. E., & Matthews, A. (1995). Memory for actual and imagined events in OC checkers. *Behaviour Research and Therapy, 33,* 665–671.

Cottraux, J., Gerard, D., Cinotti, L., Froment, J., Deilber, M., Le Bars, D., et al. (1996). A controlled positron emission tomography study of obsessive and neutral auditory stimulation in obsessive-compulsive disorder with checking rituals. *Psychiatry Research, 60,* 101–112.

Cottraux, J., Mollard, E., Bouvard, M., Marks, I., Sluys, M., Nury, A. M., et al. (1990). A controlled study of fluvoxamine and exposure in obsessive-compulsive disorder. *International Journal of Clinical Psychopharmacology, 5,* 17–30.

Cottraux, J., Note, I., Yao, S. N., Lafont, S., Note, B., Mollard, E., et al. (2001). A randomized controlled trial of cognitive therapy versus intensive behavior therapy in obsessive compulsive disorder. *Psychotherapy and Psychosomatics, 70,* 288–297.

Craske, M. G. (2003). *Origins of phobias and anxiety disorders: Why more women than men?* Oxford, UK: Elsevier.

Craske, M. G., & Barlow, D. H. (2001). Panic disorder and agoraphobia. In D. H. Barlow (Ed.), *Clinical handbook of psychological disorders* (3rd ed., pp. 1–59). New York: Guilford.

Crespo-Facorro, B., Cabranes, J. A., Lopez-Ibor Alcocer, M. I., Paya, B., Fernandez Perez, C., Encinas, M., et al. (1999). Regional cerebral blood flow in obsessive-compulsive patients with and without a chronic tic disorder: A SPECT study. *European Archives of Psychiatry and Clinical Neuroscience, 249,* 156–161.

Crino, R. D., & Andrews, G. (1996a). Obsessive-compulsive disorder and Axis I comorbidity. *Journal of Anxiety Disorders, 10,* 37–46.

Crino, R. D., & Andrews, G. (1996b). Personality disorder in obsessive compulsive disorder: A controlled study. *Journal of Psychiatric Research, 30,* 29–38.

Deacon, B. J., & Abramowitz, J. S. (2005a). Patients' perceptions of pharmacological and cognitive-behavioral treatments for anxiety disorders. *Behavior Therapy.*

Deacon, B. J., & Abramowitz, J. S. (2005b). The Yale–Brown Obsessive Compulsive Scale: Factor analysis, construct validity, and suggestions for refinement. *Journal of Anxiety Disorders, 19,* 573–585.

Demal, U., Lenz, G., Mayrhofer, Z., Zapotoczky, H. G., & Zitterl, W. (1993). Obsessive-compulsive disorder and depression: A retrospective study on course and interaction. *Psychopathology, 26,* 145–150.

de Silva, P., & Marks, M. (1999). The role of traumatic experiences in the genesis of obsessive-compulsive disorder. *Behaviour Research and Therapy, 37,* 941–951.

de Silva, P., Menzies, R. G., & Shafran, R. (2003). Spontaneous decay of compulsive urges: The case of covert compulsions. *Behaviour Research and Therapy, 41,* 129–137.

DeVeaugh-Geiss, J., Landau, P., & Katz, R. (1989). Treatment of OCD with clomipramine. *Psychiatric Annals, 19,* 97–101.

DiNardo, P., Brown, T., & Barlow, D. H. (1994). *Anxiety Disorders Interview Schedule for DSM–IV: Lifetime version (ADIS–IV–LV).* San Antonio, TX: Psychological Corporation.

Dollard, J., & Miller, N. E. (1950). *Personality and psychotherapy: An analysis in terms of learning , thinking, and culture.* New York: McGraw-Hill.

Dupont, R. L., Rice, D. P., Shiraki, S., & Rowland, C. R. (1995). Economic costs of obsessive-compulsive disorder. *Mental Interface, 8,* 102–109.

Ebert, D., Speck, O., Konig, A., Berger, M., Hennig, J., & Hohagen, F. (1997). 1H-magnetic resonance spectroscopy in obsessive-compulsive disorder: Evidence for neuronal loss in the cingulate gyrus and the right striatum. *Psychiatry Research, 74*, 173–176.

Ecker, W., & Engelkamp, J. (1995). Memory for actions in obsessive-compulsive disorder. *Behavioural and Cognitive Psychotherapy, 23*, 349–371.

Eisen, J. L., Phillips, K. A., Baer, L., Beer, D. A., Atala, K. D., & Rasmussen, S. A. (1998). The Brown Assessment of Beliefs Scale: Reliability and validity. *American Journal of Psychiatry, 155*, 102–108.

Eisen, J. L., Phillips, K. A., Coles, M. E., & Rasmussen, S. A. (2004). Insight in obsessive compulsive disorder and body dysmorphic disorder. *Comprehensive Psychiatry, 45*, 10–15.

Ellis, A. (1962). *Reason and emotion in psychotherapy*. Secaucus, NJ: Lyle Stuart.

Emmelkamp, P. M. G., & Beens, H. (1991). Cognitive therapy with obsessive-compulsive disorder: A comparative evaluation. *Behaviour Research and Therapy, 29*, 293–300.

Emmelkamp, P. M. G., de Haan, E., & Hoogduin, C. A. L. (1990). Marital adjustment and obsessive-compulsive disorder. *British Journal of Psychiatry, 156*, 55–60.

Emmelkamp, P. M. G., Visser, S., & Hoekstra, R. J. (1988). Cognitive therapy vs. exposure in vivo in the treatment of obsessive-compulsives. *Cognitive Therapy and Research, 12*, 103–114.

Emmelkamp, P. M. G., & Kraanen, J. (1977). Therapist-controlled exposure *in vivo* versus self-controlled exposure *in vivo*: A comparison with obsessive-compulsive patients. *Behaviour Research and Therapy, 15*, 491–195.

Enright, S. (1996). Obsessive-compulsive disorder: Anxiety disorder or schizotype? In R. Rapee (Ed.), *Current controversies in the anxiety disorders* (pp. 161–190). New York: Guilford.

Eysenck, H. J. (1985). Behaviorism and clinical psychiatry. *International Journal of Social Psychiatry, 31*, 163–169.

Fallon, B. A., Javitch, J. A., Hollander, E., & Liebowitz, M. R. (1991). Hypochondriasis and obsessive-compulsive disorder: Overlaps in diagnosis and treatment. *Journal of Clinical Psychiatry, 52*, 457–460.

Fals-Stewart, W., Marks, A. P., & Schafer, J. (1993). A comparison of behavioral group therapy and individual behavior therapy in treating obsessive-compulsive disorder. *The Journal of Nervous and Mental Disease, 181*, 189–193.

First, M. B., Spitzer, R. L., Gibbon, M., & Williams, J. (2002). *Structured Clinical Interview for the DSM–IV Axis 1 disorders*. New York: New York State Psychiatric Institute Biometrics Research Department.

Fitzgerald, K. D., Moore, J., G., Paulson, L. A., Stewart, C. M., & Rosenberg, D. R. (2000). Proton spectroscopic imaging of the thalamus in treatment-naive pediatric obsessive-compulsive disorder. *Biological Psychiatry, 47*, 174–182.

Foa, E. B. (1979). Failure in treating obsessive-compulsives. *Behaviour Research and Therapy, 17*, 169–176.

Foa, E. B., Abramowitz, J. S., Franklin, M. E., & Kozak, M. J. (1999). Feared consequences, fixity of belief, and treatment outcome in patients with obsessive-compulsive disorder. *Behavior Therapy, 30*, 717–724.

Foa, E. B., Amir, N., Gershuny, B., Molnar, C., & Kozak, M. (1997). Implicit and explicit memory in obsessive-compulsive disorder. *Journal of Anxiety Disorders, 11*, 119–129.

Foa, E. B., & Goldstein, A. (1978). Continuous exposure and complete response prevention in the treatment of obsessive-compulsive neurosis. *Behavior Therapy, 9*, 821–829.

Foa, E. B., Grayson, J. B., Steketee, G. S., Doppelt, H. G., Turner, R. M., & Latimer, P. R. (1983). Success and failure in the behavioral treatment of obsessive-compulsives. *Journal of Consulting and Clinical Psychology, 51*, 287–297.

Foa, E. B., Huppert, J. D., Leiberg, S., Langner, R., Kichic, R., Hajcak, G., et al. (2002). The Obsessive-Compulsive Inventory: Development and validation of a short version. *Psychological Assessment, 14*, 485–496.

Foa, E. B., & Kozak, M. J. (1986). Emotional processing of fear: Exposure to corrective information. *Psychological Bulletin, 99*, 20–35.

Foa, E. B., & Kozak, M. J. (1995). DSM–IV field trial: Obsessive-compulsive disorder. *American Journal of Psychiatry, 152*, 90–96.

Foa, E. B., & Kozak, M. J. (1996). Psychological treatment for obsessive-compulsive disorder. In M. R. Mavissakalian & R. F. Prien (Eds.), *Long-term treatments of anxiety disorders* (pp. 285–309). Washington, DC: American Psychiatric Press.

Foa, E. B., Kozak, M. J., Salkovskis, P. M., Coles, M. E., & Amir, N. (1998). The validation of a new obsessive-compulsive disorder Scale: The Obsessive-Compulsive Inventory. *Psychological Assessment, 10*, 206–214.

Foa, E. B., Liebowitz, M. R., Kozak, M. J., Davies, S., Campeas, R., Franklin, M. E., et al. (2005). Treatment of obsessive-compulsive disorder by exposure and ritual prevention, clomipramine, and their combination: A randomized, placebo controlled trial. *American Journal of Psychiatry, 162*, 151–161.

Foa, E. B., Mathews, A., Abramowitz, J. S., Amir, N., Przeworski, A., Riggs, D. S., et al. (2003). Do patients with obsessive-compulsive disorder have deficits in decision-making? *Cognitive Therapy and Research, 27*, 431–445.

Foa, E. B., Steketee, G, Grayson, J., Turner, R., & Lattimer, P. (1984). Deliberate exposure and blocking of obsessive-compulsive rituals: Immediate and long-term effects. *Behavior Therapy, 15*, 450–472.

Foa, E. B., Steketee, G., & Milby, J. (1980). Differential effects of exposure and response prevention in obsessive-compulsive washers. *Journal of Consulting and Clinical Psychology, 48*, 71–79.

Foa, E. B., Steketee, G., & Ozarow, B. (1985). Behavior therapy for obsessive-compulsives: From theory to treatment. In M. R. Mavissakalian, S. M. Turner, & L. Michelson (Eds.), *Obsessive-compulsive disorder: Psychological and pharmacological treatment* (pp. 49–129). New York: Plenum.

Foa, E. B., Steketee, G., Turner, R. M., & Fischer, S. C. (1980). Effects of imaginal exposure to feared disasters in obsessive-compulsive checkers. *Behaviour Research and Therapy, 18*, 449–455.

Franklin, M. E., Abramowitz, J. S., Bux, D. A., Jr., Zoellner, L. A., & Feeny, N. C. (2002). Cognitive-behavioral therapy with and without medication in the treatment of obsessive-compulsive disorder. *Professional Psychology: Research and Practice, 33*, 162–168.

Franklin, M. E., Abramowitz, J. S., Kozak, M. J., Levitt, J. T., & Foa, E. B. (2000). Effectiveness of exposure and ritual prevention for obsessive-compulsive disorder: Randomized compared with nonrandomized samples. *Journal of Consulting and Clinical Psychology, 68*, 594–602.

Freeston, M. H., & Ladouceur, R. (1997). What do patients do with their obsessive thoughts? *Behaviour Research and Therapy, 35,* 335–348.

Freeston, M. H., & Ladouceur, R. (1999). Exposure and response prevention for obsessive thoughts. *Cognitive & Behavioral Practice, 6,* 362–383.

Freeston, M. H., Ladouceur, R., Gagnon, F., & Thibodeau, N. (1993). Beliefs about obsessional thoughts. *Journal of Psychopathology and Behavioral Assessment, 15,* 1–21.

Freeston, M. H., Ladouceur, R., Gagnon, F., Thibodeau, N., Rheaume, J., Letarte, H., et al. (1997). Cognitive-behavioral treatment of obsessive thoughts: A controlled study. *Journal of Consulting and Clinical Psychology, 65,* 405–413.

Freeston, M. H., Ladouceur, R., Provencher, M., & Blais, F. (1995). Strategies used with intrusive thoughts: Context, appraisal, mood, and efficacy. *Journal of Anxiety Disorders, 9,* 201–215.

Freeston, M. H., Ladouceur, R., Thibodeau, N., & Gagnon, F. (1991). Cognitive intrusions in a non-clinical population: I. Response style, subjective experience, and appraisal. *Behaviour Research and Therapy, 29,* 585–597.

Friedman, S., Smith, L. C., Halpern, B., Levine, C., Paradis, C., Viswanathan, R., et al. (2003). Obsessive-compulsive disorder in a multi-ethnic urban outpatient clinic: Initial presentation and treatment outcome with exposure and ritual prevention. *Behavior Therapy, 34,* 397–410.

Fritzler, B. K., Hecker, J. E., & Losee, M. C. (1997). Self-directed treatment with minimal therapist contact: Preliminary findings for obsessive-compulsive disorder. *Behaviour Research and Therapy, 35,* 627–631.

Frost, R. O., & Gross, R. C. (1993). The hoarding of possessions. *Behaviour Research and Therapy, 31,* 367–381.

Frost, R. O., & Hartl, T. L. (1996). A cognitive behavioral model of compulsive hoarding. *Behaviour Research and Therapy, 34,* 341–350.

Frost, R. O., Krause, M. S., & Steketee, G. (1996). Hoarding and obsessive-compulsive symptoms. *Behavior Modification, 20,* 116–132.

Frost, R. O., Lahart, C., Dugas, K., & Sher, K. (1988). Information processing among nonclinical compulsives. *Behaviour Research and Therapy, 26,* 275–277.

Frost, R. O., & Steketee, G. (1997). Perfectionism in obsessive-compulsive disorder patients. *Behaviour Research and Therapy, 35,* 291–296.

Frost, R. O., & Steketee, S. (2002). Cognitive approaches to obsessions and compulsions: Theory, assessment, and treatment. Oxford, UK: Elsevier.

Frost, R. O., Steketee, G., & Greene, K. A. I. (2003). Cognitive and behavioral treatment of compulsive hoarding. *Brief Treatment & Crisis Intervention, 3,* 323–337.

Goldsmith, T., Shapiro, N., phillips, K., & McElroy, S. (1998). Conceptual foundations of obsessive-compulsive spectrum disorders. In R. Swinson, M. Antony, S. Rachman, & M. Richter (Eds.), *Obsessive-compulsive disorder: Theory, research, and treatment* (pp. 397–425). New York: Guilford.

Goodman, W. K., Price, L. H., Rasmussen, S. A., Mazure, C., Delgado, P., Heninger, G. R., et al. (1989). The Yale–Brown Obsessive Compulsive Scale: Validity. *Archives of General Psychiatry, 46,* 1012–1016.

Goodman, W. K., Price, L. H., Rasmussen, S. A., Mazure, C., Fleischmann, R. L., Hill, C. L., et al. (1989). The Yale–Brown Obsessive Compulsive Scale: Development, use, and reliability. *Archives of General Psychiatry, 46,* 1006–1011.

Grayson, J. B., Foa, E. B., & Steketee, G. (1982). Habituation during exposure treatment: Distraction vs. attention-focusing. *Behaviour Research and Therapy, 20,* 323–328.

Grayson, J. B., Foa, E. B., & Steketee, G. S. (1986). Exposure *in vivo* of obsessive-compulsives under distracting and attention-focusing conditions: Replication and extension. *Behaviour Research and Therapy, 24,* 475–479.

Greenberg, D. (1984). Are religious compulsions religious or compulsive: A phenomenological study. *American Journal of Psychotherapy, 38,* 524–532.

Greenberg, D. (1987). Compulsive hoarding. *American Journal of Psychotherapy, 41,* 409–416.

Greist, J. H., Jefferson, J. W., Kobak, K. A., Katzelnick, D. J., & Serlin, R. C. (1995). Efficacy and tolerability of serotonin transport inhibitors in obsessive compulsive disorder: A meta-analysis. *Archives of General Psychiatry, 52,* 53–60.

Greist, J. H., Marks, I. M., Baer, L., Kobak, K. A., Wenzel, K. W., Hirsch, J., et al. (2002). Behavior therapy for obsessive-compulsive disorder guided by a computer or by a clinician compared with relaxation as a control. *Journal of Clinical Psychiatry, 63,* 138–145.

Grisham, J. R., Brown, T., Liverant, G. I., & Campbell-Sills, L. A. (in press). The distinctiveness of compulsive hoarding from obsessive-compulsive disorder. *Journal of Anxiety Disorders.*

Gross, R. C., Sasson, Y., Chorpa, M., & Zohar, J. (1998). Biological models of obsessive-compulsive disorder: The serotonin hypothesis. In R. P. Swinson, M. Antony, S. Rachman, & M. Richter (Eds.), *Obsessive-compulsive disorder: Theory, research, and treatment* (pp. 141–153). New York: Guilford.

Hafner, R. J. (1982). Marital interaction in persisting obsessive-compulsive disorders. *Australian and New Zealand Journal of Psychiatry, 16,* 171–178.

Hafner, R. J. (1988). Obsessive-compulsive disorder: A questionnaire study of a self-help group. *International Journal of Social Psychiatry, 34,* 310–315.

Haidt, J., McCauley, C., & Rozin, P. (1994). Individual differences in sensitivity to disgust: A scale sampling seven domains of disgust elicitors. *Personality & Individual Differences, 16,* 701–713.

Hamilton, M. (1960). A rating scale for depression. *Journal of Neurological and Neurosurgical Psychiatry, 18,* 315–319.

Hartl, T. L., & Frost, R. O. (1999). Cognitive-behavioral treatment of compulsive hoarding: A multiple baseline experimental case study. *Behaviour Research and Therapy, 37,* 451–461.

Hatch, M. L., Friedman, S., & Paradis, C. M. (1996). Behavioral treatment of obsessive-compulsive disorder in African Americans. *Cognitive and Behavioral Practice, 3,* 303–315.

Hedlund, J., & Vieweg, B. (1979). The Hamilton Rating Scale for Depression: A comprehensive review. *Journal of Operating Psychiatry, 10,* 149–165.

Hermans, D., Martens, K., De Cort, K., Pieters, G., & Eelen, P. (2003). Reality monitoring and metacognitive beliefs related to cognitive confidence in obsessive-compulsive disorder. *Behaviour Research and Therapy, 41,* 383–401.

Hiss, H., Foa, E. B., & Kozak, M. J. (1994). Relapse prevention program for treatment of obsessive-compulsive disorder. *Journal of Consulting and Clinical Psychology, 62,* 801–808.

Hodgson, R., & Rachman, S. (1972). The effects of contamination and washing in obsessional patients. *Behaviour Research and Therapy, 10,* 111–117.

Hodgson, R., Rachman, S., & Marks, I. (1972). The treatment of chronic obsessive-compulsive neurosis: Follow-up and further findings. *Behaviour Research and Therapy, 10,* 181–189.

Hoekstra, R. J., Visser, S., & Emmelkamp, P. M. G. (1989). A social learning formulation of the etiology of obsessive-compulsive disorders. In P. M. G. Emmelkamp (Ed.), *Fresh perspectives on anxiety disorders* (pp. 115–123). Amsterdam: Swets & Zeitlinger.

Hohagen, F., Winkelmann, G., Rasche-Rauchle, H., Hand, I., Konig, A., Munchau, N., et al. (1998). Combination of behaviour therapy with fluvoxamine in comparison with behaviour therapy and placebo. *British Journal of Psychiatry, 173,* 71–78.

Hollander, E., DeCaria, C. M., Nitescu, A., Gully, R., Suckow, R. F., Cooper, T. B., et al. (1992). Serotonergic function in obsessive-compulsive disorder. Behavioral and neuroendocrine responses to oral m-chlorophenylpiperazine and fenfluramine in patients and healthy volunteers. *Archives of General Psychiatry, 49,* 21–28.

Hollander, E., & Wong, C. (1995). Body dysmorphic disorder, pathological gambling, and sexual compulsions. *Journal of Clinical Psychiatry, 56,* 7–12.

Hollander, E., & Wong, C. M. (2000). Spectrum, boundary, and subtyping issues: Implications for treatment-refractory obsessive-compulsive disorder. In W. Goodman, M. V. Rudorfer, & J. Maser (Eds.), *Obsessive-compulsive disorder* (pp. 3–22). Mahwah, NJ: Lawrence Erlbaum Associates.

Hoover, C., & Insel, T. (1984). Families of origin in obsessive-compulsive disorder. *Journal of Nervous and Mental Disease, 172,* 207–215.

Horowitz, M. J. (1975). Intrusive and repetitive thoughts after experimental stress. *Archives of General Psychiatry, 32,* 1457–1463.

Insel, T. R., & Akiskal, H. (1986). Obsessive-compulsive disorder with psychotic features: A phenomenological analysis. *American Journal of Psychiatry, 143,* 1527–1533.

Insel, T. R., Mueller, E. A., Alterman, I., Linnoila, M., & Murphy, D. L. (1985). Obsessive-compulsive disorder and serotonin: Is there a connection? *Biological Psychiatry, 20,* 1174–1188.

Jaisoorya, T., Janardhan, R., & Srinath, S. (2003). The relationship between obsessive-compulsive disorder and putative spectrum disorders: Results from an Indian study. *Comprehensive Psychiatry, 44,* 317–323.

Janeck, A., Calamari, J., Riemann, B., & Heffelfinger, S. (2003). Too much thinking about thinking? Metacognitive differences in obsessive-compulsive disorder. *Journal of Anxiety Disorders, 17,* 181–195.

Janet, P. (1903). *Les obsessions et la psychasthenie* [Obsessions and psychasthenia] (Vol. 1, 2nd ed.). Paris: Alcan.

Jenike, M. (2000). Neurosurgical treatment of obsessive-compulsive disorder. In W. Goodman, J. Maser, & M. V. Rudorfer (Eds.), *Obsessive-compulsive disorder* (pp. 457–482). Mahwah, NJ: Lawrence Erlbaum Associates.

Johnson, M. K., & Raye, C. L. (1981). Reality monitoring. *Psychological Review, 88,* 67–85.

Jones, H., & Aldemann, U. (1959). *Moral theology.* Westminster, MD: Newman.

Jones, M. K., & Menzies, R. G. (1997a). The cognitive mediation of obsessive-compulsive handwashing. *Behaviour Research and Therapy, 35,* 843–850.

Jones, M. K., & Menzies, R. G. (1997b). Danger ideation reduction therapy (DIRT): Preliminary findings with three obsessive-compulsive washers. *Behaviour Research and Therapy, 35,* 995–960.

Jones, M. K., & Menzies, R. G. (1998). Danger ideation reduction therapy (DIRT) for obsessive-compulsive washers: A controlled trial. *Behaviour Research and Therapy, 36,* 959–970.

Kampman, M., Keijsers, G. P. J., Hoogduin, C. A. L., & Verbank, M. J. P. M. (2002). Addition of cognitive-behavior therapy for obsessive-compulsive disorder patients non-responding to fluoxetine. *Acta Psychiatrica Scandinavica, 106,* 314–319.

Karno, M., Golding, J., Sorenson, S., & Burnam, A. (1988). The epidemiology of obsessive-compulsive disorder in five US communities. *Archives of General Psychiatry, 45,* 1094–1099.

Khanna, S., & Channabasavanna, S. M. (1988). Phenomenology of obsessions in obsessive-compulsive neurosis. *Psychopathology, 21,* 12–18.

Kirk, J. W. (1983). Behavioural treatment of obsessional compulsive patients in routine clinical practice. *Behaviour Research and Therapy, 21,* 57–62.

Kolada, J. L., Bland, R. C., & Newman, S. C. (1994). Obsessive-compulsive disorder. *Acta Psychiatrica Scandinavica, 89*(376), 24–35.

Koran, L. M. (2000). Quality of life in obsessive-compulsive disorder. *Psychiatric Clinics of North America, 23,* 509–517.

Koran, L. M., Thienemann, M., & Davenport, R. (1996). Quality of life in patients with obsessive compulsive disorder. *American Journal of Psychiatry, 156,* 783–788.

Kovacs, M., & Beck, A. T. (1978). Maladaptive cognitive structures in depression. *American Journal of Psychiatry, 135,* 525–533.

Kozak, M. J., & Coles, M. E. (2005). Unleashing the power of exposure. In J. S. Abramowitz & A. C. Houts (Eds.), *Concepts and controversies in obsessive-compulsive disorder.* New York: Springer.

Kozak, M. J., & Foa, E. B. (1994). Obsessions, overvalued ideas, and delusions in obsessive-compulsive disorder. *Behaviour Research and Therapy, 32,* 343–353.

Kozak, M. J., & Foa, E. B. (1997). *Mastery of obsessive-compulsive disorder: Therapist manual.* San Antonio, TX: The Psychological Corporation.

Ladouceur, R., Freeston, M. H., Rheaume, J., Dugas, M. J., Gagnon, F., Thibodeau, N., et al. (2000). Strategies used with intrusive thoughts: A comparison of OCD patients with anxious and community controls. *Journal of Abnormal Psychology, 109,* 179–187.

Ladouceur, R., Rheaume, J., Freeston, M. H., Aublet, F., Jean, K., Lachance, S., et al. (1995). Experimental manipulations of responsibility: An analogue test for models of obsessive-compulsive disorder. *Behaviour Research and Therapy, 33,* 937–946.

Lax, T., Basoglu, M., & Marks, I. M. (1992). Expectancy and compliance as predictors of outcome in obsessive-compulsive disorder. *Behavioural Psychotherapy, 20,* 257–266.

Leckman, J. F., Grice, D. E., Barr, L. C., de Vries, A. L. C., Martin, C., Cohen, D. J., et al. (1995). Tic-related vs. non-tic-related obsessive compulsive disorder. *Anxiety, 1,* 208–215.

Leckman, J. F., Grice, D. E., Boardman, J., Zhang, H., Vitale, A., Bondi, C., et al. (1997). Symptoms of obsessive-compulsive disorder. *American Journal of Psychiatry, 154,* 911–917.

Leckman, J. F., Walker, D. E., Goodman, W. K., Pauls, D. L., & Cohen, D. J. (1994). Just right perceptions associated with compulsive behavior in Tourette's syndrome. *American Journal of Psychiatry, 151,* 675–680.

Lee, H. J., & Kwon, S. M. (2003). Two different types of obsession: Autogenous obsessions and reactive obsessions. *Behaviour Research and Therapy, 41,* 11–29.

Lindsay, M., Crino, R., & Andrews, G. (1997). Controlled trial of exposure and response prevention in obsessive-compulsive disorder. *British Journal of Psychiatry, 171,* 135–139.

Lopatka, C., & Rachman, S. (1995). Perceived responsibility and compulsive checking: An experimental analysis. *Behaviour Research and Therapy, 33,* 673–684.

MacDonald, P., Antony, M., MacLeod, C., & Richter, M. (1997). Memory and confidence in memory judgments among individuals with obsessive-compulsive disorder and non-clinical controls. *Behaviour Research and Therapy, 35,* 497–505.

Magliana, L., Tosini, P., Guarneri, M., Marasco, C., & Catapano, F. (1996). Burden on families of patients with obsessive-compulsive disorder: A pilot study. *European Psychiatry, 11,* 192–197.

Marks, I. M. (1992). *Fears, phobias and rituals.* Oxford, UK: Oxford University Press.

Marks, I. M., Hodgson, R., & Rachman, S. (1975). Treatment of chronic obsessive-compulsive neurosis by in vivo exposure: A two-year follow-up and issues in treatment. *British Journal of Psychiatry, 127,* 349–364.

Marks, I. M., Lelliott, P., Basoglu, M., Noshirvani, H., Monteiro, W., Cohen, D., et al. (1988). Clomipramine, self-exposure and therapist-aided exposure for obsessive-compulsive rituals. *British Journal of Psychiatry, 152,* 522–534.

Marks, I. M., Stern, R. S., Mawson, D., Cobb, J., & McDonald, R. (1980). Clomipramine, self-exposure, and therapist-aided exposure for obsessive-compulsive rituals. *British Journal of Psychiatry, 152,* 522–534.

Masellis, M., Rector, N. A., & Richter, M. A. (2003). Quality of life in OCD: Differential impact of obsessions, compulsions, and depression comorbidity. *Canadian Journal of Psychiatry, 48,* 72–77.

Mataix-Cols, D., Cullen, S., Lange, K., Zelaya, F., Andrew, C., Amaro, E., et al. (2003). Neural correlates of anxiety associated with obsessive-compulsive symptom dimensions in normal volunteers. *Biological Psychiatry, 53,* 482–493.

Mataix-Cols, D., Marks, I. M., Greist, J. H., Kobak, K. A., & Baer, L. (2002). Obsessive-compulsive symptom dimensions as predictors of compliance with and response to behaviour therapy: Results from a controlled trial. *Psychotherapy and Psychosomatics, 71,* 255–262.

Mataix-Cols, D., Rauch, S. L., Manzo, P. A., Jenike, M. A., & Baer, L. (1999). Use of factor-analyzed symptom dimensions to predict outcome with serotonin reuptake inhibitors and placebo in the treatment of obsessive-compulsive disorder. *American Journal of Psychiatry, 156,* 1409–1416.

McElroy, S. L., Keck, P. E., & Phillips, K. A. (1995). Kleptomania, compulsive buying, and binge-eating disorder. *Journal of Clinical Psychiatry, 56,* 14–27.

McKay, D. (1997). A maintenance program for obsessive-compulsive disorder using exposure with response prevention: 2-year follow-up. *Behaviour Research and Therapy, 35,* 367–369.

McKay, D., Abramowitz, J. S., Calamari, J. E., Kyrios, M., Radomsky, A. S., Sookman, D., et al. (2004). A critical evaluation of obsessive-compulsive disorder subtypes: Symptoms versus mechanisms. *Clinical Psychology Review, 24,* 283–313.

McKay, D., Neziroglu, F., & Yaryura-Tobias, J. A. (1997). Comparison of clinical characteristics in obsessive-compulsive disorder and body dysmorphic disorder. *Journal of Anxiety Disorders, 11,* 447–454.

McLean, P. D., Whittal, M. L., Thordarson, D. S., Taylor, S., Sochting, I., Koch, W. J., et al. (2001). Cognitive versus behavior therapy in the group treatment of obsessive-compulsive disorder. *Journal of Consulting and Clinical Psychology, 69,* 205–214.

McNally, R. J., & Kohlbeck, P. A. (1993). Reality monitoring in obsessive-compulsive disorder. *Behaviour Research and Therapy, 31,* 249–253.

Mehta, M. (1990). A comparative study of family-based and patient-based behavioural management in obsessive-compulsive disorder. *British Journal of Psychiatry, 157,* 133–135.

Menzies, R. G., Harris, L. M., Cumming, S. R., & Einstein, D. A. (2000). The relationship between inflated personal responsibility and exaggerated danger expectancies in obsessive-compulsive concerns. *Behaviour Research and Therapy, 38,* 1029–1037.

Merkel, W., Pollard, C. A., Wiener, R. L., & Staebler, C. R. (1993). Perceived parental characteristics of patients with obsessive-compulsive disorder, depression, and panic disorder. *Child Psychiatry and Human Development, 24,* 49–57.

Meyer, V. (1966). Modification of expectations in cases with obsessional rituals. *Behaviour Research and Therapy, 4,* 273–280.

Meyer, V., Levy, R., & Schnurer, A. (1974). The behavioral treatment of obsessive-compulsive disorders. In H. R. Beech (Ed.), *Obsessional states* (pp. 233–258). London: Methuen.

Miller, W. R., & Rollnick, S. (2002). *Motivational interviewing: Preparing people for change.* New York: Guilford.

Montgomery, S. A., McIntyre, A., Ostenheider, M., Sarteschi, P., Zitterl, W., Zohar, J., et al. (1993). A double-blind placebo-controlled study of fluoxetine in patients with DSM–III–R obsessive-compulsive disorder. *European Neuropsychopharmacology, 3,* 142–152.

Mowrer, O. (1960). *Learning theory and behavior.* New York: Wiley.

Muller, J., & Roberts, J. E. (2005). Memory and attention in obsessive-compulsive disorder: A review. *Journal of Anxiety Disorders, 19,* 1–28.

Muris, P., Merckelbach, H., & Clavan, M. (1997). Abnormal and normal compulsions. *Behaviour Research and Therapy, 35,* 249–252.

Nestadt, G., Samuels, J., Riddle, M. A., Liang, K.-Y., Bienvenu, O. J., Hoehn-Saric, R., et al. (2001). The relationship between obsessive-compulsive disorder and anxiety and affective disorders: Results from the John Hopkins OCD family study. *Psychological Medicine, 31,* 481–487.

Nestadt, G., Samuels, J. F., Romanoski, A. J., Folstein, M. F., & McHugh, P. R. (1994). Obsessions and compulsions in the community. *Acta Psychiatrica Scandinavica, 89,* 219–224.

Newth, S., & Rachman, S. (2001). The concealment of obsessions. *Behaviour Research and Therapy, 39,* 457–464.

Neziroglu, F., & Yaryura-Tobias, J. (1993). Body dysmorphic disorder: Phenomenology and case descriptions. *Behavioural Psychotherapy, 21,* 27–36.

Neziroglu, R., McKay, D., & Yaryura-Tobias, J. (2000). Overlapping and distinctive features of hypochondriasis and obsessive-compulsive disorder. *Journal of Anxiety Disorders, 14,* 603–614.

Obsessive Compulsive Cognitions Working Group. (1997). Cognitive assessment of obsessive-compulsive disorder. *Behaviour Research and Therapy, 35,* 667–681.

Obsessive Compulsive Cognitions Working Group. (2001). Development and initial validation of the Obsessive Beliefs Questionnaire and the Interpretations of Intrusions Inventory. *Behaviour Research and Therapy, 39,* 987–1006.

Obsessive Compulsive Cognitions Working Group. (2003). Psychometric validation of the Obsessive Beliefs Questionnaire and the Interpretation of Intrusions Inventory: Part I. *Behaviour Research and Therapy, 41,* 863–878.

Obsessive Compulsive Cognitions Working Group. (in press). Psychometric validation of the Obsessive Belief Questionnaire and Interpretation of Intrusions Inventory: Part 2. Factor analyses and testing of a brief version. *Behaviour Research and Therapy.*

O'Connor, K., Todorov, C., Robillard, S., Borgeat, F., & Brault, M. (1999). Cognitive-behaviour therapy and medication in the treatment of obsessive-compulsive disorder: A controlled study. *Canadian Journal of Psychiatry, 44,* 64–71.

O'Connor, K. P. (2001). Clinical and psychological features distinguishing obsessive-compulsive and chronic tic disorders. *Clinical Psychology Review, 21,* 631–660.

Öst, L.-G. (1989). A maintenance program for behavioral treatment of anxiety disorders. *Behaviour Research and Therapy, 27,* 123–130.

Parkinson, L., & Rachman, S. (1980). Are intrusive thoughts subject to habituation? *Behaviour Research and Therapy, 18,* 409–418.

Pato, M. T., Pato, C. N., & Pauls, D. L. (2002). Recent findings in the genetics of OCD. *Journal of Clinical Psychiatry, 63,* 30–33.

Pato, M. T., Zohar-Kadouch, R., Zohar, J., & Murphy, D. L. (1988). Return of symptoms after discontinuation of clomipramine in patients with obsessive-compulsive disorder. *American Journal of Psychiatry, 145,* 1521–1525.

Pauls, D., Towbin, K., Leckman, J., Zahner, G., & Cohen, D. (1986). Gilles de la Tourette's syndrome and obsessive-compulsive disorder: Evidence supporting a genetic relationship. *Archives of General Psychiatry, 43,* 1180–1182.

Persons, J. B., & Silberschatz, G. (1998). Are results of randomized controlled trials useful to psychotherapists? *Journal of Consulting and Clinical Psychology, 66,* 126–135.

PsychCentral. (2004). *Obsessive-compulsive disorder: Treatment.* Retrieved from http://Psychcentral.com/disorders/sx25.htm

Purdon, C. L. (2001). Appraisal of obsessional thought references: Impact on anxiety and mood state. *Behavior Therapy, 32,* 47–64.

Purdon, C., & Clark, D. A. (1993). Obsessive intrusive thoughts in nonclinical subjects: Part I. Content and relation with depressive, anxious, and obsessional symptoms. *Behaviour Research and Therapy, 31,* 713–720.

Purdon, C., & Clark, D. A. (1994). Obsessive intrusive thoughts in nonclinical subjects: Part II. Cognitive appraisal, emotional response and thought control strategies. *Behaviour Research and Therapy, 32,* 403–410.

Purdon, C., Rowa, K., & Antony, M. (2005). Thought suppression and its effects on thought frequency, appraisal and mood state in individuals with obsessive-compulsive disorder. *Behaviour Research and Therapy, 43,* 93–108.

Rabavilas, A., Boulougouris, J., & Stefanis, C. (1976). Duration of flooding sessions in the treatment of obsessive-compulsive patients. *Behaviour Research and Therapy, 14,* 349–355.

Rachman, S. (1974). Primary obsessional slowness. *Behaviour Research and Therapy, 12,* 9–18.

Rachman, S. (1976). Obsessional-compulsive checking. *Behaviour Research and Therapy, 14,* 269–277.

Rachman, S. (1993). Obsessions, responsibility and guilt. *Behaviour Research and Therapy, 31,* 149–154.

Rachman, S. (1994). Pollution of the mind. *Behaviour Research and Therapy, 32,* 311–314.

Rachman, S. (1997). A cognitive theory of obsessions. *Behaviour Research and Therapy, 35,* 793–802.

Rachman, S. (1998). A cognitive theory of obsessions: Elaborations. *Behaviour Research and Therapy, 36,* 385–401.

Rachman, S. (2002). A cognitive theory of compulsive checking. *Behaviour Research and Therapy, 40,* 625–639.

Rachman, S. (2003). *The treatment of obsessions.* Oxford, UK: Oxford University Press.

Rachman, S. (2004). Fear of contamination. *Behaviour Research and Therapy, 42,* 1227–1255.

Rachman, S., & de Silva, P. (1978). Abnormal and normal obsessions. *Behaviour Research and Therapy, 16,* 233–248.

Rachman, S., & Hodgson, R. J. (1980). *Obsessions and compulsions.* Englewood Cliffs, NJ: Prentice-Hall.

Rachman, S., Hodgson, R., & Marks, I. (1971). The treatment of chronic obsessive-compulsive neurosis. *Behaviour Research and Therapy, 9,* 237–247.

Rachman, S., Marks, I., & Hodgson, R. (1973). The treatment of obsessive-compulsive neurotics by modelling and flooding in vivo. *Behaviour Research and Therapy, 11,* 463–471.

Rachman, S., & Shafran, R. (1998). Cognitive and behavioral features of obsessive-compulsive disorder. In R. P. Swinson, M. M. Antony, S. Rachman, & M. A. Richter (Eds.), *Obsessive-compulsive disorder: Theory, research, and treatment* (pp. 51–78). New York: Guilford.

Rachman, S., Shafran, R., Mitchell, D., Trant, J., & Teachman, B. (1996). How to remain neutral: An experimental analysis of neutralization. *Behaviour Research and Therapy, 34,* 889–898.

Radomsky, A. S., & Rachman, S. (1999). Memory bias in obsessive-compulsive disorder (OCD). *Behaviour Research and Therapy, 37,* 605–618.

Radomsky, A. S., Rachman, S., & Hammond, D. (2001). Memory bias, confidence and responsibility in compulsive checking. *Behaviour Research and Therapy, 39,* 813–822.

Rasmussen, S. A., & Eisen, J. L. (1988). Clinical and epidemiologic findings of significance to neuropharmacologic trials in OCD. *Psychopharmacology Bulletin, 24,* 466–470.

Rasmussen, S. A., & Eisen, J. L. (1992a). The epidemiology and clinical features of obsessive-compulsive disorder. *The Psychiatric Clinics of North America, 15,* 743–758.

Rasmussen, S. A., & Eisen, J. L. (1992b). The epidemiology and differential diagnosis of obsessive-compulsive disorder. *Journal of Clinical Psychiatry, 53,* 4–10.

Rasmussen, S. A., & Tsuang, M. T. (1986). Clinical characteristics and family history in DSM–III obsessive-compulsive disorder. *American Journal of Psychiatry, 143,* 317–322.

Rassin, E., Merckelbach, H., Muris, P., & Spaan, V. (1999). Thought–action fusion as a causal factor in the development of intrusions. *Behaviour Research and Therapy, 37,* 231–237.

Rauch, S., & Jenike, M. (1998). Pharmacological treatment of obsessive compulsive disorder. In P. E. Nathan & J. M. Gorman (Eds.), *A guide to treatments that work.* London: Oxford University Press.

Ricciardi, J. N., & McNally, R. J. (1995). Depressed mood is related to obsessions but not compulsions in obsessive-compulsive disorder. *Journal of Anxiety Disorders, 9,* 249–256.

Riggs, D. S., Hiss, H., & Foa, E. B. (1992). Marital distress and the treatment of obsessive compulsive disorder. *Behavior Therapy, 23,* 585–597.

Roper, G., & Rachman, S. (1976). Obsessional-compulsive checking: Experimental replication and development. *Behaviour Research and Therapy, 14,* 25–32.

Roper, G., Rachman, S., & Hodgson, R. (1973). An experiment on obsessional checking. *Behaviour Research and Therapy, 11,* 271–277.

Rosen, J. (1996). The nature of body dysmorphic disorder and treatment with cognitive behavior therapy. *Cognitive and Behavioral Practice, 2,* 143–166.

Rosenberg, D. R., & Keshavan, M. S. (1998). Toward a neurodevelopmental model of obsessive-compulsive disorder. *Biological Psychiatry, 43,* 623–640.

Rubinstein, C., Peynirciglu, Z., Chambless, D., & Pigott, T. (1993). Memory in sub-clinical obsessive-compulsive checkers. *Behaviour Research and Therapy, 31,* 759–765.

Salkovskis, P. M. (1985). Obsessional-compulsive problems: A cognitive-behavioural analysis. *Behaviour Research and Therapy, 23,* 571–583.

Salkovskis, P. M. (1989). Cognitive-behavioural factors and the persistence of intrusive thoughts in obsessional problems. *Behaviour Research and Therapy, 27,* 677–682.

Salkovskis, P. M. (1991). The importance of behaviour in the maintenance of anxiety and panic: A cognitive account. *Behavioural Psychotherapy, 19,* 6–19.

Salkovskis, P. M., Forrester, E., & Richards, C. (1998). Cognitive-behavioral approach to understanding obsessional thinking. *British Journal of Psychiatry, 173,* 53–63.

Salkovskis, P. M., & Harrison, J. (1984). Abnormal and normal obsessions: A replication. *Behaviour Research and Therapy, 22,* 549–552.

Salkovskis, P. M., Shafran, R., Rachman, S., & Freeston, M. H. (1999). Multiple pathways to inflated responsibility beliefs in obsessional problems: Possible origins and implications for therapy and research. *Behaviour Research and Therapy, 37,* 1055–1072.

Salkovskis, P. M., Thorpe, S. J., Wahl, K., Wroe, A. L., & Forrester, E. (2003). Neutralizing increases discomfort associated with obsessional thoughts: An experimental study with obsessional patients. *Journal of Abnormal Psychology, 112,* 709–715.

Salkovskis, P. M., & Warwick, H. M. (1985). Cognitive therapy of obsessive-compulsive disorder: Treating treatment failures. *Behavioural Psychotherapy, 13,* 243–255.

Salkovskis, P. M., Westbrook, D., Davis, J., Jeavons, A., & Gledhill, A. (1997). Effects of neutralizing on intrusive thoughts: An experiment investigating the etiology of obsessive-compulsive disorder. *Behaviour Research and Therapy, 35,* 211–219.

Salkovskis, P. M., Wroe, A. L., Gledhill, A., Morrison, N., Forrester, E., Richards, C., et al. (2000). Responsibility attitudes and interpretations are characteristic of obsessive compulsive disorder. *Behaviour Research and Therapy, 38,* 347–372.

Salzman, L., & Thaler, F. H. (1981). Obsessive-compulsive disorders: A review of the literature. *American Journal of Psychiatry, 138,* 286–296.

Savage, C. R., Keuthen, N. J., Jenike, M. A., Brown, H. D., Baer, L., Kendrick, A. D., et al. (1996). Recall and recognition memory in obsessive-compulsive disorder. *Journal of Neuropsychiatry and Clinical Neurosciences, 8,* 99–103.

Saxena, S., Bota, R. G., & Brody, A. L. (2001). Brain–behavior relationships in obsessive-compulsive disorder. *Seminars in Clinical Neuropsychiatry, 6,* 82–101.

Schwartz, S. A., & Abramowitz, J. S. (2003). Are nonparaphilic sexual addictions a variant of obsessive-compulsive disorder? A pilot study. *Cognitive and Behavioral Practice, 10,* 373–378.

Shafran, R., Thordarson, D. S., & Rachman, S. (1996). Thought–action fusion in obsessive compulsive disorder. *Journal of Anxiety Disorders, 10,* 379–391.

Shapira, N. A., Ward, H. E., Mandoki, M., Murphy, T. K., Yang, M. C. K., Blier, P., et al. (2004). A double-blind, placebo-controlled trial of olanzapine addition in fluoxetine-refractory obsessive-compulsive disorder. *Biological Psychiatry, 55,* 553–555.

Shapiro, A., & Shapiro, E. (1992). Evaluation of the reported association of obsessive-compulsive symptoms or disorder with Tourette's disorder. *Comprehensive Psychiatry, 33,* 152–165.

Sheehan, D. (1983). *The anxiety disease.* New York: Scribner.

Sheehan, D., Lecrubier, Y., Harnett-Sheehan, K., Amoriam, P., Janavs, J., Weiller, E., et al. (1998). The Mini International Neuropsychiatric Interview (M.I.N.I.): The development and validation of a structured diagnostic interview for DSM–IV and ICD-10. *Journal of Clinical Psychiatry, 59*(Suppl. 20), 22–33.

Sica, C., Novara, C., & Sanavio, E. (2002). Religiousness and obsessive-compulsive cognitions and symptoms in an Italian population. *Behaviour Research and Therapy, 40,* 813–823.

Simpson, H. B., Gorfinkle, K. S., & Liebowitz, M. R. (1999). Cognitive-behavioral therapy as an adjunct to serotonin reuptake inhibitors in obsessive-compulsive disorder: An open trial. *Journal of Clinical Psychiatry, 60,* 584–590.

Simpson, H. B., & Kozak, M. (2000). Cognitive-behavioral therapy for obsessive-compulsive disorder. *Journal of Psychiatric Practice, 6,* 59–68.

Skoog, G., & Skoog, I. (1999). A 40-year follow-up of patients with obsessive-compulsive disorder. *Archives of General Psychiatry, 56,* 121–127.

Stamm, B. H. (Ed.). (1999). *Secondary traumatic stress: Self-care issues for clinicians, researchers, and educators* (2nd ed.). Lutherville, MD: Sidran Press.

Stampfl, T. G., & Levis, D. J. (1967). Essentials of implosive therapy: A learning-based psychodynamic behavioral therapy. *Journal of Abnormal Psychology, 72,* 496–503.

Stanley, M., & Mouton, S. (1996). Trichotillomania treatment manual. In V. Van Hasselt & M. Hersen (Eds.), *Sourcebook of psychological treatment manuals for adult disorders* (pp. 657–687). New York: Plenum.

Stanley, M., Swann, A., Bowers, T., & Davis, M. (1992). A comparison of clinical features in trichotillomania and obsessive-compulsive disorder. *Behaviour Research and Therapy, 30,* 39–44.

Stanley, M. A., & Turner, S. M. (1995). Current status of pharmacological and behavioral treatment of obsessive-compulsive disorder. *Behavior Therapy, 26,* 163–186.

Steketee, G. S. (1993). *Treatment of obsessive compulsive disorder.* New York: Guilford.

Steketee, G. S., Chambless, D. L., & Tran, G. Q. (2001). Effects of Axis I and II comorbidity on behavior therapy outcome for obsessive-compulsive disorder and agoraphobia. *Comprehensive Psychiatry, 42,* 76–86.

Steketee, G. S., Eisen, J., Dyck, I., Warshaw, M., & Rasmussen, S. (1999). Predictors of course in obsessive-compulsive disorder. *Psychiatry Research, 89,* 229–238.

Steketee, G. S., Frost, R. O., & Kyrios, M. (2003). Cognitive aspects of compulsive hoarding. *Cognitive Therapy and Research, 27,* 463–479.

Steketee, G. S., & White, K. (1990). *When once is not enough.* Oakland, CA: New Harbinger.

Summerfeldt, L. J. (2004). Understanding and treating incompleteness in obsessive-compulsive disorder. *Journal of Clinical Psychology/In Session, 60,* 1155–1168.

Summerfeldt, L. J., Richter, M. A., Antony, M. M., & Swinson, R. P. (1999). Symptom structure in obsessive-compulsive disorder: A confirmatory factor-analytic study. *Behaviour Research and Therapy, 37,* 297–311.

Tallis, F. (1995). *Obsessive-compulsive disorder: A neurocognitive and neuropsychological perspective.* New York: Wiley.

Tallis, F. (1997). The neuropsychologic of obsessive-compulsive disorder: A review and considerations of clinical implications. *British Journal of Clinical Psychology, 36,* 3–20.

Taylor, S. (2000). *Understanding and treating panic disorder.* New York: Wiley.

Taylor, S. (2005). Dimensional and subtype models of OCD: A critical analysis. In J. S. Abramowitz & A. C. Houts (Eds.), *Concepts and controversies in obsessive-compulsive disorder.* New York: Springer.

Taylor, S., & Asmundson, G. J. G. (2004). *Treating health anxiety: A cognitive-behavioral approach.* New York: Guilford.

Taylor, S., Thordarson, D., & Sochting, I. (2002). Obsessive-compulsive disorder. In M. Antony & D. H. Barlow (Eds.), *Handbook of assessment and treatment planning for psychological disorders* (pp. 182–214). New York: Guilford.

Thomas, N. D. (1997). Hoarding eccentricity or pathology: When to interfere? *Journal of Gerontological Social Work, 29,* 45–54.

Tolin, D. F., Abramowitz, J., Brigidi, B., Amir, N., Street, G., & Foa, E. (2001). Memory and memory confidence in obsessive-compulsive disorder. *Behaviour Research and Therapy, 39,* 913–927.

Tolin, D. F., Abramowitz, J. S., Brigidi, B. D., & Foa, E. B. (2003). Intolerance of uncertainty in obsessive-compulsive disorder. *Journal of Anxiety Disorders, 17,* 233–242.

Tolin, D. F., Abramowitz, J. S., Hamlin, C., Foa, E. B., & Synodi, D. S. (2002). Attributions for thought suppression failure in obsessive-compulsive disorder. *Cognitive Therapy and Research, 26,* 505–517.

Tolin, D. F., Abramowitz, J. S., Kozak, M. J., & Foa, E. B. (2001). Fixity of belief, perceptual aberration, and magical ideation in obsessive-compulsive disorder. *Journal of Anxiety Disorders, 15,* 501–510.

Tolin, D. F., Abramowitz, J. S., Przeworski, A., & Foa, E. B. (2002). Thought suppression in obsessive-compulsive disorder. *Behaviour Research and Therapy, 40,* 1255–1274.

Tolin, D. F., Hamlin, C., & Foa, E. B. (2002). Directed forgetting in obsessive-compulsive disorder: Replication and extension. *Behaviour Research and Therapy, 40,* 792–803.

Tolin, D. F., Maltby, N., Diefenbach, G. J., Hannan, S. E., & Worhunsky, P. (2004). Cognitive-behavioral therapy for medication nonresponders with obsessive-compulsive disorder: A wait-list-controlled open trial. *Journal of Clinical Psychiatry, 65,* 922–931.

Tolin, D. F., Woods, C. M., & Abramowitz, J. S. (in press). Disgust sensitivity and obsessive-compulsive symptoms in a nonclinical sample. *Journal of Behavior Therapy and Experimental Psychiatry.*

Tolin, D. F., Worhunsky, P., & Maltby, N. (2004). Sympathetic magic in contamination-related OCD. *Journal of Behavior Therapy and Experimental Psychiatry, 35,* 193–205.

Turgeon, L., O'Connor, K., Marchand, A., & Freeston, M. (2002). Recollections of parent–child relationships in patients with obsessive-compulsive disorder and panic disorder with agoraphobia. *Acta Psychiatrica Scandinavica, 105,* 310–316.

Van Balkom, A. J. L. M., De Haan, E., Van Oppen, P., Spinhoven, P., Hoogduin, K. A. L., & Van Dyck, R. (1998). Cognitive and behavioral therapies alone versus in combination with fluvoxamine in the treatment of obsessive compulsive disorder. *Journal of Nervous and Mental Disorders, 186,* 492–499.

Van Noppen, B., & Steketee, G. (2003). Family responses and multifamily behavioral treatment for obsessive-compulsive disorder. *Brief Treatment and Crisis Intervention, 3,* 231–247.

Van Oppen, P., & Arntz, A. (1994). Cognitive therapy for obsessive-compulsive disorder. *Behaviour Research and Therapy, 32,* 79–87.

Van Oppen, P., De Haan, E., Van Balkom, A. J. L. M., Spinhoven, P., Hoogduin, K., & Van Dyck, R. (1995). Cognitive therapy and exposure in vivo in the treatment of obsessive compulsive disorder. *Behaviour Research and Therapy, 33,* 379–390.

Veale, D., & Riley, S. (2001). Mirror, mirror on the wall, who is the ugliest of them all? The psychopathology of mirror gazing in body dysmorphic disorder. *Behaviour Research and Therapy, 39,* 1381–1393.

Vogel, P. A., Stiles, T. C., & Götestam, K. G. (2004). Adding cognitive therapy elements to exposure therapy for obsessive compulsive disorder: A controlled study. *Behavioural and Cognitive Psychotherapy, 32,* 275–290.

Vogel, P. A., Stiles, T. C., & Nordahl, H. (1997). Recollections of parent–child relationships in OCD outpatients compared to depressed outpatients and healthy controls. *Acta Psychiatrica Scandinavica, 96,* 469–474.

Warren, R., & Thomas, J. C. (2001). Cognitive-behavior therapy of obsessive-compulsive disorder in private practice: An effectiveness study. *Journal of Anxiety Disorders, 15,* 277–285.

Warwick, H. M., & Salkovskis, P. M. (1990). Hypochondriasis. *Behaviour Research and Therapy, 28,* 105–117.

Wegner, D. M. (1994). *White bears and other unwanted thoughts: The psychology of mental control.* New York: Guilford.

Wegner, D. M., Schneider, D. J., Carter, S. R., & White, T. L. (1987). Paradoxical effects of thought suppression. *Journal of Personality and Social Psychology, 53,* 5–13.

Weissman, M. M., Bland, R. C., Canino, G. J., Greenwald, S., Hwu, H.-G., Kyoon Lee, C., et al. (1994). The cross national epidemiology of obsessive compulsive disorder. *Journal of Clinical Psychiatry, 55,* 5–10.

Wells, A. (1997). *Cognitive therapy of anxiety disorders: A practice manual and conceptual guide.* West Sussex, UK: Wiley.

Wells, A., & Davies, M. I. (1994). The thought control questionnaire: A measure of individual differences in the control of unwanted thoughts. *Behaviour Research and Therapy, 32,* 871–878.

Whiteside, S. P., Port, J. D., & Abramowitz, J. S. (2004). A meta-analysis of functional neuroimaging in obsessive-compulsive disorder. *Psychiatry Research: Neuroimaging, 132,* 69–79.

Wilhelm, S., McNally, R., Baer, L., & Florin, I. (1996). Directed forgetting in obsessive-compulsive disorder. *Behaviour Research and Therapy, 34,* 633–641.

Williams, K., Chambless, D. L., & Steketee, G. (1998). Behavioral treatment of obsessive-compulsive disorder in African Americans: Clinical issues. *Journal of Behavior Therapy and Experimental Psychiatry, 29,* 163–170.

Wisner, K. L., Peindl, K. S., Gigliotti, T., & Hanusa, B. H. (1999). Obsessions and compulsions in women with postpartum depression. *Journal of Clinical Psychiatry, 60,* 176–180.

Wolpe, J. (1958). *Psychotherapy by reciprocal inhibition.* Stanford, CA: Stanford University Press.

Woods, C. M., Vevea, J. L., Chambless, D. L., & Bayen, U. J. (2002). Are compulsive checkers impaired in memory? A meta-analytic review. *Clinical Psychology: Science and Practice, 9,* 353–366.

Wroe, A. L., & Salkovskis, P. M. (2000). Causing harm and allowing harm: A study of beliefs in obsessional problems. *Behaviour Research and Therapy, 38,* 1141–1162.

Wu, K. D., & Watson, D. (2005). Hoarding and its relation to obsessive-compulsive disorder. *Behaviour Research and Therapy, 43,* 897–921.

Zohar, J., & Insel, T. R. (1987). Obsessive-compulsive disorder: Psychobiological approaches to diagnosis, treatment, and pathophysiology. *Biological Psychiatry, 22,* 667–687.

Author Index

Note: *f* indicates figure, *h* indicates handout, *n* indicates footnote, *t* indicates table.

Subject Index

Note: *f* indicates figure, *h* indicates handout, *t* indicates table.

J. SARGEANT REYNOLDS
COMMUNITY COLLEGE
Richmond, VA